TRUE ESOTERIC TRADITIONS
by
M. Dale Palmer

-- A SEARCH FOR THE SOURCE OF WESTERN CULTURAL VALUES --

NOETICS INSTITUTE, INC.
PLAINFIELD, INDIANA USA

TRUE ESOTERIC TRADITIONS
by
M. Dale Palmer

Copyright© First English Language Edition; October 1994,
by Noetics Institute, Inc.

All rights reserved. No part of this book may be reproduced or transmitted in any form or by any means, electronic or mechanical, including photocopying, recording, or by any information storage and retrieval system, without permission in writing from the publisher.

Copies of this edition of this book are available from the publisher for US $29.00 each, which includes postage, for mailing within the United States only. This book will be available in other languages. For details, or for permission to quote, contact the publisher.

NOETICS INSTITUTE, INC.
201 WEST MAIN STREET
PLAINFIELD, INDIANA 46168 USA

Library of Congress Cataloging - in - Publication Data

Library of Congress Catalog Card Number: 94-066752.

TRUE ESOTERIC TRADITIONS by M. DALE PALMER --- Includes Selected Annotated Bibliography and Index

International Standard Book Number: ISBN 0-9642633-0-0

1. History 2. Philosophy I. Palmer, M. Dale

TABLE OF CONTENTS   Page

Introduction	7
Exhibit 1: Albert Hugh T. Doss	11
Exhibit 2: Doss Family Home, Cairo	14
Opening Statement	21
Chapter One -- God Does Exist	33
Chapter Two -- Outline of Western History	43
Exhibit 3: The Hammurabi Code	45
Exhibit 4: Plato	54
Exhibit 5: United Methodist Church	67
Exhibit 6: The Rosetta Stone	75
Chapter Three -- Atlantis	77
Exhibit 7: Rosicrucian Alphabet	82
Exhibit 8: Ancient Alphabets	83
Exhibit 9: Karnak Temple, Egypt	85
Chapter Four -- Garden of Eden	93
Exhibit 10: Ancient Akkadian Seal	100
Exhibit 11: Drawing of Ancient Akkadian Seal	101
Exhibit 12: Cheops	103
Exhibit 13: Giza Plateau	105
Exhibit 14: Drawing of the Great Pyramid	106
Chapter Five -- The Ancient Mysteries	107
Chapter Six -- Laws of the Physical Universe	119
Chapter Seven -- The White Lodge	135
Exhibit 15: The Great Sphinx of Giza	136
Exhibit 16: The Great Pyramid of Giza	137
Exhibit 17: The King's Chamber or Temple	138
Exhibit 18: Srinagar, Kashmir	142
Exhibit 19: Mummy of Joseph-Yuya	145
Exhibit 20: Pharaoh Akhnaton	146
Exhibit 21: Queen Nefertiti	147
Exhibit 22: Tree of Life	151
Exhibit 23: King Tut	156
Exhibit 24: Judging the Dead	157
Exhibit 25: Sarcophagus or Tomb	158
Exhibit 26: General Horemheb	160
Chapter Eight -- The Exodus	165
Exhibit 27: Rameses II	166
Exhibit 28: The Wadi Hammamat Road	167
Exhibit 29: The Babylonian Empire	168
Exhibit 30: The Egyptian Empire	169
Exhibit 31: The Assyrian Empire	170
Exhibit 32: The Median and Chaldean Empires	171
Exhibit 33: Alexander the Great's Empire	172
Exhibit 34: The author on the Red Sea	175
Chapter Nine -- The Blue Lodge	177
Exhibit 35: The Oklahoma Freemasonic Grand Lodge Seal	179
Exhibit 36: The Indiana Freemasonic Grand Lodge	180
Exhibit 37: The Scottish Rite Cathedral, Indianapolis USA	182

6 TRUE ESOTERIC TRADITIONS

```
    Exhibit 38: Master Mason George Washington                 186

Chapter Ten -- The Bible                                       189
    Exhibit 39: The Holy Books                                 193
    Exhibit 40: The Ten Commandments                           194

Chapter Eleven -- Master Jesus the Christ                      197
    Exhibit 41: Kashmir, Northern India                        199
    Exhibit 42: Tomb of Saint Issa                             213
    Exhibit 43: Footprints at the Tomb of Saint Issa           214

Chapter Twelve -- The Roman Church                             219

Chapter Thirteen -- The Dark Ages                              233
    Exhibit 44: King Arthur's Kingdom                          235
    Exhibit 45: Bayeux Tapestry                                241

Chapter Fourteen -- The Rosicrucian Enlightenment              261
    Exhibit 46: Francis Lord Bacon                             274
    Exhibit 47: Declaration of Independence                    277
    Exhibit 48: Jefferson Memorial                             281
    Exhibit 49: Cave in Jordan                                 290

Closing Statement                                              295
    Exhibit 50: Machupicchu                                    305
    Exhibit 51: Acropolis in Athens                            307
    Exhibit 52: Stonehenge                                     308

Appendix -- The Roman Church Popes                             311

Selected Annotated Bibliography                                315

Index                                                          339
```

*Right-thinking people
are never threatened by ideas.*

INTRODUCTION

After Dale Palmer had spent many years in research for this book, and was preparing it for publication, he asked me to write the Introduction. He showed me, a long-time friend of his, some of the pages when it was still in manuscript form. I am a Coptic Christian medical doctor and psychiatrist, a native Egyptian now living in the United States. This book traces many of the values of Western civilization back to my country, Egypt. I was impressed with the way in which he had correlated events in history and chronology, how the thoughts and actions of strong leaders had forced those whom they led to comply with the patterns they visualized, and how much humanity still needs to learn.

When does history begin? Can the broad sweep of events and personalities through the ages be outlined in one book? What concepts are most important from the past? What can we learn from the decisions made by political, military, and religious leaders down through the centuries? How can we profit from reviewing the history and results of mass movements such as the Crusades and the Inquisition? Why is the true history of our planet Earth and its people in different ages important? Has it been one of gradual but increasing progress and improvement, one of decline, or a mixture of the two? Has it manifested in cycles? What is its status today? What are the factors (observed from experience and history) that have brought about what we see today?

In asking these questions, we come to realize that **memory** is the basis of all development, all progress, of all achievement! The experience of every moment of our lives, unremembered, would be useless. Indeed, our very lives would be useless without memory. Memory functions to hold realizations in place so we can take advantage of them toward a purposeful end.

This book, however you react to it, has given you a useful tool for endeavor -- in thought or action or both. Perhaps its greatest value is in that it will make you **think**, which I feel is the author's intent. It has made me think, and I recommend that you read it for yourself, to that end.

Few of us, in our busy everyday lives, have the opportunity to travel through history in research, to find answers to these questions. We must remember, always, that **all** aspects of history are **subjective**. Historians in various countries and eras of time have tried to record events for future generations, but events are only the objective manifestation of the thoughts and emotions of individuals and groups of individuals -- which are always subjective. The historian perceives history subjectively, and the reader reads and reacts to written history subjectively. He has been conditioned all his life by his studies, experiences, relationships, observations, prejudices, environment, and the scope of his ability to understand. All these factors lead him to believe that he comprehends clearly and rightly...but is he ready to consider a **new idea**, particularly if the new idea does not fit in with his current understanding?

This book represents research by the author over the last 30 years or so. He outlines the history of the Western world, beginning with 8500 BC, to which he has added his personal annotations. His purpose is to inform the reader of what he has learned, together with his analysis of its significance. Since he is a lawyer, he has presented the text in the form of a legal brief. He has read thousand of volumes and traveled extensively throughout the world in the course of his studies in the various fields of thought which are contained in what he has written.

Dale Palmer has written a book--not for objective scientific scrutiny or for academic literary professors and historians to ponder--but for the layman, the "man in the street." He has made it easy to read and to understand, as a case would be presented to a jury. The layman who wants to gain the most from it, however, must consider, with an open mind, the depth of some of the concepts presented -- especially in the chapter "God Does Exist" and in the "Closing Statement".

This book is a provocative work. It speaks of the mundane and the spiritual; it presents both actual and circumstantial evidence; it goes into possibility and probability; it asks questions and gives the author's answers and conclusions based on the evidence he presents, and he asks the reader to do the same.

He offers four choices: (1) To accept all that he has written; (2) To reject all that he has written; (3) To accept part and to reject part of what he has written; and (4) To suspend coming to a conclusion until he or she feels an inner urge, inspiration, or conviction that brings contentment and peace within.

Ultimately, a fact is **not** a fact, to any individual, until he himself or she herself has accepted it as a fact. We each live in our own subjective world, and all evidence observed or presented to us is weighed subjectively -- just as a juror in a court case decides what evidence to accept or reject and what value, in his or her own eyes, should be placed on it.

In the final analysis, we realize that **all is subjective**. This means **everything we experience**! No one has had the same experiences in life to draw on, in forming an opinion or evaluation, so how could there be a unanimity of opinion among all the readers of this book, for example? And, again, if you accept the understanding that we have lived many lives in different cultures; under diverse physical, mental, emotional, and spiritual circumstances; in varied relationships with others through the centuries; and as both a man and as a woman, you can add all these factors to the experiences of this life and realize the impossibility of viewing **any** evidence in **exactly** the same way that another sees it.

If that were possible, we would be mere robots, without free will and independent thought. Difference of opinion and difference in evaluating evidence and experience challenges thought and promotes deeper thinking. That is why juries are used in the trials of serious cases. If all members of the jury, having different backgrounds and experiences, come to a concurrence, we accept their decision and feel that the accused has had a fair trial and that justice has been done.

We, too, should appreciate the value and challenge of new thoughts -- not necessarily to accept them, but to consider them as impartially as we can, within the framework of our own subjective conditioning. This will help us to grow in our comprehension in that particular field of evidence, and to know why (or why not) we accept (or do not accept) what has been presented. It requires intellectual courage to face this challenge!

I have known Dale Palmer as a very good friend for many years and have met with him at various times, in his home and in my home, and also in different cities and countries. We have traveled together with his wife, Kay, and my wife, Madge, in the United States and abroad. He is a former district attorney and a successful, well-known lawyer in his own right.

I have found him to be cautious in his thinking, perceptive in his observations, and discriminating in his evaluations. He pursues subjects in which he is interested with resolute determination to get to the bottom of it, with the aim of getting a full, accurate, authentic, and well-rounded picture. I truly admire his genuine sincerity of purpose. He is a unique individual, not one to accept traditional and conventional history and chronology without research and the application of personal logic. However, we do not always agree (even on everything that is included in this book), but we have had some wonderful discussions that have given each of us a broader scope of perspective, and we respect each other's point of view and understanding.

It is difficult to classify this book. Is it a review of history and chronology -- past, present, and future? Does it trace the Lesser and Greater Mysteries and their outer organizations and teachers through the eras of time? Is it a book of science, speaking of the geological ages, light, vibrations, energy, and black holes? Is it a book of philosophy that delves into time, space, origins, unity, and free will? Is it a record of world religions and their leaders, followers, priesthoods, and teachings, "from the time whereof the memory of man runneth not to the contrary"?

Is it a brief to substantiate the author's personal conclusions given in the Closing Statement? Is it a provocative work to stir human thought and action in the fields of social relationships and attitudes, law, religion, government, metaphysics, and values?

This book includes all of this and more. It gives information from documents and records (some in obscure locations abroad) that would be inaccessible to the average reader. The author's research is presented so that the reader can seriously consider it and make his or her own decisions. This remarkable volume gives a new vision into many avenues of thought for the reader. It will not appeal to shallow-minded persons whose time is filled with day-to-day, routine activities and who have deeply ingrained thought patterns that will not allow a new idea to enter.

10 TRUE ESOTERIC TRADITIONS

In an old World War II United States Army training manual, a quotation attributed to Robert P. Patterson, Secretary of War, read: "The ideal officer is not afraid of **anything**--not even a new idea." I hope that the reader of this book will remember **the challenge of a new idea** as he or she reads it. He or she may accept all, none, or a part of it--or suspend coming to a conclusion until he or she does personal research on what seems questionable or finds other evidence leading to acceptance or rejection.

This book represents one person's search for truth -- in history, religion, science, philosophy, metaphysics, and other fields. Truth is never written down or explicitly contained in any teachings, however **approved** by **authorities** or **experts** they may be, even if they are traditional and time-honored.

Truth is perceived and accepted by each individual, on a subjective level. It is a matter of realization within each person's consciousness. It is possible to **know**, within one's self, that something is true, even though others do not or will not accept it. There are many instances of this in this book. Unfortunately, it is also possible for a person to accept a truth within, yet because of circumstances, consequences, or expediency, he or she will never express it without, by either word or deed.

Truth is limitless and exists now and will exist throughout eternity. Since truth is subjective, it cannot ever really be revealed or shared with another, fully; it can only be pointed to or suggested for consideration. All teachings contain only seeds of truth that may, or may not, take root and grow from within each individual's consciousness. Likewise, symbols and words (which are symbols of thoughts) are simply keys to doors that lead to truths. All material keys are but manifestations that lead the true Seeker to truth. It is in the silence of the material senses that wisdom is unveiled. It has been said that he who talks much does not know; he who knows much keeps silent. The highest knowledge is unutterable; it exists as an entity on planes that transcend all material words or symbols, to be assimilated by those who can enlarge their vision and consciousness by turning inward, not outward, in their search.

Everything in the universe moves according to law, and the law that regulates the movement of the planets is no more immutable than the laws that regulate the material expressions of man. The aim of the Rosicrucian Order, AMORC, throughout its history has been to reveal to man, for his guidance, the laws that connect the material man to the spiritual man. The connecting link between them is the intellectual man, for the mind partakes of both the material and the spiritual. Mind is an attribute of the soul (the programmer) that acts upon the brain (the computer). It is the personal computer that is given to each one of us to record all our experiences and realizations throughout life. The remarkable feature about this computer is that we can change its chips by using our free will.

When my friend, Dale Palmer, asked me to write an introduction to his book, he said he asked me to do this because I have a totally different background from his own. He also told me that he wanted it to have **an Egyptian flavor** and that I should include something of my Egyptian background.

I was born in Egypt, in the city of Assiut, the capital of Upper Egypt, between Cairo and Luxor, on 22 August 1909. My father, Tewfik Doss, and my mother, Lena Habib Shenoudah Doss, the daughter of the Mayor of Assuit, were Coptic Christians. The word **Coptic** is derived from the word **Coptos** and can be traced forward to **gyptios** and **Egypt**. In the dictionary, "Copt" is defined as "a native of Egypt, descended from the ancient inhabitants of that country." The Coptic people are the indigenous people of Egypt, the direct descendants of pharaonic times. They are the real Egyptians in the same sense that the American Indians are the real Americans. The adjective "Coptic" applies both to the race and its religion. The word "gypsy" is also related to Egypt. The gypsies carried the sacred wisdom from Egypt through the Tarot cards, when many of them migrated to Europe and other parts of the world. The discerning Seeker, if diligent, can understand some of the sacred wisdom from these cards through study.

Exhibit 1: Albert Hugh T. Doss, M. D., Egyptian, Rosicrucian, and Freemason, now a practicing psychiatrist in Raleigh, NC. He has lived in the US since 1960.

Egypt was one of the first countries to embrace Christianity, through Saint Mark. He came to Egypt in very early apostolic days, and it was easy for the people to change from the ancient pharaonic religion to Christianity because they already had, in their religion, the virgin birth, the Trinity (in the form of Osiris, Isis, and Horus), and the personification of evil (in the form of Set).

Egypt was one of the places where a great mystery school existed, and the Egyptian Brotherhood preserved the true wisdom for those who understood and were ready and prepared to study it and to disseminate it without change or misinterpretation. This ancient heritage has been passed down to modern times through the Rosicrucian teachings.

The Mysteries gave answers to the important questions of who man is, why he is on Earth, his purpose during his sojourn here, and the history of planet Earth. This was transmitted only to the very few who were tested rigorously in various ways before they were allowed to receive it. Pythagoras and others had to wait many years before they were initiated into the Mysteries. A great many traveled to Egypt in search of this ancient wisdom, but only a few were accepted and trained as true mystics.

What, and who, is a Mystic? What is mysticism? These words have been misunderstood throughout the ages. A mystic is one who has searched and is searching diligently, trying to understand nature, natural law, and himself in his or her attempt to reunite with the One Great Source, the Creator, or God. Speaking biblically, mysticism is the return of the Prodigal Son, through his free will. Spiritual wisdom must be zealously guarded against curiosity seekers, the ignorant, the skeptics, and the superstitious. True Cosmic laws cannot conflict or interfere with other Cosmic laws. They always form a unity, a oneness, and are in harmony with each other. The Seeker will ultimately reach the conclusion that the great Master Jesus the Christ expressed in **Matthew 7:7** "Ask, and it shall be given you; seek, and ye shall find; knock, and it shall be opened unto you."

Much of what I am I owe to my father and mother, my three brothers and two sisters, and numerous relatives of mine in Egypt; to my beloved wife, Madge Conyers Doss, her father, and many of her close relatives in the United States; and to many of our friends in both countries and in Europe.

My father and mother were married when both of them were quite young. As a rising lawyer in Assiut, my father felt that caring for the children would be too heavy a burden upon my mother, and so he arranged to bring several governesses for us from England. They spoke and taught English to us and so this was my first language. In our home everyone spoke both English and Arabic.

When the time came for me to enter Egyptian public elementary school, a Moslem sheik and priest came to our home daily, except Sunday, to teach us Arabic. He was very broad-minded and taught us Arabic through the **Koran** and the **Bible** and other Arabic books. He was a great scholar with a keen sense of humor. He used to ride on a bicycle, going from one Coptic home to another, teaching the children. We called him Sheik Bicyclette. In the public schools, English was a major part of the curriculum at that time. I finished secondary school in Assiut.

During this time, many tourists from Europe and the United States took the cruise ships on the Nile. These ships would anchor overnight in Assiut, the center of the Coptic culture in Egypt at that time, and lavish parties were given to the visitors by the Coptic families there. I remember many such parties were given in our own home. In this way we contacted much of the culture of Western Europe and the United States.

When my father became increasingly involved in political and financial affairs, our whole family moved to Cairo. During the hot summer months of July, August, and September, our whole family would embark on one of the large luxury ships that crossed the Mediterranean and go to France, Italy, Germany, Switzerland, Holland, and Belgium. We would visit museums, churches, and tourist attractions, thus experiencing some of the vast culture of Europe. In the evenings we would go to operas, movies, or concerts. All of this was educational, relaxing, and entertaining for us.

I look back at those times with sweet memories and I am grateful to my parents for giving us the opportunity to expand in our understanding and awareness of the Western world, and the different cultural expressions within it. It gave us new thoughts and emotions to blend with those we had had in Cairo, a cosmopolitan city that was the crossroads between the East and the West.

As a young child in Assiut, I had a very strong attraction to pharaonic Egypt and its antiquities. I went a number of times with my classmates and my teachers to visit the monuments in Upper Egypt in various locations. I remember having a feeling of affinity and identity with them but I did not express this outwardly.

In Cairo, I felt the same attraction to the monuments in Lower Egypt -- the Great Pyramid, the Sphinx, the Step Pyramid at Sakkara, and the Fayoum District with Lake Karoun (formerly Lake Moeris). I recall one experience quite vividly. One evening after nightfall I went to visit the Great Pyramid. While there, in the moonlight, I saw a beautiful rainbow over the top of the pyramid. It was most impressive. I always enjoyed visiting the Egyptian Museum and did so often.

I was seventeen years old when my family moved to Cairo. In time I entered the Egyptian University and took a pre-medical course of studies, followed by my entry into the School of Medicine. All my medical studies were taken in the English language and were given by British and Egyptian professors.

My father became a prominent lawyer. He also was chairman of the board of directors of The Egyptian Hotels, a corporation which included the large tourist hotels in Egypt, such as the Winter Palace Hotel in Luxor and the Cataract Hotel in Aswan. He served a term as president of the Egyptian YMCA, and was a leader in the Coptic community of Egypt.

He built a beautiful home on the island of Zamalek in the Nile at Cairo, where now resides the Saudi Arabian ambassador to Egypt. It was built between two residences that later became the Chinese Embassy, on the left, and the Iraqi Embassy, on the right, in a part of Zamalek where many of the diplomatic corps later came to live.

14 TRUE ESOTERIC TRADITIONS

The Nile side of the house faced East and had a large balcony overlooking the water, about 30 feet away. A somewhat smaller balcony was built above this, on the second floor, where breakfast could be served from the upstairs breakfast room just inside. It was an excellent place from which to see the sunrise or take pictures. There was an unobstructed view of Cairo across the Nile.

Exhibit 2: The Doss Family home on Zamalek, an Island in the Nile at Cairo, now the residence of the Saudi Arabian Ambassador to Egypt.

In Cairo, house cleaning and cooking was done by men; washing the clothes and linens, by women; and, traditionally, ironing was done by Coptic men. In my early days many men were recruited in Sudan to work in the large homes in Cairo because they had a keen sense of cleanliness and were considered reliable. We had Mohammed, the chief servant, who supervised all the others and organized the serving of the food and beverages for the many parties and receptions we held as my father grew more prominent in the political and financial world. Mohammed, who had a handsome and intelligent face, usually wore a **galabeyah** in his normal household duties, but if the doorbell rang and he had time, he would don his long black overcoat and red **tarboosh** (fez) before opening the door. The first floor was used primarily for receiving visitors and for entertaining.

Adjoining the large main entrance lobby was a small salon which was used as a family living room, a large salon in which 65 persons could easily be seated, the long dining room across from the large salon, and the room-sized space between them where a table would be set for beverages when there were large receptions. Mohammed always presided over this table, dressed in a tuxedo, smiling at the guests as he and his helpers served them. From time to time, we had up to 300 guests for large events, moving from room to room and out onto the balcony overlooking the Nile.

The servants' quarters were in the basement of the house. The kitchen was also there. Food was prepared in the kitchen, brought up on a dumb waiter into a small service room adjoining the dining room, and served at the table in courses. This was always done, even when the family was dining alone.

In addition to Mohammed, two men who cleaned and the cook and his helper lived in the home. Others who helped with various chores were a gardener and his helper, a man who came to wash the car each morning, a woman who came to do the washing, and a Coptic man who came to do the ironing. For large social occasions, additional help was brought in. This was the family home I brought my American wife to after we were married.

My father was a remarkable man. In his law practice, beginning in Assiut and continuing in Cairo, my father had a number of high-profile, controversial cases -- both civil and criminal. He was appointed several times to defend citizens of foreign countries who had committed very serious crimes against Egyptians, thus stirring emotions within the country and attracting national and international attention. In a different type of litigation, he once won the case for the Constitutional Party in Egypt, whose political newspaper publishing operation had been closed by government officials, thus allowing them to re-open and resume publishing.

During the reigns of King Fouad and later his son, King Farouk, my father was a cabinet minister three times. There was an unwritten understanding and tradition that, of the fourteen ministers in the Cabinet, one of them would be Coptic; the rest were Moslem.

16 TRUE ESOTERIC TRADITIONS

At different times, he was Minister of Agriculture, Minister of Foreign Affairs, and Minister of Communication. While he served as Minister of Communication, the first long distance telephone call from Egypt to England was made from the study in our home. With journalists, photographers, and government officials attending, my father called and greeted the Egyptian Ambassador in London.

After the British occupation of Egypt ended, my father was appointed as a member of the commission to draw up a constitution for Egypt. King Fouad respected his judgment and integrity and had a private telephone line installed between the palace and my father's study in our home. The king would use this telephone when he wanted to have my father's advice on difficult situations that arose in the government during that critical period.

When Italy invaded Ethiopia early in World War II, the royal family fled to Egypt. Emperor Haile Selassie and his immediate family, who were Coptic, stayed in our home for a few days enroute to London. They also stopped with us on their way home, for several days, when they were able to return to Ethiopia. One of the Emperor's sons, who needed medical treatment, remained with us longer. After the war my father was invited to be an observer at the Nürnberg Trials.

I graduated as a medical doctor in 1932 and took a residency in surgery at Kasr el Ainy Hospital, which was affiliated with the Egyptian University. Being very interested in cancer, I joined the Egyptian Cancer Society, composed only of medical doctors in Egypt. After that, I decided to take post-graduate courses in surgery in London, in preparation for becoming a Fellow of the Royal College of Surgeons. I went to London, studied there, and passed my Primary Fellow of the Royal College of Surgeons examination, but I was not able to remain in London to take the final examination because when World War II broke out I was recalled to Cairo by the Egyptian government. During the war in Egypt, I was surgeon to the Students' Hospital in Cairo, under the Ministry of Education, and later became its Director. After opening my private clinic for the practice of surgery, I remained in practice in Egypt for about 19 years and was a member of the Societe International de Chirurgie.

Always, I had many questions about the human mind and body that had not been answered in a satisfying way to me during my medical and surgical training and later, also in my practice. I joined the Rosicrucian Order hoping to find answers.

In August 1953, the Imperator of the Rosicrucian Order, AMORC, Ralph M. Lewis, and a group of Rosicrucians from the United States visited Egypt, and I was able to assist him in getting special permission for photographs he wished to take and also permission to pass through customs with them. I invited him and the group to our home in Zamalek where our family gave them a party. He asked me and all other members of the Order in Egypt at that time to participate in a special initiation that he conducted in the King's Chamber of the Great Pyramid. This was a very special event in our lives for all of us. Two or three years later, I served a term as Master of the Cheops Chapter of AMORC in Cairo. During this time, my future wife, whom I had met the year before in Rosicrucian Park, came to Egypt for the first time and we became much better acquainted.

My first visit to the United States was in 1954, and I attended Rose-Croix University in San Jose, California, headquarters of the worldwide Order at that time. It was there that I met my future wife; both of us attended the Rosicrucian Convention, which followed the university courses that I took. Our meeting seemed to be kismet. We had reached the same place in our studies, and she loved ancient pharaonic Egypt just as I did though she had never yet been there in this lifetime.

In 1956, I was greatly surprised to be invited to be chairman of the International Rosicrucian Convention to be held in San Jose. At the beginning of the convention, the Imperator, Ralph M. Lewis, invited the Egyptian Consul General, Abdel Moneim El-Khedry, and his assistant to fly from San Francisco in a helicopter piloted by a Rosicrucian. The helicopter landed in Rosicrucian Park where they were welcomed by the imperator, AMORC dignitaries, and myself, as an Egyptian who was the chairman of the convention. I greeted them in Arabic and in English as they stepped from the helicopter. It was a memorable occasion.

The word "noetic" is taken from the Greek word "noetikos" and means "intellectual," "from the mind or intellect", or "of, related to, or based on the intellect." It is related to the Greek "nous", meaning "mind." A philosopher once quipped: "What is matter? (**never** mind); What is mind? (**never** matter)!" In truth, both mind and matter are different aspects of the same creative energy that pervades the universe.

The Greek philosophers admonished "Man, know thyself!" Man learns more of self through the mind, especially through the techniques of concentration, meditation, and contemplation. The brain, which weighs only three pounds (about two per cent of the body's weight), contains ten billion nerve cells and nearly 100 billion smaller supporting cells. It uses about twenty per cent of the body's food and oxygen.

The average person receives as many as 10,000 separate bits of information into the brain every second, all of which are recorded. The brain has no waste basket, and it never discards anything. Everything you see, hear, smell, think, and experience is stored in your brain. The brain executes orders given to it by the mind which does the planning and observes the results.

If you go one step further, you come to realize that there is mind in every cell of the body -- in the liver, in the bones (even in the marrow of the bones), the palm of your hand, and in the elbow. There is also mind in the marvelous immune system that protects you from all attacks from the outside, such as viruses, fungi, and microbes. There is even mind in that beautiful DNA structure that you inherited from both parents, through a remarkable process that provides the continuity and heredity of the human species. This DNA is the blueprint of your material and psychic body, from infancy to old age.

Man is a holograph, a microcosm of the macrocosm, a picture of something greater than himself, a little world of the Great World. Man was created in the image of God. A holographic picture has the wonderful characteristic that if it is cut into small pieces, each piece will reproduce the whole. In other words, man, the holograph, has the ultimate potentiality of reproducing the perfection of God. Man, as a holograph, also has the holographic potentiality for reproducing his memory of the seeing, hearing, smelling, tasting, feeling, thinking, emotions, form, concepts, and functions of Cosmic actuality. Thus man has the potential, by the will of God, of co-creating a more perfect condition within himself or herself and on planet Earth.

We learn, through the Rosicrucian teachings, that your thoughts are things and that they actually create electrons in your body and in your environment. The entire body is constantly sending forth sparks of light or electricity. This tremendous shooting forth of electrons (that is, of cosmic particles) is concentrated in the area of the body where your activity, for the moment, is focused. For example, electrons pass from your hand in a handshake: from your forehead during the process of thinking; from your eyes in the process of reading or closely observing an object; and from your lips during speech or singing. These electrons are of varying quality, determined by the state of your consciousness, understanding, and feelings. Enthusiasm increases this power.

Electrons are mere points in space with no extent and no structure, but these elementary particles are the most numerous particles in the universe. No one has ever seen an electron, but they live forever, and they learn, think, love, and act upon their environment in the world around them. The entire universe is filled with intelligent, vibratory electrons of light. They are spirit and are able to accept and store information. When all the electrons in the universe are put together, they constitute the world of spirit. There are almost 100 billion electrons in **each cell** of your body. When you die (or pass through transition, to be more accurate), the electrons in your body are slowly released to mingle with all other electrons in the universe, without losing their individual identity or their experiences. This is how certain gifted persons can read the Akashic Records. With the first breath, a baby breathes in electrons which then become a part of his or her evolving soul personality. Your electrons are always in communion with all of the electrons of the universe. Electrons are the basic building blocks of the universe, and there is mind in every electron!

In your thinking, which is a noetic process, you begin to know yourself and also begin to realize that your constant creation of electrons affects you, your environment, and the entire universe. What an awesome responsibility!

Dale Palmer has, in this book, shown how mass thinking by large groups--out of fear, indoctrination by the priesthood, wrongful accusation of individuals, and other causes that stirred the emotions of such groups -- influenced the course of history. This immense creative power can also be used positively, by individuals and groups, for health and healing; success and prosperity; as a blessing to yourself and others; and for your environment; but, most of all, it can be used for the glory of God. Since mind is an attribute of the soul, and the soul is an unseparated segment of the universal soul of God, the mind should be used to send out constructive thoughts, both objectively and subjectively.

In this book the author speaks of cycles. There are astronomical cycles that bring the seasons, other cycles that affect the physical body, yet others that cause the secretion of hormones by the endocrine glands, and still others that cause the tides, or heighten the emotions. We observe cycles in everything. As a physician and psychiatrist, I fully agree with the importance of cycles. Everything we know goes in cycles, because everything must return to its source.

Also, the author speaks of polarity. Positive and negative electrons, positive and negative atoms, and positive and negative molecules compose all physical matter in the universe. They combine together, using the law that like attracts unlike and repels like. Man is composed of a duality of organic and inorganic substances, thus polarity is ever present in man, both in structure and in function.

All of us probably accept the concept that God is not a material being, but a spirit and that, as such, is formless, invisible, and eternal. Man's usual practice is to refer to God as being masculine: **our Heavenly Father, King of the Universe**, and so on. In this book, the author speaks of God in the feminine sense. While this may seem quite strange to some, why should it? In the spiritual world there is no gender; the masculine and the feminine do not exist; there is only One. Is it because some cultures on planet Earth depreciate women and the feminine aspect, that we think of God as being **He**? Since a spirit is neither **he** nor **she** and has no masculine or feminine form; such ideas come from the form we attribute to God through our humanizing of God. Would it not be better if we spoke of **the Creator**? In any event, referring to God as **She** will make the reader **think**, which is a major purpose of this book.

After we were married in Washington D.C. in 1958, my wife and I went to Egypt. In 1959, we left Egypt and returned to the United States to make our permanent home here, one month before our daughter, Aïda, was born in San Jose, California. In 1964, we moved to Phoenix, Arizona and lived there for four years. In 1968, we moved to Raleigh, North Carolina, where we **put down roots**. We decorated our home and my office in pharaonic style; my wife and I both feel quite comfortable in that environment and find it satisfying. We even have pharaonic wallpaper in our kitchen.

Because of my growing interest in the mind, from my metaphysical studies, I had decided to go into psychiatry as a medical specialty. I took a residency in psychiatry at Raleigh's Dorothea Dix Hospital and served as Chief Resident during my last six months there. A new two-year Fellowship program in Geriatric Psychiatry opened at Duke University Medical Center in Durham, North Carolina, 25 miles north of Raleigh, offering this two-year course in the mental problems of the elderly as a sub-specialty. I graduated from this program and, from 1975 to the present, have been in the private practice of psychiatry in Raleigh. Our only daughter, Aïda, practices law in Raleigh.

Having become quite interested in hypnosis and having observed how effective it can be in certain psychiatric cases, I completed the training for professional qualification offered by the American Society of Clinical Hypnosis, became a member of that organization, and began using hypnotherapy in my practice where it seemed indicated. Some excellent -- and even amazing -- results in difficult situations have been most satisfying, both to my patients and to me.

The important universal law of change is clearly brought out in this book in its various chapters -- change in the forms of religion, government, and the thoughts and consciousness of mankind through the ages. As we know, everything in the universe vibrates. A vibration is a movement, however infinitely small, from one place to another -- a change. The universe is thus constantly changing -- for better or for worse -- but it never remains the same. Change is necessary if we wish to grow and evolve, rather than stagnate and deteriorate. If we always think the same thoughts, have the same attitudes, and resist any change, we can never make progress, nor can we be creative. With our God-given free will, we can choose to reach out for a greater awareness; we can see the mistakes that have been made in history, mistakes we ourselves have made, and then work for a better world of peace, beauty, cooperation, and harmony.

In this book, Dale Palmer has pointed the way, as he sees it. He has outlined the steps that his consciousness tells him should be taken. He has presented to the reader his analysis of the wrong choices mankind has made, making the path a little easier for those who follow his logic, and delineating the true nature of the problems that must be solved. He leaves it up to you, the reader (where the responsibility truly lies) to decide how, when, and if you will proceed further. He has done his part, as he sees it. And now it is up to you.

Albert Hugh T. Doss, M.D.
Raleigh, North Carolina USA
August 1994

OPENING STATEMENT

May it please my readers, this is perhaps a daring thing I do. Why are we here in discussion on these matters? What is the purpose, if any? Do we really have anything to say here that has not been said before? Indeed, do we have anything to say here that has not been said before in much better form and from much more learned sources? The answer is probably not.

You will find very little here that is really new. You will find very little here that has not been said before, over and over again, some place in this world. I have only tried to say it more simply and with less verbiage. Hopefully, that effort will be found worthwhile.

This book was not written by a priest. It was not written for priests. It was also not written for those who bow down to pray before priests. And it is kindly requested that all such persons not read this book. I have no intent or desire to trample on anyone's religious beliefs. Every person has the absolute right to believe as he or she chooses. And if you read this book and find things herein that are not true, as you know them to be, then please put the book aside; accept not the thoughts contained herein and tell not a soul that this book even exists.

I am a lawyer which does affect my thinking and manner of presentation. I am writing this in a very abbreviated or brief form in that I have attempted to give a birds-eye view of history in less than 350 pages of manuscript. I am presenting this as though to an impartial jury for their consideration. This book could have been published twenty years ago. Most of the manuscript has been in existence longer than that. Only recently have I come to believe that the thoughts contained herein might be shared beneficially with others. I do so now with some apprehension and misgivings.

I will attempt to show:

1. That God really does exist and comes from outside this physical universe that we now live in.

2. That Atlantis probably did exist in what is now the British Isles and this is the culture that later probably migrated to Egypt.

3. That the Joseph of the **Bible** really was prime minister of Egypt and his descendants became pharaohs of Egypt and, later, created the Exodus out of Egypt. I report on a revised time and place of the happening of that event.

4. That, in the Exodus, the Hebrews left Egypt and crossed the Red Sea into Saudi Arabia; not into the Sinai Peninsula, which is the reason that no evidence of the Exodus ever has or will be found in the Sinai.

5. That those Hebrews carried tons of gold with them and it was this gold that was used, 400 years later, to build King Solomon's Temple in Israel. This gold was also the basis of the legends concerning King Solomon's mines.

6. That the **Bible** is merely another book that was re-written mostly by a politician named Ezra in about 450 BC. Ezra changed many things in the **Bible** in order to create a Jewish theocracy.

7. That the greatest man who has yet lived was the man we know as Master Jesus the Christ. He was both a Freemason and an Essene or Rosicrucian, which are different names for the same people.

8. That all the races, major religions, and languages of the world probably go back to only one common source.

9. That all religions were started by men for men -- not for women who are degraded in all present-day organized religions.

10. That the Christian church is the off-spring of the Apostle Paul, Roman Emperor Constantine, and Saint Augustine of Hippo. It has little connection with Master Jesus the Christ or his true teachings.

11. That we now have the dawning of the so-called Age of Aquarius and the time is quickly approaching for the true teachings of what was known in Latin as Antiquus Mysticusque Ordo Rosae Crucis, or AMORC for short, and Master Jesus the Christ, to be exposed to the world yet one more time. The name of the Rosicrucian Order has been known by many different names in many different languages, and would perhaps loosely translate into English as The Ancient and Mystical Order Rose Cross (TAAMORC). However, in order to save as much space as possible, I will use the initials of its Latin name, which are AMORC.

12. That the United States of America was designed by Freemasons and Rosicrucians as a defensive nation and based its government on their teachings until the 1960s.

I also hope that the reader will acquire a new and very general overview of the history of Western culture. This book draws attention to some things in history that are either little known or underestimated in value by many people.

What are the most important happenings in the history of Western culture? Here is my list of fifteen:

1. The adding of the Greater Mysteries to the teachings of the ancient White Lodge of Egypt (now called, AMORC) in the 1350s BC. These were later exposed to the world as the teachings of Master Jesus the Christ.

2. The Exodus event of the Hebrews leaving Egypt. This allowed the teachings of the White Lodge or AMORC to be carried to the Blue Lodge in Israel and the Jewish mystics, and on down to the time of Master Jesus the Christ.

3. The writing of the **Bible**, and re-writing of many ancient documents, by the Jewish politician, Ezra, in about 450 BC. This event created a schism between the Jews and the rest of humanity that continues to the present day.

4. The teachings of Master Jesus the Christ that were exposed to the world for about an eighteen year period between about AD 15 and 33.

5. The decision of Roman Emperor Constantine to create the Roman Church and exterminate the Blue Lodge and AMORC after he was denied membership in AMORC in about AD 310.

6. The burning of the great library at Alexandria, Egypt, by the Roman Church in AD 400 which threw Western culture into the Dark Ages for the next thousand years.

7. The defeat of the Muslims by Charles Martel at the Battle of Tours in France in AD 732. This slowed the spread of the Muslim culture and religion to the rest of the world.

8. The capture of Istanbul by the Turks in AD 1453. This cut off Europe from the trade routes to the Far East making it necessary for Western countries to become sea-faring nations. This led to the discovery of other routes to the Far East and to the discovery of America.

9. The re-discovery of America by Columbus in AD 1492. This opened up an expansion of European ideals into the rest of the world that continues to the present day. This also allowed the Rosicrucians of France and England to create a republic in this new land which, indeed, has been the true land of milk and honey for the Jews, as predicted in the **Bible**. It has also been the land of milk and honey for millions of others, including the author's own ancestors.

10. The crushing of Roman-church power in England by King Henry VIII during the AD 1536 to 1540 period. This established, for the first time in the West, at least one small island where people were allowed to think. This was truly a pivotal event in the history of Western culture.

11. The adoption of the Rule in Shelly's Case in the late AD 1500s in England. This court decision mandated that wealth become more widely distributed in England, and subsequently in all English-speaking countries. While there have been horrible blood-letting social revolutions in France, Russia, and China, the English-speaking countries, including India, were spared such blood baths.

12. The re-discovery of Inductive Logic by Francis Lord Bacon from the teachings of Master Jesus the Christ. Lord Bacon also postulated the Scientific Method which gave rise to the works of Sir Isaac Newton. Bacon was also instrumental in creating Modern English as an almost universal language.

13. The writing of the Declaration of Independence of the United States of America by Thomas Jefferson in AD 1776. Jefferson embedded the teachings of brotherhood of the second Masonic degree into this document, and those ideals have spread throughout most of the entire world. This is the most important political document of all time.

14. The formulation of the Theories of Relativity by Albert Einstein in the AD 1905 to 1916 period. This allowed the development of atomic energy and an understanding of the origin and operation of the physical universe in which we live.

15. The development of Quantum Theory by Heisenberg and others about AD 1927, which allowed mankind to finally come to realize that we live in an indeterminate and subjective universe.

It is most difficult for any person to obtain from any one book, or even a small number of books, any coherent view of our Western history. That is the major reason for my producing this book.

Almost 40 years ago, I undertook to read Arnold Toynbee's massive treatise entitled **A Study of History**. It was massive then and only about two-thirds of the volumes were even completed at that time. It now contains twelve volumes and more than 7000 pages. It is the outstanding work on history in the world today.

Few people have the stamina to persevere through so much very heavy verbiage. Toynbee is very heavy reading. Toynbee wrote his material between 1930 and 1961. Before he died, he wrote a 576-page summary of his work. It is also intimidating. Toynbee was an Englishman and a Protestant.

Toynbee once observed that:

"The Orthodox Christian Society compromised its future by reviving and idolizing a ghost of Roman imperial absolutism: the authoritarian rule of a church-dominated state crushed and distorted social growth."

I would have tried to say it a little more simply, but truer words were never spoken.

During that same time-span two Americans, Will and Ariel Durant, also wrote their equally massive **The Story of Civilization** in eleven large volumes totaling almost 10,000 pages. The Durants' work is much more readable than Toynbee's but surely less objective. Will Durant warns us that he was reared as a devout Roman Catholic, attended a Jesuit College, and still retained his love and awe of church priests. Also, he spent many of his years teaching in church schools. The Durants' work is more kind to the Roman Church than objective historical facts would warrant.

The Durants also failed to recognize, for example, that the actor William Shakespeare did not write the literature published under that name. But its true author is unimportant anyway. The wisdom teachings in the Shakespearian works are the important thing. The same thing is true concerning Master Jesus. It really doesn't matter when or where Master Jesus was born or died. What is important, is what he said and taught.

The Durants' work represents massive effort and is worthwhile. But its mere size is also intimidating. The Durants also came to realize this problem and before Will Durant died, he too wrote a small 100-page summary of his work entitled **Lessons of History**. Every person should read that summary.

The first great history written in modern times was that of Edward Gibbon, entitled **The History of the Decline and Fall of the Roman Empire**. The first of the six volumes was published in AD 1776, the same year that Thomas Jefferson wrote **The Declaration of Independence**. The last volumes were published in AD 1788, the year before the French Revolution, which over-threw the oppressive yoke of royalty and the Roman Church in that country.

Gibbon began life as a Protestant but, while a student at Oxford University, converted to Roman Catholicism and was forced to leave the school. His work has now also been condensed into one volume. Gibbon said that the Roman Empire fell mainly for the following reasons:

1. The concentration of power into the hands of one person for whom there was no constitutional form of election;

2. An ever-widening gap between the rich and the poor;

3. A pampered army which failed to perform its duties;

4. Cuts in the Roman defense budget in spite of massive taxation;

5. Suppression of the Middle Class; and,

6. A breakdown of law and order.

I certainly disagree with Gibbon that cuts in the Roman defense budget caused the decline of Rome. Quite the contrary, in my opinion. The greatest defense any country can have is not to be found in its military might. America is in the process of re-living history yet again on that point. Witness what happened in 1991 in the former Soviet Union.

The Christian religion as espoused by the Roman Church became the state religion of the Roman Empire in about AD 380. Only twenty years later, the Roman Church burned the great library at Alexandria, Egypt, and destroyed the center of learning in the Western world. And only ten years after that the Roman Empire fell.

Surely that mixing of church and state, and the adoption of ignorance as the criterion for good citizenship, had something to do with the fall of the Roman Empire. But Gibbon saw that not. However, Gibbon's work was a monumental effort, well deserving of the general acclaim it received at that time.

Another earlier historian was the Jewish General Josephus. He was captured early in the war with the Jews by the Roman Army and became a prisoner of war. Josephus wrote **Antiquities of the Jews** and **Wars of the Jews** in about AD 76. The source of much of our Western culture comes from Jewish writers, so those two briefs can help us understand that source.

However, Josephus was wrong in thinking that Joseph of the **Bible** was a part of the same family as the ancient Semitic Hyksos Kings of Egypt. He was not. The two lived almost 200 years apart, had no connection, and were totally different.

In his **Antiquities** manuscript there is a paragraph concerning Master Jesus. That paragraph was not in the original manuscript and is an obvious forgery inserted there later by the Roman Church.

There have been some other good histories written. Perhaps one other should be mentioned. In the early 1800s, an English circuit judge named Godfrey Higgins retired and became an amateur historian. He labored long and hard and wrote a two-volume history with the short title of **Anacalypsis**. This is an excellent work on the source of Western cultural values, although I disagree with his final conclusion that the source was India. I personally think that it was the Garden of Eden in the Middle East in what is now Southern Iraq, scene of the recent Gulf War.

In some of those histories, the indexes and citations are longer than this book. I make no apologies for that. This is a brief, not a treatise. I make no effort to convert anyone from any one belief system to any other belief system. To all who are now comfortable, stay that way. But, to those who are hungry for something better, perhaps this material can supply some rational historical basis of support. I have come to know that it is not possible to share knowledge with another until that person is truly ready. And when the student is ready, a teacher always appears. That, too, is a lesson of history.

Probably the most complete history of religion was published only in 1987. It is sixteen large volumes in size and is entitled **The Encyclopedia of Religion**. I waited years for this effort to be completed and received one of the first sets off the presses. It is extremely well done and covers about every religion ever known to man.

By far the most knowledge that I have ever located in one place are the materials of AMORC. It takes more than twenty years to study those materials, and they are very good; actually, they are the best. However, those materials are all private and are not reported on here, with one exception. Information on the very ancient Rosicrucian alphabet, for the first time, is shown here to the general public, by specific permission.

I come from a very mixed background. I grew up in a small township in southern Indiana, USA. It had a Roman Catholic Church with a small grade school. It had a Lutheran Church with an even smaller grade school. Also, it had one Baptist, one Free Methodist, two Methodist, and two United Brethren Churches. There were also two small public grade schools but only one small public high school. Some of my relatives were Nazarenes, Holy Rollers, and Jehovah's Witnesses. They all left town to attend church with their own kind when possible. That was truly Bible Belt, USA.

At one time or another I have visited or represented all of those various churches in some way. Technically, I have been a member of the Methodist Church all of my adult life. I have had several good friends who are ministers, including Norman Vincent Peale. They are not the priests depicted in this book. I intend no disrespect to any of them and will understand if they choose to disassociate themselves from this material. I am not a Freemason and will never be one until the Freemasons accept members based only on merit, including women and blacks.

My hope is that many women will find some comfort in this material. However, I say this fully realizing that some women will be my most severe critics. I learned that sad lesson very early in life when I tried to free my own pet dog from a tangled barbed-wire fence. She bit me on the hand. Indeed, Master Jesus was persecuted by some of the same people that he was trying to free from ignorance. I say that you, too, can be free. Hate me for that if you must.

I have been an avid reader all of my life. After age four, I was a ward of the welfare system. The old gentleman in whose home I was placed was known simply as Big Jim. He taught me to read, write, tell time, and count before starting me in grammar school at age five. There were no radios, televisions, newspapers, or magazines in that household in the mid-1930s. Times were very tough.

The library consisted of the first four very old **McGuffey's Readers**, a **Farmer's Almanac**, and a **New Testament**. Big Jim was a simple teacher: you memorized the material. He never read to me from the **New Testament**, except the first part of the Sermon on the Mount and the Golden Rule. He said that the rest of it was unimportant anyway. Big Jim's father had been a prisoner of war at the infamous Andersonville Prison death-camp during the War Between the States. He had no brief for southern rebels, Ku Klux Klansmen, and preachers who didn't work. He thought that next to Master Jesus, Abe Lincoln was the greatest man who ever lived. He wanted very much for me some day to read and learn all of **McGuffey's Readers**. To him that was the true mark of an educated person. I now have the complete set.

I owe Big Jim much. I dedicate this book to him and to the renowned Professor John Samuel Grimes of the Indiana University School of Law, now deceased. Professor Grimes taught me a lot. Upon his retirement from teaching he honored me with a dinner at which time he paid honor to me as the best student he had taught during his long teaching career. He told me almost 40 years ago that some Exodus out of Egypt probably did take place. He said to me: "*Your job is to figure out when, where, and why.*" I think that now I have pretty much done that.

My purpose is to convey ideas and generalities, not to become bogged down in excessive historical technicalities. For example:

1. The city of Istanbul was founded in 657 BC and was called Byzantium. About AD 335, the city became known as Constantinople, named after Emperor Constantine. Its current name is Istanbul and that is what I call it in this book.

2. The small country today known as Israel has had many names throughout history. Indeed the boundaries of the present country have changed since the first draft of this book some 30 years ago. I refer to the present country of Israel, plus its surrounding area, as Israel, without regard to the hundreds of boundary and name changes it has had throughout history.

3. For many centuries there was a great empire known as the Persian Empire. However, the current name of Persia is Iran, so I call it Persia-Iran in this book.

4. The family of Joseph and Moses was Hebrew. I refer to the religion of the ruling people living in Israel as the Jewish religion. In historical times those people were Hebrews but most are not today. Anyone can become a Jew by conversion, the same as in most other religions. Many of the Jews today are blue-eyed and blond, or even red-headed. The adoption of Judaism by non-Hebrews is a true mystery of history.

5. My use of terms such as Sons of Light, Freemasons, Israelites, Rosicrucians, Essenes, etc., is very general. Historically, Freemasons were persons who had mastered the Lesser Mysteries. Today, many persons who are technically members of the Freemasonic Order have not yet mastered the Lesser Mysteries. The various names come and go throughout history. The terms Israelites, Essenes, Therapeuti, and Rosicrucians mean about the same thing: except that they were used in different periods of history.

Many historians are mystified by the sudden disappearance of the Essenes about AD 70. That same thing happened several other times in history. It happened about 1350 BC when the Israelites, as they were called then, went underground. Another disappearance occurred again in AD 400 and thereafter when the Roman Church persecuted the Gnostic Christians, Freemasons, and Rosicrucians.

6. There were Christian sects in several areas of the world prior to the Roman Church. The Church of England, for example, has roots older than the Roman Church. However, most of those earlier sects were later exterminated by the Roman Church. There have also been Russian, Armenian, Greek, Coptic, Protestant, and other groups that have survived, but world-wide, in gross numbers, the Roman Church has been the dominant one. Most important is the fact that the true teachings of Master Jesus were lost or misinterpreted even by the time of the Apostle Paul in AD 50 or so and have not survived intact in any Christian sect.

7. The term **Bible** in this book refers only to the **Old Testament**.

This book is very critical of the Roman Church. That is fully justified in my opinion. However, some of the finest men who ever lived have been members of that Roman Church. I will mention Saint Francis of Assisi, and even a pope, the second John XXIII. Dr. Norman Vincent Peale, a prominent Freemason, has done much to educate the Protestant sects.

8. When I talk about the source of our present Western culture, I am referring to a period of no further back than 8000 BC at most. I am convinced that modern thinking man originated in Africa or the Middle East about 250,000 years ago or so, and that our present culture came from the British Isles to Egypt about 8000 BC.

9. Many people refer to Joseph-Jesus as Jesus Christ. While that hurts no one, it is not technically correct. It is like saying Lincoln President. Christ Jesus would be correct. In this book I use the terms Master Jesus and Master Jesus the Christ which are earned titles.

10. I use the initials AMORC which stand for **Antiqus Mysticuque Ordo Rosae Crucis** which was the new name of the ancient White Lodge after 1353 BC. I generally do

not like to use initials because readers tend to forget what the initials really mean and stand for. However, their use herein will shorten this text and this is a brief.

Please remember that there are many bodies worldwide, and throughout history, that have called themselves Rosicrucian. Many of these groups have put out some excellent materials, but the true Rosicrucian teachings of the ancient White Lodge of Egypt, of the Jewish Kabalists, of the Essenes, and of Master Jesus the Christ were passed down through history mostly among only a very few people until about AD 1600 or so. It is only because of the decline in power of the Roman Church that learning and truth have been allowed to re-emerge and be available to the general public.

I have prepared a very small Selected Annotated Bibliography for readers who may want to read more on some of these subjects. In this book are my opinions. They may not be wise and they may not all be found to be totally correct historically when further evidence is available. Nevertheless, they are mine at this moment in time. I share those opinions with you only for any possible benefit they may be to you. They are the result of many years of travel, study, and research. I believe them to be largely accurate.

To those readers who may care, I should warn you that this manuscript has not been submitted to the censor of the Roman Church for approval. Therefore, it could contain doctrinal or moral error as those terms are defined by the Roman Church. The reader is so forewarned.

However, it is not my intent to cause even one person to leave a Christian church. Quite the contrary. I advise all to remain members of their churches and become voices for change to the way the teachings of Master Jesus the Christ should be explained within those churches. A belief in something is better than a belief in nothing. A set of erroneous beliefs is better than no beliefs at all.

Do not put aside your current belief system until you have something better to take its place. Man must have a belief in something beyond himself in order to live and function properly. As long as good people come together in church or elsewhere to pray, or meditate, or talk, or just think, there is hope because the truth will eventually come out and that truth will indeed set us free. God is the only complete truth. All other truths are approximations of truth only. That is true of all knowledge and it is also true of the contents of this book.

God is truly great and also only good. We should thank her every day for creating a physical universe in which we may more quickly aspire to the Christ consciousness. However, God is not all-knowing nor all-powerful. We do have free will which is limited by the physical universe in which we reside at this time in our evolution. Not even God knows what we will do and cannot dictate what we think.

I do thank God for allowing me to live for a short while in this physical dimension and to be able to inquire into these matters. I dedicate this book also to my family whom I love dearly. Master Jesus the Christ loved me and all of mankind equally with his own family. That too may be my goal someday, but regretfully, I shall not begin to approach that status in the near future.

I have tried to think of at least one group of people that I have not offended herein and that might not be critical of this material. I can think of none. So mote it be. I present my case to inform and not necessarily to please. If only one person on the planet is shown the road that can lead to his or her enlightenment, it will be enough.

Although I had developed the theory in the early 1950s that Master Jesus obtained some of his ideas in the Far East, I am indebted to fellow lawyer and friend, John Vandivier, for pointing out to me similarities between the teachings of Laotse and Master Jesus.

I also give my sincere thanks to:

1. The George F. Cram Company, Indianapolis, Indiana USA for allowing me to reproduce their maps herein;

2. The Supreme Grand Lodge of AMORC, for allowing me to reproduce their Rosicrucian alphabet herein;

3. The Indiana Freemasonic Grand Lodge for providing me with pictures for reproduction herein;

4. My friend, Albert Doss, for working long and hard to write the Introduction for this book. I also thank Albert for allowing me to use his pictures taken inside the Egyptian Museum in Cairo;

5. My wife, Kay Palmer, for typing and re-typing this material several times far beyond the call of duty; and,

6. My long-time friend, Sherry Ploetz, and my cousin, Joe Palmer, for their editing suggestions; although, the final responsibility for all matter herein is mine alone. Although it is double emphasis I have had the quotes typed in italics and taken other grammatical liberties where I felt it would improve the presentation.

M. Dale Palmer

The universe
is so constructed that
what appears to be an end
is always only a new beginning.

CHAPTER ONE -- GOD DOES EXIST

In the beginning, God created the heavens and Earth. Very shortly thereafter, according to the prevailing theory of cosmology, many things happened very fast.

Everything in the universe is in motion. The only thing that never changes is that everything never stops changing. Matter and energy share an equivalence and, indeed, if as suggested herein spirit also shares a similar equivalence with energy, then things that are equivalent to the same thing are equivalent to each other, and spirit and matter are one and the same thing, except only in different forms.

The universe we live in appears to contain a tremendous amount of empty space and more all the time. But is it indeed empty? If space and time are equivalent to motion and if motion is equivalent to energy, then would it not seem that space and energy are one and the same thing, except in different forms?

The things of the universe all seem to be the same except in different forms. Thus, if one of those things does in fact exist, the others must also necessarily exist, at least in potential. And if any one of those things ever, in fact, ceased to exist in any form, then all of them must also necessarily cease to exist in every form. Energy can exist as energy, as matter, as motion, as spirit, or even as space, but it never ceases to be in some form.

AMORC went even further and taught that spirit, and therefore everything else that exists, manifests in the form of vibrations. The lowest form of vibration is the physical universe we see around us. All other forms in which vibrations may be found, such as motion, energy, spirit, and all the way up to the Soul Essence or God, are merely higher and finer vibrations. The Soul Essence or God was thought to be nine hierarchies or levels above man and the physical universe. God is the highest vibration at the highest level.

The only way matter can manifest is for energy to slow its vibration down to the vibration of visible light, at which level, matter can manifest. Light is generally thought to be and is the fastest thing possible in the physical universe. But it is the slowest thing or the lowest vibration of the many universes above it. Light is the fastest thing in the physical universe, but certainly not the fastest thing that exists.

Light, speed, and motion all suggest space and time, but those concepts apply only at the physical level or the lowest rate of vibrations possible. At the higher levels, there is no space and motion because all is here; there is no time because all is now; there are no individual minds because all minds are of the Universal Mind, and there are no personalized souls, because all souls are in Unity and Oneness in the one Soul of God.

Motion does create energy and energy does create motion. But which came first -- the energy or the motion? How one answers the question will disclose somewhat a person's view of the nature of things in the universe. A deist or person who believes in God would probably say that energy came first, and from that energy, everything that exists came to be. A materialist, on the other hand, might feel that motion came first and that motion is the root cause of all energy and everything else in the universe. The universe is space which contains energy, and energy by its own nature moves, and as it moves it creates changes. Matter is merely energy that has slowed down into a relatively stable form.

For centuries, science has been characterized by the objectivist assumption, which is that the universe can be approximated with quantitative models; by the positivist assumption, which is that reality can be observed only physically, and by the reductionist assumption, which is that all complex phenomena can be explained in more elementary terms. But finally, in this century, subjectivity has entered science with quantum mechanics. Purpose and other teleological causes now need to become acceptable considerations in serious discussions about the beginning and fate of the universe.

The Scientific Method has been preeminent in revealing new precepts. It has utilized the understanding that much human knowledge derives from the discernment of patterns. Patterns may be God's footprints. But it is almost axiomatic that we need to find new knowledge in places and in ways which have previously been regarded as either unfruitful or unworthy of investigation. If our anticipated new knowledge were where we would expect to find it, we probably would have already discovered it. It remains hidden from us simply because it is not where we expect it to be.

Assume that the law of the Conservation of Mass and Energy is true; that mass and energy may change forms but can never be destroyed. Further, assume a big bang beginning of our present physical universe, and that there are only the four known forces to-wit: gravity, electromagnetic, plus the weak, and strong forces existing in the universe. The electromagnetic and the weak force have now been joined into the electro-weak force so that now we have only three. Some day these three forces will be joined into one.

What is the force that causes the universe to expand? We assume that force to be energy but is that necessarily true? We assume that the universe will keep on expanding forever unless there exists enough matter that, through gravity, will cause it to stop expanding and become static -- that is, neither expanding nor contracting -- or, that it will begin contracting back again into a singularity and, eventually, into nothing at all.

Science tells us that there are only the four forces in nature and thus the force that propels the expansion of the universe must be energy. If that is true, then logically it would seem that if it took **E** units of energy to create a big bang and begin the original expansion of this universe, it would require only **E** plus one unit of energy to some day stop that expansion and begin a big crunch.

This would be true because if there were at some time in the past E units of energy in the universe to start that initial expansion, that energy still must be here someplace in some form, since mass and energy can and do change forms but can never be destroyed.

Given any positive quantity, regardless of how many times it is divided in half, it never reaches zero. And in any closed system given some positive quantity of heat therein, a total absence of heat therein can never thereafter come to pass. No matter how much the universe expands, it can always expand more if the energy is still present to cause it to happen. Thus, the universe can never reach a state of infinite size or absolute cold.

We look for the missing mass to stop the expansion of the universe, but we find it not. Some hard scientists think that such mass does not even exist, but if there are only the presently known four forces in the universe, they are mistaken. We eventually must either find that missing mass, or find a fifth force because, logically, one or the other has to be here if some of our known physical laws are indeed laws.

Logically, the mere expansion of the universe itself alone implies the energy to cause it to happen in the first place without any other cause. And also logically, the fact of that expansion, alone and of itself, implies the existence of the equivalent mass necessary to eventually almost stop that expansion.

Thus, if there are only the four known forces in the universe, the author submits that the universe is exactly evenly balanced between outward explosive energy and the equivalent inward gravitational pull on that same energy or mass. Thus, the universe tends to continue indefinitely in the direction in which it has been previously set in motion by some external factor.

If matter and energy are one and the same thing only in different forms, is one form dominant over the other? We know that gravity does act on both matter and energy. Since that is true, it must also logically be true that both matter and energy can be only causation factors pulling for the reduction and eventual collapse of the entire physical universe. However, the universe is not reducing in size but, quite to the contrary, is expanding. Therefore, if such expansion of the universe continues indefinitely then it must be caused by some force other than energy -- a fifth force. What force could that be? Who knows, perhaps God.

The development of conditions for the evolution of life to exist in this universe seem highly improbable, but the even balance of explosive energy and implosive gravitational pull is very logical and very probable. For example, if I buy a half dozen apples and put them in my shopping bag it is only logical that there would then be six apples in that shopping bag. If God created our universe and put 100 units of energy herein, it is only logical that exactly 100 units of energy, or its equivalent, is still here in some form.

The Law of the Conservation of Mass and Energy logically implies some external factor, or God, in order to explain the present expansion of our physical universe.

At the present time, within our universe, there is enough energy to cause the universe to continue to expand, but ever more slowly. It will never completely stop expanding, unless and until there is an injection of energy from outside our universe system.

The endless expansion of this physical universe, or an almost static universe that would also expand endlessly, both would seem to violate the Law of Cycles. That is, they both would imply violation of that law without the presence of some external factor from outside our universe system. The reason they do not violate AMORC teachings is that those teachings included the existence of an external factor, or God, outside our physical universe.

Also, an endless expansion of the universe would tell us that there must indeed be an as yet undiscovered fifth force present and operative in this physical universe. Let's call that fifth force God. Is it not amazing that all the laws taught by AMORC and all the physical laws yet discovered by science require God in order to make sense logically.

The Hindu Vedas say that after this universe goes into annihilation it returns again. This idea can be expressed in Western cultural terminology as: The universe is so constructed that what appears to be an end is always only a new beginning. Or, as AMORC teachings say in the Law of Cycles: Everything in the universe operates in cycles.

Let's assume that the Second Law of Thermodynamics is true and that in a closed system chaos always increases. Thus, if gas molecules are confined to the left half of a box; then when the barrier is raised the molecules will spread and occupy both halves of the box.

While it is perhaps improbable, it is still possible that given enough time the molecules would, on their own, again all collect on the left side of the box. But, the important point is that, even when and if that ever happened, it would have no meaning, because it would be only chaotic order and without purpose.

To take a more simple example, open a new deck of playing cards. The cards come out of the box in a very specific order so that one can look and observe and immediately see whether all of the cards are indeed there. The cards have **intentional** order put there by man for a purpose, which gives that order meaning.

But one could shuffle those cards a very long time before they would go back to the original order as when they came from the box. Again, the point being suggested is that even if the cards did some day accidentally, on their own, happen to go back to the same order as when they came from the box, it would have no meaning because it would be only chaotic order and without purpose.

Yet man can return the cards to that original intentional order in a very few minutes, and the order of the cards again has purpose. Thus we can say that there can be chaotic order in the physical universe without purpose, but where purpose exists, **intentional** order is one of the natural consequences of that purpose.

This creates a dilemma. If there is order, is it then only chaotic order, or is it intentional order? Perhaps it is possible to have both kinds of order present in this physical universe, but we can be sure that the order created by man is not accidental and does indeed have purpose.

The Uncertainty Principle states that there are some things that we do know and some things that we do not know. Of the things we do not know now, we will learn more in the future. However, there are some things that we do not know now, and will never know, because they are not knowable. Much of modern science is based on this Uncertainty Principle. This chaotic order perhaps falls within the purview of the Uncertainly Principle and is probably not knowable.

Truly, if enough monkeys pound on enough typewriters for a long enough period of time, one of them might very well eventually pound out Einstein's Theories of Relativity. But even if one did, it would have no meaning, and no value, because it would be without purpose.

If the Second Law of Thermodynamics is true, and chaos always increases in a closed system, what does that tell us, if anything? Man does observe some intentional order in the universe, and since only chaos, including chaotic order, comes from within this system, then logically that intentional order which we do observe must come from outside this universe system. This means that our universe is not a closed system and that God does exit.

The order created by man is intentional order and thus must be from outside this universe system. Thus, man must also be from outside this physical universe system. The intentional order created by man is evidence of the source of man, and that source may be called the One True God who is from outside this universe system.

And if intentional order has heretofore come into this universe system, which can in fact be observed, then this would suggest:

1. That there is an external factor or God;

2. That God has heretofore interceded in this universe to inject the intentional order that can be observed; and,

3. That if God interceded herein once, she might do so again, given the proper circumstances.

Thus, the Second Law of Thermodynamics also implies the existence of some external factor, or God, which is needed to explain the presence of intentional order in this chaotic universe system.

When man really stops to think about it, isn't the Uncertainty Principle and Quantum Theory the greatest of all great ideas? Just think of it! There are some things that are known and there are some things that are not known at this time, but will be known someday in the future. However, there are some things that are not only not known, but are not knowable. This must be one of the great leaps forward in the advancement of human knowledge. Down goes determinism. Indeterminacy does exit. With Quantum Theory man can almost prove scientifically that God does in fact exist.

Movements in the macro universe, which is to say the galaxies and other large amounts of mass, are explained by Newton's Classical Mechanics, and more precisely by Einstein's General Relativity. However, movements in the micro universe, which is to say the elementary particles inside the atom, are explained by Quantum Mechanics or what is commonly known as the Law of Probabilities.

In the macro universe of Einstein the movements of the galaxies are explained by determinism and one cause always gives exactly one and the same result. This is very tidy and very secure. But the micro universe inside the atom is explained by indeterminism and here movements are explained only by probabilities and the Uncertainty Principle. One cause gives one result only most of the time.

If the macro universe is explained by certainties and the micro universe is explained only by probabilities, where do these two universes meet? If a sheet of paper is totally black on one end and totally white on the other, where do these two meet on the paper? Is there an area of gray in the middle where black and white are mixed? If so, how much of the paper is some shade of gray rather than either pure black or pure white? Would the gray part be 25 per cent, 50 per cent or conceivably even 100 per cent?

In other words, is there truly an area of the universe explained only by determinism and another area of the universe explained only by indeterminism? The answer to this question is not known for sure at this time. The author suggests that the whole sheet of macro-micro paper is merely different shades of gray, and that indeterminism rules the entire universe, not just the micro universe. God grants free will -- not just to man -- but to everything.

This idea would seem to be confirmed by calculations completed a few years ago by Stephen Hawking. He calculated that when a black hole is created by general relativity, it really is not so black, because quantum effects intercede and over-power general relativity and, as a result, energy can and does seep out or escape from the black hole. A black hole occurs when matter becomes so condensed, and creates such intense gravity, that nothing can escape therefrom, not even light.

If these calculations are correct, then general relativity is not a complete theory; determinism does not rule even in the macro universe, and the entire universe is indeterminate. There are areas where determinism is very powerful but none where that power is absolute. However, while determinism never rules completely, it still has influence in all areas of physical world. That sheet of macro-micro paper has no pure black or pure white but is all in shades of gray. This is to say: that there will always be at least one exception to every rule, and that there is no situation where one cause will always give exactly only one and the same result.

The reason this is true is because this universe is influenced by both God and man, each of whom has free will and the prerogative to have a change of mind. Is the glass half full of water or half empty? The answer depends on your view which is subjective. In the final analysis this is a subjective universe in which we live.

If man knows that some small part of the physical universe, such as the position or momentum of an electron, does not achieve actuality until perceived subjectively, would it not follow perhaps that the much larger physical universe could not and does not achieve actuality, or actual existence, until perceived in the subjective and cosmic mind of God?

Quantum Theory has brought man perhaps to the realization that the existence of the physical universe actually requires the existence of God. Physical science, the whipping boy of the priests, is actually proving the existence of God. This is something the priests have never really done to anyone's satisfaction other than perhaps their own.

God has thus become not just a desirable philosophical ideal but also a proven physical necessity. Man thinks -- therefore, God exists. According to Einstein, God does not play dice with the universe, but does allow man to do so if man so chooses.

AMORC taught that there are multiple universes. The physical universe we live in is at the bottom of the stack and is the most gross and least evolved of all universes. While light is the fastest thing in this physical universe, it is the slowest thing in the next higher and in all of the other universes above this physical universe.

And if this physical universe is exactly balanced between explosive energy and its counterpart which is implosive matter, as this logic would suggest, then that exact balance requires the existence of an external factor or God in order for this universe to have the outward motion which man can, in fact, observe.

Man has always suspected that the universe has a unity that can be sensed but not proven scientifically. Now it appears, that such unity not only does in fact exist but is at least approaching scientific provability.

The logical implications of action at a distance -- or, non-locality -- suggests that this physical universe does indeed have a Oneness just as taught by AMORC and its Law of Oneness.

What is action at a distance? We now know that when two correlated protons become separated, whatever happens to one of the protons also happens to the other one immediately. This is to say, that whatever happens to one proton also happens to the other. This is true, even though the distance between the two protons is far enough that a signal could not travel between them, even at the speed of light.

For example, if the spin of one of the protons altered, the spin of the other proton is likewise so altered immediately, and quicker than any message could travel between them, even at the speed of light. Einstein called this spooky action at a distance and considered it to be one step away from voodoo. He thought that this action at a distance would not be true when more facts and information were known about the situation.

According to the Law of Oneness, taught by AMORC, this would be the expected result. The entire physical universe is but one unit or one organism, and whatever happens to that organism happens to the whole organism. Thus two correlated protons separated fifteen billion years ago -- with one proton on one side of the universe or organism, and one on the other, and the spin of one is altered, then the spin of the other proton would likewise be so altered, even though it is fifteen billion light years away. This is true and it is not, in fact, spooky. It is merely the **Law of Oneness** at work.

Could we not generalize then from this knowledge that whatever happens to man also affects God and vice versa? Since man emanates from God, even though the two are separated by distance, they still have Oneness with each other.

Some of man's most revered physical laws imply the existence of an external factor, or God, to be present and actually operative in this physical universe. However, the fate of this universe falls within the purview of the Uncertainty Principle and is not a knowable. Not even God knows what man will do.

An ancient Egyptian legend states that the god Osiris created the universe out of a boundless ocean called Nu, but this was only after the god had created herself from this ocean by uttering her own name. As the **Bible** states: *"In the beginning was the Word."*

This was referring to the long-lost Word or the unspeakable Word alluded to throughout history. Tradition states that Hermes brought the knowledge of this lost Word or Tetragrammaton to Egypt from Atlantis.

The long-lost sacred word is not really just one word as written in the Modern English language. It is more like an idea or thought. Since every person is at a somewhat different level of development in consciousness, the lost word or thought for every person must be different. Every person who looks at a rainbow will perceive a slightly different projection of colors. Every person who listens to music will have a slightly different part of his inner being affected thereby. So to one who may ask, what the lost sacred word is, the answer is that it is different for each and every person.

The current prevailing theory on the origin of the universe is that it all started some fifteen billion or so years ago in a big bang. At that time all the matter in the universe was compressed into one super-atom. With the big bang an expansion started that will go on forever without end. All the galaxies, including the solar system and Earth, have been formed from that matter in the intervening years.

Such an endless expansion violates the Law of Cycles as taught by AMORC and in most Eastern religions. Modern cosmologists say that there is not enough mass or matter in the universe to cause it to stop expanding and to begin contracting. This is now known as the big missing mass problem.

Much effort in science is spent trying to locate that missing mass, but there is a long way to go. The mass in all of the observable galaxies is only about ten percent of the amount of mass it will require to make the universe someday stop expanding. But other models of the universe are possible which, when properly understood, will explain these problems and the Law of Cycles will prevail.

Earth and moon were formed some five billion years or so ago, and on Earth, inorganic matter at some point in time received the animating vital life force and became organic, which is to say, that lower life forms began to evolve. Eventually, this evolution sometime, somewhere, somehow, resulted in homo sapiens or present-day, conscious, thinking-man.

In time, thinking man has come to realize that, Einstein notwithstanding, determinism does not rule the universe, and the mere existence of thinking man inside this physical universe requires the existence of God somewhere outside this physical universe.

It is an indeterminate, subjective, and, in fact, unfinished universe in which we live. The Hindu religion recognizes this truth when it teaches; that all things take their existence from that which perceives them. There is no black and no white on that sheet of macro-micro paper. It is all in shades of gray. God does indeed play dice with the universe. This began when man was granted free will.

Man would like very much to rid himself of the responsibility for his own conduct, and his own ultimate fate, so he creates excuses for himself in the form of ideas such as Satan and original sin. Man also created institutions to help him rid himself of responsibilities, such as religions and priesthoods.

In the Garden of Eden, Adam ate from the tree of knowledge of good and evil, and realized that he was naked and responsible for his own conduct. Adam tried to hide from that responsibility for his own conduct and disavowed the Godliness within him. But he could not and never shall it so be. Adam's progeny, man, has likewise been so hiding and disavowing ever since.

Equivalences are fixtures of this universe. Mass, energy, time, space, and spirit all share some equivalence. And to those we can now add a new one: God, man, and all other creatures share some degree of equivalence of free will.

God does exist. So teaches AMORC. Much near truth is presented in this book, or so the author verily believes. But the only one true fact that the author knows for sure to be true, without exception, is that God does indeed exist. All other facts are only approximations of truth.

Does the proton decay? We search for only one decayed proton and find it not. But if the Law of Cycles is true then protons do indeed decay. However, if the average life span of a proton is, say 100 billion years, and if this universe is now only 25 or so billion years old, then we would normally expect all of the originally created protons in the universe to decay at somewhere between say 50 and 150 billion years of age. If that is true, we have a long search ahead because the first proton would not decay for another 25 billion years or so.

Is it possible that new protons are being created all the time? It is possible and perhaps even probable. God could create more matter just as was done originally. Man too, who shares some equivalence with God, also might be able to create new matter. Was Master Jesus evolved to the level that he had the capacity to create matter?

This physical universe could explode and then later implode. Or, it could come into an existence of physical matter and then return to an existence in spirit form from whence it came. It is an indeterminate universe in which we live.

Big bang or not, the ultimate fate of this universe is not yet determined and lies in the hands of God and man. And there is no one in the universe, not even God, who knows exactly what that fate will be. Our future and our fate lies within us, not in the stars. So mote it be.

CHAPTER TWO-- OUTLINE OF WESTERN HISTORY

To make it easier for the reader to visualize the sequence of important events in Western culture, the author has created a brief outline of a very few historical events that cover the time period from the great flood in 8000 BC, to the shift of the United States of America away from that of a defensive nation to that of an aggressor nation in the late AD 1900s.

While these dates are probably not exactly correct to the year, the author feels that most of them are about as accurate as it is possible to be with the information available at this time.

The author does understand that the designations **BCE** (Before the Common Era) and **CE** (Common Era) are accurate and religiously neutral. However, the terms **BC** (Before Christ) and **AD** (Anno Domini, or the year of our lord) are more familiar to Western readers and are used herein.

The purpose of this chapter is to give the reader the most general outline in the fewest pages possible of the material presented in this book. Here is the author's outline of Western historical events:

8500 BC A 400-year war rages throughout the Mediterranean area. It is thought that this is the war to which Plato makes reference in his writings. The best book on matters in this time period is **Plato, Prehistorian** by Mary Settegast.

8000 BC A huge flood covers much of Earth. What caused this great flood that is recorded in the records of all ancient cultures? One possibility is that a huge ice sheet slid off the Antarctic ice cap and raised the water level on Earth significantly. Another is that an asteroid hit Earth and created havoc. The author favors the asteroid impact as the cause of this great flood.

7400 BC The domestication of animals, the use of cereal grains for food, advanced architectural techniques, functional pottery, and, even some metal work come into use in the Middle East. Many advanced communities suddenly appear all over the Middle East, seemingly coming from nowhere. Where did they suddenly obtain this knowledge? This is truly one of the mysteries of history.

6500 BC A dish that has become known as the parah dish is buried in ancient Israel. Some people claim that this dish has writing on it in the Modern English language. It was discovered in AD 1987.

6000 BC The Lesser Mysteries and the Greater Mysteries are perhaps taught in the Garden of Eden, Sumer, India, or the British Isles.

4004 BC This is the date that the world and everything in it is created and comes into existence, according to the Christian church. Obviously, such views are merely

Christian-church theology and have no relationship to either reason or historical fact. Many other Christian-church views have equal validity with this one. The teachings of the Apostle Paul and the Christian church that women are inferior to men is an excellent example.

3807 BC The one and a half mile-long Sweet Track Road in Southwestern England is constructed about this time from whole trees laid side by side. The date has been approximately determined by modern radio carbon and tree ring dating techniques. This road was uncovered in a peat bog around AD 1970. The story of this work is in a poorly written book entitled **Sweet Track to Glastonbury.**

3800 BC The ancient civilization known as Sumer comes into being in the Middle East. Even at this early date, these people know about the Solar System and the outer planets, including Pluto, which was not re-discovered until AD 1930.

3760 BC This is the beginning of the Jewish calendar. What significant event happened at this time to cause these people to use this date as a starting point for their calendar? This is also about the date that the great Sumerian culture burst into full bloom in the Middle East, and which is the source from which the Jewish calendar is taken. Could these various events be connected? Surely they are.

3500 BC The Lesser Mysteries, which later became known as Freemasonry, come to Egypt and also later become known as the Circle of Light or, what the author has called, the ancient White Lodge.

3113 BC This is the date of the beginning of time as calculated by people in Central America, culminating in the Long Count Calendar of the Maya Indians. What significant event happened at this time to cause these people to use this date as a starting date for their calendar? Is this the date that the legendary white god, named Quetzalcoatl, either came to or left Central America? We do not know. It is also thought that this is about the date of beginning of construction of the first pyramids in Egypt. Are the two events connected? We do not know.

2700 BC Construction of Stonehenge is started on Salisbury plain, about 60 miles southwest of London, in England.

1815 BC The great Babylonian king, Hammurabi, is born, and will raise the city of Babylon to a world renowned capital, when he reigns from 1792 to 1750 BC. He has superior ability as a military leader, as a diplomat, and as an administrator; he also genuinely cares for the well-being of his land and his people. He is also a great law-giver, as the father of the Hammurabi Code of Law.

1626 BC On Thera, an island in the Eastern Mediterranean Sea, a violent volcanic explosion rocks the area for miles in every direction. Huge tidal waves overflow the

OUTLINE OF WESTERN HISTORY 45

Exhibit 3: The Hammurabi Code - Man's Oldest Law. King Hammurabi ordered that the laws of the land be codified on a column of stone about seven feet high. The original is in the Louvre Museum in Paris. The picture shows the king receiving the laws from the sun-god Shamash who holds a measuring rod symbolizing justice. Speculation that Hammurabi may have been king at the time the patriarch of the **Bible,** named Abraham, lived are not true. Abraham lived almost 300 years after Hammurabi.

coasts of all countries in the area, including Egypt. Red pumice spews into the air and causes the sea and lower Nile River to turn blood red. To quote from Egyptian records: *"...the towns are destroyed... blood everywhere... pestilence throughout the country. Ra has turned his face from mankind... the sun in the heavens resembles the moon...."*

The **Bible** also records this event although with supernatural overtones: **Zechariah 1:15**, *"...That day is a day of wrath...a day of darkness and gloominess, a day of clouds and thick darkness."* And at **Zechariah 52:5**, *"...Woe unto the inhabitants of the sea coast... Lord is against you...I will even destroy thee, that there shall be no inhabitant."* **Jeremiah 47:2** also discusses this same event. Following this event there is a terrible seven-year famine throughout the area.

1575 BC Ahmosis becomes Pharaoh of Egypt and begins the Eighteenth Dynasty. This period evolves into a great advance for mankind.

1570 BC Ahmosis institutes formal classes for the teaching of the Lesser Mysteries. This will someday become the Circle of Light or the White Lodge, and then the Ancient and Mystical Order Rose Cross, and later the Blue Lodge, the Essenes, the Therapeuti in Greece, and later the Great White Brotherhood in Tibet. However, these teachings were not as profound as those later put into effect by Hermes and Akhnaton.

1550 BC The Semitic Asiatic Hyksos kings are expelled from Egypt but, contrary to the views of historian Josephus, they have no connection to the later Hebrews in Egypt who were also Semites.

1500 BC Abram and Sari, as brother and sister, pass through the breadbasket of Egypt and continue to the political and esoteric capital at Thebes in central Egypt, where the White Lodge is located, and also where the pharaoh resides. Pharaoh Tuthmosis II takes the very beautiful Sari as one of his lesser wives.

1495 BC Both Abram and Sari are initiated into the White Lodge, and change their names to Abraham and Sarah to honor their initiation, and to recognize their symbolic spiritual rebirth as new people. They then reveal to Pharaoh that Sarah has all along been Abraham's wife. Sarah and Abraham are expelled from Egypt by the pharaoh and they return to Canaan.

1494 BC Isaac -- biological son of Pharaoh Tuthmosis II -- is born in Canaan to Sarah. Following the custom of his Egyptian father the boy is circumcised. The Hebrews in Canaan take up the Egyptian custom of circumcision, which they continue to practice to the present day.

1490 BC Hatshepsut, the female pharaoh, takes the throne of Egypt. Contrary to many learned books and reports, she is not the pharaoh of the Exodus.

OUTLINE OF WESTERN HISTORY   47

1468 BC Jacob is born to Isaac in Canaan. In Egypt, Hatshepsut dies and Tuthmosis III takes the throne of Egypt. He begins to formalize the White Lodge, which teaches the Lesser Mysteries. Contrary to many learned books and reports he, also, is not the pharaoh of the Exodus.

1454 BC Isaac's son Jacob buys the birthright to the Egyptian throne from Essau, his older brother. Jacob goes to Egypt to study, is initiated into the ancient White Lodge, and takes the name of **Israel** to honor his symbolical spiritual rebirth as a new man. In Egypt, he comes to know the Egyptian royal family, of which he is a lesser member. Jacob is a grandson of Pharaoh Tuthmosis II, but the Great Royal Wife is not his grandmother.

1438 BC Joseph is born to Jacob in Canaan. He is the son of an initiate, Jacob, the natural great-grandson of another initiate, Tuthmosis II, and the foster great-grandson of another initiate, Abraham. He is also perhaps the kindest and wisest person ever born among the Hebrews. His mummy may be seen at the museum in Cairo.

1436 BC Amenhotep II takes the throne of Egypt.

1422 BC Jacob breaks tradition and gives the claimed birthright to the throne of Egypt to his son, Joseph, age 16, who is a mystic as well as a very kind and brilliant young man. Jacob sends Joseph to Egypt to seek initiation into the ancient White Lodge like his father, grandfather, and great-grandfather before him.

1421 BC Joseph, age 17, goes to Egypt to attend the ancient White Lodge and to try to claim his birthright as pharaoh of Egypt. Joseph takes initiation and assumes the name of Yuya to honor his symbolic spiritual rebirth as a new man. As an initiate, he comes to know the royal family very well, of which he is a lesser member.

1417 BC Amenhotep III is born in Egypt.

1413 BC Tuthmosis IV takes the throne of Egypt. He is a distant cousin of Joseph-Yuya.

1412 BC A daughter named Tiye is born to Joseph-Yuya. Like her father, she is a true mystic and a brilliant woman. Tiye later achieves high position in the ancient White Lodge and becomes one of the most powerful women of all time. Her father, Joseph-Yuya, is Grand Vizier or Prime Minister; her brother, Aye, will be Prime Minister to three pharaohs and then becomes pharaoh himself. Her son, Akhnaton, will be the man who brings monotheism to the world, and who, with Hermes, designs the teachings that will be followed by the ancient White Lodge up to the present day.

The family lines are very confused. It is probable that Semenkhkare and Tut were the sons of Amenhotep III and his other queen, Sitamun. Also, both may have married their nieces, who were daughters of Akhnaton, in order to tighten their grip on the throne.

1410 BC The war chariot comes into use in Egypt.

1408 BC Joseph-Yuya is appointed prime minister of Egypt by Tuthmosis IV, who is his distant cousin. For the next 73 years, the Hebrew Joseph-Yuya, his daughter, Tiye, and his son, Aye, control the government of Egypt. This all ends at the time of the Exodus event in 1335 BC.

1405 BC Tuthmosis IV dies and Amenhotep III, age 12, takes the throne of Egypt. Joseph-Yuya is still prime minister and is really the ruling pharaoh of Egypt except in name.

1403 BC Amenhotep III breaks with tradition and makes Tiye, aged about nine years, his Great Royal Wife, instead of his sister. Because of the influence of Joseph-Yuya, his daughter, Tiye, will be the mother of the next pharaoh.

1399 BC Hermes, the thrice-great man and the sage of all sages, is born at Thebes in central Egypt. He will be present when Akhnaton takes office as Master of the White Lodge in 1365 BC, and will, himself, become Master in 1350 BC when Akhnaton dies. He is often confused with the Egyptian god Thoth who may have been only a myth. However, Thoth also was probably an earlier actual king of Egypt who became deified over time.

1391 BC Amenhotep IV is born to Amenhotep III, now age 26, and Tiye, now age 21. At initiation, he takes the name of Akhnaton to honor and recognize his symbolic spiritual rebirth as a new man.

1385 BC The great mystic and initiate Moria-El is born near Cairo in Egypt. He will add adult baptism to the rites of the ancient White Lodge, and remain a leading Rosicrucian in the world after the lodge in Egypt goes silent in 1335 BC. Is Moria-El in fact Moses' initiatic name? The author thinks so, and will call him Moses Moria-El.

1374 BC Joseph-Yuya dies at age 64 and is mummified the same as royalty. He has lived long enough to tutor his grandson, Akhnaton, who is now 17 years of age. Pharaoh Amenhotep III has tired of life as a king and turns completely to matters of pleasure. Like Solomon over 400 years later, he is a womanizer to the extreme. Queen Tiye runs the government and is virtually the pharaoh, except in name.

1371 BC Akhnaton becomes co-pharaoh with his father, Amenhotep III.

1367 BC Amenhotep III dies and Amenhotep IV, or Akhnaton as he is now called, the heretic pharaoh who is an Egyptian by Egyptian law, but a Hebrew by Hebrew law, takes the throne of Egypt. Akhnaton's Great Royal Wife, Nefertiti, the daughter of Aye is his first cousin and also is half Hebrew. Aye, youngest son of Joseph-Yuya and a trained priest is now the prime minister in place of his father, Joseph-Yuya. The Hebrews rule Egypt completely.

1366 BC Akhnaton, under the persuasion of his Hebrew mother, Queen Tiye, begins the purge of the empire of many gods and idols, and he requires the worship of the One True God. The family of Joseph-Yuya becomes one of the wealthiest and most powerful families in Egypt and the entire world.

1365 BC Akhnaton becomes Master of the White Lodge at age 26. The great sage of all sages, Hermes, is his assistant and very possibly his spiritual superior.

1364 BC Belief in One True God becomes the law of Egypt and is taught publicly but with disastrous results. Hermes and Akhnaton add the Greater Mysteries to the teachings of the ancient White Lodge, and upgrade severely the requirements for admission. These Greater Mysteries are not made public.

1353 BC The name of the ancient White Lodge is changed to **The Ancient and Mystical Order Rose Cross**, or AMORC for short, by Hermes and Akhnaton. We will use the name AMORC throughout this book. It teaches both the Greater and the Lesser Mysteries. A new calendar is started with 1353 BC as year one. The new year begins with the Spring equinox about March 21st. This new calendar is still in use today.

1351 BC Akhnaton makes Semenkhkare, his younger half-brother, the co-pharaoh. He is the most loyal of all of Akhnaton's followers. The prime minister is still Aye. Why the great sage, Hermes, does not become co-pharaoh has not yet been determined. It is probable that Hermes is either not Egyptian, or not of the royal family.

1350 BC Akhnaton is assassinated probably by slow poisoning by members of the priesthood, but Semenkhkare continues as pharaoh and makes his younger brother, Tut, the co-pharaoh. Akhnaton's body has never been found. Aye continues as prime minister.

1347 BC Pharaoh Tutankhamen, known to us as King Tut, who is another younger half-brother of Akhnaton takes the throne of Egypt at 11 years of age. The government is now almost completely controlled by the army and not the pharaoh. The pharaoh is forced to change his name from his initiate name back to his Egyptian name -- Tutankhamen.

The complete reinstatement of the priests is implemented, and much wealth is turned over to them. The persecution of the Hebrews begins. This persecution is not slavery in the sense that we think of it today, but is more like just being denied power or access to power, much as the King of England is denied power after his abdication in AD 1936.

1345 BC The Lesser Mysteries are again made secret and taught only in AMORC. The Greater Mysteries remain, as always, secret and underground.

1340 BC King Tut makes Prime Minister Aye, who is his uncle and an old man, co-pharaoh. Aye is the youngest son of Joseph-Yuya, and the first and only full-blooded Hebrew to sit on the throne of Egypt, during this period. While Akhnaton is also Hebrew by Hebrew law through his mother, he is also Egyptian, and of the royal family, through his father. Semenkhkare and Tut were both fully Egyptian, but they were completely dominated by the Hebrew family of Aye.

1339 BC King Tut is poisoned and dies at age 19, but Aye keeps the throne. Putting Aye on the throne of Egypt breaks another tradition and sets a precedent that would very shortly destroy the Hebrews in Egypt. This sets the stage and precedent for Horemheb, who is a general in the army, and also not of the Egyptian royal family, to take over and sit on the throne of Egypt as pharaoh. This is the last gasp for the family of Joseph-Yuya and the Hebrews in Egypt.

1335 BC Pharaoh Aye is on his deathbed. By now, the army and the priesthood are too powerful to allow Pharaoh Aye to name another Hebrew as co-pharaoh. Hermes is the man who will plan, organize, and motivate the Exodus. Moses Moria-El, who is picked to lead the Exodus, is very close to Hermes and may have been a younger brother. The Exodus of the Joseph-Yuya family, of about 60 people, begins from Egypt in the spring of the year, with the complete approval of the Pharaoh, but against the wishes of the priesthood and the army. This family is extremely wealthy and removes much gold and other wealth from Egypt.

Hermes makes AMORC go silent and become a super-secret organization, which it has remained throughout history. Moses Moria-El takes these teachings from Egypt in the Exodus to what is known today as the northern Saudi Arabian peninsula, but the heathen Hebrew tribes already living there never accept them.

Pharaoh Aye dies and General Horemheb immediately takes the throne and tries to capture the departed Hebrews but fails. Many of his troops drown during a violent storm on the Red Sea. Horemheb removes the names of his four predecessors from the official lists of kings of Egypt, and tries to wipe them from history. These four Hebrew-dominated pharaohs are Akhnaton, Semenkhkare, Tut, and Aye.

1334 BC From this date forward, Pharaoh Horemheb seeks to purge the Hebrews, and all traces and memories of them, from Egypt. This includes particularly AMORC. The master of that lodge, Hermes, takes the order deeply underground and makes it so secret that much of the world, for 1500 years, will think that Hermes is only a mythical person.

1219 BC The famous Merenptah Israel Stele is made in Egypt by Pharaoh Merenptah, son of Rameses II. It brags that "...*Israel is destroyed, its seed is not....*" This is not true. The reference is probably to the Israelites of AMORC. It might be saying that the external organization is destroyed but still is known to exist underground. But even if it refers to the departed Hebrews now back in Canaan, who have also taken the name of Israelites, it still is not true.

1202 BC AMORC sends missionaries from Egypt out into the world for the first time. The Greater Mysteries are still taught in Egypt, and also by the Joseph-Yuya family (the Kabalists) in Israel. It is possible that the Greater Mysteries are also taught in India-Tibet at this point in time.

1035 BC These dates are not certain. King David of Israel-Judah, one of the most evil men who has ever lived, is born about this time in Bethlehem-Judah. He will rule from maybe 1017 to 970 BC.

1013 BC King Solomon, the founder of the Blue Lodge of Freemasonry is born in Jerusalem. He is the second son born to David and Bathsheba, and will rule from about 970 to 930 BC. The only dates that are known with reasonable certainty about King David or King Solomon are when King Solomon did attend school at AMORC in Egypt, from 999 to 995 BC.

999 BC Solomon, age 14, son of King David of Israel-Judah, enters AMORC in Egypt but fails for some reason ever to graduate and take initiation into AMORC. AMORC teaches seven degrees. The first three degrees are the Lesser Mysteries, and the next four degrees, four through seven, are the Greater Mysteries. Solomon finishes the first three degrees of the work on the Lesser Mysteries.

950 BC Solomon begins the Blue Lodge in Israel, which has only three degrees, and teaches the Lesser Mysteries. The Masons become the Freemasons. Solomon's Blue Lodge is similar to AMORC in many respects, but the Blue Lodge is not open to all persons equally, with membership based only on merit. Neither women nor former slaves are admitted. This fact alone shows that the Hebrews in Egypt were not in fact slaves in the usual sense; otherwise, the Jews and Solomon could not now be members of the Blue Lodge they are creating. The Greater Mysteries are taught and preserved among the Hebrews by the Kabalists, descendants of Joseph-Yuya and Moses Moria-El.

922 BC Parts of the Elohim **Bible** Version are written in Israel.

848 BC Parts of the Jehovah **Bible** Version are written in Judah.

722 BC Assyria destroys Israel.

700 BC Parts of the Priests' **Bible** version, which includes both Elohim and Jehovah versions, are re-written by the priests in Jerusalem.

630 BC Solon, the great law-giver of the Greeks, is born in Athens. He freed people from prison for debt, prevented oppression, redressed wrongs, prevented revolution, and allowed ordinary citizens to sit on the newly created jury courts. Just like Pharaoh Akhnaton of Egypt, over 700 years earlier, not all of his reforms will last. However, once a people taste freedom, it is very difficult ever again to make all of them slaves.

Solon at some point becomes an initiate in AMORC in Egypt. He returns to, and establishes lodges in, Greece where they are known as the Therapeuti. These lodges are open to all equally, based only on merit. They teach both the Greater and Lesser Mysteries. Solon dies in 561 BC.

628 BC The great teacher Zoroaster is born in Persia or what we call Persia-Iran. He reforms the religion of Persia-Iran away from the view that God is a trinity, as taught by the Hindus in India and the ancient pagan religion of Egypt, to the view that God is only one person. The later Christian church will adopt the pagan idea of God as a trinity of persons.

604 BC Laotse, pronounced Lauu-its, is born about this date in China. He is credited with being the author of the still popular book entitled **Tao Te Ching**. He is an old man when the great Chinese teacher, known as Confucius, is born in 551 BC. Laotse taught AMORC teachings when he told his students that it is better to light one small candle than to curse the darkness. He is important to us because it is very probable that Master Jesus the Christ either studied in China, or studied his teachings at the Hemis Monastery in northern India. The author suggests that the Sermon on the Mount, as taught by Master Jesus, is taken from this man's teachings. Like Moses Moria-El before him, when it came time for him to die, he went away to die in private.

587 BC The Babylonian Exile of the Jews begins.

580 BC Jeremiah writes Deuteronomy and several following books of the **Bible** while in exile in Egypt.

563 BC About this date, Prince Gautama is born near the present country of Nepal. He will give up his right to be king in order to study and become enlightened, which he finally does achieve. He is also said to have been born of a virgin. This, of course, is not true in the sense that we understand the meaning of virgin today. In earlier times, the term virgin applied only to a girl who had not yet begun her menstrual cycle, and had nothing to do with sexual intercourse or the absence thereof.

Prince Gautama is given the title of Buddha much like Master Jesus will be given the title of Christ many years later. Buddha taught that in the beginning God created man, the heavens and Earth, and everything else in the universe. Master Jesus perceived the error in this teaching, in that anything that has a beginning must also necessarily have an end, and that time is only a condition in the present physical universe. Master Jesus correctly taught that both man and God have no beginning, and therefore will have no end.

560 BC The great mystic and teacher, Pythagoras, is born on the island of Samos in the Eastern Mediterranean Sea. He will attend school at AMORC in Egypt for a period of one thousand weeks and will take the sixth initiation, just as Solon had done earlier, and as Plato will do later. Like many other great men, after his death it is told of him that he was born of a virgin.

The famous 47th proposition, usually accredited to Euclid, is actually conceived by Pythagoras. The author thinks that possibly Albert Einstein got the idea for his theories on relativity from Pythagoras' 47th proposition.

553 BC The man who will become known as King Cyrus the Great becomes king of Persia-Iran. There were also stories attached to Cyrus, just as Moses Moria-El before and Master Jesus after him, that efforts were made to kill him as a baby. None of these stories is historically true. The great Greek historian Xenophon described Cyrus as handsome, generous, ambitious, and devoted to learning. Persia-Iran will remain a great empire until 330 BC when it is captured by Alexander the Great.

In tracing the source of Western cultural values, Cyrus becomes important to us because he is the man who allows the Jews of the captivity to return to Jerusalem and rebuild Solomon's Temple. He also appoints Ezra as co-ruler of Jerusalem, and Ezra literally creates the Jewish theocracy. This theocracy in Israel has very little connection with Moses Moria-El or the things he taught.

538 BC The Babylonian exile of the Jews is ended by King Cyrus the Great of Persia-Iran. Cyrus dies in 530 BC.

529 BC Pythagoras takes initiation into AMORC in Egypt. He then goes to Italy and establishes lodges there. These lodges are open to all equally, based only on merit. They teach both the Greater and Lesser Mysteries.

522 BC King Darius the Great becomes the ruler of Persia-Iran. Although Darius is a very successful military leader, it is for his civil ruling ability that he is remembered. He divided his empire into at least twenty different provinces, with an appointed governor in charge of each province. Prior to this time the central government has depended on gifts for its support. Darius started a new system in which each of the provinces is assessed for tax purposes, and is required to provide a fixed annual tax to the king.

490 BC King Darius the Great, of Persia-Iran, is defeated at Marathon in Greece. After this battle a Greek runner runs all the way to Athens to deliver the news of victory. From this feat comes the Marathon Run of today.

This is a decisive battle in that it allows Greece to remain free from foreign domination. It also later allows such great Greeks as Socrates, Plato, and Aristotle to live and work. This battle is also the cause of Alexander the Great's later attacking and subduing Persia-Iran.

Exhibit 4: Plato, the Greek sage, who taught AMORC teachings; one of these is that man has an immortal soul that lives forever.

460 BC The natural philosopher, Democritus, is born in Greece. He will later propose the atomic theory of matter. In the AD 1900s, Albert Einstein and others will use this theory to create atomic energy and also atomic bombs.

458 BC Ezra leaves Babylon to go to Jerusalem and is appointed co-ruler over Judah by the Persian-Iranian king.

450 BC Ezra creates the Jewish theocracy, re-writes the **Bible**, and adds many new things about the Hebrew god to it. This includes the idea that the Hebrews are the chosen people and that Israel is granted to them as their land **forever**. True law can never recognize a perpetuity because perpetuity violates the Law of Cycles.

390 BC The Greek sage, Aristocles, takes the sixth initiation into AMORC in Egypt. He takes the name of Plato to honor his initiation and to recognize his symbolic spiritual rebirth as a new man. Plato goes to Italy and then returns to Greece in about 387 BC and establishes a school.

In Greece it is the highest of high crimes, punishable by death, to reveal the Greater Mysteries to the profane or uninitiated. What started as secrecy for the safety of the lives of the members of the lodge has now become secrecy for secrecy's own sake. Master Jesus will later try to reverse this.

356 BC Alexander the Great is born in Macedonia, which is just north of Greece. His teacher is the Greek, Aristotle, who was a student of Plato's. The reader will remember that Aristocles, or Plato, was a sixth degree initiate of AMORC in Egypt.

In 334 BC, at the mere age of 22, Alexander begins the march toward his conquest of Persia-Iran. Within ten years, Alexander has created the largest empire in the history of Western culture. However, just like all conquerors, both before and since, he never captures the northern mountainous area of what today is known as the Saudi Arabian peninsula. Alexander dies in 323 BC at age 33.

340 BC About this time, Aristotle teaches a philosophy of Deductive Logic which dominates Western thinking for the next 2000 years, until the time of Francis Lord Bacon, who re-discovered Inductive Logic in about AD 1600. Aristotle also has knowledge of the existence of the Western Hemisphere, as did many other ancient writers almost 2000 years prior to Columbus.

325 BC The accepted father of geometry, Euclid, is probably born this year in Greece, but the actual date is uncertain. He wrote several books, the most important of which is named **Elements**. He set forth the basic postulates of geometry, which are taught and followed even unto the present day. Most of the knowledge in his book is actually conceived by other people, but Euclid organizes it so that it can be understood by lay people. This book will become the second most popular book in Western culture, next to the **Bible**.

247 BC Hannibal, a Carthaginian general, is born in Carthage. He will later prove to be a real thorn to the Romans. This is the man who takes AMORC teachings from Egypt to Carthage.

200 BC According to the Sumerian scholar Sitchin, the big planet of the Solar System, called Marduk, that orbits the sun once every 3600 years, would be in Earth's area during this time period. Sitchin has told the author, in personal correspondence, that he is working on a book concerning the events of this time period.

198 BC According to some astrologers, the world entered the Age of Pisces at this time. However, according to AMORC teachings, this Piscean Age would not begin until about 6 BC. Master Jesus the Christ is born in 7 BC, or only one year before the world entered this new Piscean Age. Interesting coincidence?

100 BC Julius Caesar, the greatest of all the caesars of Rome is born. As a military leader, he captures much of what is now Germany and France and annexes it to the Roman Empire. In the process he destroys forever the old Roman Republic. Later, historians will say that no man ever made war so horrible as did Julius Caesar. His conquests of Germany and France make it possible for the Christian religion to spread into these countries some years later.

73 BC King Herod the Great is born and will rule over Israel from 41 to 4 BC. Herod is a very capable administrator and serves the Roman emperors as governor very well. He does not hesitate to execute people who disagree with him, or who, in any way, threaten the Roman rule. This includes his wife, two sons, his mother-in-law, and about 45 members of the 70 member Sanhedrin, which is the legislative body of Israel.

However, there is no historical evidence that he ever slaughtered all boy babies under two years of age as indicated by Matthew in the **New Testament.** The slaughter of innocents is a very old story, told in many cultures prior to Israel, and is added to the stories about Master Jesus long after Herod's death.

King Herod avoided any problems with the Essenes or Rosicrucians, of which Master Jesus and his family were members. Legally, by Jewish law, as the descendant of a converted Jew, Herod is technically Jewish, but he is not Hebrew, and never is accepted by the Jewish-Hebrew leaders in Jerusalem.

Master Jesus the Christ is also only technically Jewish, but is not Hebrew, and also is never accepted by the Jewish-Hebrew leaders in Jerusalem. Except when the Jews defy Roman law, Herod is a good Jew and a good governor, and rebuilds both Solomon's Temple at Jerusalem and the fortress at Masada.

63 BC The Romans conquer Jerusalem and put an end to the Hasmonean Royal Family as rulers of Israel.

55 BC Julius Caesar invades the south of Britain and it eventually becomes a Roman province several years later.

46 BC Julius Caesar reforms the calendar and makes a year containing 365 days except that, every four years, an extra day is added to create Leap Year. In order to adjust for past errors he makes the year 46 BC have 445 days which is the longest year on record. In March of 44 BC, Julius Caesar is surrounded by conspirators and stabbed and beaten to death.

This event will give rise to the later conflict between Mark Anthony and Octavian, which Octavian wins. Octavian will rule under the name Octavian for four years and later will be called Caesar Augustus. He will be the head of government when Master Jesus the Christ is born in 7 BC. Augustus dies in AD 14.

41 BC King Herod the Great, a Jewish prince from another family of recent Jewish converts, is made King of the Jews by the Romans about this date.

7 BC A boy child named Joseph, who will later become known as Master Jesus the Christ, is born to an Essene, or Rosicrucian, couple.

4 BC King Herod of Israel dies in March. He was appointed as king of the Jews by the Roman Emperor, but he was only technically a Jew himself. The gospel writer Matthew says, in the **New Testament**, that Master Jesus was born in Israel in the days of Herod the King. If correct, then Master Jesus was born sometime prior to March of 4 BC, and if shepherds were in fact in the hills, as Matthew says, then the time of year has to be after March but before November.

AD 6 The Roman government orders a complete census of Israel in order to facilitate taxing of all the people. Prior to the time of Julius Caesar the government had sold to the highest bidder the right to collect taxes in various areas. Julius Caesar abolished this system, but now it is re-instated, and is as unpopular as all taxing systems had been before that time or have been since.

AD 14 Again, AMORC teachings are made public, this time by Master Jesus, and again with disastrous results. Master Jesus is run out of India by the Hindu priests, much as Abraham was earlier threatened.

AD 17 Master Jesus is outlawed and run out of Persia-Iran.

AD 33 Master Jesus is crucified and run out of Israel and goes underground and silent.

AD 34 In India, the manuscript about Saint Issa, or Jesus, is written and preserved at Hemis Monastery. This is the earliest known record of Master Jesus that exists.

AD 38 This is probably the year that the Apostle Paul is converted and the Christian church as a political institution is born. It is created by Paul who is a Roman citizen, a Jew, and a lawyer. The Roman Empire had brought peace, prosperity, and open communication among most nations of the Western world and this makes rapid expansion of the Christian church possible.

Although Paul did visit briefly with Peter in Jerusalem in about AD 51 modern Christianity comes almost exclusively from the mind of Paul, and has very little in common with the teachings of Master Jesus the Christ. Paul is the man who creates the theology of Master Jesus as the son of God, the vicarious atonement of Master Jesus for mankind, and Master Jesus having resurrected from the dead.

None of this theology is accepted by the apostles and most of the original apostles never accept Paul as an apostle of Master Jesus. Neither Peter nor Paul ever become bishops in Rome, and Paul is not executed there. Paul later leaves Rome and goes probably to Damascus where, according to Jewish sources, he marries and has a family. The much later gospels of Matthew, Luke, and Mark are written in an effort to reconcile Jewish and Gentile Christianity.

AD 64 Insane Roman Emperor Nero burns Rome, and begins to persecute the Christians. The persecution will last, off and on, until AD 312. About this time, Epictetus who had been a slave in the palace of Nero, is educated and becomes a teacher of Philosophy. Epictetus and the Pythagoreans, or Rosicrucians, in Rome teach the universal brotherhood of all men throughout the world. This will later put the Rosicrucians on a collision course with the Christian churches where they have been ever since.

AD 68 Insane Emperor Nero commits suicide in order to avoid arrest and execution.

AD 74 Master Jesus the Christ -- Saint Issa -- dies at age 81, and is buried in Srinagar, Kashmir, in India.

AD 97 One of the first references to Master Jesus in the Western world, outside the New Testament, that the author has located, is by the ancient historian Tacitus, who becomes consul at Rome in AD 97, and who, in reporting about Nero, states that:

*"he (Nero) laid the guilt on others, and visited them with the most exquisite punishment, those, namely, who, held in abhorrence for their crimes were popularly called Christians. The author of that profession was Christ, who, in the reign of Tiberius, was capitally punished by the procurator, Pontius Pilate. The deadly superstition, though checked for a while, broke out afresh; and that, not only throughout Judea, the original seat of the evil, but through the city also ... In consequence, though they were guilty, and deserved most signal punishment, they began to be pitied, as if destroyed **not** for any public object, but from the barbarity of one man..."*

At the time this is written, Tacitus accepts the theology of Paul which is becoming popular by this time, to the effect that Master Jesus was earlier put to death in Israel, which of course is not true.

AD 100 Although some of the contents of the **Gospel of Matthew** has been circulating verbally since about AD 65, they are not written down until about this time by an unknown person of a strong Jewish religious faith. The author of **Matthew** pretty obviously is neither familiar with the geography of Israel nor the time period of Master Jesus. This gospel does not reach its present form until much later in about AD 173.

AD 120 The **Gospel of Luke** is written about this time by a person unknown. The author of **Luke** pretty obviously is neither familiar with the geography of Israel nor the time period of Master Jesus. The purpose of Luke is not clear, but it may have been written to make Paul's gentile teachings more acceptable to Jews.

AD 122 Roman Emperor Hadrian begins construction of a wall across northern England to protect his Roman province from attack by the Picts and Scots.

AD 130 The **Gospel of Mark** is written about this time in Rome by an unknown author. The purpose of Mark is also not clear but may have been written to build a bridge between Matthew and Luke. Christians have not and cannot explain why God would inspire three different people to write about the same person and events and yet report them so differently. Some scholars say the Gospel of Mark came first but the issue cannot be decided at this time and is academic in any event.

AD 167 Pope Soter sets Easter as a holiday on the Sunday following the 14th of the Jewish month Nisan, which is the day of the Passover.

AD 179 The time, place, and author of the **Gospel of John** is not known for sure. The first mention of this gospel in history is by Irenaeus who probably wrote it at this time, himself, and added it to **Matthew**, **Luke**, and **Mark** which he already had. Irenaeus goes to great lengths to justify the need for four gospels. Thus, we see that the four gospels were not only written long after the time of Master Jesus, but also long after the time of the Apostle Paul as well.

AD 255 Pope Stephen I decides to make it appear that the Christian church actually is the legitimate heir of Master Jesus the Christ and one of his assistants known to us as Peter. He has inserted into **Matthew 16:18** the following: "*And I say also unto thee, That thou art Peter, and upon this rock I will build my church; and the gates of hell shall not prevail against it.*"

This is an obvious forgery for the very simple reason that Master Jesus did not believe in a hell, and the Christian church was born from the teachings of the Apostle Paul; not Peter, and also not Master Jesus. This pope was a very egotistical and uncompromising priest.

AD 258 Roman-church Bishop Cyprian of Carthage is beheaded. He is the first to set forth the idea that there can be only one universal Christian church, which is the Roman Church, and everyone should be forced to be a member.

AD 288 Roman Emperor Constantine the Great is born in Central Europe. He will later literally create what is now called the Christian church as a basically pagan institution.

AD 310 Roman Emperor Constantine is refused admission into AMORC, and later sets up the Christian church to exterminate both the Blue Lodge and AMORC. The reason Constantine is refused admission is because he is found to be totally unfit. This is just one of many examples where extremely powerful men thought that they could bully their way into membership in AMORC. But, it cannot be done. Such membership really amounts to acceptance in the minds and hearts of other Rosicrucians and thus is totally subjective.

AD 311 Roman Emperor Galerius ends government discrimination against the Christians and makes their religion equally acceptable with all of the many other religions in the Roman Empire. His edict states:

"...We ...extend a pardon even to these men and permit them once more to become Christian and reestablish their places of meeting ...however, that they shall in no way offend against good order...."

AD 319 Roman Church priests are exempted from doing public works.

AD 321 Emperor Constantine decrees that everyone must observe Sunday and that dying people may leave property to the Roman Church.

AD 323 The Roman government makes it a criminal offense to force Roman Church priests to participate in pagan rites. The penalty for violation is a fine or being beaten with rods.

AD 325 The Nicene council meets at Nicaea, which is the present town of Jznik in northwest Turkey.

AD 337 Roman Emperor Constantine the Great dies.

AD 343 The Council of Sardika decrees that other bishops may appeal to the Bishop of Rome for final opinion on controversies. This makes the Bishop of Rome number one in the Roman Church.

AD 349 The sons of Roman Church priests inherit their father's position. This creates a hereditary class of priesthood in the Roman Church. Obviously, this is before it was decided that women were too evil to socialize with male priests. As a result, male priests have been relegated to socializing only with other males and history records the results of this folly.

AD 354 A new birth date is invented for Master Jesus by the Christian church. It is December 25, the day of the Roman pagan festive holiday celebrating both the idea that Rome cannot be conquered and also the winter solstice.

The year of Master Jesus' birth is also invented as being in the year AD zero. However, the Christian monk, named Dionysius Exiguus, who calculated the date by order of the Roman Emperor made several mistakes. First, he forgot that Augustus Caesar reigned for four years under his old name of Octavian. Second, he calculated from 1 BC to AD 1 without counting the year zero. Apparently, he miscounted one or two other years also.

AD 362 Julian is elected emperor at age 30 on the death of Constantius but will rule for only 19 months. Julian is a unique man and even more unique emperor. He is a Greek philosopher, mystic, and Rosicrucian. Julian ordered complete religious toleration for all faiths and for this he is hated by Christians and may have been murdered by them.

AD 365 The Roman Church hierarchy meets at the Council of Laodices and decides which manuscripts are forgeries and which ones should be inspired by God and included into the **New Testament**. Apparently, many at the meeting thought and claimed they were speaking for God. However, there is no evidence that God in fact either attended or was properly represented at the meeting.

AD 377 The Roman Church priesthood is exempted from paying taxes.

AD 380 The Christian religion becomes the official religion of the Roman Empire by order of Theodosius I. All Roman citizens are ordered to believe in the trinity of gods expounded by the Roman Church.

AD 385 Pope Siricius issues the first papal decree to a bishop in Spain and declares the decree to be binding on all bishops.

AD 395 The Roman Empire is reconstructed into two jurisdictions. The East is headquartered in Constantinople, now called Istanbul, and the West in Rome.

AD 398 Many non-Roman Church books are banned and burned. Possession of banned books is made a capital offense punishable by death.

AD 400 The great library at Alexandria is burned by the Christian church. The Western world is thrown into the Dark Ages. The Russian mystic, Madame Blavatsky, who studied in India and Tibet for several years in the late 1800s, says in her writings, that there are many rare and priceless documents still in existence in safe custody in Tibet that were thought to have been destroyed in the burning of the great library at Alexandria. This burning is probably the second greatest sin ever committed against mankind. The greatest sin ever was the confusion of languages. But the teachings survived in other parts of the world even after this fire.

The leaders of AMORC receive advance warning that the great library will be burned. Many major records are copied and removed to Tibet. One such record is called: "*The Economy of Life.*" It was written by Pharaoh Akhnaton about 1355 BC. A second set of these manuscripts was also made, but apparently has been lost.

AD 405 Saint Jerome completes his translation of the **Bible** into Latin.

AD 409 The Roman legions withdraw from England and the Roman Empire begins its fall.

AD 410 The barbarian, Alaric, captures Rome. However, legends that Alaric sacked and burned Rome are greatly exaggerated. As a result of this fall of Rome, Saint Augustine writes his book entitled **City of God** in an effort to show that the fall of Rome could not be attributed to the anger of the heathen gods, or desertion by the Christian church god. The premise of the book is, of course, true since none of those gods even exist.

AD 423 A new law states that all pagans, including non-Roman Church Christians and Jews, deserve to be put to death; however, they may instead forfeit all of their property and go into exile.

AD 425 The priest known as Saint Patrick arrives in Ireland and begins instilling Roman Catholicism, or paganism, in that country. He does this in order to replace the Christian church which is already there, and which teaches the knowledge of Master Jesus the Christ. This began a conflict in Ireland that could properly be called The 1500 Year War, because it is still in progress and killing many people, even unto the present day.

AD 438 The Theodosian Code of Laws is promulgated by Theodosius II. The code section entitled **On the Catholic Faith** outlaws all religions except that promulgated by the Roman Church. This will eventually wipe out most non-Roman Church Christians but the very tough Jews do survive.

AD 445 Emperor Valentinian issues an edict stating that the Bishop of Rome is pope and head of the Roman Church.

AD 451 Attila the Hun invades Western Europe.

AD 452 Pope Leo the Great meets with Attila the Hun and persuades him to spare Rome from destruction.

AD 476 King Arthur the Great is born.

AD 527 Justinian becomes emperor of what is left of the eastern jurisdiction of the Roman Empire.

AD 541 The first outbreak of the horrible bubonic plague occurs which, over the next 50 years or so, will kill perhaps as many as a third of all humans living on Earth.

AD 542 This is the presumed date of death of King Arthur the Great.

AD 551 Silkworms are raised in Europe from eggs imported from the Far East. This is a significant advance for Western Culture. Many years later in AD 1788, Thomas Jefferson, while serving as US Ambassador to France, purchases dozens of pairs of silk stockings for Abigail Adams, wife of his dear friend, John Adams.

AD 597 Augustine (this is a different man from Saint Augustine of Hippo), an Italian priest, becomes the first Archbishop of Canterbury in England.

AD 622 The Muslim religion begins.

AD 660 The Koran is collected into one book which is the one still in use by Muslims to the present day.

AD 673 The famous historian Bede, who speaks many languages and is master of knowledge in many areas of learning, is born. He writes his **Ecclesiastical History of the English People**, which preserves much of England's ancient history. The legend persists that Bede translated the Gospel of John into English. But if so, it has been lost and does not survive. Bede also states in his work **On the Nature of Things** that:

> "*We speak of the globe of the earth, not that it is perfectly round, owing to the inequalities of mountains and plains, but because, if all its lines be considered, it has the perfect form of a sphere....*"

Even in the darkest hours of the Dark Ages educated people know that Earth is round. Bede also observes that stars far to the south are not visible to northern people due to the curvature of Earth. He dies in AD 735.

AD 678 A large comet, probably Halley's, is visible for several months.

AD 721 Abbot Egbert translates the four gospels into Anglo Saxon.

AD 732 Charles Martel defeats the Muslims at the Battle of Tours in France.

AD 742 The great German king, Charlemagne, is born. During his life he will unite much of Western Europe into what is called the Holy Roman Empire. Pope Leo crowns him Emperor on Christmas Day in the year 800. Charlemagne knows about the ancient AMORC teachings and sends out many agents trying to locate those teachings and return them to him. His effort is never successful and he dies in AD 814.

AD 769 The Council of Rome declares that only priests are capable of being made bishops. The Council also deposes of Pope Constantine and has him blinded and beaten in public.

AD 871 In what is now southern England, King Alfred the Great, at age 21, takes the throne of what is now England, succeeding his brother. Alfred fought many battles with the Danes and is usually credited with unifying England and being its greatest king. King Alfred restored justice, issued a code of laws, constructed churches, and rebuilt London. He also may be responsible for collecting the historical data and preserving it in the **Anglo-Saxon Chronicles**. These **Chronicles** now provide a history of events in southern England from the time of Julius Caesar, in about 50 BC, up to AD 1154.

AD 1066 William the Conqueror, of Normandy, a speaker of a dialect of French, defeats England's King Harold at the Battle of Hastings on the southeastern coast of England on October 14. William becomes king of England. This will change the course of English history and result in lawyer double-talk, which persists to the present day.

AD 1095 Pope Urban II issues a summons for the First Crusade, which lasts until AD 1099. He calls on all Christians to go to Jerusalem and rid it of Muslim domination. With this edict, the Christian church becomes a power waging aggressive war. If such an international crime were committed in the current century, the Pope could be executed as a war criminal. Urban has also earlier renewed Pope Gregory's edict against priests being married.

AD 1099 In July, Godfrey of Bouillion and his co-leaders of the first crusade send a report to Pope Urban II on their success in Israel, parts of which state as follows:

> "...although the princes and kings of the Saracens rose up against us, yet, by God's will, they were easily conquered and overcome...."

> "...Moreover hunger so weakened us that some could scarcely refrain from eating human flesh. It would be tedious to narrate all the miseries which we suffered in that city...."

> "...God at first revealed to us, as a recompense for our tribulation and as a pledge of victory, his lance which had lain hidden since the days of the apostles..." (The holy lance with which the Roman soldier is reported to have pierced Christ's side.)

> "...And while we were delaying there, there was so great a famine in the army that the Christian people now ate the putrid bodies of the Saracens..."

> "...And if you desire to know what was done with the enemy who were found there, [Jerusalem] know that in Solomon's Porch and **in his temple our men rode in the blood of the Saracens up to the knees of their horses....**"

> "...When our army was in sight of the enemy, we invoked upon our knees the aid of the Lord, that he who in our other adversities had strengthened the Christian faith,

might in the present battle break the strength of the Saracens and of the devil, **and extend the kingdom of the Church of Christ from sea to sea, over the whole world...."**

"...More than one hundred thousand Moors perished there by the sword...."

"...Therefore, we call upon you of the Catholic Church of Christ and of the whole Latin Church to exult in the admirable bravery and devotion of your brethren, in the glorious and desirable retribution of the omnipotent God, and in the devoutly hoped for remission of all our sins through the grace of God...."

The report went on to state that unfortunately several thousand people escaped who could have been killed except that the crusaders stopped to plunder. The report may be exaggerated with the number of people slaughtered in hopes of pleasing Pope Urban, but even when discounted, it is still a stain on the Roman Church and a shame on Western Culture. However, Pope Urban II dies only two weeks after the taking of Jerusalem by the Crusaders and so never lives to enjoy the blood-bath he created. It should be noted here that the pope's military leaders thought that the pope's goal was to rule the whole world and **all human beings**, not just Christians.

AD 1146 Pope Eugenius III grants remission of sins and eternal life to those who will go to Israel and kill the Jews and Muslims living there in a second crusade.

AD 1158 In Europe, Frederick Barbaross assures all students of protection in their travels to study. Other secular rulers also begin to encourage scholarship. Such study will eventually lead to the Reformation.

AD 1162 The Mongol leader, Genghis Khan, is born in eastern Siberia. In AD 1206, he defeats many rivals and continues to wage aggressive war. He captures all the territory from Peking in China to the Turks on the Black Sea. This is probably the largest amount of territory ever brought under the control of one ruler. He sets up a code of laws that is followed by the Mongols for generations. His grandson, Kublai Khan, begins the Mongol Dynasty of China, and is the host for the traveler from Venice, Italy, named Marco Polo.

AD 1182 King Philip of France seizes all Jews in their synagogues and confiscates their gold, silver, real estate, and garments which Philip says the Jews stole from the Egyptians at the time of the Exodus event.

This is a very interesting observation by King Philip. It is true that the Hebrews removed much gold from Egypt at the time of the Exodus, but it is not true that these Jews in France have any connection whatsoever to those ancient Hebrews. In April, or the Jewish month of Nisan, King Philip orders that all Jews must be out of France by the coming feast of Saint John the Baptist. Many Christians accept that, under the new calendar, Saint John the Baptist was born on June 24. Philip used, as his rationalization for such a criminal act, the obvious falsehood that each Easter the Jews sacrificed a Christian in order to make fun of the Christian religion.

AD 1215 The bad King John of Robin Hood fame agrees to abide by Magna Carta. This provides, or really only implies, freedom of the church, strict administration of justice including due process of law, the protection of life, liberty, and property, consent of the people to taxation, and trial by a jury of peers. It becomes much of the basis for many laws in the United States of America.

AD 1235 Frederick II of Hohenstaufen issues a statute against heretics in Sicily. The statute states that anyone who deviates from even one belief of the Roman Church and refuses to recant: "...*shall suffer the death they court; that sentenced to the flames, they shall be burned alive in the sight of the people...*"

AD 1244 Montsegur in southern France, the mountain stronghold of the true followers of Master Jesus the Christ, is captured. The captives are summarily exterminated by the Roman Church in an act of genocide. Montsegur is supposedly the site where the so-called Holy Grail is kept. There is much fantasy about the true identity of the Holy Grail. It is not a vessel that Jesus drank from, and it also does not refer to the direct blood-line descendants of Master Jesus the Christ.

This strange mystery of history began when the Knights Templar went to Jerusalem on the First Crusade in AD 1095. They went there on behalf of the pope for very immoral reasons: to exterminate the Muslims and Jews living there, which is exactly what they tried to do. Then a very strange thing happened. Somehow, they gained possession of the Holy Grail. This caused a transformation in their character and they became true followers of Master Jesus the Christ. They took this knowledge back to France and, eventually, this knowledge brought them into conflict with the Roman Church. These people who had earlier been exterminators now become the exterminated.

The author offers the hypothesis that the Holy Grail is the Gnosis or knowledge taught by AMORC and Master Jesus the Christ about how man can attain to the Christ consciousness and become ever more in attunement with God, as Master Jesus was able to do. This system provides for teachers, but no priests, and thus is contrary to the teachings of the Roman Church.

AD 1296 Pope Boniface VIII issues his papal bull entitled **Clericis Laicos** in which he states:

"...*We...decree that all ...ecclesiastical persons ...who shall pay ...taxes ...without authority of this same Apostolic See ...likewise emperors ...who shall impose ...taxes ...shall ...incur the sentence of ex-communication...*"

Exhibit 5: United Methodist Church, Plainfield, Indiana USA. Not one penny in taxes has ever been paid to maintain the street in front of this building. The value of that maintenance is stolen from neighbors who are taxpayers. When any religious house has its fingers in the public treasury it is a clear violation of the separation of church and state.

With this papal bull, the Roman Church and all of its off-spring become thieves. Is there today even one Methodist Church anywhere that does not steal the value of fire and police protection from its neighbors? Indeed, is there any Christian church anywhere on Earth that is not also guilty?

AD 1302 Pope Boniface VIII issues his papal bull entitled **Unam Sanctum** in which he states among other things: "*We moreover, proclaim, declare, and pronounce that it is altogether necessary to salvation for **every human being** to be subject to the Roman Pontiff.*"

This obvious falsehood is believed by many Roman Catholics and a few still so believe even to the present day. Pope Leo X, in the AD 1500s, tries to tone down Pope Boniface's earlier false claim by **incorrectly** stating that Boniface had only been referring to Christians rather than to all human beings. **Unam Sanctum** is set forth in the Selected Annotated Bibliography.

AD 1314 Jacques de Molay, the Grand Master of the Knights Templar, is burned at the stake for heresy in Paris. About 70 of his assistants are also burned to death.

AD 1324 Abel's Case, which favors marketability of real estate, is decided in England. This will eventually become a firm rule of law in AD 1581 in the famous Rule in Shelley's Case. In Paris, Marsiglio of Padua, Rector of the University of Paris, publishes his book entitled **Defender of Peace** which is an open attack on the pope and priesthood. He asserts that popes are not supreme; that the Apostle Peter probably never was in Rome and, in any event, never delegated any powers to successor bishops; that no one should be forced in this world to accept church teachings; and that popes and priests have no authority over lay people including heretics.

Can anyone even imagine the horror this book caused in Rome? Marsiglio was in error about Peter being in Rome. Peter did visit Rome but never became a bishop there.

AD 1346 The plague, known as the Black Death, begins in China and reaches Western Europe by AD 1348. In some cites, half the total population dies from this terrible plague.

AD 1415 The Council of Constance issues its decree **Sacrosanct** in which it states that a general council has even the power to reform the papacy and its decree **Frequens** which provides that thereafter general councils should be assembled regularly.

AD 1438 Pope Eugene IV issues instructions to the Armenians concerning the seven sacraments of baptism, confirmation, the mass, penance, extreme unction, ordination, and matrimony. The pope fails to tell them that these sacraments are only economic in nature in order to raise money for the Roman Church. And, the pope makes no effort to rationalize how matrimony can be a sacred sacrament and yet be prohibited to the priests of the church.

AD 1450 Pope Nicholas V establishes, for the first time, a library in the Vatican and begins collecting books. The long absence of a library in the Vatican vividly demonstrates the lack of commitment to learning and scholarship in the Roman Church. However, Nicholas dies and his project temporarily dies with him.

AD 1453 The Arabs capture Istanbul and cut off Europe entirely from the trade routes to the Far East. This economic blockade by land is the big factor in pushing Spain, Portugal, France, England, and the Dutch states into becoming sea-faring nations. Less than 40 years later, Columbus re-discovers America and breaks Arab control of wealth in the world. The Turks are eliminated from world power at the Battle of Lepanto, just 118 years later.

AD 1492 Columbus sails the **ocean blue** in fourteen hundred and 92.

AD 1517 Martin Luther nails to the door of Wittenberg Cathedral his **95 Theses**, detailing abuses of the Roman Church. This act begins the Reformation in Germany.

AD 1525 Scholar William Tyndale, in Cologne and Worms, translates the **New Testament** into English so that ordinary people can read it. In AD 1535, he is rewarded for his effort when he is arrested for heresy and executed.

AD 1530 Ivan the Terrible is born.

AD 1536 This is the time of the most important changes in English history. Henry VIII confiscates nearly all the monasteries in England, which own a very sizeable percentage of all wealth, and parcels it out among his supporters. Also, by AD 1540, Parliament passes the Statutes of Wills and Uses which make it possible for people to dispose of, and control, wealth even after death.

AD 1543 Nicolas Copernicus publishes his book in which he suggests that the sun, not Earth, is the center of the Solar System. He dies very soon thereafter. This is the theory that is later proven by Galileo, and from which Galileo recanted after being threatened with death at the stake by the Roman Church.

AD 1549 **The Book of Common Prayer** for the Church of England is issued by Archbishop Cranmer of Canterbury.

AD 1559 Elizabeth becomes Queen of England after the death of Bloody Mary.

AD 1560 The Church of Scotland is founded.

AD 1580 In England, converts to the Roman Church are subject to the penalties for high treason.

AD 1581 The famous Rule in Shelley's Case is handed down by an English court. This ruling was sought by Queen Elizabeth I in order to make it possible for her to tax real estate. It also made real estate saleable.

AD 1588 England, under Queen Elizabeth, defeats the Spanish Armada and turns the balance of power to England for control over most of North America, including what will become the United States of America. The attempt by Pope Sixtus V to exterminate Protestantism in England is defeated.

AD 1600 The Blue Lodge is re-established in the West and the degrees in the Scottish Rite are raised in number from three to 33. The author offers the hypothesis that these 33 degrees are taken from the Tree of Life referred to in **Genesis**.

AMORC is re-established in the West, and the degrees are raised from seven degrees to nine. The early esoteric Christians thought there were nine celestial hierarchies between God and man. The great Rosicrucian, Dante Alighieri, reported these matters in **The Divine Comedy**. The author suggests that it may have been Dante who started the process of raising the number of degrees from seven to nine. In Dante's literary works one can perceive the basis for nine degrees.

AD 1607 Sir Walter Raleigh, an assistant to Francis Lord Bacon, establishes a colony at Jamestown, Virginia. He transports and stores in America many ancient and secret documents of AMORC and the Blue Lodge. Much later in 1789, when the United States adopts its constitution, the English common law as of 1607 becomes the law in the United States also. The next year, the John Smith of Pocahontas fame is elected governor of Virginia. In England, the King James Version of the **Bible** is being translated and is later turned over to the chief editor for finalizing. He was probably Francis Lord Bacon.

AD 1616 Galileo is threatened with death for supporting the Copernican heresy. The actor William Shakespeare dies at Stratford-upon-Avon but, of course, makes no claim in his will to any ownership of the literature published under that name.

AD 1618 Sir Walter Raleigh is executed by King James for refusing to reveal the identity of his friends in AMORC. Francis Lord Bacon fails to come to the aid of his friend and assistant, which raises serious questions about the character of Francis Lord Bacon. King James always hated Raleigh because Raleigh wanted to make England into a republic and had strongly opposed inviting James to England to become king, and also because, in his heart, King James was really a Roman Catholic.

AD 1620 King James learns that Francis Lord Bacon is the top Freemason, is head of the Rosicrucian Order, and destroys him publicly. But King James never solves the puzzle of the world-wide Rosicrucian network.

The Pilgrims sail from England in the Mayflower to Plymouth, Massachusetts, and settle there. The next year, William Palmer settles at Plymouth, Massachusetts, and becomes the first Palmer to move here from England.

AD 1622 The Roman Church sets January 1 as the beginning of the new year, rather than March 25.

AD 1623 The first folio edition of the plays attributed to Shakespeare are published. The actor, Shakespeare, has been dead seven years at this time, and probably has never even read much of the literature that bears his name.

AD 1626 The Freemasons are turned over to other leadership. Francis Lord Bacon works from 1621 to 1626 to complete many literary works, including many of the Shakespeare works, and then decides to go silent. After a fake funeral, he goes to Europe and later to America, but always in disguise. In America, he furthers the work begun by Raleigh, which is laying the groundwork for the American Revolution.

AD 1647 The Constitution of Rhode Island separates church and state and allows religious freedom. This is an indication of things to come in AD 1776.

AD 1649 The very corrupt Charles I, King of England, is executed; however, it is premature to set up a republic, and the effort is short-lived. In 1660, Charles II takes the throne of England. He too commits treason against his own country, but does live out his natural life.

AD 1662 In England, the Royal Society receives its charter from King Charles II. The Royal Society is comprised mostly of Rosicrucians and Freemasons. The society is still operative to the present day.

AD 1665 Rosicrucian Sir Isaac Newton discovers differential calculus and begins work on his theory of gravity and other matters.

AD 1672 Peter the Great of Russia is born.

AD 1705 Edmund Halley correctly predicts the return of the comet that now carries his name.

AD 1712 An uprising of blacks is suppressed in New York when 21 blacks are executed.

AD 1717 The Blue Lodge of the Freemasons again goes public in Western culture for the first time since the burning of the great library at Alexandria, Egypt, by the Roman Church in AD 400.

England starts the practice of sending its convicts to America, usually to Georgia. After American independence those convicts are sent to Australia. Thus, both the United States and Australia, two of England's best descendants, were settled somewhat by felons from the jails of England. That must say something about the quality of judicial procedure in England at that time. There is really nothing wrong with England today that Thomas Jefferson and 10,000 bulldozers couldn't fix.

AD 1727 The Quakers petition for the abolition of slavery in the American colonies.

AD 1730 The first Freemasonic Lodge is organized in Philadelphia. The very next year Master Mason Benjamin Franklin establishes the first subscription library, also in Philadelphia. The next year after that, in AD 1732, Franklin begins publishing **Poor Richard's Almanac.**

AD 1735 The French settle Vincennes, Indiana. This outpost is later captured by the British General Hamilton, called the hair buyer, because he purchased white scalps from the Indians.

Governor Patrick Henry of Virginia, in AD 1778, has George Rogers Clark capture this outpost during the America Revolution. This capture later made it possible for Thomas Jefferson to complete the Louisiana Purchase and allowed the United States to spread west to the Pacific Ocean.

AD 1740 Fifty blacks are hanged in South Carolina for wanting to be free. The very next year 101 blacks are convicted of plotting arson in New York City.

AD 1750 The first Conestoga wagons, the vehicles used to settle the American West, come into use in Pennsylvania.

AD 1751 Ben Franklin has already invented a very efficient heating stove and has also carried out experiments with electricity. This year he establishes Franklin Academy which will later become the University of Pennsylvania. The very next year he will conduct his famous experiments with lightning.

AD 1754 Rosicrucian Benjamin Franklin suggests that all the colonies in America unite. Franklin later advises that if we did not hang together, we would surely hang separately.

AD 1765 The child musical genius Mozart completes his first symphony at only age nine. He later will be an outstanding member of the Freemasons. His opera, named **The Magic Flute**, is centered around the ideals of Freemasonry.

AD 1767 Daniel Boone begins exploring Kentucky. He later leads several families over the Cumberland Gap and into Kentucky. Two of those families were the Lincolns and the Palmers. Both families stayed in Kentucky until the early 1800s when they starved out and moved north into southern Indiana. Later, some moved on to Illinois and other points west. Abraham Lincoln is born in Kentucky, grows up in southern Indiana, and becomes president of the United States prior to the bloody War Between the States.

AD 1775 The first skirmishes of the American Revolution begin at Lexington, Concord, and Bunker Hill.

AD 1776 The Freemasons control and operate the United States government. Jefferson is a Rosicrucian but not a Freemason. Franklin is both. Washington and most of the other founding fathers of America were Freemasons but not Rosicrucians. Thomas Jefferson and Benjamin Franklin design the American government along the philosophical lines envisioned by Francis Lord Bacon, but they adopt the republic as the political form of government as envisioned by Jefferson.

AD 1781 English General Cornwallis surrenders at Yorktown, and the American Revolution virtually comes to an end. The English really did not lose the war on the battlefield. More correctly, the British officers, who were also Freemasons like the American officers, decided to not win it.

AD 1786 The English lawyer, William Jones, who is an expert on Eastern cultures proposes the so-called Indo-European hypothesis, which is that the European languages and the so-called Aryan language of India have a common source.

AD 1787 Virginia cedes its northwest territories to the Unites States in the Northwest Ordinance of 1787 which prohibited indentured servants and slaves in this area. This is the first step toward the War Between the States, later in the AD 1860s.

AD 1789 The Constitution of the United States is adopted. That constitution, with its later attached Bill of Rights, will become the model for good government throughout the world. In France, revolution is fostered by Thomas Jefferson and the Rosicrucians.

AD 1795 On June 8, the son of Louis XVI and Marie Antoinette dies in the Temple Prison in Paris. This brings to an end the corrupt ruling family of France. Rumors that the Dauphin, as the boy is called, actually survived are political propaganda without any basis in fact.

74 TRUE ESOTERIC TRADITIONS

AD 1796 Master Mason George Washington, in his farewell address as president, urges the nation to be wary of foreign entanglements. America has violated that advice many times since World War II, all to its own shame and detriment.

AD 1799 The Rosetta Stone, which allowed Egyptian hieroglyphics to be translated into Greek, is discovered at Rosetta, Egypt, by the French.

AD 1822 The study of the history of languages takes a second big step forward when one of the Grimm brothers of Germany, Jacob, formulates Grimm's Law which is that consonants in language displace themselves in a predictable time sequence.

AD 1848 There are three movements begun in this one year: the labor movement, the cooperative movement, and the communist movement. All of these begin in England, but are the results of revolutions in Western Europe.

AD 1850 Rudolf Clausius, a German, enunciates the Second Law of Thermodynamics, sometimes known as the Dreaded Second Law. This law states that energy in a closed system tends to degrade into heat; or, stated differently, chaos always increases in a closed system.

AD 1905 Einstein publishes his Special Theory of Relativity which gives rise to atomic energy. He follows this, in 1916, with his new theory of gravity called General Relativity.

AD 1918 On July 16, the entire Romanov family is executed at the small town of Sverdlovsk in Russia. This brings to an end the 300-year reign of one of the world's most oppressive ruling families. Rumors that the youngest daughter, Anastasia, did not die at that time are political propaganda without any basis in fact.

AD 1927 Werner Heisenberg develops his Uncertainty Principle, which states that it is impossible to measure the position and momentum of an electron at the same time. This becomes the cornerstone of Quantum Theory which is the most successful physical theory of all time.

AD 1939 Rosicrucians in Germany warn of the coming attack on France and many secret records are removed from France only days ahead of the German troops entering France.

AD 1948 The World Council of Churches is created by Protestant church leaders from around the world. The objective of the World Council is to take the Christian church back to true christianity.

AD 1961 The United States of America, for the first time in its history, abandons its posture from that of a defensive nation to that of an aggressor nation. In the next few

OUTLINE OF WESTERN HISTORY   75

Exhibit 6: The Rosetta Stone, now in the British Museum. It was discovered by Napoleon in Egypt in AD 1799. Note that it is written in three different languages: Egyptian hieroglyphics, Greek, and Demonic.

76 TRUE ESOTERIC TRADITIONS

years, this new aggressive war policy will result in America waging aggressive war in Vietnam, Central America, the Middle East, and the Far East. Because of the military might of America, there is no country in the world strong enough to place American leaders on trial for war crimes, as was done at Nürnberg after World War II.

```
            The long-lost
        sacred language -- the
       Eve of the language world --
     is none other than Modern English
```

CHAPTER THREE -- ATLANTIS

The evidence available at this time suggests that present-day thinking man originated about 250,000 BC in the Middle East or Africa, perhaps in a Garden of Eden. But how can that be? The dinosaurs ruled Earth for 200 million years or more and became extinct about 65 million BC. Highly intelligent mammals can be traced back less than ten million years.

Early man, as distinguished from present-day thinking man, can be traced from maybe 7,000,000 BC down to maybe 50,000 BC. If true, that means that early man and present-day thinking man co-existed on Earth for a quarter of a million years.

Which would you rather know; where you came from, or where you are going? Certainly, both are intriguing questions. Perhaps if man could figure out whence he came, he might at the same time figure out where he is going.

In considering the source of mankind, there are several possibilities:

1. Man gradually evolved in a straight line, Darwinian style, from a lesser man to present-day thinking man;

2. God specially created man from dust on a certain day, Roman-church style, in or about 4004 BC;

3. Early man evolved but then was at some point in time -- about maybe 250,000 BC -- mutated into present-day thinking man by a chemical reaction from drugs ingested from plants; or,

4. Early man was taken into a laboratory and had his genes intermingled in a test tube, Sitchin style, with those of more advanced men or gods then on Earth, and then with cross-breeding with those gods present-day thinking man was thus created as a hybrid with two brains and two potentials.

Archaeologists confirm that there is indeed a missing link in the development of present-day thinking man. Three out of four of the above theories would account for this missing link. The only one that does not and maybe cannot is the Darwinian theory of evolution, which is the very one that is accepted by most educated people in the Western world. Perhaps the missing link is indeed missing and cannot be found simply because it does not exist. The author can see the possibility of truth in all of these theories, except the one advanced by the Roman Church.

We do not know when or where the ancient White Lodge began, but we can trace it in formal structure to ancient Egypt. The culture of Egypt sprang forth in full bloom from its very beginning perhaps as early as 6000 BC. That is, there exists no evidence in Egypt of a gradual cultural development.

From historical records available at this time, it is not possible to say for sure where that Egyptian culture came from. But it can be established with reasonable certainty that it was imported to Egypt from someplace else and did not originate in Egypt.

One theory that has much public support is that the Egyptian culture came from a major continent in what is now the Atlantic Ocean, and which was called Atlantis. This lost continent of Atlantis supposedly sank beneath the waves of the Atlantic Ocean in about 9500 BC. Some of the survivors who escaped from that cataclysmic event migrated to Egypt and eventually started the Egyptian culture.

The Greek philosopher Plato, who lived from 428 to 347 BC and studied for twenty years, or one thousand weeks, in AMORC in Egypt, tells the story of this lost continent in one of his books called **Timaeus**, where Egyptian teachers are explaining history to Solon. According to Plato, who got the story from his own studies, the Egyptian teachers told the earlier Greek sage Solon the story. The story goes:

"...For these histories tell of a mighty power which was aggressing wantonly against the whole of Europe and Asia, and to which your city [Athens] put an end. This power came forth out of the Atlantic Ocean, for in those days the Atlantic was navigable; and there was an island situated in front of the straits which you call the columns of Heracles (Gibraltar); the island was larger than Libya [Africa] and Asia put together, and was the way to other islands, and from the islands you might pass to the whole of the opposite continent (North America) which surrounded the true ocean; for this sea which is within the Straits of Heracles (Gibraltar) is only a harbor, having a narrow entrance, but that other is a real sea, and the surrounding land may be most truly called a continent.

"Now in this island continent of Atlantis there was a great and wonderful empire which had rule over the whole island continent and several others, as well as over parts of the continent, and, besides these, they subjected the parts of Libya (Africa) within the columns of Heracles (Gibraltar) as far as Egypt, and of Europe, as far as Tyrrhenia.

"The vast power thus gathered into one, endeavored to subdue at one blow our country and yours and the whole of the land which was within the straits (the Mediterranean Sea Basin); and then, Solon, your country (Athens) shone forth, in the excellence of her virtue and strength, among all mankind; for she was first in courage and military skill, and was the leader of the Hellenes.

"And when the rest fell off from her, being compelled to stand alone, after having undergone the very extremity of danger, she defeated and triumphed over the invaders, and preserved from slavery those who were not yet subjected, and freely liberated all the others who dwell within the limits of Heracles (the Mediterranean Sea Basin).

> "But afterwards there occurred violent earthquakes and floods; and in a single day and night of rain all your warlike men in a body sank into the earth, and the island of Atlantis in like manner disappeared, and was sunk beneath the sea. And that is the reason why the sea in those parts is impassable and impenetrable, because there is such a quantity of shallow mud in the way; and this was caused by the subsidence of the island (continent)...."

Plato further relates that in the legend these things happened about 9000 years earlier or about 9500 BC, according to Plato. Recent studies show a more correct date of 8000 BC.

There are some independent legends that say that until about 2000 BC the Atlantic Ocean, west of the Straits of Gibraltar, was muddy. But was there in fact a major continent there? The author feels that the answer is no.

When the great deluge of ancient times took place as related in the **Bible** and many other historical documents, undoubtedly some of the present day Azores and some of what today are the British Isles did become submerged below the waters of the Atlantic. But this simply could not have been a major continent, half the size of Africa, because in this area there is no such major missing link. It is more probable that this great deluge or flood took place about 8000 BC and not 9500 BC.

One of the major stumbling blocks to accepting a major continent in the middle of the Atlantic Ocean is that it just doesn't fit from a physical, geological standpoint. Studies concerning the land masses of Earth and their movements have developed to the point where we can now reasonably well outline the shape and size of the land masses of Earth over the last 200 million years.

A study of most any ordinary map will show that North America and South America once fitted into the Western coast of Africa and Europe like the pieces in a jigsaw puzzle. And in that puzzle, while there could be small islands missing, there simply is not a major missing piece. An Atlantis culture probably did in fact exist, but it was not on a major continent.

The land mass of Earth about 250 million years ago was one continent and is named by modern geologists as Pangaea. The break-up of this massive Pangaea has continued for the last 250 million years down to the present time.

Both archaeologists and geologists have rejected the existence of a continent of Atlantis. Plato's student, Aristotle, always thought that Plato's idea of Atlantis was an imaginary state to be used to test his ideas for the government of the ideal state: "*It was,*" said Aristotle, "*a hypothetical state Plato used for teaching purposes only.*"

The Gulf Stream that flows north and warms the northwestern coast of Europe and makes it habitable does provide some support for an Atlantis simply because prior to 8000 BC northern Europe was much colder and much less inhabited than now.

However, this flow of the Gulf Stream towards Europe could have been aided by some parts of the British Isles going under the Atlantic or merely by Earth's rotation to the East. It also could have been caused by a reversal in the magnetic poles or from any number of other causes.

Ignatius Donnelly, a United States congressman from Minnesota in the 1880s, noted that there is no question that there are many positive comparisons between architectural styles, customs of the people, and religious teachings in Europe and Africa on the one hand, and in North and South America on the other.

Such a comparison is definitely true but that doesn't necessarily require a land bridge of islands or a continent between the two. Actually, water is easier to transport and communicate across than a mountainous continent. The absence of a continent of Atlantis does not invalidate the findings of Donnelly. Donnelly's findings are just as valid if Atlantis were the British Isles as if it were a continent farther south in the Atlantic. Atlantis did exist some place on Earth as a culture, but probably not as a major continent.

The teachings of the ancient White Lodge of Egypt included the idea that a great enlightened leader would come who would bring salvation to the world. This idea somehow found its way into the culture of the Mayan Indians of Central America, which also tends to confirm Donnelly's findings. Perhaps the teaching became confused through time. Instead of believing that a great enlightened teacher of the ancient White Lodge would come, the Mayans believed that a white teacher would come who would be a god.

Because of the total misunderstanding of this teaching, when the white Spanish arrived the Mayans were totally unable to defend themselves from them because they feared the Spanish as gods. And thus with very little effort, the Spanish murdered and enslaved those people and very nearly wiped out their entire culture.

We perhaps smile that people could be so naive. But, if there is yet another undiscovered planet inhabited by advanced men, and one of them steps forth from his rocket ship in front of the world press, how many of us might think it was Master Jesus who had returned as predicted? Perhaps even more so, if that person were a tall, thin, bearded, blue-eyed, Aryan as most of us believe Master Jesus to have been. Surely many would mistake such a person for Master Jesus.

This idea of a great enlightened leader, or savior, who would some day come, is found in many religions. To Christians, it is the second coming of Master Jesus; for Jews, the

Messiah; for Muslims, the Imam Mahoi; for Buddhists, the Buddha; for Hindus, the Avatar of the age; to the Indians of America, it was Quetzalcoatl, and to the New Age people, it is the next World Teacher.

The great deluge that Noah survived, which is also recorded in many cultures, could have been caused by a large asteroid hitting Earth near the Gulf of Mexico area. Such impacts have probably happened before. One major asteroid impact took place in the Pacific Ocean about 65 million years BC and caused the extinction of the dinosaurs.

Either one of those asteroid impacts could have been the blow that started Earth wobbling on its axis and began the precession of the equinoxes, which now takes about 25,920 years per wobble.

The **Bible** tells of mankind at one time prior to the Tower of Babel all sharing a common language. What language was that? Was it Egyptian, Greek, Sanskrit, Hebrew, Celtic, Austronesian, or Modern English?

You might find some scholars in favor of each of those languages except probably Modern English. The author offers the hypothesis that the oldest language on Earth, and the one referred to in the **Bible** as being in common use by mankind prior to the Tower of Babel, is in fact Modern English. Modern English is indeed the long-lost sacred language.

Soviet Professors Gamkrelidze and Ivanov, only in the last few years, have made some big advances in the study of linguistics as it applies to locating the time and place of the long-lost sacred language or, may we say, the **Eve** of the language world.

The study of linguistics is almost as complicated as the study of the human genetic code. Spoken languages can already be traced back farther than written languages. It will require the use of giant computers to store and correlate all the details of these studies as scholars untangle the history of languages.

The two Soviet scholars came to the tentative conclusion that the birthplace of languages was in the Near East, in present-day Eastern Turkey, about 6000 BC, not too far from the legendary Garden of Eden. Some proponents of an **Eve language** prefer Africa as the birthplace. From the ancient Eve language, the various families of languages evolved. This includes the Greek, Sanskrit, Iranian, Slavonic, Germanic, Romanic, Celtic, and Anatolian, which is now dead. The two professors also came to the rather novel conclusion that in some respects the Germanic family of languages, which includes English, are more ancient than Sanskrit and Greek. Very interesting.

In August 1987 in Israel, according to news reports, a group of archaeologists headed by Yaakov Levitt reported the accidental finding of an object known as the parah dish that some people claim had writing on it in Modern English. They were naturally

82 TRUE ESOTERIC TRADITIONS

mystified and sent it to a laboratory for carbon dating. The date came back as 6500 BC. The reporter instantly and erroneously jumped to the conclusion that this proved that

Exhibit 7: This is reported to be the ancient Rosicrucian alphabet, containing 26 letters. Note the similarities to Modern English. The author offers the hypothesis that all later alphabets evolved from Modern English, which is the long-lost sacred language.

EVOLUTION OF THE ALPHABET

EGYPTIAN				I	II	III	IV	V
𓅃	= smooth breathing, like h in "honor". As vowel see below	𓏴	= ch (like ch in German "ich")	∢	A	A	A	A
𓏲	= y (in Greek times it was used as a vowel)	⊘	= kh (like ch in Scotch "loch" or German "Bach")	9	S 𐤁	B	B	B
𓂝	= guttural, pronounced in back of throat; not used in English	—	= s	7	1	Γ	C G	C G
𓅱	= w (later 𓏲 was also used; 𓏲 both signs as vowels, see below)	𓊪	= s (originally of slightly different sound from the preceding)	Δ	Δ	Δ	D	D
				⊣	⋺	E	E	E
				Y	Y	Y	F V	F.V.U
𓃀	= b	⊐	= sh	I	I	I	...	Z
𓊪	= p	△	= q (in Greek times also used for k)	H	8	8	H	E.H
𓆑	= f	⌒	= k	⊕	⊗	⊗	...	TH.PH
𓅓	= m (later ⊂ was also used for m)	△	= g	Z	?	?	I	I
		⌒	= t	7	K	K	...	K.KH
𓈖	= n	⊂	= th	6	√ 11	L ∧	L	L
𓂋	= r	𓆟	= d	?	M	M	M	M
𓃭	= l in late times (originally r or rw)	𓆓	= dh or dsh (like j in "jug")	?	Y	N	N	N
𓉔	= h			∓	∓	∓	X	X
				O	O	O	O	O
				)	1	Γ	P	P
				M	N	M	...	S
				φ	φ	φ	Q	Q
				q	4	P	R	R
				W	3	ξ	S	S
				X	T	T	T	T

Exhibit 8: Evolution of the Alphabet. The Egyptian Hieroglyphic alphabet containing 24 consonants which was in use prior to 3000 BC. The Egyptians pronounced but did not write their vowels. Column I is the Phoenician; Column II is the early Greek; Column III is the late Greek; Column IV is the Latin; and Column V is the English alphabet.

not only did the legendary Atlantis actually exist, but also that it existed in the eastern Mediterranean area near present-day Crete.

Such a conclusion was not warranted. What it may have meant, if anything, indeed was the possible use of Modern English in Israel in 6500 BC.

Why did language become confused? The major reason may be that as agricultural populations dispersed from their common source, which we will call the Garden of Eden, throughout the rest of the world, their languages changed due to the new environments they encountered. However, a more subtle explanation might also be that the priesthoods did not want ordinary people to be able to read and understand and communicate with each other without the priests as go-betweens. They feared a loss of control over the people.

From **Genesis 11** in the **Bible** we read:

> "...*And the whole earth was of one language and of one speech ... And the Lord came down to see the city and the tower, which the children of men builded. And the Lord said, Behold, the people is one, and they have all one language; and this they begin to do: and now nothing will be restrained from them, which they have imagined to do. Go to, let us go down, and there confound their language, that they may not understand one another's speech....*"

The unnatural confusion of language was the greatest sin ever committed against mankind. God does not sin; therefore, God was not responsible for the so-called Tower of Babel incident.

Egyptian hieroglyphics deciphered from the Rosetta stone in the early 1800s by Champollion were found to be very simple to read. We now know that continually, throughout Egyptian history, when it got to the place that ordinary people had learned how to read, the priests would further confuse matters by adding new letters to the alphabet. The priests finally added a total of 450 new letters to the previously very simple 31 letter Egyptian alphabet. They also quit writing the vowels. And so the reader had to infer the vowels. The priests knew how to do this, but the uninitiated did not.

If the priesthood in ancient Egypt would do this to confuse people, might not this suggest the same explanation for the world-wide confusion of languages in the first place? The **Bible** also suggests that some god confused the languages so the people could not communicate with each other. That the One True God would do such a thing is unthinkable to right-minded people. That the priests would do so only confirms their other actions over the centuries.

In all ancient cultures there is much learning hidden in symbolism. Why so much symbolism? The reason is that as ordinary people learned to read, the priests feared the loss of their positions and hid all the knowledge they possibly could in symbolism, so that only members of their group could read and acquire such cultural knowledge.

The many different alphabets in use on planet Earth all seem to share some things in common. Take special note of the similarity between the ancient Rosicrucian alphabet which has been presented here and Modern English. It is submitted that they are far too similar for it to be accidental.

Exhibit 9: Kay Palmer, learning to count Egyptian style, in Karnak Temple, Egypt.

Although the author cannot verify its authenticity, the Rosicrucian alphabet shown is claimed to be from Atlantis and is presented here with the specific permission of AMORC. Note that this alphabet is all taken from the symbols that can be derived from a cross within a triangle. It was perhaps in use from 8000 to 6000 BC.

It is not the purpose of this book to report on matters such as Astrology, Numerology, Tarot, and Kabala. However, we need to touch on some ancient Kabala in order to bolster our hypothesis that Modern English may be the oldest language known to man, and the language of the most ancient Kabala.

One reason we do not report on the subject of Astrology herein is because at least 95 per cent of the books and articles written on the subject are pure nonsense and over-emphasize the impact that astrology has on man.

It is true that there does exist some valid information on astrology and that the planets do indeed affect our lives. But it is also true that by far most information on the subject is not valid, and that the effect of the planets on man is so minute and inconsequential as to be unworthy of a great deal of time and attention.

The ordinary astrologer wants to know your time and place of birth to the most minute detail, and then seeks from that information to project aspects of character as well as the best and worst times to undertake matters of life.

But there are many important things that most astrologers never even consider: What were the eating, drinking, and emotional states of the mother for the months prior to birth? What were the family characteristics and traits of the parents and forefathers of the person? Those family inheritances certainly do profoundly affect man. And, what was the environment of the person, such as opportunity for education and responsibility? Perhaps most important of all is, what God-given ability and inclinations were given to the person at birth with which to begin life. All of these matters are important but usually remain unconsidered.

There is no question but that the sun and moon do influence our lives. Sun spots and solar flares do affect the amount of radiation surrounding Earth. The wise farmer plants his potatoes when the moon is right. The ocean tides and the menstrual cycles of most women are determined by the moon. Also mental patients, or so-called lunatics, are deeply affected by the lunar cycles.

And if the sun and moon can affect us so profoundly then most certainly the other planets affect us somewhat. To suggest otherwise is to lack wisdom and understanding of the nature of things.

But the influence of the planets on our lives is minuscule. Many people in Western culture own automobiles. Many drive those automobiles to market to obtain food and other necessities. If there is a one mile per hour breeze blowing directly against your windshield, it will take more fuel to move the automobile and you to the market than if there were no such breeze. There is no question about that. Still, few people even consider such a small breeze when they are deciding on going to market. Astrology is like that little breeze. Certainly it is there and certainly it affects us, but not enough to cause us to give it much attention or concern.

Besides astrology there are many other belief systems promulgated to mankind whereby a person can rid him or herself of responsibility for his or her own conduct. All of these systems, from time to time, gain favor with some people. There are many examples.

Some reincarnationists think that events in their lives are caused by events that took place in prior lives. The psychologist, Sigmund Freud, thought that the sex drive was the causation factor in most human conduct. This idea was perhaps a natural consequence of the Victorian era where people, especially women, were not supposed to plan in advance on having sex or to particularly enjoy the process. A woman had sex simply because she was seized with the urge which was beyond her ability to control.

Freud's student, Carl Jung, took the idea of past lives and presented it in more scientifically acceptable terms. He proposed that all of the experiences of mankind were present in what he called the collective subconscious, and these subconscious factors are causation factors in human conduct. Man is thus controlled by subconscious motivations that are beyond his own control and which are outside the area of his own individual responsibility.

Joseph Campbell developed Jung's idea of subconscious archetypes, and thought that a culture's mores are set forth in the symbols of the culture, and these symbols represent various Jungian archetypes. Again, man's conduct is controlled by cultural archetypes that are outside his own individual responsibility.

Ideas on the cause of human conduct are many. The reason is that people, quite naturally, want to find excuses to justify their own conduct, or misconduct, and the excuses they seek to find are always beyond their own control.

Astrology, past lives, the sex drive, the collective subconscious, and various cultural archetypes may indeed influence us in our lives. Also, some people's lives are controlled by such things as drugs, food, alcohol, and a multitude of other factors. However, the idea that such things are the causation of human conduct are substantially overstated. Such influences may exist, but man is granted free will which may be used by him to subdue and control those influences.

The ancient Kabala is sort of an alphabet of symbols in which the language is on a spiritual level so that each reader may read and understand at his own individual level of development in consciousness. It is said that God and man can communicate through the symbology of the Kabala, which is the language of soul, and thus can be comprehended only on a subjective level. The Kabala may go all the way back to the Garden of Eden.

In Kabala there were what were known as the six fundamental mathematical constants:

1. The first and best known constant is Pi, the irrational and infinite number which describes the relationship between the diameter and the circumference of a circle. It is expressed numerically as 3.14159.

2. The second constant is the golden section, or golden mean, known by its Greek name of Phi. It is expressed numerically as 1.61803 and is the relationship between the radius and the sides of a ten sided figure. It can be obtained by adding one to the square root of five and dividing the sum by two. The speed of light is 161,803 nautical miles per second. The golden mean is truly a relationship that happens literally hundreds of times and places in nature. For example, it is the division of a line into two parts so that the small portion is to the large portion exactly the same as the large portion is to the entire line. Early Masons knew of these natural relationships and copied them into their man-made objects such as the Great Pyramid of Giza.

A Line Divided by the Golden Mean

A   B   C

In the above line, the distance between **A** and **B** is 1.61803 times the length of the line between **B** and **C**; and, the line between **A** and **C** is 1.61803 times the length of the line between **A** and **B**.

Both Pi and Phi are shown on the faces of the Great Pyramid or Masonic Temple at Giza, Egypt. Is it not amazing that these ancient builders seemed to know and understand not only the basic mathematics of the universe but it would seem, also, the Modern English language which was thought not even to have developed until over 4000 years later?

3. The third constant is the base of natural logarithms and is known in Greek as Epsilon or e. It is expressed numerically as 2.71828. The universe is said to fluctuate between one and 2.71828. There are several ways to obtain this mysterious number.

4. The fourth constant is one.

5. The fifth constant is zero.

6. The sixth constant is the square root of negative one, or **i**. This is sometimes called an imaginary number because there is no number that when multiplied by itself will equal negative one. This is because the product of two negative numbers is always

positive. It is said to represent the soul essence of man and cannot be perceived, except on a subjective level.

This is also actually true of pi and phi. Neither have true values that can be mathematically determined. They are really relationships or concepts of the mind.

These six constants represented the totality of all existence from the nothingness of the unmanifested zero to the totality of the All or One. They are all set forth and expressed in the Great Pyramid of Giza, the great Masonic Temple of ancient Egypt. There are many books on the reason for the existence of the Great Pyramid of Giza, but the author now identifies it as an ancient Masonic temple. The best book on this subject is **Mysteries of the Great Pyramid** by Peter Tomkins.

Two of these six constants, Pi and Phi, have been found to express themselves rather well in the modern Roman alphabet, which is generally assumed not even to have been developed until thousands of years after the ancient Kabala was expressed in Hebrew and Greek and other supposedly more-ancient languages.

For example, translate the Modern English alphabet into numbers with **A** equal to one, **B** equal to two and so forth down to **Z** which equals 26. Next, take the symmetrical letters which are **M, T, U, V, W, X, Y, A, H** and **I,** and exchange them for their numerical equivalents. Note here that, in the ancient Kabala, complex numbers were reduced down to simple digits by eliminating the nines. Thus, a 17 with the nine eliminated would be eight. **H** equals eight and **I** equals nine, which together then equals 17. Then eliminate the nine and there is eight left.

The symmetrical letters look the same from either side; that is, they mirror-image themselves. So, how many groups of symmetrical letters would there then be? **M** equals one; **O** equals one; **T, U, V, W, X** and **Y** equal six; **A** equals one and **H** plus **I** equals eight. Thus, the symmetrical letters of the Modern English alphabet in ancient Kabala were 1-1-6-1-8 or 1.1618 or Phi, the Golden Mean. Is this just an accident of nature or is there some method to this madness?

Now, how about the non-symmetrical letters? The non-symmetrical letters grouped similarly would be: **J, K** and **L** equals three; **N** equal one; **P, Q, R** and **S** equal four; **Z** equal one; and **B, C, D, E, F,** and **G** equal six. Thus, the non-symmetrical letters of the Modern English alphabet in ancient Kabala were 3-1-4-1-6, or 3.1416, or Pi.

Again, is this just another accident of nature or is there indeed some method to all of this madness? The author thinks that there is. And the reason that the ancient Kabala translates into Modern English is that Modern English is the long-lost, sacred language, and the language in which the ancient Kabala was originally written.

Martin Gardner and William Eisen have noted the brilliance of this interpretation of the relationship between the ancient Kabala and the modern English alphabet. However, they failed to realize that the reason for this is that Modern English is the most ancient of all languages. Modern English is the language in which the ancient Kabala was originally written. The Sanskrit, Hebrew, and Greek languages came after Modern English, not before.

Some of the oldest recorded history in the world is Hindu. This ancient Kabala may also find its way into Hindu history. We can note it even if we cannot fully explain it. For example:

Time of Brahma:

Age of Brahma	3,110,400,000,000 years
Year of Brahma which is (1/100 of an Age)	31,104,000,000 years
Day of Brahma which is (1/360th of a year)	86,400,000 years
Total of Age, Year, and Day	3,141,590,400,000 years
	or 3.141,59 etc. or pi

This comes from the Hindu culture, so some of the secrets of this forgotten knowledge may be found there. The fact that the year is depicted as 360 days rather than 365 and one-fourth days shows that the information is very ancient. Many ancient cultures recorded the year as 360 days. Do not assume that to have been error. At some time in our ancient history, perhaps prior to the collision that started the precession of the equinoxes, it may have taken Earth only 360 days to circle the sun.

Modern English was developed in England from about the time of Roger Bacon, who lived from AD 1214 to 1292, to the time of Francis Lord Bacon in AD 1626, from the ancient Rosicrucian alphabet and language. Both Roger Bacon and Francis Lord Bacon were experts in ancient manuscripts and ciphers. The Magna Carta, written in AD 1215, in old English and Latin, is as different from Modern English as any foreign language. Why and how did Modern English come to be?

The author offers the hypothesis that Roger Bacon somehow discovered the ancient Rosicrucian alphabet and language in very old and very secret Rosicrucian or Masonic records and started the rebirth and standardization of that old Rosicrucian language as Modern English. This process was substantially completed by Francis Lord Bacon and the Rosicrucians in the Rosicrucian enlightenment by the early AD 1600s. In the Shakespearean plays alone, Francis Lord Bacon added more than 10,000 new words to the Modern English language.

Modern English is now becoming the international language. There are not one but two reasons for this. One is that the British Empire covered the globe and spread the

British culture world-wide. But another reason is that all languages on Earth at some distant time in the past perhaps descended from Modern English. We have come full circle from Atlantian English back to Atlantian or Modern English again. The Law of Cycles prevails once again.

According to the White Lodge, the Law of Cycles teaches that the universe is so constructed that what appears to be an end is always only a new beginning.

Genesis 2:7
*"...And the Lord God
formed man of the dust of
the ground, and breathed into
his nostrils the breath of life;
and man became a living soul. ..."*

Evolution tends
to show that there
is a plan -- or God --
in the universe rather than
that there is not.

God is not fickle.
True love is totally impersonal.

CHAPTER FOUR -- GARDEN OF EDEN

Where did thinking man begin? One possibility is that thinking man began in the Garden of Eden in what is now the Tigris-Euphrates valley of the Middle East. The Russian-born scholar, Zechariah Sitchin, has spent a lifetime studying the records of an ancient culture known as Sumer that flourished for several thousands of years in that area.

There are literally thousands of clay tablets from this civilization in the ancient cuneiform script, many of which have not been fully translated. Sitchin has put some of this material in a series of books known as the **Earth Chronicles**. His studies show a Middle Eastern birthplace for present-day thinking man, the same as the **Bible**.

There are at least four different theories on the origin of man. All of these theories have weaknesses. The four theories we have identified are as follows:

The first theory is the **Bible** version. As interpreted by the Christian church, the Christian-church god created the heavens and Earth and man during six days in October of 4004 BC. The infamous Bishop Usher calculated that Earth was actually created at nine o'clock in the morning. There is no geological evidence, no historical evidence, and even very little reasonable biblical evidence for such a theory.

In the last few centuries, most educated Christians have rejected such a belief; however, it is still taught and believed by some less-educated and less-informed fundamentalist Christians.

The second theory is the Evolution Version. This theory was put forth by the naturalist Charles Darwin. His followers have taken much abuse from the Christian-church community.

The theory very simply holds that a species adapts to its environment by a process of natural selection and, as a result, very slowly changes its physical and mental makeup. Over long periods of time, by this natural selection, and by the survival of the fittest among the species, man developed from a lesser being into present-day thinking man. It was never suggested that man evolved from the monkey.

Man was a species of his own, developing from a less-developed line of man. It also was not implied that the survival of the fittest meant the strongest physically. The fittest really means the best suited to its environs.

Evolution has, in some situations, been shown to be scientifically true, and is therefore generally accepted by almost all scientists and the vast majority of educated persons in the entire world. Evolution tends to show that there is a plan -- or God -- in the universe rather than that there is not. What better way to prove the existence of God than by evolution? The priests who condemn the evolutionists do not know what they are doing. A person who accepts evolution almost has to believe in God.

There is a major problem with the theory of evolution as applied to man. This is the so-called missing link. There is no link between early man and present-day thinking man. The problem -- and it is a major one -- is that early man can be traced down to perhaps 50,000 BC, but present-day thinking man very suddenly appeared on Earth, seemingly without ancestors, about 250,000 BC. He thus co-existed with early man on Earth for some 200,000 years or more. In Africa, archaeologists have now traced modern thinking man back to 250,000 BC.

So, even accepting evolution, the sudden appearance of present-day thinking man about 250,000 years ago has not yet been sufficiently explained. Perhaps, modern-day thinking man pushed both the gods of the **Bible** and the evolutionists' early man entirely off the planet. This leaves man searching for his roots both above and below him. As above, so below, it is said.

What are some of those evolutionary traits that man has developed that sets him apart and distinct from other species of mammals? Most mammals have eyes and can see. Bats are one exception. Just think of the difficulty in describing the awe and beauty of sight to a person who has never been able to see. Just think of the difficulty Master Jesus had in trying to use the language of the day to describe and explain the Law of Love.

Most mammals have legs and can walk. Whales and porpoises, among others, are exceptions. How about the perception of colors? When did the human species first perceive colors? Animals apparently do not perceive colors. Also, a small percentage of humans do not perceive colors yet today.

When did the first human perceive colors? Was it 100,000 years ago or only 10,000 years ago? Think of the beauty of colors perceived by that first human! Also imagine the difficulty he or she must have had in explaining to other humans the beauty of a rainbow. The colors have always been physically present, but humans simply did not yet have the ability to perceive them. Humans apparently do not perceive colors until several months after birth.

The sense of taste and smell are not yet fully developed in all of the human species and is certainly more finely developed in some than it is in others. These are also traits that are still developing.

How about memory? Some few people can remember hardly anything, while others, such as Jerry Lucas, can memorize the New York telephone directory in only a few hours. Some people cannot remember things that happened only yesterday, while others can remember the instant of their own conception in the mother's womb, and apparently even back into prior lives.

Such memory recall is undoubtedly true, and yet it is difficult to accept by those of us who have never experienced it. It is often said that experience is the best teacher. Perhaps experience is really the only teacher. However, experiences can be emotional as well as physical and intellectual. Memory is a trait that is still developing in mankind.

Some animals certainly do have memory. Even the horse, which will eat or drink itself to death, can easily remember the proper route back to its own barn. Chimps, apes, and dogs know shame, remorse, curiosity, humor, and altruism, and some chimps can even use tools.

Music is another trait that is well developed in a few people and hardly at all in most of us. Look at Mozart and his high musical genius. Is there any possible way that he could have learned all of his knowledge of music in this lifetime? It would seem not. Mozart must have brought his musical ability with him to this life, either from God or perhaps from some past life. It would seem he did not acquire it all here.

A very few humans, such as Master Jesus the Christ, have perceived some level of Cosmic Consciousness. And Master Jesus says that some day all other humans will be able also to so perceive. That also must be true, and yet it is so very difficult for many of us to accept as true.

Any time any human states that something cannot be true, what is that person really saying? Such a negative person is really saying that he has not yet evolved sufficiently to perceive such a truth, and therefore neither has anyone else on the planet. Ignorance, or lack of evolvement, is a very common human shortcoming.

The evolution theory, and the special creation theory of the Christian church, probably account for almost all the belief systems held by people in Western culture.

The third theory is the chemical version. This theory has few followers. A few researchers believe that they have discovered the true meaning of the Garden of Eden story in the **Bible**.

The theory goes something like this: Early man was evolving like other animals when he discovered certain plants that contained mind-altering chemical substances, and the eating of those plants and the chemical substances caused tremendous mind-altering growth in his brain. As a result of this major mind jump, man became conscious of himself and thus became present-day thinking man almost overnight. This would explain the missing link.

There is some possible historical evidence to support this theory when that evidence is interpreted by proponents of the theory. It comes mostly from the work of Carlos Castaneda, Terrence and Dennis McKenna, and R. Gordon Wasson.

96 TRUE ESOTERIC TRADITIONS

From Chapter Three of **Genesis**, we read:

> "...And the woman said unto the serpent, We may eat of the fruit of the tree of the garden. But of the fruit of the tree which is in the midst of the garden, God hath said, Ye shall not eat of it, neither shall ye touch it, lest ye die. And the serpent said unto the woman, Ye shall not surely die: For God doth know that in the day ye eat thereof, then your eyes shall be opened, and ye shall be as gods, knowing good and evil. And when the woman saw that the tree was good for food, and that it was pleasant to the eyes, and a tree to be desired to make one wise, she took of the fruit thereof, and did eat, and gave also unto her husband with her; and he did eat. And the eyes of them both were opened...."

According to this theory, the priest who copied parts of **Genesis** from much earlier Sumerian records understood the secret mystery of why man was forbidden to eat this particular food. It was because it would alter his mind and could make him a little like God. Man did eat and that is how he came to acquire some of the knowledge of God -- to know good and evil.

There is no question but that there are some mind-altering drugs that can cause traumatic changes in the mind. Many such drugs used by ancient cultures are being discovered and re-discovered by modern researchers. Also, the discovery that such drugs were in fact used by the forerunners of our Western culture has only recently been found. Whether or not such drugs caused the quantum jump in man's mind and thus also created the missing link remains to be verified.

The fourth theory is the Sumer version. There is probably more written historical evidence for this version than any of the rest, and yet it has very few followers simply because of its extraordinary improbability.

In the late 1800s, thousands of clay tablets were discovered in the Middle East in writing known as cuneiform. Many of those tablets have still not been completely translated. Those records tell some amazing stories, many of which may sound familiar to modern Western readers. Zecharia Sitchin has spent much of his life studying these records. Sitchin's calendar in abbreviated form is as follows:

445,000 BC: The Nefilim gods referred to in the **Bible** arrive on Earth to search for gold.

432,000 BC: Gold is found and a base is set up on Earth.

400,000 BC: Gold mining operations were established in South Africa, with refining of the gold completed in the Middle East.

300,000 BC: The workers, who were lesser gods not close enough in blood line to be ruling gods, revolted against the hard work in the gold mines. History has again repeated itself in the last few years in those same gold mines. The present-day workers have revolted for the very same reasons.

250,000 BC: There were twelve ruling gods, six men and six women. One of the female gods was a scientist and went into a laboratory and created a more advanced female earthling, called Eve, who could procreate just like the female gods. Eve was then bred to the male gods. This created present-day thinking men and women who have spread over the entire Earth.

In 1987, two biochemists, named Vincent Sarich and Allan Wilson, announced that they had located the Eve of the **Bible** who is the mother of all human beings now living on Earth. They say that Eve lived in Africa only 200,000 years ago. The biochemists determined this date by a new dating technique where proteins evolve by accumulating mutations at a steady rate. These proteins are then counted like the ticking of a clock.

These findings would certainly seem to confirm Sitchin's thesis of a very recent source for present-day thinking man, and would also explain the missing link problem. These findings are, of course, controversial.

Sitchin has attempted to interpret those records. Here are some of the other things he reports:

1. That Sumer was a civilization which flourished in the Tigris-Euphrates area of the Middle East in present day Iraq from perhaps 8000 BC, or earlier, to perhaps as late as 2100 BC. Many records were made and preserved there of the earlier history of the Nefilim gods.

2. That history tells of gods that were really much-advanced men who lived on Earth and had atomic energy and space ships. They came here from their mother planet about 432,000 BC. They came here to mine gold needed back on their home planet. This is why man to this day has such a pre-occupation with, and love for, the yellow metal.

Their home planet circles the sun once every 3600 years, and thus comes close to Earth with each pass, to-wit: 11,000 BC; 7400 BC; 3800 BC; and 200 BC. The next pass should occur in AD 3400.

Note also that there is substantial scientific evidence that there may be another planet in the solar system. The planet Neptune was discovered in modern times when mathematicians calculated that something was skewing the outer planets outside their expected orbits. So Neptune was discovered, and Pluto also in 1930. But, still there is skewness. Still, something out there is pulling the outer planets outside their expected orbits. Some mass is missing in the solar system. So, is there another planet out there? Is it massive? Most importantly, is it inhabited?

These questions will be answered, we hope by the turn of the century. Perhaps we can call this the little missing mass problem. This little missing mass problem in the Solar System should not be confused with the much larger missing mass problem in the universe.

> 3. That in order to have workers, one of the female gods went into a laboratory and created Eve by crossing her own god-like genes with those of the earth creatures, thus creating a more intelligent woman with two brains, a left or beastly brain, and a right or god-like brain. This hybrid woman could better follow orders and was taught to earn her keep by the sweat of her brow. She was also taught to work for, or worship, only her god that created her.

Woman is thus a hybrid with both the capacity for good and evil. The idea that present-day thinking woman has been around on Earth for some 300,000 years or more would also fit in with Hindu history and legend. Also, those hybrid females were found to be attractive to the male gods and cross-breeding between them helped to create present-day thinking woman with the big brain almost overnight. This is the missing link.

Chapter Six of **Genesis** says:

> "...*And it came to pass, when men began to multiply on the face of the earth, and daughters were born unto them, that the sons of God saw the daughters of men that they were fair; and they took them wives of all which they chose.... There were giants [or more correctly translated as intellectual giants, or Nefilim] in the earth in those days; and also after that, when the sons of God came in unto the daughters of men, and they bare children to them, the same become mighty men which were of old, men of renown. ...*"

> 4. That there were twelve of these gods in the pantheon. They loved a lot and fought a lot among themselves for the very usual and human reasons. They also created the idea of kingship.

They were the kings, and men and women were taught to obey them because it was the right thing to do. The divine right of kings was to rule over others. When these gods left Earth about 11,000 BC and returned to their home planet, they picked out some of the brighter and stronger earth beings to be kings in their places. People were taught to obey these substitute kings.

The idea of kingship was a crutch for the people to lean on. When the true kings left Earth, ordinary people were put in their place, and while the true kings could no longer be a crutch, the idea of kingship has remained a crutch unto the present time. The idea of kingship is a pleasant one indeed for the kings. It is much less pleasant to those who are imposed upon to support it with their taxes, labor, and all too often their very lives. Queen Elizabeth II is worth perhaps more than ten billion dollars and is the richest woman on Earth. Yet, she demands and accepts twenty million dollars each year from the poor over-taxed British people. And, incredible as it sounds, the queen pays no taxes on her vast plunder. Gifts and taxes are not the same thing.

In ancient times, the kingship passed down by blood line. At first, these kings were stronger, smarter, and better than other men and women, but the system became so bad that kings would father children to be future kings with their own sisters and their own daughters. This, of course, eventually resulted in long family lines of almost feeble-minded kings. This practice also continues to the present time.

One only need look at the barely mediocre and anemic royal families of the Middle East and Western Europe to see the results of this inbreeding practice. The British Royal Family is so inept that most of its members would be on the public dole if they didn't steal their livelihood from the British people. Joseph-Yuya, and his protege Moses Moria-El, tried to put an end to this practice, and perhaps were successful among the Hebrews, but not in the world in general.

If the original idea that kings were kings because they were better was valid, then indeed all royal families on Earth today long ago lost any valid moral claims to their positions.

> 5. This kingship idea was also adopted by the Roman Church, in that the pope was said to be unable to be wrong on matters of morals. Also the priesthoods of most Christian sects by their acts and deeds, even if not by their verbal statements, generally claim to be more righteous and moral than other people. The infamous priest, Pope Boniface VIII, in AD 1302, went so far as to say: "...*it is necessary for salvation to be subject to the authority of the Roman pontiff.* ..."

The idea of kingship flourished over much of Earth until the French Revolution and the rise of America in the late 1700s. The idea of kingship still holds forth in many parts of the world to the present day, even in a few relatively advanced nations. It is an ancient tradition that can only be overcome by a strong, intelligent, and mature people, or by enlightened monarchs who are willing to perform their moral duty, which might be to insist that their nations change to republics as the best form of government.

> 6. That once created, man became a problem to control. The story of this difficulty is well reported in the **Bible** as it was taken from the records in Sumer. One thing those gods did was to confuse man with many languages so that people could not communicate with each other.

100 TRUE ESOTERIC TRADITIONS

The Hebrews probably learned of this history when they were in exile in Babylon, very close to Sumer, in about 587 BC. These stories became very much a part of Hebrew folklore and were copied into the **Bible** by Ezra, the politician-scribe who went to Jerusalem from Babylon about 458 BC and wrote and re-wrote much of the **Bible**.

Exhibit 10: An ancient Akkadian seal that clearly depicts the solar system. Note that there is an extra large planet between Mars and Jupiter.

While some stories in the **Bible** are very ancient legend, the **Bible** itself is less than 2500 years old, and was written much later than many books and records in other cultures.

7. That the **Bible** is the word of God is, of course, not historically accurate. Ezra was indeed a literary genius, a great politician, and perhaps even greatly inspired, but only the uninformed and ignorant could call his work the literal word of God. For Ezra was not God. He was only a man and perhaps not even a godly man.

The idea of attributing deity to a physical object such as a book like the **Bible,** or any other physical object, is as old as man himself, and may also go back to the idea of kingship where other people and physical things were worshipped as gods.

8. By about 8000 BC, these gods were getting fed up with man because they could no longer control him, and upon learning that an asteroid would soon strike Earth and

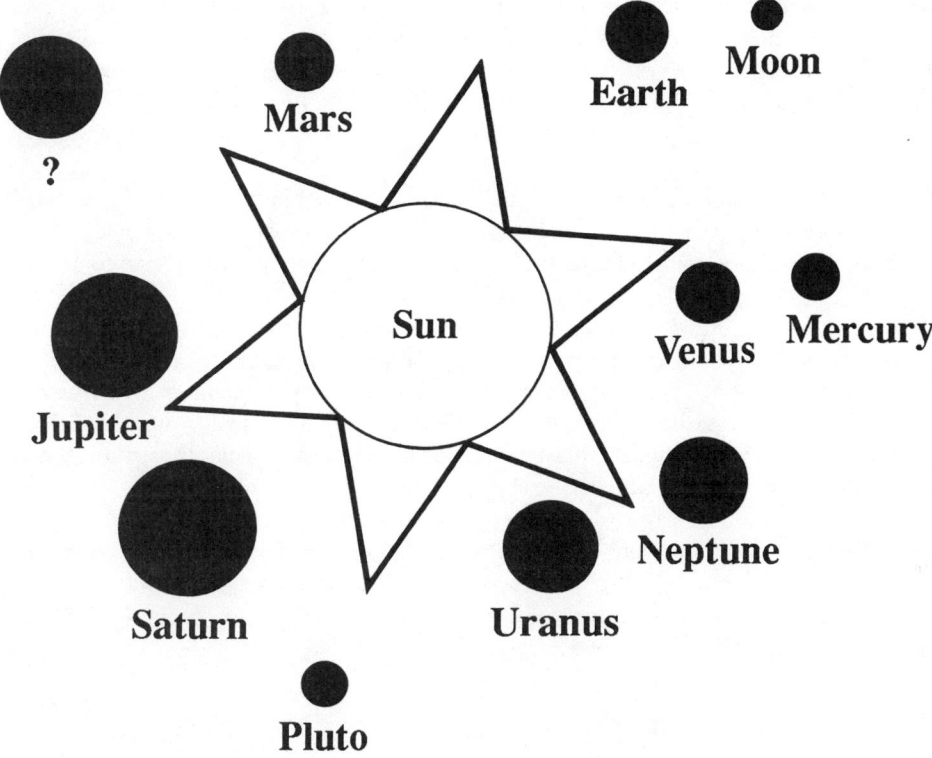

Exhibit 11: Re-creation of the Akkadian seal of the solar system.

create world-wide chaos and death, they decided to allow man to be exterminated. But one god ignored the plan and informed one of the earth people about what was going to happen.

The story of Noah is well known in the Western world and need not be repeated here. That same story with very little variation is also known and recorded in almost every other culture on Earth.

9. After the great flood of 8000 BC man was not doing so well on Earth. In 7400 BC the Nefilim gods, or intellectual giants, stopped by Earth long enough to show man the art of growing cereal grains and how to domesticate animals. Then they departed to their home planet, and left in charge human kings who were supposed to make sure that humans followed all the rules left by the gods.

The problem was that because of inbreeding and other reasons the lines of kings actually devolved while ordinary man had continued to evolve. This devolution was well demonstrated when the king of England quit the throne in a fit of animal passion in 1936. Today, ordinary people are much stronger and certainly much smarter than the remaining kings. The Nobel Prize has been awarded by a king but has never been awarded to a king.

10. In 7400 BC, and again in 3800 BC, these gods again visited man on Earth and imparted knowledge to him to help him survive and prosper. So what happened in 200 BC, if anything, when these gods should have again passed close to Earth?

Scholar Sitchin has told the author in personal correspondence that he plans to publish material that will cover this time period. The Sumerian account of early history seems improbable to modern man, but if true, it would certainly explain a lot of history that otherwise remains unexplained at this time. An Akkadian seal from the 3500 BC to 2500 BC era, now in the State Museum of Berlin, clearly depicts the solar system as it was known to the ancient Sumerians.

The only modern-day problem we have with the seal is that Pluto is shown as being between Saturn and Uranus. At the present time Pluto is between Uranus and Neptune, but spends most of its time outside of Neptune and, as far as we know, Pluto is the outermost planet of the solar system.

Two big questions are:

1. How did those ancient people know about the planets beyond Saturn that we thought were only discovered in recent times?

2. What is the extra tenth planet doing between Mars and Jupiter?

This extra planet is much larger than Earth, but smaller than Jupiter or Saturn. The modern scientific law known as Bode's Law says that there should be a planet between Mars and Jupiter, but it does not exist as far as we know, according to modern knowledge.

There is a lot of debris known as the asteroid belt in this area, but no planet. Is there yet another planet of the Solar System, the one that circles the sun every 3600 years, and is the home planet of the Nefilim gods of the **Bible**?

GARDEN OF EDEN

Modern science does believe that there are other advanced intelligent beings elsewhere in the universe. The Planetary Society in Pasadena, California USA, headed by astronomer Carl Sagan, has a program called Search for Extra Terrestrial Intelligence (SETI), which is a multi-million channel radio search of the audio spectrum trying to pick up radio signals from other planets.

The SETI search is a monumental undertaking. There are literally millions of different radio frequencies and the beings on another planet might be sending out signals through the universe on any one of them.

So the SETI search is set up to monitor millions of radio frequencies simultaneously and all with automated equipment that is programmed to look for certain anomalies. These computer programs are designed by human beings on Earth so they are all based on the assumption that beings on other planets will think something like us and will have knowledge of basic physical laws.

At least half of that assumption has to be wrong. Surely any people that were scientifically advanced enough, long enough ago, to be sending out signals that we can now receive, would be more civilized than the beings on this planet. But those beings on those alien planets should be subject to the same laws of physics.

SETI searchers think that the best frequency should be near the 1420 Megahertz hydrogen line because hydrogen is the lightest and most abundant element in the universe. In order to distinguish man-made signals from natural cosmic signals it is thought that if the hydrogen line were multiplied by pi (3.14159) it would give a radio frequency of 4.462336275 GHz, and that is the most likely frequency to broadcast or receive signals on across the universe.

To think that we are the only intelligent beings in the universe is a very parochial view. Indeed, even to think that we beings of this planet are intelligent beings is an assumption

Exhibit 12: Cheops, or Khufu, great pharaoh of the Fourth Dynasty and builder of the Great Pyramid.

that would be most difficult to support logically. It would be the height of wastefulness to create such a vast universe only for the semi-enlightened human beings on planet Earth.

Since God is outside of this physical universe, why would she search out such an insignificant out-of-the-way spot to rear such an insignificant litter of rabble such as the human race? Why indeed? God is not wasteful. Other beings do exist out there someplace.

However, until we develop some means of communication that is faster than the speed of light we will not be able even to begin really searching the universe. But someday, we shall make contact with other planets. When we do, the impact on the belief and value systems of Earth will defy imagination.

If there is a tenth planet in the solar system inhabited by beings superior to man, it would explain a lot of things, both historical and scientific. However, acceptance of these ideas of advanced men in rocket ships is very close to the flying-saucer phenomenon, which despite widespread individual affirmation remains unverified scientifically.

According to Sitchin's thesis, this other planet would not visit Earth again until AD 3400, and their rocket ships normally should not be visiting here until AD 3300 or so. Thus, any such flying saucers should not be coming from this other planet at this time. In other words, Sitchin's theories do not help explain the current flying-saucer controversy.

In Sitchin's reading of the Sumer version of the origin of civilization, the Great Pyramid of Giza in Egypt was built as a landing beacon to guide the Nefilim gods in their rockets to their landing site, which was in what is now the Sinai Peninsula. The pyramid was also used as a prison for one of the gods who had violated the rules. This would explain the air shafts to the King's Chamber in the Great Pyramid.

It is difficult to say at this time just why or even when the Great Pyramid was actually built. Two things are pretty certain:

1. The Great Pyramid was not built as a tomb for anyone. A dead pharaoh does not need air, and the king's chamber has two air shafts cut through hundreds of feet of granite to the top at great effort, planning, and cost. Only Master Masons built this temple.

2. By the time of Pharaoh Tuthmosis III in 1468 BC, the Great Pyramid was used as a temple for initiation by the ancient White Lodge, the parent and forerunner of the Blue Lodge of the modern Masonic Order.

GARDEN OF EDEN 105

Exhibit 13: The author and Kay Palmer on the Giza plateau northwest of Cairo. In the background to the east is the Great Pyramid Temple and two other pyramids that were built for and used as tombs.

106 TRUE ESOTERIC TRADITIONS

The author cannot accept that the Great Pyramid was built as a beacon. The Great Pyramid cost far too much in labor, materials, and intellectual effort to be planned only to hold up a beacon for landing aircraft. Surely there were less expensive ways even then to obtain landing signals, such as a tower or a mountain top. The author believes that the Great Pyramid of Giza was built for use as a Masonic or Rosicrucian Temple, a temple of initiation for those properly prepared.

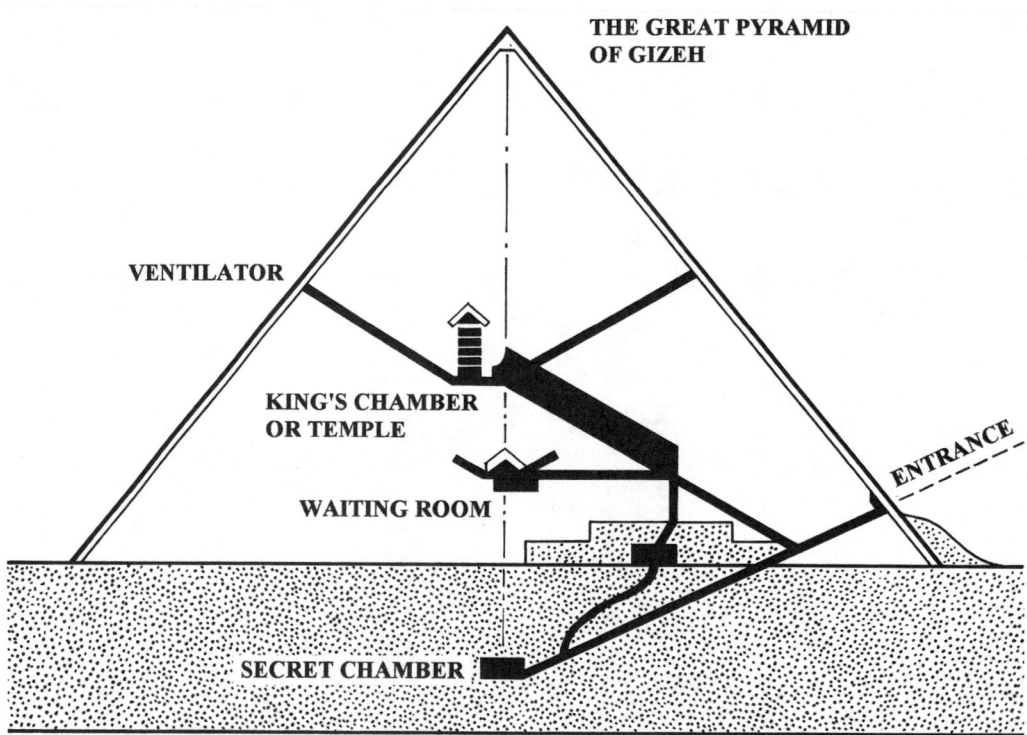

Exhibit 14: Drawing of Great Pyramid

It would be one of the most traumatic happenings ever in history if the new Hubble telescope in space actually verifies the existence of this extra tenth planet. This question should be answered by the turn of the century.

CHAPTER FIVE -- THE ANCIENT MYSTERIES

The mysteries of history are much more fascinating than any modern novel or play. If we can ever come to understand those mysteries, we will not only understand our own past much better, but we will also understand ourselves much better.

When man studies history he tends to satisfy his yearning for eternal life at least on an objective level. On a subjective level man knows that he is immortal and will live and exist forever. However, on an objective level it is quite a different story. Many people fear death. One would think that Christians would not fear death, and certainly they would not if they understood the teachings of Master Jesus the Christ. But in fact, most do not understand and do indeed fear death. Man fears loss of consciousness and seeks to extend as long as possible the known conscious state.

By studying history and the teachings of the masters, man can visualize and have affinity with those people and those periods and thus, to some extent, enlarge the time period of his consciousness back to, and including, historical periods.

Why has most of mankind believed in a multiplicity of gods? Why was it so difficult and even impossible for Moses Moria-El and many others since to sell the idea of One True God? The primitive idea of God was that she was very emotional and given to fits of anger and pleasure. Another primitive idea is the trinity, where god is wisdom, or intelligence, or love. When the idea of the existence of many gods was at last put away, many pagan-oriented groups, such as the Christian church, put forth the idea of an evil god, or Satan.

These people believed that God was vengeful and jealous; good in her heart but evil in her thinking; sometimes kind, but often unkind; both just and unjust, depending on her whims; and both forgiving and totally unforgiving. These pagan ideas have still not been removed from Christian-church theology, even to the present day.

The ancient Egyptians thought that creation came about by manifestation of the Word and the manifested triune gods of Ptah, Sekmet, and Nefertum. Why a trinity of gods? The idea of trinity is a valid one as to manifestations. One such manifestation is the pure will of God, or love; the second is the creative radiance of love, which is wisdom; and the third is the reflection of light and love which is intelligence.

In many religions, these manifestations of God have been confused with, and worshipped as, God. Such worship reverts to the ancient Egyptian worship which Joseph-Yuya and his group tried to replace with the worship of the One True God. Both the Hindus and Christians still worship these three manifestations, rather than God. The worship of only the One True God has not yet been done, except in the ancient White Lodge and among its descendants. Such an event should happen during the coming so-called Aquarian Age.

Of course, all Freemasons and all Rosicrucians believe in God. But there is more to this matter than belief in God. Christians believe in a god, but Freemasons and Rosicrucians do more than believe. They know, and what they know is the One True God of the universe, not some tribal god given to fits of anger and jealously, or who has a chosen people.

Many Christians who do not know God suffer from a superiority complex. And it is truly a suffering because all who do know can so easily recognize these pathetic people trying to appear as people of knowledge. This includes many priests of the Christian church. A superiority complex is caused by an inferior intellect, and can only be cured with a dose of wisdom. Ignorance begets superiority; wisdom begets humility.

Many people, even today, live with the idea that in all of our daily actions, a lesser god named Satan pushes and shoves us around at his will because he is always close to us. God, on the other hand, is perceived as more distant from man and requires more time and incentive than Satan to come close to man. Satan is perceived as ready, willing, and able to pounce on man at any moment and ruin him for eternity. But God is perceived as a lesser power who can redeem man only by the most unusual, extraordinary, and bizarre of happenings.

The danger in such thinking is not just that it is not true; the real danger is the propensity it instills in man to have an excuse outside himself for his lesser motives and actions. **The devil made me do it** is indeed an alibi often used, but always without merit.

Some people need many gods or a negative god because One True God is simply too inconceivably remote to comprehend. The One True God must finally be perceived as the Grand Architect of the Universe, as the Maker of universal laws, as the Ultimate beyond all ultimates, and as the Repository and Source of complete love.

Could God increase the total amount of love in the universe? If God were total love then such an increase would not seem possible. But, by creating man in her own image -- who could also learn to love -- and by adding that love by man to the love of God, the total amount of love in the universe could be expanded. So maybe God created man simply because that was the best way to expand the total amount of love in existence.

Man, with his limitations, could only equate the love of God with some of his man-made emotions. We define love as emotions toward our mates, our children, our friends, and even our country. Those are all worthy emotions, but they are not love. True love can only be completely impersonal. Love is when you care for all children equally with your own, or when you wish well for all countries equally with your own. Impersonal love is true love and really the only love.

It would seem that love and religion should have something in common. In practice they seldom do. Organized religion is, and has always been, a political institution, but has never manifested love.

Popular religion in Egypt developed over several thousands of years, with little influence from the rest of the world. This was somewhat because of geographic isolation. Then, as now, access to the Delta region of Lower Egypt was relatively easy by way of the trade routes along the Mediterranean Sea. But then, as now, most of Egypt was not accessible except by crossing vast and desolate areas which later became deserts on both the east and west sides of the Nile River.

The demand for social justice gave birth to the gracious and paternal kingships of early Egypt. These same qualities were ascribed to the gods, and indeed the pharaohs were thought of as gods or at least as the offspring of the gods.

These early religious beliefs were national in that they were only for Egyptians and only in Egypt. The idea of One True God was inherent in the teachings of the Lesser Mysteries which came into Egypt prior to 3500 BC. The notion of One True God was an idea whose time had not yet come.

The reader should remember that the Lesser Mysteries were taught only in what later became known as the White Lodge, and not among the general population or priesthood. The general population worshipped many gods then just as in most of the rest of the world.

While there were many gods in Egypt, one of the best and most important gods was Ra, the sun god. He was a great and mighty sovereign god often directly interceding on behalf of the dead. He was dominant in the affairs of living men, and his majesty expanded until he was the keeper of the exalted realm of moral values.

Very slowly over many years, the sun god, Ra, became more and more the chief god, and by 1600 BC, matters of religion in Egypt were approaching a crisis point. While the priesthood still taught the idea of many gods, the royal family and the ancient White Lodge were secretly teaching only One True God.

At some point, from some source, numbers were assigned to some of the heavenly bodies. The sun sign, and the sign of the sun god, Ra, was the number 666. The **New Testament** in **The Revelation** makes reference to this ancient sign of the sun.

The Revelation, Chapter 13; Verse 18 states:

> "...*And I stood upon the sand of the sea, and saw a beast rise up out of the sea, having seven heads and ten horns, and upon his horns ten crowns, and upon his heads the name of blasphemy. ... Here is wisdom. Let him that hath understanding*

count the number of the beast: for it is the number of a man; and his number is six hundred threescore [60] and 6 [666]. ..."

We also do not know where or when astrology and numerology began. But many of the heavenly bodies came to be associated with numbers. The numbers for some: Saturn was 45; Jupiter was 136; Mars was 325; Venus was 1,225; Mercury was 2,080; the Moon was 3,321; and, of course, the sign of the Sun was 666.

There were seven orders of magic squares with each standing for one of the planets in astrology. The smallest numbers were one to nine, and the largest were one to 81 with the numbers so arranged that the numbers in each row, column, and diagonal add up to the same total.

The numbers one to 36 add to 666 and form a so-called magic square, as follows:

The Sun Sign

Column	1	2	3	4	5	6	7
Row 1:	6	32	3	34	35	1	111
Row 2:	7	11	27	28	8	30	111
Row 3:	19	14	16	15	23	24	111
Row 4:	18	20	22	21	17	13	111
Row 5:	25	29	10	9	26	12	111
Row 6:	36	5	33	4	2	31	111
Row 7:	111	111	111	111	111	111	666

People who ascribed the number 666 to the sign of the beast and evil on Earth do not understand the symbolism involved.

Apocalypses were secret books meant only for the initiated who were capable of understanding them. The reason matters were written symbolically was so that the uninitiated could not understand them. This became necessary in order to confuse people, after reading became a common skill that the uninitiated could master. But from symbolism the uninitiated would always come up with just the opposite of the true meaning, as indeed they have done with 666. When all people have knowledge, then priests are no longer necessary.

The Christian church claims that The **Revelation** was written about AD 95 by the beloved disciple John on the island of Patmos in the Aegean Sea where he was exiled by the Roman Emperor Domitian. Historically this was, of course, impossible, since John was beheaded along with James in Jerusalem about AD 44 by Agrippa I. By AD 95, John the Beloved had been dead over 50 years.

The reason the notion of John the Beloved as author of **The Revelation** was advanced was so that **The Revelation** would be included in the **New Testament**. A document authored by an unknown John would not even have been considered. **The Revelation** was probably written shortly before AD 70 by an Elder who was an initiate of the Jewish-christian church, and who was also named John. There is much symbolism in **The Revelation**. There is indeed a beastly nature in man, represented by the 666. That beastly nature must be overcome and subdued by the Christ nature also in man.

The man Joseph, whom we know as Master Jesus the Christ, showed us how this could be done. Master Jesus took the seventh, or Christ, initiation and thus became Master Jesus the Christ. The term Christ is a state of being, and a title, not a proper name.

There is also a prediction in **The Revelation** that the 144,000 people of the Christian church of Jerusalem will be saved from destruction. Symbolically, 144,000 equals one plus four, plus four, plus three zeros, or nine. Nine is the sign of man and thus the prediction is that mankind will be saved from destruction. In Kabala both 666 and 144,000 reduce to nine. The 666 refers to the unregenerate nature in man. The 144,000 refers to the redeemed nature in man. The prediction is that mankind will be redeemed and saved from destruction.

Many strange things can be done with the number 666 -- none of them -- however, are valid. The name of Roman Emperor Nero can be reduced to 666, and many people incorrectly believe that Nero is the person to whom **The Revelation** refers. The names of many popes, priests, and emperors can be reduced to 666 by various methods. What does it mean in the **First Book of Kings** in chapter 10, verse 14, when it says that Solomon is given 666 talents of gold in one year? Does that mean that Solomon became an evil man? **The Revelation** is the 66th book of the **Bible-New Testament**, and the 666 reference is reported in verse 18, which is the sum of six, six, and six.

Sir Isaac Newton, the great Rosicrucian, lived in England in the 1600s. The great plague ended there in AD 1666, and Newton's golden year was that same year. Since Newton was a mathematician and a Rosicrucian, would that not prove, biblically, that both scientists and Rosicrucians were agents of Satan? Such logic made sense to some Christians. The author offers the hypothesis that some of the mathematical prime numbers may also fit into the 666 symbolism.

A few years ago there was produced a popular film in which a baby boy had 666 branded into his scalp. The boy was indeed very bad and exhibited many undesirable traits. He was projected as a human incarnation of the evil god Satan. Common sense would suggest that no civilized person could take such things seriously. Certainly many boy babies were born in the world on the sixth day of the sixth month in 1966; some even at either six o'clock in the morning or six o'clock in the evening. Life could be difficult for those born into fundamentalist-Christian communities on that date, because of the 666 reference in **The Revelation**.

112 TRUE ESOTERIC TRADITIONS

What would have happened to a true follower of Master Jesus the Christ in Christian Spain who was born on June 6, 1566? Is there doubt that such a person would have been burned to death at the stake by the Roman Church? Indeed, is there much doubt that such a person would still be treated badly if the Roman Church there had the power to do it?

In AD 1749, the Dali Lama, or high priest, of Tibet allowed the Emperor of China to have translated a very ancient manuscript in his possession. The high priests of Tibet had had possession of the document since AD 732 when they obtained it from the Brahmans in India. It has now been translated into English. The document seems to be of Egyptian origin and was prepared for use in teaching in a secret mystery school. It was probably written by Pharaoh Akhnaton, or perhaps Hermes, between 1360 and 1350 BC.

The document is several dozen type-written pages in length and is very beautifully written. It sounds like **Psalms** in the **Bible**. It was probably one of the documents taken to Tibet by the Rosicrucians from the great library at Alexandria before it was burned in AD 400.

Akhnaton stated at the beginning of his material:

> "*Wheresoever the sun doth shine, wheresoever the wind doth blow, wheresoever there is an ear to hear, and a mind to conceive -- let the maxims of truth be honored and obeyed. ...*"

This was then signed: "*Unto thee I grant the economy of life. The Master.*" Presumably the master was Akhnaton. We call this document **The Economy of Life**. Pharaoh Akhnaton also wrote:

> 1. "*Promises of Hope are sweeter than the rose in the bud, and far more flattering to expectation, but the threatenings of Fear are a cross upon which the rose is crucified.*"

> 2. "*...Whatsoever thou resolvest to do, do it quickly. Defer not till the evening what the morning may accomplish. ...*"

Akhnaton deserves his honor as the world's first individual. He believed fervently in the One True God. He was both Hebrew and Egyptian and both king and high priest. Like Ptah-Hotep, he believed that to hear is the best of all qualities, and that the man who loves God will hear and learn, but the man who loves God not will hear not. He was a fine grandson for Joseph-Yuya.

The Freemasons, or more accurately the Masons, were powerful in Egypt by 3000 BC. They remain a powerful force for good up unto the present day. But survival has not been easy and at times has been nearly impossible. The adjective **Free** probably was not added to the word **Masons** until about 950 BC, by Solomon. Perhaps the reason it was added was an attempt by Solomon to separate the Blue Lodge of Israel from the ancient White Lodge of Egypt in both membership and status. Any human being on Earth could join the ancient White Lodge if that person was qualified. Only free men could join the Masonic Blue Lodge. Incidentally, this is still largely true today.

Many years later in AD 310, the Roman Emperor, Constantine, wanted to have membership in AMORC but was refused as being unqualified. This decision had disastrous results for Western culture. With much vengeance Constantine organized a rival Christian church, along largely pagan lines, and sent his church into the world to burn the storehouse of knowledge and destroy forever both the Blue Lodge and AMORC. That effort very nearly succeeded. The great library at Alexandria was burned. But AMORC and the teachings survived in the Muslim and Buddhist parts of the world.

In 3000 BC, the famous Masonic wise man, Amenhotep, was Grand Vizier, or Prime Minister, and chief architect under King Zoser. He was the first great architect in stonemasonry construction and the father of stone construction in the world. Every Mason should go to Egypt at least once in his lifetime to witness personally the great achievements of this man and his successors. Any Mason who views the masonry work in these early temples must stand tall and proud. Some 5000 years later the joints between the stones are still so perfect that not even a thin knife can be inserted between them.

Where did the Greater Mysteries and the Lesser Mysteries come from? We know that they came to Egypt from someplace, but where? They probably came from Atlantis or what we today call the British Isles. If so, did these Mysteries originate there or were they imported from some more ancient source, such as India?

Scholars are divided on the question. The great English judge, Sir Godfrey Higgins, after many years of study on the subject concluded that these teachings came from India and were not native to the British Isles.

The opposite view to this theory is that the British Isles were the ancient seat of knowledge, and that such knowledge went from the British Isles to India. The evidence is conflicting but the author believes that the original source of our present culture was the British Isles. The British Isles were Atlantis. The author's limited knowledge of the sources of languages leads him to the conclusion that Modern English is an older language than Sanskrit.

There is substantial evidence that the Aryan race of people originated in Europe and at some remote time spread east, eventually, into the Indus valley of India. The Aryans were blond-haired, blue-eyed, and had skin of a pallid white color like people who had lived in the shade for too many centuries. Along with this spreading east, they also spread south, around the Mediterranean Sea and into Egypt. Indeed this spreading from India down into Egypt may be the real story of Abraham and Sarah set forth in the **Bible**.

We know that the Hebrew patriarch, Abraham, and his wife, Sarah, were initiated into at least the Lesser Mysteries, but possibly also into the Greater Mysteries. But did Abraham and Sarah acquire some of this knowledge in India before going to Egypt, or only after arriving in Egypt? The evidence is conflicting.

Probably in some way Abraham got some small taste of the teachings in India. This was enough to whet his appetite and send him all the way to Thebes in Central Egypt, and to the ancient White Lodge. The fact that Abraham and Sarah changed their names and also confessed to Pharaoh that Sarah was really Abraham's wife makes it appear that they did take initiation into at least the Lesser Mysteries.

But if this is true, then the story of Abraham offering to sacrifice Isaac to appease God probably cannot be true. It is extremely unlikely that an initiate into the Lesser Mysteries would do such a thing. However, this was around 1493 BC, about 150 years before Hermes and Akhnaton had severely upgraded the requirements for entry into the Order. That could be the answer to the question about Abraham's behavior.

Pharaoh Tuthmosis III, another initiate, waged aggressive war, which is something else a high member of the ancient White Lodge normally would not do. But AMORC, as we later came to know it, did not come into being until the time of Hermes, in 1353 BC.

King Solomon of Israel has come down to us as a very wise king. Yet we know that he completed studying only the Lesser Mysteries, and never did complete the Greater Mysteries. Why did he quit his studies and return to Israel? Was it to become King? Solomon did build the first temple in Israel patterned after the temples in Egypt.

Why would Solomon require that slaves or descendants of slaves not be allowed to enter his Blue Lodge of the Lesser Mysteries? If the Hebrews were indeed themselves true slaves in Egypt, and Solomon was of that family, then he could not be a member of his own Blue Lodge.

The answer probably is that the Hebrews were not really slaves in Egypt. The Hebrews had a fixed mind-set that they should be treated differently, which is to say better, than other people. So when they were treated the same as other people they felt deprived of their rights and thus enslaved. This came from their own limited viewpoint. This trait continues among some Jews, who are not Hebrews, in Israel to the present day.

In the former Soviet Union, no one is treated very well, but the Jews are treated no worse or differently from other people. The Soviets opposed a Jewish Exodus much as the ancient Egyptians did and for exactly the same reasons. But from their perspective, the Jews project the image that they are virtual slaves. The Jews in Israel have never learned to live by objective standards of conduct and probably will not so learn in the foreseeable future. However, this proclivity does not seem to be true of the Jews living in America.

Also, King Solomon of Israel was not of the family of Joseph-Yuya, Akhnaton, Hermes, and Moses Moria-El. His family was one that had never been in Egypt either to live or to attend school. These were some of the people that Moses Moria-El had so many problems with in the mountains of northern Saudi Arabia after leaving Egypt.

Solomon's father, the infamous King David, was one of the meanest and bloodiest tyrants who ever graced the throne of any land. Solomon's mother was Bathsheba. Standards of life and war were different in those days, it is true, but even then worthy kings did not needlessly slaughter thousands of innocent people. They also did not encourage some bloody tribal god to murder thousands of innocent people. Decent human beings also did not have their friends killed so that they could then sleep with their wives.

Ezra, the scribe, could play an important part in this story. We know that Ezra greatly exaggerated many things he put into the **Bible** for his own political purposes. Did he exaggerate the stories about King David? The big question is, if he did exaggerate, does that mean he under-reported the number of people murdered by King David, or did he over-report them?

If Ezra over-reported the murders, that would tell us much about Ezra himself and the values he esteemed in a king. However, if King David actually did even five percent of the things Ezra has given him credit for in the **Bible**, then King David was indeed a foul and evil man. The author assumes that Ezra did exaggerate but still the stories reported were based on some actual facts in history. If true, then King David was a man to be abhorred and not honored.

The **Bible** is replete with the tyranny of King David and his gods. In the **First Book of Samuel** it says: **I Samuel 2:31 to 30:17**:

> *"But the servants of David had smitten ...so that three hundred and three score men died ...And David commanded his young men and they slew them and cut off their hands and their feet and hanged them up over the pool in Hebron ...And David said on that day, whosoever getteth up to the gutter ...and smiteth the Jebusites and the lame and the blind ...he shall be chief and captain ...Wherefore David arose and went, he and his men, and slew of the Philistines two hundred men and David*

brought their foreskins, and they gave them in full tale to the king, that he might be the king's son-in-law ..."

"David went out, and fought with the Philistines, and slew them with a great slaughter ...Therefore David inquired of the Lord, saying, Shall I go and smite these Philistines? And the Lord said unto David, Go and smite the Philistines ...And David smote the land, and left neither man nor woman alive ...And David saved neither man nor woman alive ...Lest they should tell on us ...Is not this David, of whom they sang one to another in dances, saying, Saul slew his thousands and David his ten thousands? ...And David smote them from the twilight even unto the evening of the next day: And there escaped not a man of them..."

In the **Second Book of Samuel**, more of the same level of conduct is reported: **II Samuel 5:20 to 24:15**:

"And David came to Baal-pera-gim, and David smote them there ...for then shall the Lord go out before thee, to smite the host of the Philistines. And David did so, as the Lord had commanded him; and smote the Philistines... And the anger of the Lord was kindled against Uzzah; and God smote him there for his error; and there he died by the ark of God ...And after this came to pass, that David smote the Philistines ...And he [David] smote Moab ...casting them down to the ground ...he to put to death ... David smote also Hadadezer ... And when the Syrians of Damascus came ...David slew of the Syrians two and twenty thousand men ...And the Lord preserved David whithersoever he went ... And the Syrians fled before Israel; and David slew the men of seven hundred chariots of the Syrians, and forty thousand horsemen ...And he [David] wrote in the letter saying, set ye Uriah [his friend and the husband of Bathsheba] in the forefront of the hottest battle, and retire ye from him, that he may be smitten and die ...Where the people of Israel were slain before the servants of David, and there was there a great slaughter that day of twenty thousand men ...

"These four were born to the giant in Goth, and fell by the hand of David ...These be the names of the mighty men whom David had ...he lifted up his spear against eight hundred, whom he slew at one time ...And he [David] lifted up his spear against three hundred, and slew them ...And the Lord sent a pestilence upon Israel ...and there died ...seventy thousand men."

The **First Book of Chronicles** at 18:5 to 20:3 further reports on King David as follows:

"...David slew of the Syrians two and twenty thousand men...David slew of the Syrians seven thousand men which fought in chariots and forty thousand footmen... And he [David] brought out the people that were in it, and cut them with saws, and with harrows of iron, and with axes..."

Note that King David not only killed scores of innocent and defenseless people but he also cut off their hands and feet to keep as trophies. He circumcised 200 men and presented the severed body parts to his king as dowry or payment for the king's daughter. David went so far as to award promotions in rank for those soldiers who would slaughter the lame and blind. It is difficult to imagine the blood and horror of thousands of defenseless women and children being hacked to death with saws and axes.

It is pathetic that any modern educated person could associate, in any way, King David or his god with Master Jesus the Christ or the One True God of the universe. David's predecessor, Joshua, was even worse than David, if that is possible. After waging aggressive war, and the conquest of Jericho, the **Bible** reports:

1. **Joshua 6:21**: "...*And they utterly destroyed all that was in the city, both man and woman, young and old, and ox, and sheep, and ass, with the edge of the sword...*"

2. **Joshua 6:24**: "...*And they burnt the city with fire and all that was therein; only the silver and the gold...they put into the treasury of the house of the Lord...*"

Very simply, history does not record more evil men than Joshua and David. Ghengis Kahn, Attila the Hun, Ivan the Terrible, Adolf Hitler, and others have been thought to be without equals in terms of senseless and sadistic murders of innocent and totally defenseless people. Only Hitler at his worst ever completely destroyed a whole city and everything in it, including all the children; he is the only man who can really measure up to King David and Joshua in cruelty.

The Jewish tribal gods Elohim, Jehovah, and Yahweh were angry with David for his sins, so for spite, these gods murdered 70,000 innocent people. To equate such mean and bloody tribal gods with the One True God projected by Joseph-Yuya is grossly inappropriate.

The Hebrew race gave birth to one of the finest human beings who ever lived, Joseph-Yuya, and also one of the worst that ever lived, King David. Why the Hebrew race would pick a place of honor for such a murderous tyrant as King David is a mystery of history. Even a short list of the depraved leaders of history would certainly contain the name of King David of Israel.

There probably is no such thing as national karma, but if there were, it would not be difficult to understand why the Hebrews have suffered oppression. It is one thing to suffer tyrants, but it is quite another to honor and exalt them. For 3000 years the Israelites have prayed and waited for King David to return to Earth to lead them. Surely this must give the world cause for pause. What sane human being would want a King David on Earth with atomic bombs? Surely few.

The present-day Jews have little or no connection to the Hebrews that ruled ancient Israel. How the present Jews came to adopt this Hebrew history as their own is another intriguing mystery of history. Most Jews today originated in Europe; not Africa, or Israel.

The European Jews are some of the strongest, smartest, and finest people on Earth. Albert Einstein was just one example. Perhaps their strange characteristics were only in response to the pagan ways of the Christian church. In the United States the Jews seem to have lost many of their long-held and hated customs. But the Christian church has hated the Rosicrucians even more than it has the Jews.

Solomon was the son of King David and Bathsheba. Considering the household and family he came from, he did very well. He attended school in Egypt, even if he did not finish. He also built a great temple and started the Blue Lodge, which is still an important and influential group even today. And he earned the reputation of being a wise man; not bad for the son of David and Bathsheba.

Both the Greater and Lesser Mysteries have often struggled for survival in this world of ignorance. Their natural enemies are the organized religions of the world that have a vested interest in keeping the people of the world subjugated in a political-religious-economic oppression. But, slowly, oh so very slowly and painfully, the truth and knowledge of those mysteries is penetrating the consciousness of the world.

```
          How many laws were taught
         in the ancient White Lodge?
      How many steps is it up the Tree
    of Life to mastership? How many steps
    from the kundalini power in man up to the
    third eye? How many degrees in the Scottish
    Rite? The answer is the same for all: 33.
```

CHAPTER SIX -- LAWS OF THE PHYSICAL UNIVERSE

By 1350 BC, AMORC taught that there were 33 laws or principles that ruled the physical universe. It is very difficult at this time to determine exactly if, or how, those 33 laws were broken down into categories. The author feels that the categories of laws were perhaps as follows: Twelve laws pertaining to the physical universe; ten laws pertaining to man's conduct; seven laws pertaining to God's relationship to man; three laws pertaining to the nature of God; and the Law of Love which is the supreme law of the universe.

These laws could be understood on four levels of understanding depending upon the capacity of the student. AMORC taught to the fourth level. The Masonic Blue Lodge taught to level three.

Level One: These were the profane, the mass of the population who were not only unable to comprehend any level of the mysteries but indeed thought that such knowledge did not even exist. Most priests were on this level.

Level Two: These were the neophytes who knew there is indeed a path to higher things but had not yet begun their own individual ascent.

Level Three: These were the initiates into the Lesser Mysteries in The Blue Lodge who were called Freemasons. This group also included many people who were on the path but who had not yet reached true initiation.

Level Four: The people who reached this level were very rare and were called Israelites or the Elect. Few people have reached this level of learning, understanding, and love in all of recorded history. Master Jesus was the highest initiate ever in AMORC and the only person to date who has taken the seventh, or Christ, initiation.

At that time in AMORC there were seven initiations. At the sixth initiation, the student would sometimes take a new name. Some of the people who took new names were Pharaoh Amenhotep IV, who took the name of Akhnaton, the Greek philosopher Aristocles, who took the name of Plato, Joseph, who took the name of Jesus, and Jacob of the **Bible** who took the name Israel.

There seems to be some legend that the idea for the 33 degrees of the Scottish Rite were derived from the age of Master Jesus at the time of the crucifixion event. But that is not the source. In any event, Master Jesus was probably born in May of 7 BC and thus was almost 40 years of age in April of AD 33 at the time of the crucifixion event.

The author for many years held to the view that the 33 degrees in the Scottish Rite must somehow be connected to these 33 laws of the physical universe taught in AMORC. But there is no connection between the two. The 33 degrees of the Scottish Rite were probably taken from the Tree of Life in the **Bible**.

The whole body of knowledge assembled by Francis Lord Bacon and known as the Scientific Method is the search for these laws and the vast amount of knowledge that can be derived from the implications drawn from these laws. Most of these laws are quite familiar to the serious college student. There are exactly 33 steps that the student upon the path must climb to go from the outer darkness to the inner light.

The 33 laws taught in AMORC were:

1. **Law of Magnetism**: Magnetism is the power to attract, in either the physical or the psychic realm. Everything that exists has polarity of negative and positive. The ultimate duality in nature is male and female. This law is often misunderstood in relationship to God. Many people think that there are two gods in the universe; a good or positive god and a bad or negative god named Satan.

2. **Law of Motion**: Every body continues in its state of rest or of uniform motion in a straight line except as it is compelled by force to change that state. Every action has an equal and contrary reaction. Everything in the universe is always in motion that never ceases. God creates thought; thought creates energy; energy creates motion and matter, and motion controls the physical universe we see around us.

3. **Law of Vibration**: Electrons are of two kinds: those vibrating at an even number per second and those vibrating at an uneven number. The even vibratory force manifests in the female of the species and the odd or uneven vibratory force manifests in the male. The higher a person has evolved in the level of his or her consciousness, the higher the rate of vibrations will be. The man, Master Jesus the Christ, achieved the highest rate of vibrations yet known to man. Time is also measured by vibrations. The length of the second is the amount of time it takes a hot celcium atom to vibrate 9,192,631,770 times.

How long is a **split** second? Is it the amount of time after the stop-light turns green before the car behind you blows its horn? At sporting events, many people have become aware of tenths of seconds but that is about as refined as human senses have become for most of us. However, scientists can now measure time down into **femtoseconds**. How long is a femtosecond? It is a quadrillionth, or a thousand trillionths, of one second. That is a decimal point with fourteen zeros after it and then a one.

And now scientists can photograph such events as the coming together and then breaking apart of molecules which take place over a period of only a very few femtoseconds. A femtosecond has about the same relationship to a second as a second does to thirty-two million years.

We think our life span is pretty short but just think of something that comes into being and then passes on out of existence, and then through some one-hundred thousand generations in the space of only one second. Goodness sakes! So, how long is a **split** second? It is maybe shorter than you had heretofore thought.

4. Law of Gravity: Gravity is the force that tends to draw all physical bodies in Earth's sphere toward the center of Earth. Presumably, this same law applies throughout the universe.

It is possible however that some areas of the universe are controlled by anti-gravity rather than gravity. Is it even possible that the expansion of the universe is caused by an excess of anti-gravity over gravity, rather than a big bang, or that it merely grows as any living organism grows?

Or, is it possible that the universe is a single entity as envisioned under the Laws of Oneness and Unity? Does not the mass in the far reaches of the universe affect us here on Earth? And does not such effect move across the universe, or rather exist throughout the universe, without being subject to the speed of light? The Law of Gravity tends to prove the Law of Oneness.

The Law of Gravity can perhaps answer the age-old question of what happens when an irresistible force meets an immovable object. The answer is that gravity is that irresistible force, and there is no such thing as an immovable object.

In 1916, Einstein published his new theory of gravity called General Relativity. This theory is often called the highest achievement of the human mind ever. As late as the mid-1940s, it was said that less than a dozen people on Earth truly understood the equations of General Relativity. Seventy-five years after its publication computer scientists still had not developed sufficient software to calculate all the implications of the equations.

One of the projected results of those equations is the existence of so-called black holes. A black hole occurs when a massive star, or even a whole galaxy of stars, collapses into such a small area, under the force of gravity, that nothing, not even light, can escape from the collection of mass contained therein. Black holes exist only in the equations of General Relativity and have never actually been shown to exist physically. Since black holes emit almost no light we probably will never actually see them, but we will be able to see the consequences of their existence.

However, the author offers the suggestion that if a star, or a galaxy of stars, can collapse into a black hole then the entire physical universe can likewise collapse into a huge black hole. And if the entire physical universe can collapse into a black hole then it can also logically further collapse into a single atom and then even into nothing. This is to say, that one of the logical implications of General Relativity is that the entire physical universe can one day cease to exist and return once again to the thought of God, from whence it came.

However, this would not adversely affect mankind because, while man lives and exists now within this physical universe, he is not really of this physical universe. Mankind is merely an itinerate visitor in the physical universe so its ceasing to exist would not be fatal to him. The logical implications of General Relativity are then exactly the same as the teachings of AMORC which are that the physical universe emanated from the thought of God, and pursuant to the Law of Cycles will one day return to the source from whence it came.

However, it might be possible for the physical universe to experience another big bang and begin the Law of Cycles all over again. Stephen Hawking has calculated that indeed black holes are not totally black, and that General Relativity is overcome by quantum effects, and that such quantum effects allow radiation or energy to escape from black holes, and thus again re-establish the physical universe. Under this scenario, the next physical universe would come into being by a big whimper, or by evolution, rather than by another big bang.

5. **Law of Chemistry**: Chemistry is the science dealing with the composition and properties of substances and with the reactions by which substances are produced from, or converted into, other substances.

It has been said that the Rosicrucians had the knowledge to transmute base metals into gold. Many Rosicrucians have been persecuted by political leaders in an effort to obtain this knowledge. The highest operation of this law is the conversion of the objective and lower man into the subjective and Christ-like man.

AMORC teachings were that all matter in the universe is composed of 144 different elements. Only 90 elements have so far been found in nature and another 19 synthetic elements have been created for a total of 109 elements. If AMORC teachings are correct, there are still 35 new elements out there some place waiting to be discovered.

6. **Law of Energy**: In the physical dimension, energy is usually thought of as light, heat, electricity, and electromagnetic radiation. But the largest field of energy in the universe is thought. Actually, energy in the physical dimension emanates from thought.

The Law of Energy and its offspring should make it possible someday to calculate the age of the physical universe. How so? In 1789, Lavosier propounded the Law of Conservation of Matter, which is that matter may change forms but can never be destroyed. Then, in 1842, the Law of Conservation of Energy was also propounded, which likewise is that energy can and does change form but also can never be destroyed. This naturally led to the Law of Conservation of Matter and Energy, which is that matter and energy can and do change forms, but can never be destroyed.

Then in 1905, Einstein, in his Special Theory of Relativity, gave the formula for changing matter or mass into energy, as being that energy equals the mass multiplied by the speed of light squared, or $E = mc^2$. The speed of light is 186,000 plus miles per second and then when squared creates a very large number. This shows that a great amount of energy is stored within a very small amount of matter, as demonstrated in the explosion of an atomic bomb.

In the mid-1950s, the author theorized in a college paper that there must exist some very small background of heat or radiation throughout the entire universe. A few years later, Bell Laboratory scientists did discover that such a very small background of radiation does, in fact, exist. Logically, this had to be true. If at some time in the past all of the matter and energy in the universe were collected in one spot and then began exploding out through the universe in the so-called big bang, then no matter how long and how far that heat spreads out it could never ever reduce down to absolute zero. Therefore, there logically must exist some small amount of heat or background of radiation throughout the universe. Absolute zero, which is 360 degrees below zero Fahrenheit, does not exist in a natural state; it can only be created in the laboratory.

And it follows also from this that, as the years go by and the universe expands, the rate of reduction in the amount of heat can be determined. Once the rate of reduction is determined, it should then be possible, mathematically, to calculate the reverse order of that reduction, and so determine about when the big bang happened.

The universe itself emanates and manifests from the thought of God. Energy is the capacity for doing work and overcoming resistance. It is the force imparted to a body in giving it motion, measured by the work it will do in coming to rest. Energy creates motion and motion never ceases. The only thing that never ceases to be is that things never cease to be. The only thing that never changes is that things never stop changing.

7. **Law of Attraction**: Unlike polarities attract each other and like polarities repel each other. The law of attraction is the tendency or force through which particles are attracted or drawn toward each other; the inherent tendency is for bodies to approach each other, unite, and resist separation.

Man needs, and seeks, union with God. The idea that man can fall from grace is an incorrect interpretation. Once man knows God, he can never again not know her.

8. **Law of Creation**: Creation is the act of bringing into existence all of the world, the universe and everything in it. God thought; therefore, everything is. As Descartes said, "*I think, therefore I am.*" Man, too, has the power to create, and the evidence of that creation is the culture around us.

9. **Law of Polarity**: Polarity is the predominant quality of the vibratory rate or number of an electron, atom or molecule. Positive polarity is due to the expanding quality of the vibratory rate. Negative polarity is due to the relatively arrested or receptive quality

of the vibratory rate. Positive polarity is usually thought to be male, and negative polarity is usually thought to be female.

The danger in such thinking is that some people tend to think of positive as being better than negative in moral terms, which is not the case at all. In fact, the contrary is perhaps true. Certainly, the female is more governed by the love principle than is the male. Man is indeed star stuff, but man is indeed more than just star stuff. Before anything is, God was. Before matter and motion, before energy and emotion, before galaxies and the universe, before time and light, God was.

But, should God exist alone? With all that God was, still she was not complete. True, she existed, but mere existence alone was not enough. Perhaps God thought: For me to manifest and realize my being, I need man to relate to. And if man is to manifest and realize his true being he will need me. So, let there be polarity in the universe. And it was so. From Genesis: "*And God said, Let Us make man in our image, after our likeness ...So God created Man in His own image....*" And she saw that it was good. And it is good.

The universe is so constructed that what appears to be an end is always only a new beginning. The ego must experience death before the soul can experience illumination. The soul is immortal, but the ego is not, and this is necessary in order to have polarity. The Rosicrucians have defined polarity as: "*The predominance of one or the other phase of electrical or magnetic force possessed by any manifestation of creation, and which gives it its distinguished character of positive or negative....*"

And thus we say that all that exists is dual in essence. Nous constantly maintains its duality of nature and each division has its distinctive domain of essence named the positive and the negative. The term **nous** apparently began with the Greeks about 450 BC. The Greek Master Empedocles became convinced that there was a double or binary element in man. Most cultures throughout history have been aware of the nature of polarity. This was true even of cultures that had little or no written language such as the American Indians and the natives of the South Sea Islands.

The term **Ma** has long been associated with the mother or female instinct; the term **Ra** with the father or male instinct. The combination of **Ma-Ra** creates a complete duality or polarity of the power of positive and negative, or of male and female.

Sir Godfrey Higgins, an English lawyer, over 150 years ago, in his monumental work with the imposing title, **Anacalysis, An Attempt To Draw Aside The Veil of the Saitic Isis or, An Inquiry Into The Origin of Languages, Nations, and Religions** recognized this polarity when he said:

"...The first philosophers could not account for the existence of moral evil without the doctrine of the immortality of the soul. Moral evil is a relative term; its correlative is moral good. Without evil there is no good; without good there is no evil. There is no such thing known to us as good or evil per se. But absolute perfection can be expected only by priests who can call to their aid apples of knowledge. Philosophers must content themselves with something less...."

Thus, it would seem that if good exists, there must be the polarity of evil and if evil does in fact exist there must be the polarity of good. In either event there must be polarity.

The ancient Persians knew what modern psychologists are just beginning to truly understand, and that is, that man too is a polarized being. Is not love and hate, courage and fear alike, but seen from different perspectives? Man recognizes these polarities in his everyday thoughts and sayings. For example, we hear that there are two sides to every question; that all swords have two edges, and that everything both is and is not. To which the author might add; that all things that are, are true, but all truths are only partially true.

Each person has a dual nature. One is a worldly, physical, material, beastly, sinful,, coarse, vulgar, unkind, weak, evil, objective, and negative nature. The other is a spiritual, divine, noble, sacrificing, generous, subjective, and positive, God-like side. Both, a left brain and a right.

God did not have to create man with two natures, but she did. She did not have to give man choices, but she did. It's not surprising that God did know what she was doing. Both natures are very needed and very necessary for man to exercise his free will and decide which nature will dominate.

Likewise, in the physical world, is not heat and cold one and the same thing, only perceived from a different perspective? And wet and dry; high and low; East and West; light and darkness; large and small; are they not also alike unto each other, except as seen from a different view?

Throughout history the philosopher made a road map for the hard scientists telling them where to search for knowledge. In this century that all has changed. With Relativity and Quantum Mechanics the hard scientists not only draw their own road maps, they also now had become a major influence on, and even dominate, philosophy.

Are there multiple universes? Does the proton decay? What, if anything, is faster than light? Matter and energy share an equivalence; so do spirituality and energy likewise share a similar equivalence? One of the oldest documents known to man is **Stanza III of: Stanzas of Dzyan**, which is taken from the **Kalachakra Tantra** from Tibet, which suggests such equivalence to be true when it states: "...*spin a web whose upper end is* *fastened to spirit -- and the lower one to its shadowy end, matter; And this web is the universe ..."*

Is the law of cause and effect a universal, or only a local law? Does the monopole exist? Is there yet another massive inhabited planet in the solar system? What effect will the answers to these questions have on mankind? Much profound effect.

10. **Law of Division**: This law is expressed best when cells split and divide, thus forming new cells. This law also operates in the world of man. Families, businesses, and other man-made institutions tend to obey the same law.

What causes the law to operate? Perhaps the rate of vibration gets so high that it cannot be contained in the same material, and division becomes necessary. At the transition or death of a human being, it is thought that the vibrations of the person increase so much and become so high that he or she cannot remain in the physical body. This is the cause of death. For the physical body, from dust back to dust; for the Soul, from God back to God.

11. **Law of Light**: Light is that which makes it possible for us to see. It is anything that emits, or is a source of, visible energy. God thought, and then that thought changed form into spirit, and then spirit changed form into energy. One form of energy is light. Energy, or light, then changed form into matter.

The world of matter that we live in is the lowest form of existence possible. Our physical bodies are composed of such matter. But inside that physical body, while we are alive, resides part of the thought of God, which is man. Everything in the universe shares an equivalence of some kind. Trying to discover these equivalences is the task assigned to man.

12. **Law of the Circle**: The circle is the symbol of the universe. It represents the continuity of life, and it is the ideal of harmony and proportion. The law operates in the subjective realm as well as the objective or physical realm. It is often said with truth that: All that goes around also comes around.

13. **Law of Self-Preservation**: Self-preservation is the preservation of one's self and physical body from danger, injury, or death. It is the urge to preserve oneself. It is regarded as an instinct. It includes the creation of positive psychic energy around one's self to protect one's self from physical, mental, emotional, or psychic attack in any negative form.

It is often said, erroneously, that the urge in man for self-preservation is man's highest urge. Many men and women have voluntarily given up their lives to protect loved ones. Even if Master Jesus the Christ did surrender his life voluntarily for others it would be no more than many other people have done. Master Jesus was a unique man but not for that reason.

14. Law of Transition: Death, or transition, is the separation of the soul from the body. It neither destroys nor annihilates the soul or the body. Both continue to express themselves on different and independent planes; the body expresses on a physical plane, and the soul on the plane of Cosmic Consciousness. The universe is so constructed that what appears to be an end is always only a new beginning.

15. Law of Incarnation: Incarnation is to be made flesh, or be endowed with a human body, or to have appearance in a human form. In order for the human soul to enter a human body at birth, as taught in both AMORC and in the **Bible**, with the first breath of life it must lower its vibration to the point that it can reside and manifest on the physical plane of existence.

Those who say that abortion is murder are denying that the soul enters the human body only at birth. Abortion may or may not be wrong but it is not murder. At transition or death, this vibration again increases until it necessitates separation from the physical body. Abortion kills a physical body, making it unsuitable as the abode of a soul; a soul that continues to exist on a higher plane of existence.

16. Law of Immortality: Immortality is the condition or quality of being immortal or exempt from death, annihilation, or unending existence.

Man is, in fact, immortal and will live forever without end. There is nothing man can do to change this. Fear of death, or fear of loss of consciousness, comes from a lack of knowledge and understanding of the nature of things. It comes from a lack of exposure to, or understanding of, the teachings of Master Jesus the Christ. This fear is most prevalent in those areas of Earth influenced by the Christian church.

17. Law of Will: Will is the God-given ability of man to use the power of God. God willed that the universe and man should be and it was so. Man, too, can will things to be and they will be, commensurate with man's level of development of consciousness and realization. The man, Master Jesus the Christ, is the best example of the development of consciousness, and therefore of will, in the human species up to this time.

The true gift from God to man is the freedom and power of will. With it man can and does do many things both good and evil. In exercising his free will, man creates Karma, and the Law of Compensation must be paid in full, every last cent, without exception. The most beautiful teaching of all time is that realized and taught by Master Jesus: that the Law of Love can satisfy and fulfill the Law of Compensation. Man must learn the Law of Love and how to use it, just as Master Jesus did. Man's assignment on Earth, and in the universe, is to learn the will of God and bring his own will into harmony with the will of God.

18. **Law of Cycles**: Everything in the universe operates in cycles. One example of a cycle is the period required for the revolution of the moon's node, which is about eighteen years and eleven days, after which eclipses usually return in a similar order. Other examples, are the period of 28 years, after which the days of the month again fall on the same days of the week; and, the period of nineteen years, at the end of which the new moon reappears on the same day as at the beginning of the cycle. Perhaps the ultimate cycle will be when the entire physical universe implodes back to the thought of God and ceases to exist.

Unto everything there is a time and a season. There is a time to be born and a time to die. May the wise perceive the season. Some times are indeed better for some things, than are others. Gardens planted in the spring do better than those planted in the fall. Man, too, sleeps better at night than when the sun is high above.

The big bang theory and an endless expansion of the universe would seem to violate this law. This is one of the very few places where modern science seems to be in conflict with the ancient teachings. The author suggests that this is only a temporary conflict. At some time in the future more mass in the universe will be discovered, and the universe, too, will be found to operate in cycles. The ancient teachings were to the effect that there are really nine levels of existence or universes. Some modern cosmologists are now postulating seven to eleven universes with infinite dimensions.

19. **Law of Life**: Life is motion or action, and reaction or evolution. It is throughout all creation. It has the two aspects of matter and mind. When the Vital Life Force enters the physical body it has life. Likewise, when the Vital Life Force leaves the body, there is transition or death.

The Law of Life is the principle that a man can become an individual concentration of energy. It is the **I Am** presence. **I Am** is the lost sacred word. I Am the truth and the light. I Am the resurrection and the life. I Am that I Am.

20. **Law of Cause and Effect**: This might be called the Law of Causation. All causes have multiple effects and all effects have multiple causes. Science is now at the point where it hopes to prove that there are situations where this law is invalid. Some scientists are suggesting that the Law of Causation may not be universally true. But at this time the law remains valid.

21. **Law of Compensation or Karma**: For each action there is an equal and opposite reaction. For each sorrow or joy we bring to others, we shall have experience in like degree and manner at the appropriate time, so that the lessons to be gained will teach us our error and increase our understanding. Master Jesus the Christ tried to teach man

how to satisfy and fulfill the Law of Compensation by our forgiving the sins of others, and more importantly, by forgiving the sins of one's self.

The Roman Church taught and believed in the Law of Compensation until the time of Justinian. The belief was declared heretical and banned by the Second Council of Constantinople in AD 553. The reason it was banned was that Justinian's wife, the queen, had been a lady of questionable virtue in her earlier years. When she became queen she had all who knew her in those earlier years, about 500 people, put to death. Under this law, she would have had to make amends for those wrongs, so she had her husband have the Law of Compensation declared invalid. How ignorant can people be? Neither the Roman Emperor nor the Roman Church can repeal the laws of God and the universe. But both have tried many times. Indeed, the Roman Church still tries, even to the present day.

22. **Law of Assumption**: Any person for proper moral purposes can assume the personality and identity of another person and in the process expose the consciousness of the other person to truth. That person may then accept or reject such truth as he desires in the exercise of his own individual free will. This is what happens in meditation or prayer when a person whispers to or prays for the illumination of another. It can and does work.

23. **Law of Continuity**: As is the inner, so is the outer; as is the great, so is the small; as it is above, so it is below; if truth is true, then it is always true.

When the Pope was about to burn Galileo at the stake, Galileo convinced the Pope that religious truths were different from, and higher than, scientific truths. This meant that they were agreeing that the Law of Continuity was not in effect. Of course this was absurd, but Galileo was not burned. This was only one of many times that the Christian church believed that the laws of God and the universe were not in effect and were not, in fact, laws. Galileo, of course, knew better, but avoiding being burned at the stake gave him an ulterior motive.

This event created a schism between science and religion that haunts the world to the present day. Today, many priests can look at, see, and believe in scientific truths such as evolution, and yet feel that these truths do not operate in the religious realm. How strange! Almost all scientists believe in Quantum Theory, but a few of them do not believe in the existence of God as is mandated and required by Quantum Theory. Again, how strange!

24. **Law of Transmutation**: Transmutation is the changing of one thing into another. It is the conversion of one element into another or the possible conversion of base metals into gold and silver by alchemy. It is the transmuting of our bare physical natures into the highest ideal expressions. It is also the transmuting of our desires and thoughts into living spiritual ideals. This is exactly the lesson that Master Jesus the

Christ tried to teach to man. Master Jesus did it, and therefore, by the implication of inductive logic, man, too, can do it.

25. Law of Thought: Everything that exists on the physical level of existence emanates from thought. The physical universe emanates from the thought of God. On Earth, everything that is, was first conceived in the mind of man. For example, in the physical dimension, a man conceives in his mind a rocket to go to the moon. It will take months or even years for this conception to actually come into being, but his thinking creates reality.

But on the higher levels of existence where there is no time, the thought and the actualization of the thought happen simultaneously. We all are as we perceive ourselves to be. There is only one mind in the universe and that is the one and only Universal Mind which is both the mind of God and man.

26. Law of Transfer of Thought: The Law of Thought and the Law of Transfer of Thought share some similarities. This law states that energy can be created by the power of mind through thought and thus transferred from thought to energy. Creation can be a continuous process from the mind of God or even from the mind of man. Since man is created in the image of God, man, too, has the potential capacity to transfer his mind from thought to energy and, of course, from energy to matter.

Thus, it is physically possible for man to create matter with his mind. To be sure few people have evolved to this level of knowledge but surely many would agree that Master Jesus the Christ may have possessed such power. And by inductive logic, if Master Jesus could do it, all others might do it also when they are sufficiently evolved.

27. Law of Harmony: Harmony is the concordance of vibrations. Life is harmony and harmony is joy. The figure three is the representation of complete harmony and represents the unity of opposites in nature. The law of harmony is a cosmic law and might be called the voice of God.

28. Law of Evolution: Man evolves upwards in a spiral. Man studies and learns lessons or laws on one level and then, as he goes ever higher in a spiral, he will encounter those same lessons and laws to be learned yet again, but this time on a higher level. AMORC taught these laws of the universe to the highest level ever known to man.

The idea that man is ever reborn as a lower form of animal is not correct and is not in accordance with AMORC teachings. Once man truly knows, it is never possible that he can ever again not know. Man is an ever-spiraling consciousness, always spiraling upwards.

This plan of evolution was set forth in the Tree of Life referred to in **Genesis** of the **Bible** and other ancient documents. That Tree of Life has been subverted and perverted by the Roman Church and others so that the soul is depicted as devolving, or going down, rather than up on the Tree of Life. The reader can be assured that any time he sees a Tree of Life and the arrows thereon go any direction other than upward, then that Tree of Life is not based on accurate information from AMORC.

All the religious and philosophical systems and structures ever known to man have been less than perfect. And as great and complete as the teachings of AMORC are, and they are the very best ever known to mankind, still they are less than perfect.

This is why both the Freemasons and Rosicrucians have never condemned **per se** the teachings of any religion. This is why neither have ever encouraged anyone to give up a particular religious belief system unless and until he or she has a better and higher belief system to take its place. And this is why the Communist ideology is not and has never been a really serious long-term threat to the religious systems of the world.

It is good and even necessary that man believe in something higher than himself. The belief in a trinity of gods is not as desirable as the belief in the One True God of the universe, but it is better than believing in more than 500 gods which the Hindus at one time in history did. The belief in a negative god called Satan is far from believing in only the One True God, but it is better than not believing in any higher power at all.

All religious systems in the world need to be improved pursuant to the teachings of Master Jesus the Christ, and the Masonic and Rosicrucian teachings, but none should be discarded outright. Truth is never written down or contained explicitly in any teachings regardless of how profound those teachings may be.

Truth only arises and can only be perceived on a subjective level by man. Teachings contain only seeds of truth. Thus, truth can never be revealed to, or shared with, another. It can only be perceived from within. From the teachings of Master Jesus man can acquire the seeds of the highest truth yet revealed to man, and from these seeds truth can take root and grow within.

29. **Law of Trinity**: There is only one God, not three. The one True God does manifest in many ways. Most apparent to the human species are the three most important ones, in which God manifests as wisdom, as intelligence, and as love. The ancient Egyptians worshiped a trinity of gods, as do the Hindus and Christians yet, to the present day. The Christians call this trinity the Father, the Son, and the Holy Ghost. But there is only One True God, not three. Master Jesus the Christ was indeed the most godly of all men who ever lived, but a man he was indeed. He certainly was not the One True God of the universe.

It is pagan to teach that any man, including Master Jesus, could be God. Master Jesus would be the first person to reject such a pagan idea. The number three has much significance in AMORC teachings and traditions. With the number seven it can be found prevalent in Masonic history. Master Jesus had not twelve but 73 disciples, and the council of AMORC had a Sanhedrin or council of 73 members. Also, much later, the so-called Israelites had a Sanhedrin or Council of 73 elders who ruled over Israel.

30. Law of Balance: The law of balance requires that man keep a balance between the physical dimension and the spiritual dimension. In order for the physical body to be healthy, the mind must be healthy. For the mind to function at its highest and best level, it must reside in a reasonably healthy body. Man incarnates and is born into this life in order to learn. One of the things to be learned is balance. Fanatics of every description violate this law. Buddhist philosophy is usually thought of as being one of balance and is known as the Great Middle Way. It is sometimes called the Eight-Fold Path.

The Jews have often violated this law. The Jews in King David's day were the meanest and most sadistic people on Earth. In Hitler's day, they were the most persecuted people on Earth. Now in Israel, the Jews again become persecutors of others. History always repeats itself over and over again. It will continue to do so until the lessons are learned.

31. Law of Unity: Unity is concord or agreement or harmony. It is the quality of being one in purpose, sentiment, affection, or the like.

The Law of Unity can best be understood with the Golden Mean, discussed earlier. It can be physically observed in the growth of a crystal and the spirals in sunflower seeds. In mathematics, it is known as the Fibionacci Series. It is perfectly expressed in **Saint John 1:1** "*In the beginning was the Word, and the Word was with God, and the Word was God.*" It is not a number, but a relationship. The Law of Unity shows the relationship of this physical universe as it now exists compared to its source and in relation to its possible future.

Through meditation and prayer man can unite with others to serve a common purpose. One of the best known unities and one that most people enjoy is that of man and woman. The ultimate unity is that of man and God. In some Christian churches they sing an old hymn which states that we pray that all unity may one day be restored. Actually, the unity of the universe has always been true and always will be true because it is a law. So, while the basic premise of the song may not be correct, the sentiment it expresses is very fitting.

32. Law of Oneness: There is only one **Soul** in the universe. This is the soul of God and also the soul of man. This is the one thing that all men share with each other and that all men also share with God. How does Oneness manifest in the physical world of matter?

Science has learned some rather amazing things in this century. Einstein tells us that in the physical realm nothing moves faster than light. But suppose two correlated photons are sent in opposite directions across a room; whatever happens to one photon also happens to the other.

For example, when the spin of one photon is altered, the spin on the other one is also likewise altered; and this happens instantly, much faster than the speed of light. How can this be, since any signal passing between the two would have to travel faster than the speed of light? Does the message about what has happened to the one photon travel across the room to the other, faster than the speed of light, and violate Einstein's law that nothing in the physical realm can travel faster than light?

Now suppose the two photons are separated by light years of distance. That should not matter, since no measurable information is involved. The answer is that it would not and does not matter. The distance between the two photons is irrelevant. Also, they do not violate Einstein's law because no message, in fact, travels between them. How can that be? The whole universe is ONE field or ONE thing. It has Oneness.

What happens in one part of the universe can be instantly known throughout the universe without the traveling of any message. Again, in other words, it has Oneness. Remember, that it is only in this physical universe, where the cosmic vibrations have slowed down below the speed of light, that we actually have time and space. In the higher realms, there is no time or space.

This is not very easy to visualize but suppose you had a steel rod that was, say 200,000 miles long. It would take any message traveling between the two ends well over one second to travel the distance. But suppose a giant takes a big hammer and hits the rod on one end. The other end of the rod will be affected immediately and will not have to wait more than a second for the message to travel between the two ends. This is true because the rod has Oneness. The same thing is true of the universe, but it is not so easy to visualize the Oneness of the universe.

The most powerful and widely accepted theory of nature ever discovered is the Quantum Theory. It was discovered principally by Werner Heisenberg in this century. His discovery was called the Uncertainty Principle. The gist of this principle is that there are some things in nature that are never possible to know because they are not knowable. They are uncertain and therefore are not knowable.

You can know the probabilities of something happening, but you cannot know for certain what will happen at any one time. For example, when you roll the dice, there is no way for sure to know which numbers will come up. It is very sure that over a period of time you can very accurately predict the number of times any number will come up. But we cannot now, and never will be able to predict, exactly what number will come up on any one roll of the dice, because that knowledge is not knowable.

You can easily learn this principle yourself by rolling the dice. There is no way to know which number will come up. This is true regardless of how many times you roll, or how much information you have regarding, the dice.

There are many things that are not known. There are many people, including Einstein, who felt that while there are many things that are not now known, all of these things will someday become known. They will, these people felt, become known when our science is advanced enough to fully analyze and describe them. But Heisenberg said that this is not true. There are some things that not only are not known, but also are not knowable.

33. Law of Love: Love is God's benevolent concern for mankind and man's devout attachment to God. It is the feeling of benevolence and brotherhood that people should have for each other. Love is not just an emotion, it is also the highest vibratory frequency of psychic energy. It actually creates a field of energy.

Science has yet to prove the existence of this law, but every human being who has ever loved knows the feeling and knows for sure that it does exist. True love is totally impersonal. It would be well to remember that the Law of Love is a law of the physical universe and that it operates according to known principles. Master Jesus the Christ knew these principles and spent his life trying to teach them to man.

Master Jesus had a monumental problem in that he was trying to describe to man things for which there were no known words to describe. How do you describe the beauty of a rainbow to a person who is totally color-blind and has never seen color? The answer is: Only with the greatest of difficulty.

Learning these laws of the physical universe was mandatory for all students on the path from ignorance to understanding. It remains a requirement unto the present day. It would be well to remember that under the Law of Unity, all things of the universe are united and all these laws would then be merely different expressions of the One Supreme Law: the Law of Love. So may it always be.

CHAPTER SEVEN -- THE WHITE LODGE

The formal name for this group is not certain. It would perhaps translate as the Circle of Light, and the members were perhaps known as the Sons of Light. This was because of their high degree of enlightenment and was used without regard to gender. One female pharaoh actually ruled over Egypt in the early 1400s BC. The author has selected the more generally descriptive and gender-neutral name of White Lodge to describe this group.

It has not been possible for the author to rediscover all the teachings of the White Lodge. Many would be beyond the comprehension of the author in any event. However, seven basic teachings the author has identified were:

1. That, there are nine universes, each layered on top of the other in a spiral. The White Lodge taught the Law of Spiral. Mankind lives on the lowest, the slowest, and the most gross of these universes. Time is a reality only in this physical universe.

Could there be a clue here to the big missing mass problem in the universe? Modern scientists tell us that 90 per cent of the mass in the universe is missing, that is, it cannot be located at this time. Could that missing 90 per cent be hidden somewhere in these nine universes? All the vast galaxies that can be observed or theorized still add up to only about ten per cent of the matter that must logically exist. Where is that missing 90 per cent? If these nine universes inter-connect on a spiritual level might they not also inter-connect on a material level?

2. That, all creation manifests in the form of energy and vibrations. The slowest vibrations are those that manifest in the physical universe we see around us. The higher up the spiral of universes one goes the higher are the vibrations. All of these universes are inter-connected, and God exists at the top of the spiral at the highest frequency of vibration and energy possible.

3. That, man lives; that he has always lived and he will always live. At times man manifests and lives in this physical universe and then passes through transition or death into manifestation in one of the higher universes. The particular higher universe to which man manifests depends on the status of his soul development. It follows from this that death is not a true reality. Man cannot die; all he can do is determine the quality of his living.

4. That, it is possible to pass through transition or death without losing consciousness. The great masters, such as Master Jesus and others, were able to do this. When a person **dies** this is only a transition or passing over, and some people do sometimes lose their way for a short period of time, which usually does not exceed 49 days. This lost period is best described in the Tibetan Book of the Dead. It is this lost period that the Roman Church calls purgatory. In earlier times priests would try to be present at a transition in order to guide the person

136 TRUE ESOTERIC TRADITIONS

through transition and send him on his way into his own new reality as quickly and easily as possible.

Exhibit 15: The Great Sphinx of Giza. Although there are many theories, no one has a reasonable hypothesis as to why this monument was constructed. Since the Sphinx is part man and part beast perhaps it is to show man's two natures.

So-called ghosts are simply persons who have passed through transition and, for one reason or another, are lost and cannot find their way into their own new reality. Sometimes people who meet violent deaths do not yet even know and understand that they have passed over, and actually do reappear to loved ones.

Other departed ones are held close to Earth dimension by the excessive grieving of loved ones. Obviously, one should never seek advice from ghosts because if the ghosts were evolved enough to give good advice they probably wouldn't be captured between two competing dimensions of reality. In any event, death or transition, in and of itself, does not confer wisdom on an individual. Unevolved humans pass through transition and become unevolved ghosts, so to speak. Although there may be much pain leading up to transition, the transition process itself, is totally free of pain.

The great masters knew how to pass through transition without losing consciousness and did not need a priest to help them. Some went away in private to go through transition alone. Moses Moria-El and Laotse are just two examples. Sadly, many Christian-church priests do not know and understand this transition process themselves and are of little help to people approaching transition.

Exhibit 16: The Great Pyramid of Giza which was 481 feet tall, with a base of approximately 756 feet on each side. It contains approximately 2.5 million limestone blocks weighing an average of 5000 pounds each for a total of about 12.5 trillion pounds.

138 TRUE ESOTERIC TRADITIONS

5. That, after transition it is possible to be born again into a new body on Earth and many people have done so. It is also possible not to be reborn again on Earth. Each person decides for him or herself when, where, and if he or she will reincarnate on Earth again. Each person decides this based on his own needs, and tries to select the best situation on Earth in order to learn lessons needed to further his own soul development. Children do choose their parents. The Roman Church taught reincarnation until about AD 553.

6. That, man must be born again. Symbolical death and resurrection was celebrated in the so-called Rite of the Little Dead in the White Lodge. It was for the celebration of this ancient rite that the pit was built deep in the bowels of the Great Pyramid of Giza. Remember, the Great Pyramid was apparently built about 2900 BC and is a Freemasonic or Rosicrucian temple.

In this rite the student would spend three days in this deep pit, without food or water, and in total darkness, experiencing altered states of consciousness, and ultimately, suffering death of the ego. This was a very touchy procedure because air was very scare, and after a few hours would be almost non-existent. The student needed to lower his metabolism in order not to suffocate. An untrained person could easily lose it all and go mad. But, a few well prepared students did pass all the tests.

After the third day in the pit the student was symbolically reborn as a new person and then became an initiate in a ceremony in the King's Chamber. Remember, there are

Exhibit 17: The King's Chamber in the Great Pyramid which is about 17 feet by 34.5 feet by 19 feet high. The ceiling is made of granite blocks weighing about 50 tons each and were imported from Aswan.

two air shafts that bring air from the top of the Great Pyramid into the King's Chamber. At this time the student became a master and took an initiatic name, such as Aristocles took the name Plato, and Joseph took the name Jesus. Hence the name, Master Jesus. Only masters could aspire to the Christ Degree. But only one master, Master Jesus, has succeeded in reaching that degree to our certain knowledge. And hence the name, Master Jesus the Christ.

It should be noted that there are some ancient traditions to the effect that in earlier Ages at least two other men may have taken the Christ Degree. These two men were Enoch and Melchizedek. An Age is about 2160 years, and the ancient traditions were that a great teacher comes in each Age. Some traditions state that Melchizedek was an earlier incarnation of Master Jesus the Christ. The author reports these traditions but has not been able to confirm them.

It is the symbology of this ancient rite that is depicted in the **New Testament** story of the symbolical death and resurrection of Master Jesus the Christ. If Master Jesus were put in a tomb which was above ground, on Friday afternoon, and was then gone from that building by Sunday morning, that would not be three days or even two full days. Thus, the story of Jesus having died, and being placed in a tomb for three days, and then resurrecting from the dead, relates to this ancient rite.

Master Jesus had earlier experienced this rite of symbolical death and rebirth in the Great Pyramid of Giza in Egypt. The **New Testament** story of his death and resurrection in Israel is only symbolical of this earlier event, much like the baptism of Master Jesus by John the Baptist was an reenactment of other baptisms Master Jesus had earlier celebrated in other cultures.

Baptism is merely a public acknowledgement of an inner achievement; like receiving a college degree. Only adults who had achieved a certain level of development were baptized. Baptism of babies is of Christian-church origin and is only for the purpose of raising revenue for the church. Baptism of a baby has the same merit as awarding a college degree to a baby; which is, almost none at all. There is no question but what those ancient teachings do exert influence on Western culture yet today. How many modern preachers have you heard expound that everybody must be baptized and born again?

7. That, the Law of Love can over-power the Law of Compensation. To the scientific minded, perhaps it is like Quantum effects over-powering General Relativity in the area around black holes. The Law of Compensation was also known as the Law of Karma and was to the effect that every wrong one does must be compensated for; which is to say, that all people must pay their karmic debts. This is a most difficult concept to understand and even more difficult to explain.

If one person wrongs another and thus owes a karmic debt, how does he **compensate** for that debt? The wrong is the cause; the karmic debt is the effect. One way might be to compensate for it by doing good deeds thereafter. But, there is a serious problem with this concept. How could a Hitler ever compensate for his many sins? How could he ever right all the wrongs done to so many people?

This seventh teaching was that a person can wipe out all of those debts to others, through the Law of Love, by forgiving the sins of self. This is to say, that when a person wrongs another person the soul of the person committing the wrong **knows it**, and registers that wrong in his soul computer as one which must be compensated for at some time. Hitler's soul computer must be a main-frame and not one of the small personal computer models.

However, apparently it is very difficult for the soul to forgive the sins of self. It is like having a file in the soul computer stored full of karmic debts, which requires a password for entry. No password; no entry. The password into the soul computer, containing the karmic debts, is the forgiving of the sins of self, and a true seeking of forgiveness for wrongs done. Master Jesus tried to give mankind the password. It is very difficult to simply wipe out all of those debts to others, but it can be done by being truly sorry in the soul and seeking forgiveness for wrongs done. It may be a difficult procedure but it can be done, according to Master Jesus. A person can forgive the sins of self and go on to soul development.

How can one learn to forgive the sins of self? How can the mind and soul retrain itself to come to know that it does not have to compensate for all debts? One method the White Lodge used was for the student to learn to communicate with more highly evolved Beings in other dimensions of reality. Those higher Beings supposedly then would convey knowledge of the password and procedure to the student, and he could acquire that great wisdom in that manner. There are many traditions about the search for the great lost word.

So, how does one communicate with higher Beings in other dimensions of reality? High initiates were able to do this through prayer and meditation. This communication was facilitated by looking into highly polished surfaces, mirrors, or pools of clear water. The higher Being or person in another dimension of reality, would supposedly then appear in this dimension and give counsel to the seeker.

A thousand years later in Greece, great temples were built with various kinds of apparatus for facilitating these communications to other dimensions of reality. These temples eventually failed because, for some reason, such communications either, no longer worked, or no longer had any real meaning. Perhaps it was because the persons in those other dimensions were not evolved and did not possess the required knowledge either.

Plato refers to these teachings in his story of the pool of water in the cave. What is reality and what is illusion? Is this physical universe the only true reality and those other universes only an illusion? Or, are those higher dimensions the true reality and this universe the illusion? Is not each person's reality his own individual reality, created by himself? Similar teachings were also taught in Italy and many other cultures on Earth. It was a criminal offense in Greece to reveal the mysteries to the uninitiated and Plato very nearly got himself into trouble.

Could these great teachers actually converse with people in other dimensions of reality? Modern science tells us that certainly they could not. However, modern science has not yet sufficiently explained these ancient teachings. Hopefully answers will be forthcoming in the near future. The author has insufficient information to either confirm or refute those ancient teachings, but they are most thought provoking.

Many scholars from throughout the world came to Egypt to study in the White Lodge. A few of these were Master Jesus the Christ, Plato, Solon, Pythagoras, Joseph-Yuya, and Abraham. The biblical patriarch Abraham probably was a Hindu priest who came from Ur, which was not a specific place but probably just meant the East. Actually, Abraham probably came from the northern part of India in Kashmir near the border with Tibet. The probable reason why Abraham left is that he fell out with the elderly priests, perhaps over whether God was three entities, as the Hindus believed, or only one entity as Abraham believed.

It is also possible that Abraham took initiation into the ancient White Lodge in Egypt, and this is why his name was changed from Abram to Abraham. The same could also be true of Sarah, for women had equal access with men to the ancient White Lodge. This may also explain why Abraham and Sarah went all the way to Thebes in central Egypt and did not stop at the breadbasket area in the Delta, north of present-day Cairo. The ancient White Lodge, as well as the Pharaoh, and the seat of government were located in Thebes.

It is also very probable that the part of northern India where Abraham came from is the same area where Moses Moria-El went to study as a young man, to the home of his ancestor Abraham, and where he returned after disappearing from the **Bible** and going east to die. There are legends in the area that this is so, and that Moses Moria-El is buried there. German scholar Holger Kersten says that the grave of Moses Moria-El is located about 60 miles north of Srinagar in northern India, near the small village of Hasbal.

Master Jesus went to this same area to study when he was about thirteen years old, in about AD 6. He studied there for about seven years or until about AD 13. Until the AD 1880s, the records still existed concerning Master Jesus and his time of study at Hemis Monastery in northern India, near the border with Tibet. When one reads the translation of those records, there is very little doubt that they refer to Master Jesus. They are most convincing.

The story of the three wise men coming to see Master Jesus as a child is really the visit by initiates of the ancient White Lodge with Joseph and Mary, who were also members of that lodge, to make arrangements for the education of Master Jesus when he reached the proper age. Master Jesus attended school at Mount Carmel on the Mediterranean Sea, in present-day Lebanon, from age five to twelve.

There is also considerable legend in the Kashmir area, including a claimed grave site, that Master Jesus lived there in his last years and died and was buried there about AD 74. The author visited this area and lived on a houseboat in Srinagar in the summer of 1976. There was also a writer visiting there at about the same time, by the name of A. Faber-Kaiser. He reports on these sites in a book entitled **Jesus Died In Kashmir.**

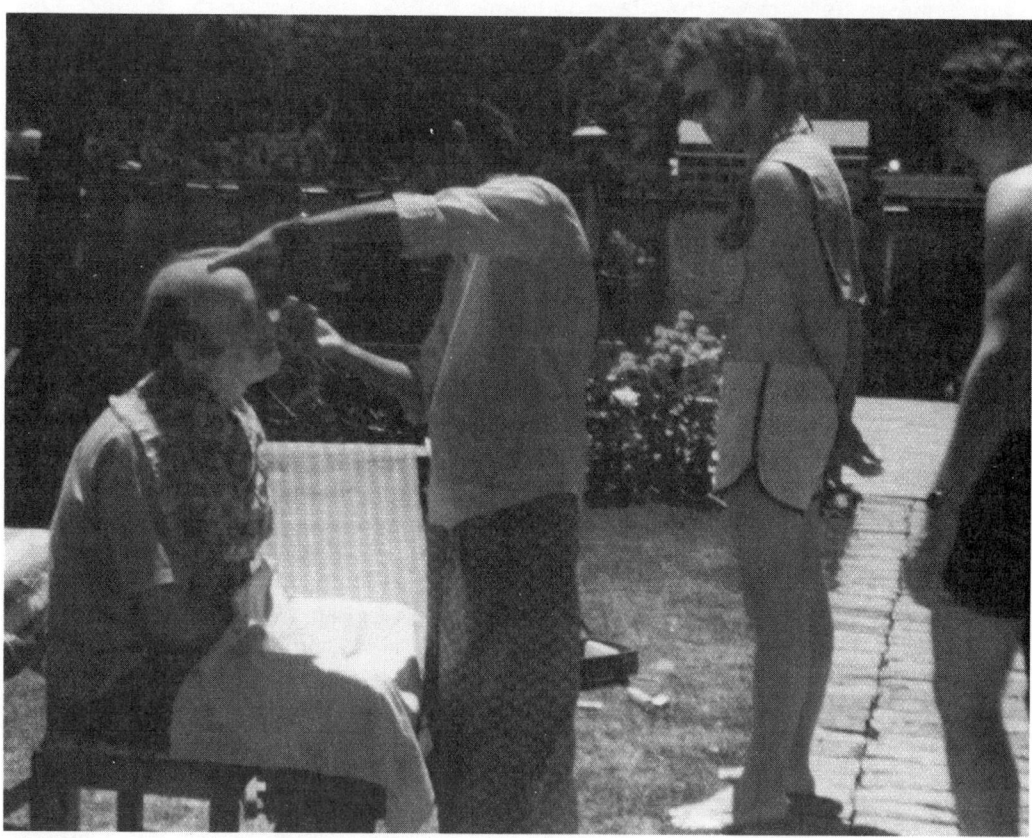

Exhibit 18: Srinagar, Kashmir in northern India, June 1976. The author receives a shave from Solomon the barber while Richard Lee, on the right, and Hunt Palmer skeptically await their turn.

The idea and claim that Master Jesus died on a cross in Israel about AD 33 is Christian-church theology and propaganda, created later. It is not historical fact. The **New Testament** does not say that Master Jesus died on the cross. In fact, quite the contrary. It reports that many people saw and talked to him after the crucifixion event. Even with the editing later performed by the Christian church, much of the history is still there for anyone who wishes to read it.

Following the long established custom of the ancient White Lodge, Master Jesus decided that it was time to go silent. After the crucifixion event, and the ending of his public teaching in about AD 33, Master Jesus can be traced to Mount Carmel on the eastern Mediterranean Sea, to the Essene Monastery where he studied as a small boy. Some years after that, Master Jesus, like Moses Moria-El earlier, may have returned to Kashmir where he lived out the rest of his life.

Abraham was possibly not always an example of virtue. He had a very beautiful wife, Sarah, and they went west to Egypt. Abraham told the Pharaoh, probably Tuthmosis II, that he and Sarah were brother and sister. This was either for his own safety or to try to entangle the Pharaoh for his own purposes. In either event, it was not exactly the action of an initiate.

This probably happened before their initiation and the obligation of honesty that goes with that initiation. It may have been the real reason they confessed to Pharaoh. It is also possible, but doubtful, that they were both husband and wife and brother and sister, as this was common in the area at this time. This was about 1495 BC.

Pharaoh had married Sarah and she had become pregnant when he was told that she and Abraham were husband and wife. Due to editing by Ezra, the **Bible** equivocates on Sarah's marriage to the pharaoh, but the **Koran** sets it forth clearly. Also, this is the only way most of the following story can make any sense. Many people have been executed for far less, but Tuthmosis II only sent Abraham and the pregnant Sarah on their way out of Egypt.

In due course, Isaac was born. He was a Hebrew by law, through his mother, but also a possible heir to the throne of Egypt, through his biological father, Tuthmosis II. His problem was that he was born to an ordinary wife rather than to the Great Royal Wife of the pharaoh.

This situation gave rise to the strange story in the **Bible** where Abraham is willing to sacrifice his son; actually his foster son, Isaac, to appease God. This story is difficult to understand because no initiate of the ancient White Lodge of Egypt would ever do such a thing. But this was before the teachings and requirements were changed and upgraded severely by Hermes and Akhnaton, so that may be the solution to the problem.

The fact that Isaac was not his own natural son gives this story more credibility. It also explains why Sarah was so upset with Abraham's actions. Human sacrifices were not common at that time in that area. This also explains the prediction in the **Bible** that the descendants of Isaac shall rule over Egypt from the Nile to the Euphrates, and indeed they did. Isaac's lineal descendants, Pharaohs Akhnaton and Aye, did rule Egypt at times between 1367 and 1335 BC.

Although there is no record, it is probable that Isaac also studied in Egypt and took initiation into the ancient White Lodge. He had twin sons, Esau and Jacob. Esau sold his birthright, which was his theoretically possible right to the throne of Egypt, to his younger brother Jacob for a mess of pottage; that is, a bowl of soup. This birthright was similar to being 73rd in line for the British throne today.

Jacob went to Egypt and took initiation in the ancient White Lodge. He changed his name to Israel to honor his symbolic spiritual rebirth as a new man. Of course, **Israelite** was the title given to, and used by, all high initiates of the ancient White Lodge. In later years, the people living in Israel incorrectly began calling themselves Israelites. Because of this, high initiates of the ancient White Lodge thereafter called themselves Essenes and, still later, Rosicrucians, which they still use today.

Jacob then had twelve sons, one of whom was named Joseph. Joseph went to Egypt at age seventeen to study in the ancient White Lodge and to try to claim his birthright as pharaoh of Egypt. Probably Jacob passed over his other sons in favor of Joseph, for the birthright, because of Joseph's outstanding abilities in all matters.

> **Genesis: 37:3** "...*Now Israel loved Joseph more than all his children, because he was the son of his old age: and he made him a coat of many colors....*"

Genius or not, any parent really has to wonder about any father who has twelve children and loves one of them more than all of the others combined. This reference to a coat of many colors, of course, has nothing to do with a garment to wear. It is symbolic. The symbolic meaning is that Joseph became a master of many different fields of knowledge. Joseph wore a coat of many colors, which is to say that he was a man of vast and diverse knowledge. He was a master of all trades.

In about 1408 BC, Joseph, whose Egyptian initiate name was Yuya, was appointed Grand Vizier, or Prime Minister, of Egypt; second in power and importance to the Pharaoh. This appointment was made by Tuthmosis IV, who ruled until 1405 BC, at which time he was followed on the throne by his son, Amenhotep III, who was also the son-in-law of Joseph-Yuya.

The author spent over twenty years trying to identify Joseph, Hermes, and Moses Moria-El in Egyptian records. If the Exodus story is true, and it is basically true, although it has been amended and inflated several times, these persons must be there in the records some place. But the credit goes to Cairo-born Muslim scholar, Ahmed Osman, who only very recently identified Joseph as Yuya.

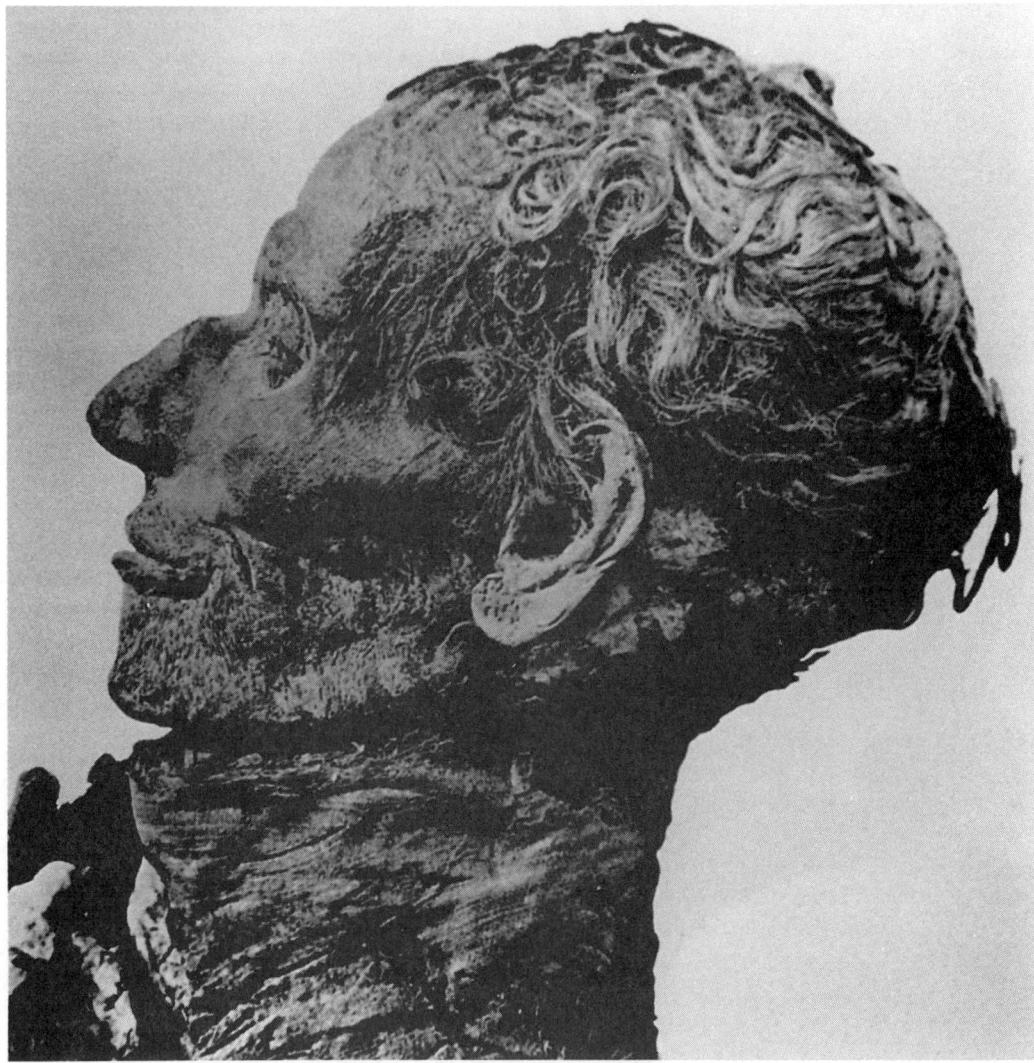

Exhibit 19: The mummy of Joseph-Yuya in the Egyptian Museum in Cairo. Note the distinctly non-Egyptian features. He and his wife were two of very few commoners who ever had their bodies mummified and preserved for history.

146 TRUE ESOTERIC TRADITIONS

These ancient events are generally thought by many to have taken place about the time the Asiatic Hyksos kings invaded and took over the rule of Egypt in about 1659 BC. The famous Jewish historian, Josephus, writing about AD 100, connected the Hebrews in Egypt to these Semitic Hyksos shepherd kings, but he was mistaken.

These Hyksos kings ruled for more than a century. They were finally completely expelled from Egypt by about 1550 BC. But a Hebrew connection to the Hyksos is not a historical fact. The Hebrews in Egypt have no connection with the Asiatic Hyksos and came into Egypt later on, in about 1500 BC after Pharaoh Ahmosis I, the great mystic and scholar, had established the Eighteenth Dynasty. The Hebrews came only after the Hyksos had gone, when Pharaoh Tuthmosis II was on the throne.

Exhibit 20: Pharaoh Akhnaton

The biblical records clearly state that Joseph-Yuya rode in a chariot. The war chariot was not introduced into Egypt until the early 1400s BC, or over 100 years after the Asiatic Hyksos were expelled. The actual time of introduction was during the reign of Tuthmosis IV, between 1413 and 1405 BC. Tuthmosis IV was a dreamer and a mystic, much like his ancestor, Ahmosis I. He appointed as his second in command another dreamer and mystic, his distant cousin, Joseph-Yuya.

Joseph-Yuya was probably born about 1438 BC in Canaan. He became Prime Minister to Tuthmosis IV about 1408 BC, at age 30. Joseph-Yuya married an Egyptian woman of a priestly family and they had at least three sons, one of whom was named Aye, and one daughter named Tiye. Amenhotep III, son of Tuthmosis IV, followed his father on the throne and this is when big problems in Egypt began.

Until his death at about 64 years, in about 1374 BC, Joseph-Yuya continued to serve under Amenhotep III. Each Pharaoh had always first married his own sister, who became the Great Royal Wife, or Queen; she was then mother to the next pharaoh. Amenhotep III did marry his own sister, Sitamun, but did not make her his Great Royal Wife. Instead, he also married Joseph-Yuya's daughter, Tiye, whom he had always loved, and made her his Great Royal Wife.

Joseph-Yuya continued as Prime Minister during much of the long reign of Amenhotep III, which lasted until 1367 BC. This is generally considered the best period ever in Egyptian history, and it is basically because Joseph-Yuya and later his daughter, Tiye, really ran the government. Both were extremely competent.

Akhnaton, Joseph-Yuya's grandson, and the man who would change history, was about seventeen years of age at that time and undoubtedly was tutored by his grandfather. Joseph-Yuya must have taught his grandson very well. Any teachings Joseph-Yuya failed to give Akhnaton were supplemented by his mother, Tiye, and the great sage, Hermes.

The successor to Amenhotep III on the throne was his son, Akhnaton, now 24 years old, who was also the grandson of a non-Egyptian, Joseph-Yuya. Akhnaton, who was known as the heretic pharaoh, instituted the monotheistic religion in Egypt by force. This force-feeding of the new monotheistic religion to Egyptians was strongly supported by his wife, Nefertiti, his mother, Tiye, the Prime Minister, Aye, and Hermes, who was the mystical leader of the ancient White Lodge. However, it was probably a mistake.

Amenhotep IV changed his name to Akhnaton to honor his symbolic spiritual rebirth as a new man. He also moved his capital from Thebes and forcefully removed all monuments to the Egyptian gods. This was very unpopular with many people, particularly the Egyptian priesthood who had lived off the gifts to the temples for centuries. The priests got even with him later.

Nefertiti was the daughter of Prime Minister Aye and the granddaughter of Joseph-Yuya. Akhnaton married the beautiful Nefertiti, who was his first cousin.

Exhibit 21: Queen Nefertiti

In 1353 BC, Akhnaton turned the ancient White Lodge into the structured order of study which is still followed today. He also changed the name of the order to The Ancient and Mystical Order Rose Cross, or for short, AMORC. The change in the teachings was a dramatic one. Previously the ancient White Lodge had imported the Lesser Mysteries into Egypt from another land that is unknown.

The author believes that this land was the British Isles, which was the legendary Atlantis. The Lesser Mysteries were the teachings of the ancient White Lodge until 1353 BC. Then Hermes added the Greater Mysteries to the ancient White Lodge teachings and increased the degree levels from three to seven. It was the celebration of these events that led to the creation of the new calendar, with 1353 BC as year one, which is still in use to the present day.

In these teachings there were one thousand lessons to be learned in order to arrive at a full comprehension of the Lesser and Greater Mysteries. The path to enlightenment is sometimes dark -- and it is always darkest just before dawn -- but these one thousand lessons constituted one thousand points of enlightenment along the path from darkness and ignorance to knowledge and wisdom. It took one thousand weeks to learn the one thousand lessons, or approximately twenty years. History reports that Plato and other Greek students, a thousand years later, each studied for twenty years; actually for one thousand weeks, in Egypt. And thus the wisdom was passed on.

The whole idea behind the ancient White Lodge teachings was to raise the level of the student's consciousness from its left-brained animal instincts up to its right-brained Christ-like potential. The unevolved person's consciousness reposes at the very base of the spine in the lower-most vertebra. This is the area of the spine that holds the serpent power or sex drive in people. In the east this is called the kundalini power. It is the driving force of the sex organs and is like a raging fire in some people. As one would expect, many unevolved people spend most of their time thinking about eating, drinking, and sex.

One of the first things the neophyte has to learn is the control of this raging fire within. It is somewhat like an atomic reaction. When loose and out of control, it is a horrible thing to behold, but when it is controlled, it becomes a thing of pure beauty. It allows the consciousness to begin its long rise, ever upward. Men and women accomplish this rise in consciousness through use of the will.

Do not be confused. There are two types of sex. There is the animal-type sex that is needed for procreation and propagation of the species. This is the sex drive that reposes at the base of the spine and is not different in humans from that of other mammals. In this type of sex, the participants have little regard for each other and desire only to satisfy their respective animal instincts. We all have two potentials. One is animal and the other is the Christ potential. The animal instinct will dominate until subdued by the will. Then the Christ instinct is allowed to bloom and unfold, symbolically, like a rose upon a cross.

There is also another kind of sex that expresses the intimacy and love between two people. This kind of sex is unrelated to procreation and the animal instincts. Many ascetics in the East, as well as priests in the Roman Church in the West, teach that one must remain celibate in order to evolve. Not true. The best evidence of this was Master Jesus the Christ who was certainly a married man, and perhaps even married more than once in his lifetime.

In **Genesis 2:9** it states: "*...In the middle of the garden were the tree of life and the tree of the knowledge of good and evil.*" What was this Tree of Life referred to in **Genesis**? Surely none would suggest that it was in fact a tree physically growing in an actual garden in Eden. Surely not. The Tree of Life does somewhat resemble a tree. It is the path of evolution of the consciousness from the base of the spine to the top of the spine and into the third eye. This so-called third eye is the area at the top of the forehead between the other two eyes. It is the channel of entry and exit of the soul at birth and death, according to ancient esoteric teachings.

The physical universe is composed of solids or Earth, liquid or water, and gas or air. The fire, or Vital Life Force, comes from outside this physical universe. It is from the gross matter of Earth with the addition of air, water, and fire, or Vital Life Force, that man moves out of the state of matter and into a state of consciousness. It is by joining the two polarities of positive and negative, of yin and yang, of the male aspect and the female aspect with the burning, animating Vital Life Force that the neophyte person comes into being.

The neophyte person then has the ever-long and arduous task of raising his or her consciousness from the grossness of its beginnings to the beauty of its potential, even to the Christ-consciousness. The first step away from the animal instincts starts the neophyte person on a quest from which he or she may pause and rest but never again cease to seek. From this point on the neophyte becomes a walking question mark.

The positive male aspect resonates at an uneven number of vibrations per second and moves upward to join the female aspect that resonates at an even number of vibrations. This forms a trinity from that duality, and creates the neophyte person, animal-like in his or her instincts, but Christ-like in his or her potential.

The neophyte lives in controlled and subdued chaos. Such a person receives information from many different sources and seldom knows whom to believe. Should such a person believe the priest or the teachings of Master Jesus the Christ? Most popes and priests have been neophytes themselves and have been totally unqualified to teach or lead others. But, order can arise out of that chaos. The way is opened by looking within the self, by meditation, prayer, and by experiencing and learning, until the consciousness comes to realize and know that there is a path upward, ever upward.

It cannot be done by the Roman Church, as presently constituted, or any of its offspring. It also cannot be done by the television preachers who contaminate the airways; but, it can be done.

The student upon the path must first subdue the negative fixations of mind. There is no evil god or Satan. One does not have to pay a priest. One does not have to be a member of a religion. Sex is not dirty or sinful. Men are not superior to women. Blacks are not inferior in potential to others. The Jews did not persecute Master Jesus any more than did others of that day. The Jews are not God's chosen people. There are no free lunches and no instant salvations; and on and on.

One must rid him or herself of such negative fixations of mind before becoming a student upon the path. This is a most difficult but essential first step. Evolution is a law of the physical universe. Shortly after the student upon the path begins the process of learning to eliminate the negative fixations of mind, he or she will also begin the positive steps toward becoming a Mason, or what have become known as Freemasons since the time of King Solomon. Always remember that half or more of the persons in the ancient White Lodge were women.

It must also be remembered that advancement came only by advancing up both sides of the Tree of Life at the same time, at the same speed, and then integrating both to the center of the Tree, which is to say, into the inner being of the student on the path. In other words, it would not matter how much knowledge a student acquired, unless he or she also acquired an equal amount of wisdom. Until he or she integrated that wisdom with his or her knowledge, he or she would not be a true Master.

A neophyte or apprentice was a student who had learned the 33 laws of the physical universe. A person who had earned the Brotherhood or Fellowcraft Degree was a student who had subdued and erased the negative fixations of mind. A Mason was a person who had mastered the Lesser Mysteries and the three degrees. A Master Mason was a student who had opened his brain to intelligence and his mind to understanding.

In the ancient White Lodge this process required about four years of study, and these were the teachings that Solomon mastered in Egypt before dropping out of school. Solomon was a school dropout, so to speak. Later when Solomon created his Blue Lodge, these were the studies that constituted the three degrees of that Blue Lodge. A Mason in the ancient White Lodge was what is called a Master or a Master Mason in the Blue Lodge of today. The Blue Lodge today has no office or status equal to the Master of the ancient White Lodge.

An Israelite was a person who had begun study of the Greater Mysteries. This meant that he or she was at a very high level of intelligence and understanding and had opened him or herself to the path of knowledge and wisdom. In the ancient White Lodge this

THE WHITE LODGE

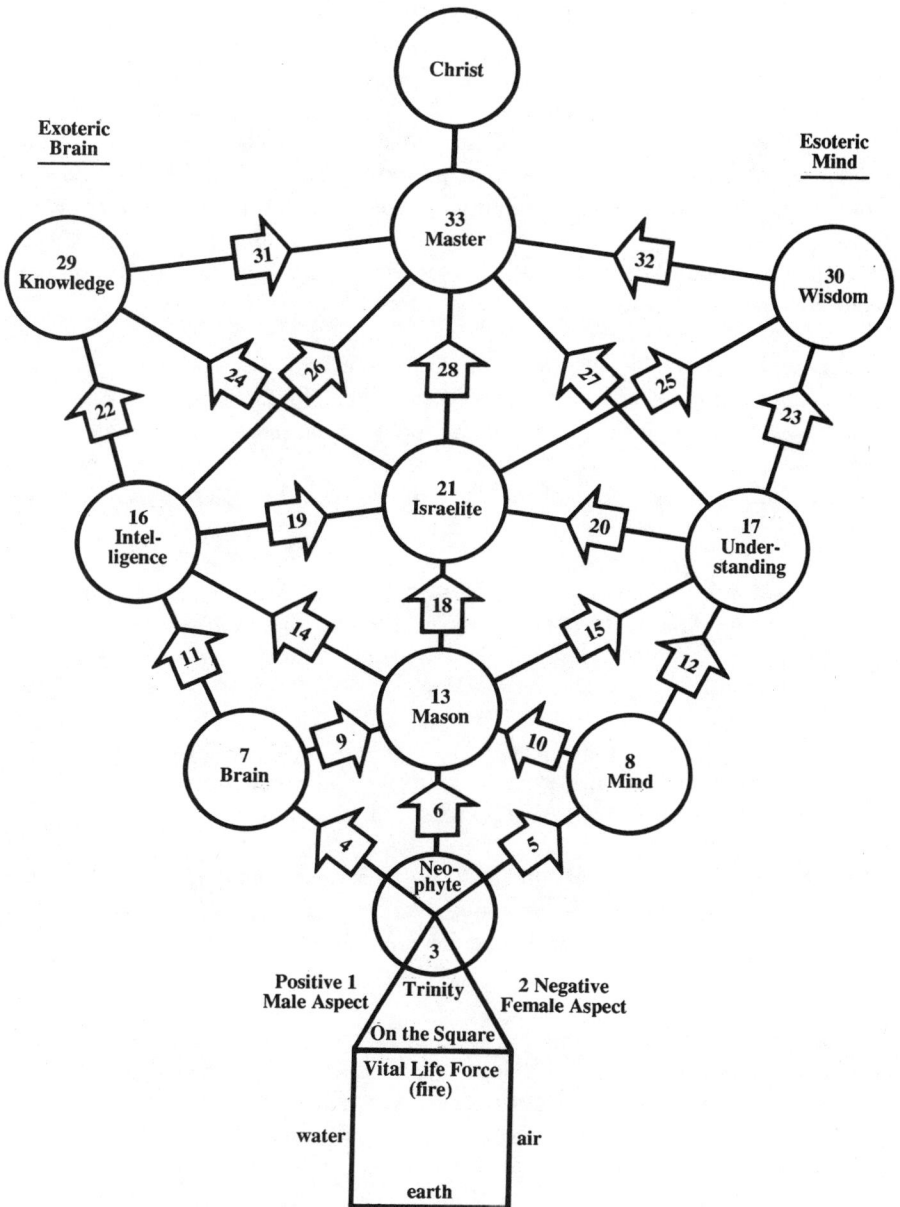

Exhibit 22: Genesis 3:5 "...*God knows that when you eat from it (the Tree of Life) your eyes will be opened and you will be like God, knowing good and evil.*"

required about six years of work and study. A true Master was a person who had conquered the Greater Mysteries and had mastered both knowledge and wisdom, and integrated them into his or her own being. This required a total of one thousand weeks of work and study, or approximately twenty years.

It is then possible for a person to raise his consciousness out of the spine and into the so-called third eye, which is an adjunct to the pineal gland in the front-center of the brain. It is the opening of this third eye that changes a person into a true master. It is this opening of the third eye that causes a person to be born again into the spirit and become a new person. Master Jesus reportedly stated at **John 3:3** "...*I tell you the truth, no one can see the kingdom of God unless he is born again.*" It is also through the opening of this so-called third eye that a person must raise him or herself through to the Christ consciousness and ultimately become as one with God.

If the reader will look at the Tree of Life, he or she will see that there are exactly 33 steps upon that path to mastership. These 33 steps are the 33 degrees of the present-day Scottish Rite. It is beyond the scope of this book to delineate the details of those 33 steps, except to say that the consciousness must move only and always upward, and on all of the paths at the same speed at the same time. The 33rd step would then raise the student to mastership, as Master Jesus demonstrated.

The author would refer the reader to the book entitled **Morals and Dogma** by Thirty third Degree Mason, Albert Pike, who uses nearly one thousand pages to describe the first 32 Scottish Rite degrees. Another great Masonic historian was Manly Palmer Hall, who died in AD 1990.

Akhnaton initiated the use of the sign of the cross as a symbol of membership in the Rosicrucian Order. This sign of the cross, centuries later, was turned around in use and meaning and was appropriated by the Roman Church.

From 1353 BC on, it would be very difficult, perhaps even impossible, ever to complete all of the degree work. Only one person to date, Master Jesus, has done so. But, by inductive logic, we can reason that if one person did it, then all persons can someday do the same.

Why did Akhnaton choose the rose on a cross as the symbol for his new order? The cross is said to symbolize a man with arms outstretched, facing the light of the sunrise. It is a symbol of the sacrifice or service man must perform. The rose symbolizes the soul personality of man. The partially unfolded rose infers an evolving consciousness as it receives the greater light from the Greater Mysteries.

During meetings of the ancient White Lodge, a rose was always hung high in the center of the meeting room. Throughout most of history it meant persecution or even death if one was discovered to be a Rosicrucian. Thus Rosicrucians never revealed to unworthy persons anything learned sub rosa, or under the rose.

The symbolic rose is locked up in the heart of every person. It can be made to bloom and come forth by serving mankind. Those who perform complete service and become fully illuminated are known as Rosicrucians. To be a true Rosicrucian is a state of being; it is to come to understand the plan of God's creation, to be capable of complete love and to acquire the all-seeing eye of complete knowledge, comprehension, and understanding.

There are two Rosicrucian organizations: an **inner** and an **outer** order. The inner order has no buildings and elects no officers. It is a state of enlightenment. All throughout history various groups of people have banded together to study the Rosicrucian teachings. A few of those people have been Rosicrucians, but some have not been. Many have called themselves Rosicrucians. Studying to become a Rosicrucian is a worthy effort. The outer Rosicrucian Order has many temples and officers throughout the world. At some times in history the outer order became suppressed by governmental or religious authorities and was thought to have gone out of existence entirely; however, the inner order has always survived and will always survive.

There are some excellent Rosicrucian organizations with excellent material. In fact, it should be the goal of every human being on Earth to become a Rosicrucian like Master Jesus. But studying to be one and claiming to be one does not make a person a Rosicrucian. In fact the very few true Rosicrucians who have lived were not generally known to be Rosicrucians to most of mankind during their lives.

It is true that no race, religion, or nationality has more virtuous people or more enlightened persons than any other. Many whites feel that whites are more honest than blacks and other races. Not so. The Chinese feel that they are superior to other Asians. Again not so. Jews feel that they are more chosen than God's other children. Again, not so.

Many priests in all religions feel that they are more virtuous than prostitutes, but a growing proportion of the world would feel that just the reverse may be true. Perhaps the most ignorant belief on Earth is that found among Christians who believe that they and their religion are closer than the other people of Earth to Master Jesus the Christ and his teachings. All such false beliefs must also pass away.

A true Rosicrucian is one who lives kindly, gives kindness, lives happily, and successfully, and helps to make his world what God wants it to be. Such conduct constitutes a real Rosicrucian in the real sense at all times and eternally. Such a person may never have heard of the Rosicrucian Order. Being a Rosicrucian is the attainment of a status, not technical membership in a formalized group.

The Rosicrucians always rise again, even from the ashes, much as the phoenix does. Even if all material possessions of the Rosicrucians were destroyed and scattered to the four corners of Earth, they would still rise again from the ashes of destruction. This is the story of the phoenix and it is the story of the Rosicrucians.

Almost by definition, anyone who claims to be a Rosicrucian is not one. The true ones have always sought to deny their status. That is completely understandable. At times advanced Rosicrucians do go public, but this is rare. Akhnaton and Master Jesus were two examples. If a Rosicrucian tells you there is only One True God and a priest tells you that God is a trinity, whom would you believe? The answer would depend on your own evolvement and not on the status of the Rosicrucian or the priest.

The only persons who have any need to know Rosicrucians are other Rosicrucians. But one true Rosicrucian can recognize another one immediately, without asking. John the Baptist immediately recognized Master Jesus, without any word or sign between them, even though they had never previously met. So, to curiosity seekers who ask idle questions about Rosicrucian membership of others; the answer is usually one of denial.

Historically, the Rosicrucians wanted and needed no publicity. It was counter-productive to their work. This high secrecy should change as we enter the so-called Aquarian Age. The secrecy will cease to be, proportional to the decline in the power of the Christian churches to persecute the Rosicrucians.

Many kings and priests in many countries have tried to stamp out both Rosicrucians and Freemasons. The Christian church has spent more time, effort, and energy trying to find and exterminate the Rosicrucians and Freemasons than it has in spreading the teachings of Master Jesus, by far. But those groups and persons have never succeeded and they never will. A few Rosicrucians will come together into a group during certain time periods to perform certain functions, but then they again go silent and are gone as with the wind. True Rosicrucians know when to band together and when to disband and go silent.

It is within the very nature of groups that once they have fulfilled their original plan, and continue to hang on and exist, they become counter-productive to their original purpose. All life is in cycles. Every cycle has its season, a time to come together and a time to be gone as with the wind. May the wise perceive the season.

It simply has not been possible to exterminate the Freemasons and Rosicrucians, regardless of the amount of effort expended and regardless of by whom. For, as long as God rules in the universe, the Freemasons, the Rosicrucians, and the teachings of Master Jesus the Christ shall survive.

All true Rosicrucians and all true Freemasons have exactly the same goal. It is identical to the goal of all who aspire to follow the teachings of Master Jesus the Christ. Some members of the Christian church and even a few of its leaders over the centuries have shared this goal.

In this century a few Christian-church leaders, generally represented by the World Council of Churches, have also pursued this common goal, but only with much recrimination from the orthodox Christian institutions. There is more true Christianity in the world today than ever before in recorded history. The teachings of Master Jesus the Christ can grow only as the power of the Christian churches decline.

The very high teachings of Master Jesus can be traced to Hermes, who became Master of the ancient White Lodge in Egypt after the death of Akhnaton in 1350 BC. Why is Hermes often referred to as the thrice-great man? It is because he was considered to excel in all three major areas of human interest. Hermes had the illumination of a high priest, the power of a mighty king, and the love of wisdom of a true philosopher. Thus, he was thrice great. Such an exalted status was symbolized by the all-seeing eye of complete knowledge, comprehension, and understanding. He was also one of the most illusive and mysterious men in recorded history.

Another illusive man of Egyptian history is the man who is known to us as Moria-El, the Illustrious. He was born near Cairo, Egypt, in 1385 BC. He came from a long family of mystics and leaders much like Joseph-Yuya. He entered the ancient White Lodge at a young age and apparently finished the twenty years of work and changed his name to Moria-El to honor his symbolical rebirth as a new man.

Moria-El operated a school for young students of the mysteries, much as Plato did a thousand years later. The distinctive feature in the teachings of Moria-El was that he taught an ancient rite of baptism. His school was located at what was then known as Lake Moeris, now known as Lake Karoun, in Egypt. Baptisms were performed in the lake. In this ancient rite, the student was submerged under water in order to symbolize a return to the purity of the mother's womb, and then be symbolically reborn as a new person.

The rite of baptism was taught in most ancient cultures even prior to this time in Egypt. The Christian church rejected many of the teachings of Master Jesus the Christ, but they did retain the rites and symbols, although without understanding.

The search for Moses in Egyptian history must at some point lead to the name of Moria-El. The name **Moses** is associated with water and so is the name Moria-El. They could very easily be one and the same person. Moria-El was fourteen years younger than the thrice-great sage, Hermes, and six years younger than the great priest-king, Akhnaton. All of these men were brothers in the spirit and may have been blood relatives as well.

Ahmed Osman has suggested that Moses and Akhnaton were one and the same person and that Akhnaton-Moses surrendered the Egyptian throne in order to lead the Hebrews out of Egypt in the Exodus. The author feels that this cannot be true for several reasons. As Sigmund Freud pointed out, the two men shared identical religious beliefs, they were born about the same time, and Akhnaton's body has never been found.

Egyptian pharaohs were perceived as gods by the Egyptian people and for this reason the pharaohs who got out of line were killed by the priesthood, not deposed. This would have been the first and only time in recorded Egyptian history that a pharaoh left the throne and continued to live. Most importantly we must consider the fact that if Akhnaton-Moses had in fact been deposed from the throne, he would not have been followed on the throne by members of his own family; Semenkhkare, Tut, and Aye.

Exhibit 23: King Tut, whose tomb was located only in 1922.

Perhaps one of the best arguments against the theory that Akhnaton-Moses was deposed is that the Rosicrucians claim that there are still ancient White Lodge records that show that Pharaoh Akhnaton died as a result of slow poisoning on July 24, 1350 BC. The author is persuaded that the Exodus event took place in 1335 BC, not 1350 BC, and that it happened at the end of the reign of Pharaoh Aye, who was the son of Joseph-Yuya of the **Bible**.

The first three degrees taught the Lesser Mysteries. These Lesser Mysteries go back to the beginning of man on Earth, even to the Garden of Eden. Tuthmosis III had these teachings reduced to that of a formalized system of study, although the movement toward this formalization had begun much earlier.

In some of the codes of law in existence at that time, the rules of law were stated in the conditional tense. For example, King Hammurabi's Code was produced in Babylon about 1750 BC so that "...*the strong may not oppress the weak and to see that justice is done for the orphan and widow...*" The Hammurabic Code provided that a slave girl could not be sold if she had given birth to a son of her master; a wife could not be seized for the debts of her husband; a husband could not divorce his wife who was incurably ill; upon divorce, a husband must set aside property to provide for his wife; an eye for an eye for an injured freeman, later picked up in the **Bible**, but only a fine if the injured party was of lower estate.

In Egypt, the obligation was much more personal, such as Master Jesus would later teach. Here, the person made his own personal commitment to the true way. However, it was phrased in the negative such as, I have not, etc. From the very old **Egyptian Book of the Dead**, we read the **Confession To Maat**, which is simply a dedication to truth. Actually, it is a dedication not to do evil. It goes as follows:

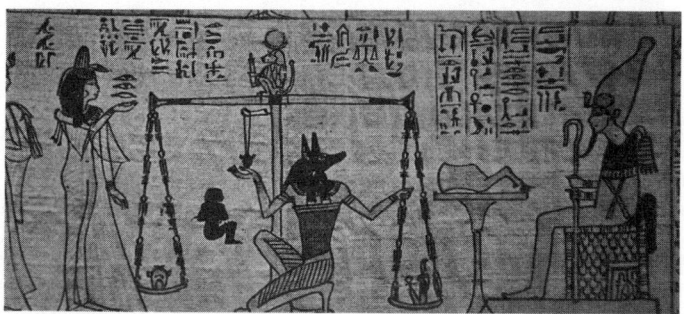

Exhibit 24: From **The Egyptian Book of the Dead**, the Egyptian god, Osiris, judging the dead princess. Note that he weighs her heart on a scale balanced against a feather.

CONFESSION TO MAAT

"...Homage to Thee, O Great God, Thou Master of All Truth! I have come to Thee, O my God, and have brought myself hither, that I may become conscious of Thy decrees. I know Thee and am attuned with Thee and Thy two and forty laws which exist with Thee in this chamber of Maat.

In Truth have I come into Thine attunement, and I have brought Maat in my mind and soul.

> I have destroyed wickedness for Thee.
> I have not done evil to mankind.
> I have not oppressed the members of my family.
> I have not wrought evil in the place of right and truth.
> I have had no intimacy with worthless men.
> I have not demanded first consideration.
> I have not decreed that excessive labor should be performed for me.
> I have not brought forward my name for exaltation to honors.
> I have not defrauded the oppressed of property.
> I have made no man to suffer hunger.
> I have made no one to weep. I have caused no pain to be inflicted upon man or animal.
> I have not defrauded the temples of their oblations.
> I have not diminished from the bushel.
> I have not encroached upon the fields of others.
> I have not filched away land.
> I have not added to the weights of the scales to cheat the seller.
> I have not misread the pointer of the scales to cheat the buyer.

I have not kept the milk from the mouths of children.
I have not turned back the water at the time when it should flow.
I have not extinguished the flame when it should burn.
I have not repulsed God in His manifestations.

<u>*AFFIRMATION*</u>

I am pure! I am pure! I am pure! My purity is the purity of the Divinity of the Holy Temple.

Therefore, evil shall not befall me in this world, because I, even I, know the laws of God which are God. Cromaat!..."

Exhibit 25: Sarcophagus; a limestone coffin or tomb. Note that it is ornamented and has a heavy lid.

The tombs of pharaohs were very heavy with equally heavy lids. The sarcophagus in the King's Chamber of the Great Pyramid Temple has no lid and no ornaments and was used for ceremonial purposes; not for burial.

The word **cromaat** is usually interpreted to mean that **the truth shall be**, or that, **it is done in truth**. What generalities can we observe in the ancient White Lodge teachings just prior to the Exodus event and the great revolution in Egypt? Some of the lessons we can learn from those ancient teachings are as follows:

1. That there is one God, singular, not many gods or even a trinity of gods as earlier taught.

2. That the unfolding rose of spirituality in man must bloom upon the cross of service, which is to say the rose cross.

3. That all people must be born again symbolically in the spirit.

4. That baptism by complete submersion under water symbolized returning to the womb and hence being born again as a new person with a new name.

5. That a Messiah, or the Christ, or a great world teacher, would someday come. The seventh or Christ initiation required that someday someone would come who could meet the requirements of that initiation. He would set a new and higher standard of love for mankind. Master Jesus the Christ fulfilled this prophecy.

6. That in the Age of Intelligence, or what we today call the Aquarian Age, which the world is about to enter, another great world teacher will come whose symbolic name will be John and whose symbol is the eagle. This ancient teaching is somehow depicted on the seal of the United States of America, as can be seen on the back of any dollar bill.

An understanding of these teachings in the ancient White Lodge can help one in understanding the later teachings of Master Jesus the Christ. It can also be helpful in understanding some of the later events surrounding the Hebrew people and the Christian church. These teachings were all promulgated by the ancient White Lodge during the time of Akhnaton.

The situation became so bad politically that Akhnaton made his younger half-brother and devoted follower, Semenkhkare, co-pharaoh in 1351 BC and they served together as rulers until the death of Akhnaton on July 24, 1350 BC. Pharaohs often picked their own successors in order to eliminate bloody palace purges. The Egyptian priesthood assassinated Akhnaton, probably by slow poison, in revenge for his actions against them in eliminating their positions and incomes.

The reader must understand that then, as now, the priesthood was very smart and very scheming. They had appointed and controlled pharaohs for centuries. Any time one did not please them, they would very simply kill him with poison in his food. Their deaths were slow and painful. These examples taught successors that they should not cross the priests. Priests did not change much in the next 3000 years. The Roman-church popes later tortured and killed millions of people in some of the worst crimes ever known in history.

Semenkhkare ruled only until 1348 BC, and he was also assassinated, probably also by poison. Pharaoh Tutankhamen, the now famous King Tut, followed on the throne. He was probably also a younger half-brother of Akhnaton, but he reigned for only nine years or until about 1339 BC. He was also probably poisoned by the priesthood. During his reign, the old Egyptian gods and temples were restored and vast concessions were made to the priesthood in an effort to stop the assassinations and to try and keep the kingship in the family. But it was not to be. During this period, the Hebrew pharaohs and their family were oppressed.

By this time Army General Horemheb was so sure of his dominance that he even had a beautiful life-size statue, now in the Metropolitan Museum of Art in New York City

160 TRUE ESOTERIC TRADITIONS

USA, made of himself during the reign of King Tut, with the following self-observation inscribed thereon:

> *"...I am the recorder of royal laws, who gives directions to the courtiers. Wise in speech, there is nothing I ignore. I am the adviser of everyone, who teaches each man his course, ...Who speaks to him who is forgetful (King Tut?)...I am the herald of the Council. ...King's deputy before the two lands (Egypt). ..."*

Exhibit 26: Army General Horemheb, later a pharaoh, who fancied himself to be a scribe, giving counsel to King Tut.

The prayer is addressed to the old Egyptian gods, Thoth, Ptah, and Osiris. Even having a statue made of himself shows his pharaoh-like position in Egypt at this time and his complete dominance over affairs. The language on the statue reinforces the same idea. The reader may see this statue in the Metropolitan Museum of Art in New York City.

The fourth and last pharaoh of this Hebrew group was Aye, who was the youngest son of Joseph-Yuya. Even though he was an old man and not an Egyptian, he was still made co-pharaoh in 1340 BC. This was the work and influence of Hermes. It would give the family time to get most of the family, and the family wealth, out of Egypt. We are now in a position to date the Exodus of the Hebrews out of Egypt with reasonable certainty.

Aye, like his father, served as Prime Minister. Now he became pharaoh in his own right, but he ruled only four years from 1339 to 1335 BC. Since Aye was not of the royal family and held the throne as sort of a usurper according to the Egyptian rules, the time was ripe for the priests with the power of the army behind them, to get rid of Pharaoh Aye and put Army General Horemheb on the throne, which is exactly what happened.

The early Egyptians believed that there was much importance in the name of a person and in keeping the name known to future generations. In this way, a man could achieve a certain immortality. It was thought that as long as a man's name lived the man, too, to some extent continued to live. The worst possible thing that could happen to a man was to have his name forgotten. Thus the Egyptians tried to destroy and erase from history the names of persons they hated.

The four Hebrew-dominated Egyptian Pharaohs: Akhnaton, Semenkhkare, Tut, and Aye were hated by their successor, Pharaoh Horemheb, who tried to erase their names from history. His effort was successful for many centuries.

Similarly, the Roman Church in AD 1415 had a priest by the name of Pope John XXIII who was a complete scoundrel, even by Roman Church standards. He was actually fired and ousted as pope. In the AD 1960s, one of the best popes ever produced by the Roman Church also used the name Pope John XXIII. This was done in the hope that the name of the first Pope John XXIII would eventually be erased from history and forgotten.

The later Hebrews borrowed this system of the perpetuation of names, like the practice of circumcision, from the Egyptians and carried it, somewhat weakened, down to our own culture of today. It is very common in Western culture to want to be remembered by as many people as possible for as long as possible.

Throughout history women have lost their names upon marriage, not just after they died, but during life. One of the great injustices man has committed against woman has been the taking away of her identity during life. During life one's identity is crucial to both men and women, but after death it is not really a consideration for some people.

And so ended the Eighteenth Dynasty of Egypt, one of the most traumatic periods in the history of mankind. The bright and shining light, Akhnaton and his One True God, was not to be lost to history. His fellow initiate, Moses Moria-El, would lead the family of Joseph-Yuya out of Egypt, and eventually, back home to Canaan. Moses Moria-El was only the fourth generation after Joseph-Yuya, not 430 years afterwards. Therefore, he was probably a great-grandson of Joseph-Yuya. It has been said that it is four generations from shirt sleeves to shirt sleeves, which to say, that cycles in families last for four generations.

However, the idea that the body of Joseph-Yuya was carried back to Canaan by the departing Hebrews is not historical fact and was inserted by Ezra a thousand years later. Ezra did this to try to show that the Hebrews wanted no part of Egypt, in retaliation for the Egyptians wanting no part of the Hebrews. This is all very understandable, but does not make it historical.

Joseph-Yuya was mummified by his son-in-law, Pharaoh Amenhotep III, and buried in the Valley of the Kings as royalty, where he remained until 1905. His mummy now reposes in the Egyptian Museum where the reader may see it for him or herself.

Pharaoh Horemheb, with encouragement from the priesthood, made it very difficult for The Ancient and Mystical Order Rose Cross. It went underground and became a super-secret order. It has remained a super-secret order unto the present day. The priesthoods from the time of Pharaoh Horemheb throughout history have sought out the Rosicrucians for persecution. For a Rosicrucian to be discovered often meant death, so they were serious about their secrecy.

The headquarters of the Order remained in Egypt until shortly before the burning of the great library at Alexandria by the Christian church in AD 400. Shortly before that arson, two more sets of the ancient manuscripts were made. One set was removed to caves in the highest mountains of Tibet where some of them may still remain to this day. In AD 1725, raiding Mongolians carted many of these records away. They may have used them for building fires or they may still be in Mongolia somewhere. The other set has never been located, but the author believes that either it has been held in the vaults of the Vatican in Rome since AD 400, or that, it has been passed down from generation to generation by a very few custodians.

The Ancient and Mystical Order Rose Cross and the priesthoods are not compatible. They never have been and they never will be. Very simply, the Order has always taught that man has a direct personal relationship with God and that no intermediary priesthood is needed or desirable. This put the priesthood out of work in Akhnaton's time in Egypt, and if this principle were followed, it would still do so today. The priesthood at that time tried to identify the Rosicrucians and extinguish them. The priesthood of the Christian church has been trying to do the same thing for 2000 years. Thank God that effort has been without total success.

The highest initiates of the ancient White Lodge and AMORC were known as Israelites, and later as Rosicrucians. These people used the Great Pyramid at Giza as their temple for initiations. They lost this privilege while Horemheb was in power, but eventually they received their temple back and have retained the privilege of using it over the centuries. The Masonic or Rosicrucian temple is the pyramid. Symbolically, the pyramid represents an effort by man to reach up to God; a sort of tower of Babel.

Some of these White Lodge teachings showed up on the great seal of the United States of America some 3000 years later. The reason for a great seal is to summarize the purpose of a nation. These symbols can also be seen on any United States one-dollar bill.

The work of the early Rosicrucians was overseen by a Great Royal Council, or Sanhedrin of 70 members with three administrators, for a total of 73 members. The Hebrews later copied this governmental structure, and Israel was ruled by a Great Council, or Sanhedrin, of 73 elders.

On one side of the dollar bill is a picture of George Washington, a well known Freemason. On the back left side is a pyramid of 73 stones, which is very difficult to distinguish, on thirteen courses, and at the top, an all-seeing eye. The all-seeing eye of Horus depicts the man of complete wisdom, intelligence, and love who was Master Jesus the Christ. On the right side is an eagle, the symbol of America. The eagle has an olive branch with thirteen leaves in its right claw, and a group of thirteen arrows in its left claw, with a crest on its breast of thirteen stripes and thirteen stars above its head.

These, of course, depict the thirteen states which made up the new nation, undivided, where wisdom, intelligence, and love would be allowed to flourish. The olive branch depicts a nation of peace, but the arrows depict a nation ready and willing to defend itself and its ideals. In 1962, America, for the first time ever, turned away from these national goals and that national purpose when it began aggression in Vietnam.

And thus the ancient Hebrews, mystics, or kabalists ask: What is in a name; what is in a number? Perhaps for those who can perceive it, there is knowledge beyond comprehension.

King Solomon came from Israel about 999 BC and attended school in Egypt, but did not, for some reason, take initiation. Perhaps King David died in Israel and Solomon had to go home to be king. Pythagoras, Plato, and Master Jesus, among many others, did take initiation. Pythagoras conceived the so-called 47th Proposition which was later put in book form by Euclid and, some 2500 years later, may have been used by Einstein in formulating his Theories of Relativity. The fact that Solomon did not take initiation would later give rise to the Blue Lodge in Israel about 950 BC.

As his last feeble act, Hebrew Pharaoh Aye granted permission for the Hebrews to leave Egypt. Horemheb, the army general, pharaoh after Aye's death, with the help and support of the Egyptian priesthood, tried to reverse this decision, but it was too late. The Hebrews had left the legal boundaries of Egypt, crossed the Red Sea, and were in the northern part of modern Saudi Arabia.

Albert Doss
Senior Rosicrucian

Memory is the basis
of all development, all
progress, of all achievement!

The historian
perceives history
subjectively, and the
reader reads and reacts to
written history subjectively.

Man is a holography,
a microcosm of the macrocosm,
a picture of something greater
than himself, a little world of
the Great World. Man was created
in the image of God.

This remarkable
volume gives a new
vision into many avenues
of thought for the reader.

CHAPTER EIGHT -- THE EXODUS

The **Bible** says that there were 600,000 Hebrews in the Exodus. This cannot possibly be true. The number has had several zeros added to it by Ezra. Ezra was a great literary agent and a great politician, but as a historian he left much to be desired. He gave the Jews the idea that they were God's chosen people, a concept that haunts them to the present day.

The Egyptians kept records, many records about everything. The Exodus is never mentioned in Egyptian history. This fact alone has led many historians to conclude that the Exodus never did, in fact, take place. Remember too, that Pharaoh Horemheb did everything possible to erase the Hebrews from Egyptian records.

Likewise, the Jews later did everything possible to wipe from history their own connection with an Egyptian bloodline. The only evidence we have for the Exodus is the **Bible**, and we know that Ezra did much editing, re-writing, and adding to the **Bible** in 450 BC. Any such event involving 600,000 people should be recorded in Egyptian records. Certainly, traumatic events such as the plagues and other unusual happenings would be recorded. But they are not recorded during the time period of the Exodus.

We do know that there was a major volcanic eruption on the island of Thera in 1626 BC, followed by a great seven-year famine. As a result, red pumice spewed into the eastern Mediterranean Sea and into the lower Nile River so that they did turn blood red. But this happened 291 years before the Exodus, and there was no connection between the two. This might have been the event to which the **Bible** refers, and perhaps these stories became co-mingled and confused over the centuries.

Some 25 years ago, a well-known historian told the author that his conclusion, after 40 years of study on the subject, was that historical events that are built up in history, such as Atlantis, the Exodus, and King Arthur, are almost always based on some actual historical fact. That was his feeling about the Exodus. It probably did in fact happen, but not with all of the hyperbole that Ezra put in the **Bible**.

So it seems more reasonable to look for 60 or 600 people in the Exodus, rather than 600,000. If Joseph and his brothers each had eight children, that would be about 96 people. If each of these second-generation offspring also had eight children, that would be 768 people in the third generation. And again eight children each would make about 6144 or so people who would be in the fourth generation and take part in the Exodus. But this may assume far too many people. There were only four generations between Joseph-Yuya and Moses Moria-El.

When and where did the Exodus take place? There are presently two major theories about the time of the Exodus, both of which are wrong. And there are three or even four major theories on the route of the Exodus; all of them are wrong. When did the Exodus take place? There have long been two different time periods suggested by scholars on that question, and now a third is being added:

1. The earliest Exodus time suggested is at the time of the reign of Hatshepsut and Tuthmosis III in about 1490-1450 BC. The Asiatic Hyksos kings, with whom Joseph-Yuya and the Hebrews were thought to be associated, had earlier been expelled from Egypt. Tuthmosis III was probably the most successful in terms of power and finance ever to rule in Egypt during its long and splendid history. But this time period is not correct for the Exodus.

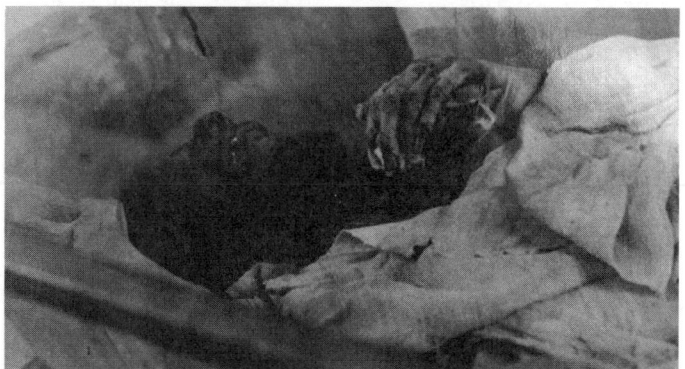

Exhibit 27: Rameses II, the little king with the **Napoleonic complex**.

2. The late Exodus time suggested is at the time of Rameses II in about 1260 BC. Rameses II was probably the second most successful pharaoh, next to Tuthmosis III, in terms of power and finance, ever to rule in Egypt. He was a small man with a monstrous ego. This included 90 wives, over 100 sons, and presumably an equal number of daughters. Rameses would never have allowed the Exodus. Also, it is not possible that the departing Hebrews went to Sinai since that was still in Egypt and under the control of the pharaoh. There are many articles and books that try to explain the Exodus at this time period, but none of them is correct, because it is established that the Hebrews did go into Canaan about 1220 BC, and Rameses II was not ruling then.

3. The middle Exodus time proposed by the author is shortly after the reign of Akhnaton, in about 1335 BC. This is the correct time, or very close to it. The author many years ago came to four firm conclusions:

   a. That the Exodus had to have taken place initially with, not only the consent, but also the full blessing and cooperation of the Egyptian pharaoh;

   b. That neither the early nor the late time periods proposed could possibly be correct;

   c. That of the several suggested Exodus routes from Egypt to Canaan, none seemed to fit; and

   d. That Moses Moria-El was, in fact, an Egyptian as well as a Hebrew and a high initiate of AMORC.

Other time periods that have been considered are still earlier, at the time of the expulsion of the Asiatic Hyksos kings. Why almost all scholars have avoided the time period following the heretic pharaoh, Akhnaton, is unclear. Once it is understood that there was no way the Hebrews could have left Egypt without the consent of the Pharaoh, the time period becomes Akhnaton's, or very shortly thereafter, by necessity.

Exhibit 28: The Wadi Hammamat Road. The asphalt has been added since Moses passed this way in 1335 BC.

The idea that a few Hebrews overcame the mighty Egyptian government was merely racial puffing and hyperbole added by Ezra and others, a thousand years after the fact. It is totally without any basis in historical fact. The reason that most scholars have not been able to come close to the true date of the Exodus is because they have concentrated on Hebrew history as set forth in the **Bible**, rather than Egyptian history, which is much more detailed, and also much more reliable.

The Muslim scholar who has identified Joseph as Yuya puts the Exodus also in this time period, but during the reign of Rameses I in about 1307 BC, or 28 years after our date of 1335 BC. The author believes that this slightly later time period is not correct because Rameses I would not have given his blessing to the Exodus, something essential for it ever to have happened.

By the spring of 1335 BC, many pressures on Moses Moria-El's family had grown stronger. General Horemheb, his army, and the traditional priests were very jealous of Moses Moria-El's wealth and power. The Hebrew pharaoh on the throne, Aye, could not last much longer. It was scandalous that a non-Egyptian had been allowed to sit on the throne of the country. A new government controlled by Horemheb would surely seize Moses Moria-El's, that is to say, Joseph-Yuya's family's wealth, and deprive his family of their power. They decided in the face of these pressures to leave Egypt immediately.

However, at this time, they would not be safe in the capital of Thebes in central Egypt. So they proceeded east over the Wadi Hammamat Road to the port of Qoseir on the Red Sea. They moved slowly, because they were taking with them much gold and other wealth. In fact, everything was going with them but the land. It was this wealth that

168 TRUE ESOTERIC TRADITIONS

Pharaoh Horemheb tried to bring back to Egypt, not the Hebrews themselves. He was very glad to be rid of them.

It is a very strong historical fact that the great empires of the past never included the area we now call northern Saudi Arabia. The great Babylonian empire of 1700 BC, the Egyptian empire throughout all of its long history, the Assyrian empire of about 650 BC, the Median and Chaldean empires before Cyrus in about 550 BC, the tremendous empire of Alexander the Great in about 325 BC, and the mighty Roman empire throughout its long history, never included the area of northern Saudi Arabia. Even today, the Saudi government reportedly has little control in this vast area.

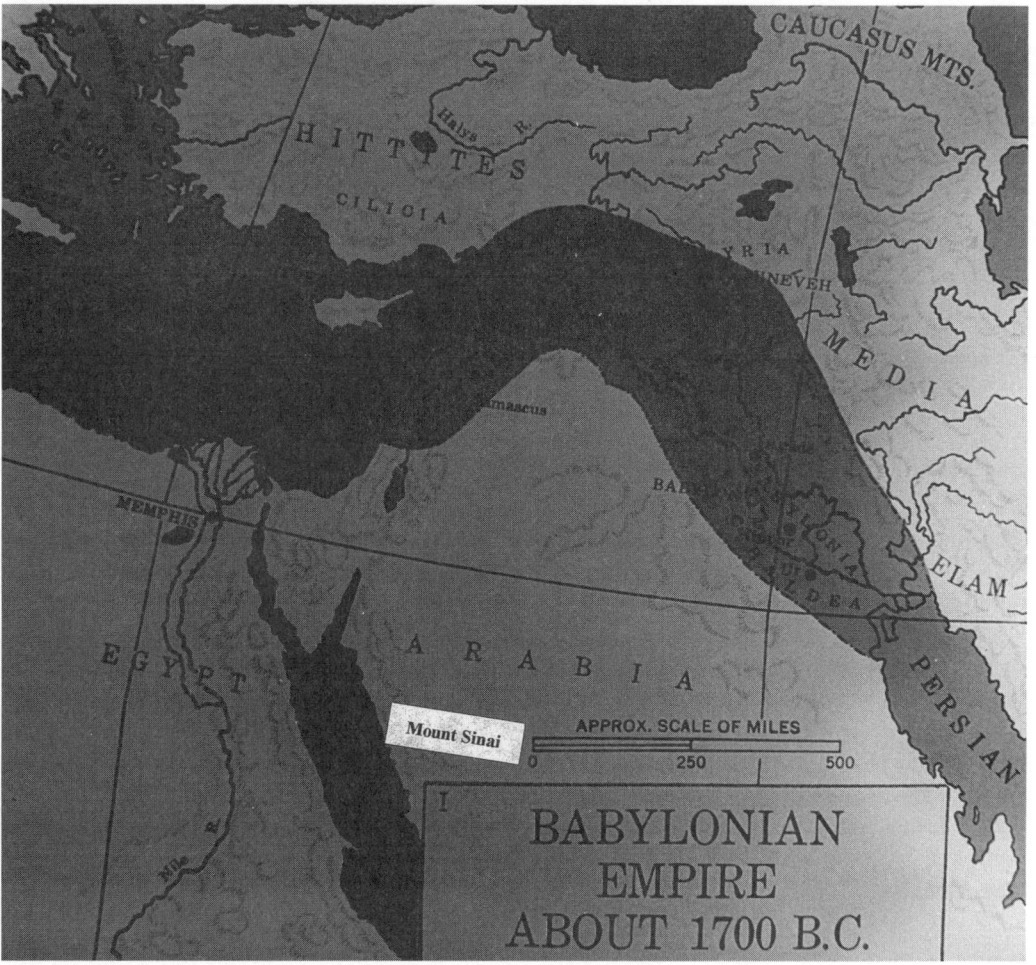

Exhibit 29: The Babylonian Empire of about 1700 BC. Note that the Babylonians did not capture the northern part of what is now Saudi Arabia, which contains 30,000 square miles of mountains.

Why did all of these great conquerors avoid that area like the plague? It must be because of the hostile, mountainous, desert-like, environment of the area. If you were the royal family of Egypt fleeing with goods and valuables beyond description, from a revolutionary general who wanted that wealth, where would you go? If you had a knowledge of the history of that time and knew that northern Saudi Arabia was a safe haven, whereas the Sinai peninsula could be easily reached by Egyptian troops, where would you go?

The **Bible** speaks about the Hebrews being in the desert for 40 years. The area of northern Saudi Arabia well fits the description. And the reason they would need to

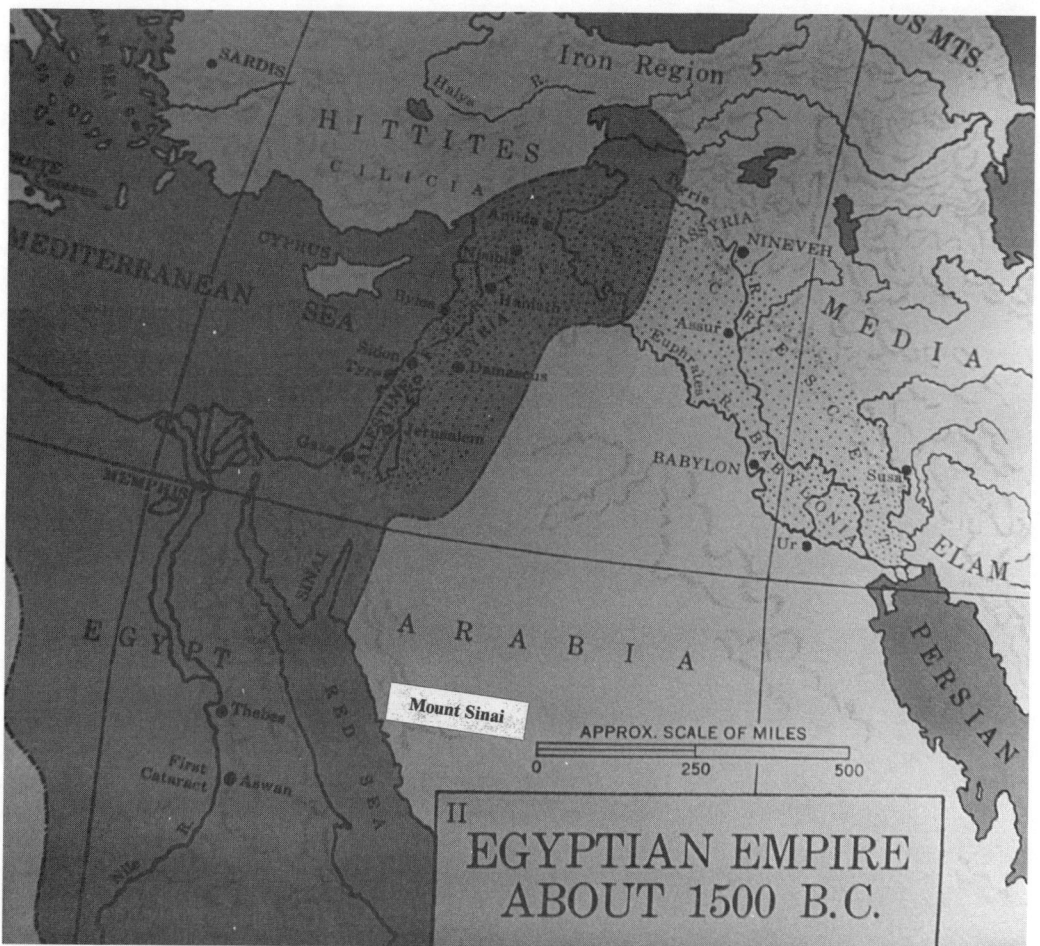

Exhibit 30: The Egyptian Empire of about 1500 BC. Would Moses escape from Egypt and flee to Sinai which is still in Egypt? Would one escaping from New York go to Texas?

170 TRUE ESOTERIC TRADITIONS

remain there for 40 years is also obvious. They would need to remain out of reach until the Egyptian government had given up on the idea of recovering the wealth the Hebrews had removed from Egypt. Actually, they were there for about 115 years before going ahead into Canaan.

In the book **The Kingdom of Saudi Arabia**, it is reported that a colony of Jews resides right in the middle of this vast mountainous desert area in the fortress towns of Khaybar and Yathrib. This could easily be the area where the Hebrews took refuge after the Exodus in 1335 BC. This is also the site of King Solomon's mines, which were really warehouses where the wealth from Egypt was stored. Throughout history, and yet today

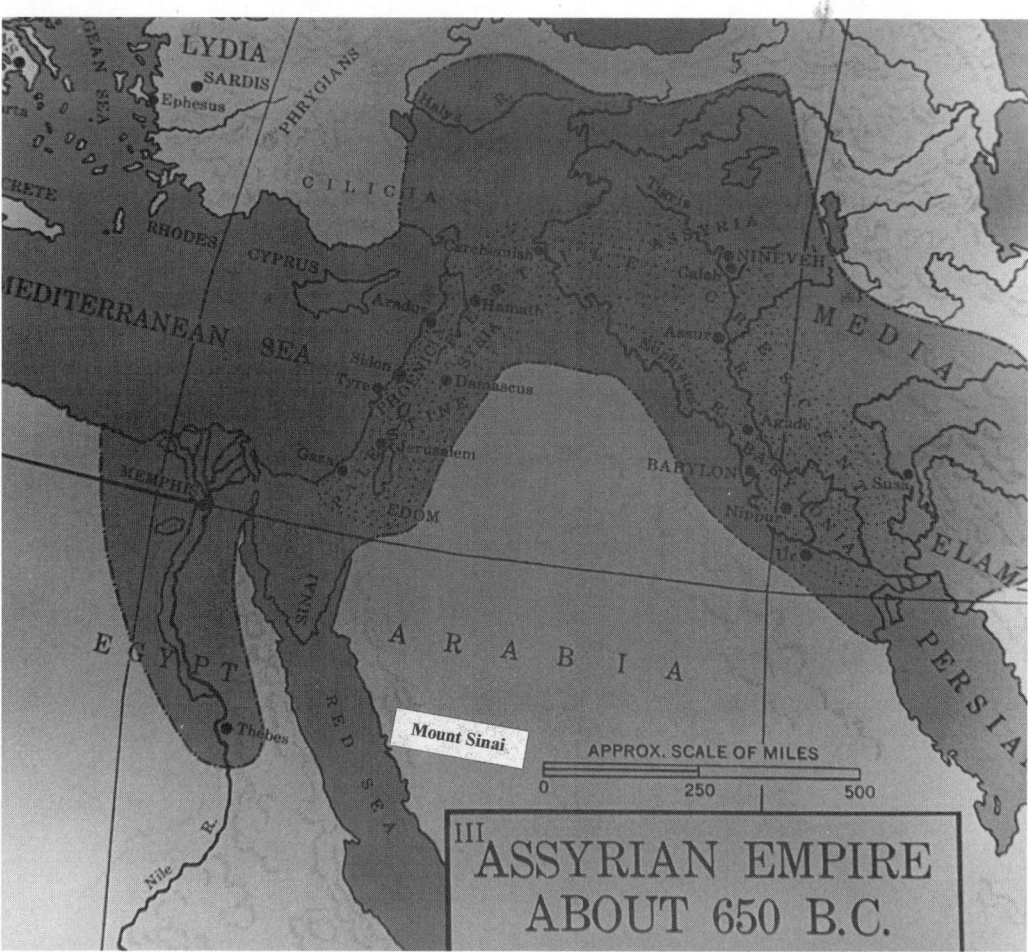

Exhibit 31: The Assyrian Empire of about 650 BC. Note that the Assyrians did not capture the northern part of what is now Saudi Arabia, which contains 30,000 square miles of mountains.

this area has been a desert-like mountainous fortress that none of the many greedy conquerors of the past ever tried to conquer. Even today, it would still be very difficult for outsiders to enter this area, even with permission of the Saudi Arabian government.

John Baldwin, in his 1869 book on pre-historic nations, reports that inscriptions along the Red Sea in Saudi Arabia have been found, but they are not well preserved. He also reports that many ruins found in this same area have a strong resemblance to other ruins in Egypt.

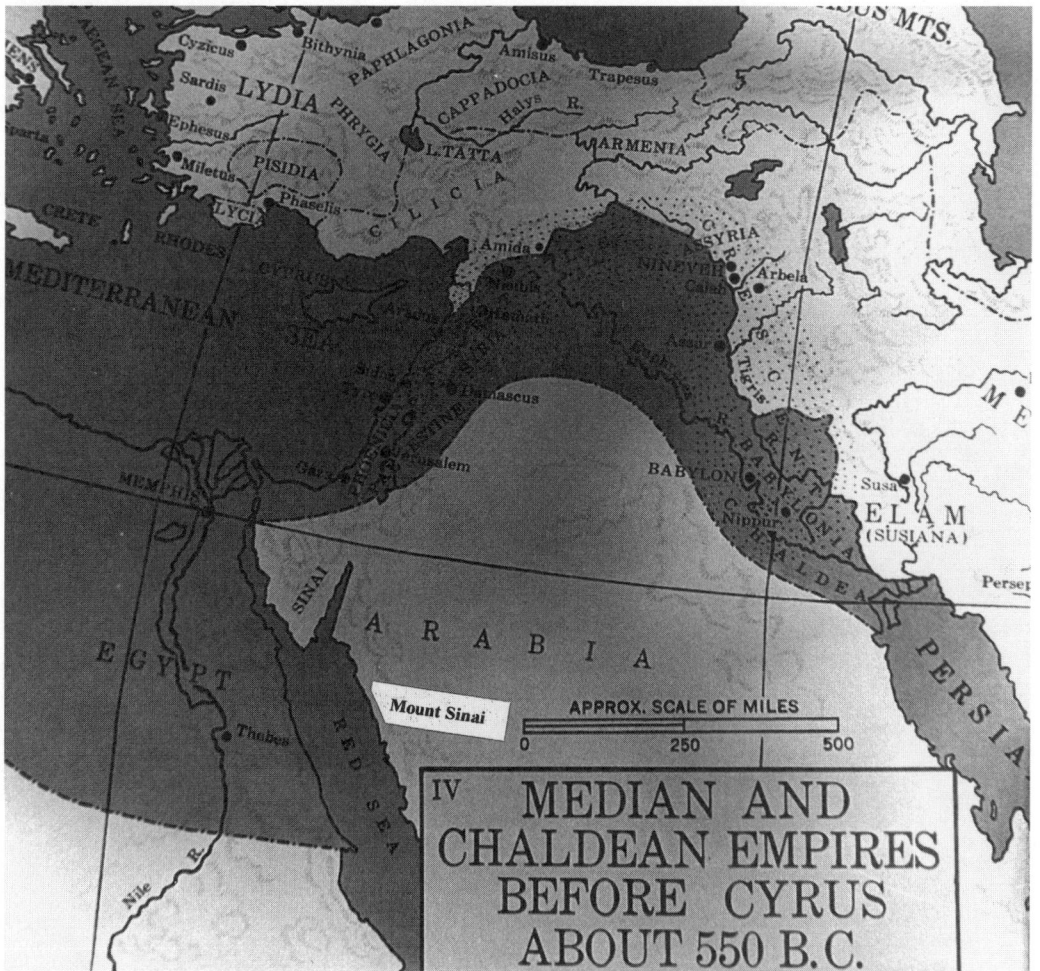

Exhibit 32: The Median and Chaldean Empires of about 550 BC. Note that these people did not capture the northern part of what is now Saudi Arabia, which contains 30,000 square miles of mountains.

172 TRUE ESOTERIC TRADITIONS

Once at the Red Sea, the fleeing Hebrews loaded on to ships, crossed the Red Sea and went into the mountains of northern Saudi Arabia, where the Mount Sinai of the **Bible** was and still is. For centuries, researchers have searched the Sinai Peninsula for Mount Sinai, but of course it is not there. Mount Sinai can only be located in northern Saudi Arabia. The author has heard tales of strange markings that may be Egyptian hieroglyphics on rocks in the mountains of northern Saudi Arabia and believes that the evidence still exists in those mountains. When finally discovered and analyzed, they will solve this mystery once and for all. It would be very difficult for any but Muslims to enter this area, so such a trip would be a worthy effort by the proper Muslim scholars.

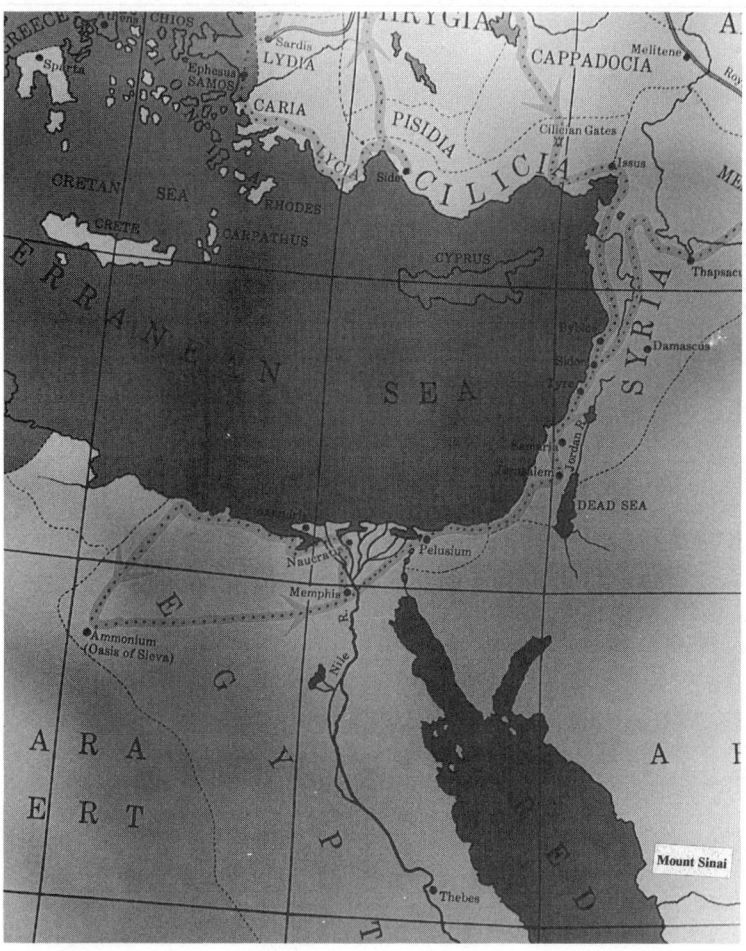

Exhibit 33: The empire of Alexander the Great in about 325 BC. Note that even Alexander the Great did not capture the northern part of what is now Saudi Arabia, which contains 30,000 square miles of mountains.

Meanwhile back in Thebes, Pharaoh Aye was now dead, either by assassination or because of old age, and the new pharaoh, Army General Horemheb, set out to recapture the wealth the Hebrews had taken out of Egypt. Horemheb tried, but failed because of a bad storm on the Red Sea. Many Egyptian troops were lost at sea, but not the new pharaoh, who reigned until 1308 BC.

The Hebrews moved into the mountains and stayed there about 115 years, or until about 1220 BC, before going down into Canaan. There is no historical evidence that this very well-led and wealthy family wandered aimlessly around a desert for 40 years. This was really the dispossessed royal family of the wealthiest and most advanced nation on Earth. From Chapter 15 of **Exodus**:

> "...*Pharaoh's chariots and his host hath he cast into the sea: his chosen captains also are drowned in the Red Sea. The depths have covered them: they sank into the bottom as a stone. ...*"

> "...*Thou didst blow with thy wind, the sea covered them: they sank as lead in the mighty waters. ...*"

> "...*Thou shalt bring them in, and plant them in the mountain of thine inheritance, in the place, O Lord, which thou hast made for thee to dwell in, in the Sanctuary, O Lord, which thy hands have established. ...*"

> "... *And Miriam answered them, Sing ye to the Lord, for he hath triumphed gloriously; the horse and his rider hath he thrown into the sea. ...*"

The author recognizes that both the time and route of the Exodus set forth above is substantially different from current theories. As the ancient Egyptians would say: **cromaat**, which is to say, that the truth shall be, or so mote it be. It is interesting that if one takes the Egyptian word for **the truth shall be**, which is cromaat, and reverses the spelling, one comes up with **TAAMORC**, which are the initials of the Order created by Hermes and Akhnaton: The Ancient and Mystical Order Rose Cross. The double maat, or double truth, was cosmic consciousness giving birth to individual consciousness. There are several suggested possible routes for the Exodus, proposed by various scholars. All agree that no one knows for sure.

First, most scholars are wrong because they do agree that the Exodus began in the Delta area, north and east of present day Cairo. From there, the departing Hebrews supposedly went east and crossed into Sinai at any number of points between the present day entrance to the Suez Canal into the Mediterranean Sea on the north, and the entrance of the Suez Canal into the Gulf of Suez on the south. The author has visited this area and found nothing that would suggest that Moses Moria-El and the departing Hebrews were ever there.

The Exodus began from the Thebes area in central Egypt and proceeded east across the desert to the Red Sea. The author has also traveled this route. It fits very well with some of the descriptions in the **Bible**, when properly understood. But, according to these theories, there are a number of possibilities:

1. That the Hebrews followed the trade routes along the Mediterranean Sea, around to the east and to Canaan. Very few scholars accept this possibility. This route does not have any mountains along it. Also, where would the Hebrews have been from the time of the Exodus to 1220 BC, when they arrived in Canaan?

2. That the Hebrews left from the area of Ismailia about two-thirds of the distance north from the Red Sea on the Suez Canal, and proceeded more or less directly east across the Sinai Peninsula.

3. That the Hebrews went straight south in Egypt to the present town of Suez, and from there east by southeast to the northern tip of the Gulf of Aqaba to the town of Aqaba.

4. That the Hebrews followed the southern route and left from the modern town of Suez and proceeded directly south along the east coast of the Gulf of Suez to the present town of El Tur; then northeast across the peninsula again to the present town of Aqaba.

Most scholars accept some variation of this southern route, but there is a slightly different route proposed by every scholar. The fact remains that really none of these routes fit with history, from the Egyptian side. Most scholars agree that they have found no evidence, absolutely none, of the Exodus in the Sinai Peninsula. There is no evidence because the Exodus was never there. Surely, some evidence of some kind would be there if this were the correct area.

Most scholars also agree that even though every mountain in the Sinai Peninsula has been checked and re-checked, none of them qualify very well to be the Mount Sinai of the **Bible**. So they continue to look, but they are looking in the wrong place.

There is absolutely no physical evidence of the Exodus in the Sinai Peninsula. There is no mountain there that qualifies to be the Mount Sinai of the **Bible**. Egyptian history was meticulously recorded and any series of events such as the plagues and 600,000 people leaving Egypt would be recorded there. It would be recorded, regardless of the efforts of Pharaoh Horemheb and others to wipe those events from the history books.

Ezra, in re-writing the **Bible**, is known to have fabricated many things that he included. All these things might lead a reasonable person to the conclusion that the Exodus never in fact happened. But it did happen, and the true story is much more interesting than the many fictional accounts of it.

A couple of scholars have suggested the possibility of the area east and north of the Gulf of Aqaba, at the northern end of Saudi Arabia or the southwestern-most tip of Jordan as the place where the Hebrews went. This is getting closer, but the correct area is probably farther south, in Saudi Arabia; east across the Red Sea from the port of Qoseir.

The story of the Exodus was first written down about 900 BC in Israel. A similar, but not nearly identical, story was also written a few years later in Judah. Afterwards, in 700 BC, the priests tried to merge the two stories into one version. Then, in 450 BC, Ezra re-wrote the whole story and added his own ideas to it. This is the version now in the **Bible** and the one claimed by

Exhibit 34: The author on the Red Sea east of Qoseir, Egypt

some people to be the true word of God. It is also the version that continues to cause friction between the Jews and Muslims and causes the Muslims to brand the Jews as forgers of Holy Writ.

Most biblical scholars and archaeologists agree that the Hebrews entered Canaan about 1230 to 1220 BC. This would date the start of the Exodus at 1270 to 1260 BC, allowing for the 40-year hiatus in the desert. This simply is not correct. Pharaoh Rameses II used much money in his building programs. He easily could have, and would have, stopped such wealth from being removed from Egypt. These dates were arrived at by very laborious and strained interpretations of the **Bible** versions. The Hebrews did enter Canaan about 1220 BC, but they had lived in the mountains prior to that time since 1335 BC.

Moses Moria-El's pain and suffering in trying to get the Hebrews to behave was not caused by a conflict with his friends and family that came out of Egypt with him. There were still many tribes of Hebrews living in the mountains and areas where Moses Moria-El and his group went. It was with these uneducated and somewhat-heathen desert tribes that he had his problems. The family of Joseph-Yuya was probably the best educated, the wisest, and the wealthiest on Earth at that time. But they were only 60 or so family members among many thousands of desert tribesmen.

The Hebrews in the Exodus out of Egypt were not many in number, but they were mightier even than the sword with their vast knowledge, education, and wealth. This knowledge has always survived and has been passed down through history to us by the Kabalists.

Present-day thinking man originated in the Garden of Eden in the Middle East about 250,000 years ago. From there, he spread over the entire world. After the great flood of 8000 BC, survivors from the British Isles fled to Egypt and imparted much culture to that land. The idea of only one God became accepted by a small group in Egypt between 3500 BC and 1335 BC, at which time, the idea left Egypt in an Exodus event when the Hebrew-Egyptian royal family fled with much of the vast wealth of that wealthy country.

The idea of the One True God has always been present in the teachings of the Hebrew Kabalists and was passed down to Master Jesus the Christ and to us. There indeed was an Exodus out of Egypt and we owe much of our Western cultural values to that event.

CHAPTER NINE -- THE BLUE LODGE

After King David had his friend Uriah put into the front of battle so that he would be killed, he took Uriah's wife, Bathsheba, as his own wife. Some time thereafter a second child, Solomon, was born to this marriage.

King David was familiar with deception and intrigue. Even one of David's sons, Absalom, was executed by David's own troops. Can any reader imagine the quality of a person who would have his own son executed? In 999 BC, Solomon arrived in Egypt and enrolled as a student in AMORC. This group taught seven degrees of study, which usually required one thousand weeks or about twenty years of work to complete. The neophyte work required one year; the Lesser Mysteries three years, and the Greater Mysteries sixteen years.

A person who had evolved to the sixth level of consciousness, where the consciousness had risen to the top of the spinal cord, was said to be a master. It was at this time that a person was said to be born again in the spirit and became a new person. It was at this time that Joseph took a new name pronounced as Ieasu in Aramaic, Issa in Sanskrit, Horus in the pharaonic Egyptian language, and Jesus in Greek. Master Jesus also took the Christ initiation and became known as Master Jesus the Christ, or for short, simply Christ Jesus, or Master Jesus.

It is indeed sad that the Blue Lodge today teaches little more than the neophyte work of its early history. It is today largely a social order, rather than an esoteric order. Socializing is fine for neophytes, but no mason should be able to complete the 32 degrees without mastering the Lesser Mysteries, which usually takes about four years of intense work. Freemasons awake! It is time to hear your higher calling.

For some reason, Solomon finished only the first three degrees of the work and then dropped out. This may have been because he just could not qualify for the higher work. His background as the son of King David plus the rules he later laid down for admission into his Blue Lodge make it appear that this may have been the case.

The author suggests another possible reason for Solomon dropping out of school. This explanation explains the ancient legend of King Solomon's gold mines. Moses Moria-El took hoards of gold out of Egypt in the Exodus and stored it in the mountains of northern Saudi Arabia. The secret of this storage place was entrusted to AMORC in Egypt. While in school in Egypt, Solomon must have learned of the location, or the approximate location, of this stash of gold in the mountains. It was this vast hoard of gold that Solomon used as King of Israel to build his great temple and for other building projects in Israel. It is also the source of the legend of King Solomon's mines.

If Solomon entered the studies in 999 BC, he could have spent four years in the Lesser Mysteries and then another three years in the fourth degree. He never completed it. He did not become King of Israel until somewhat later, but we do not know the exact year. We do not know for sure the year in which Solomon became king, because record keeping in Israel at that time was not nearly as well developed and accurate as it was in Egypt. It appears there was a sufficient time period of one thousand weeks or twenty years for him to complete AMORC studies, but, for some reason, he did not do so.

Any man who had 700 wives and 300 mistresses probably would not have had the time, the energy, nor the inclination to complete AMORC studies. Perhaps, as the Roman Emperor Constantine 1300 years later, Solomon may have expected to be admitted because of who he was rather than what he was. We do know that when King David was on his death bed, Solomon was not around. The **Bible** says: **1 Kings 1:19** "...*but Solomon thy servant hath he not called...*" and at **1 Kings 1:26** "...*thy servant Solomon hath he not called...*"

Bathsheba was able to have her son named king. Solomon did import to Israel many ideas from his years of study in Egypt. **Psalm 104**, which is usually thought to have been written by Solomon about 950 BC, is usually thought by scholars to have been taken from the Song of Akhnaton, written some 400 years earlier in about 1350 BC. Here are brief excerpts from each:

Akhnaton "*Thy appearing is beautiful in the horizon of heaven, The Living Aton, the beginning of life; Thou risest in the horizon of the east, Thou fillest every land with thy beauty....*"

Solomon: "*Bless the Lord, O my soul. O Lord my God, thou are very great; thou are clothed with honor and majesty...Who coverest thyself with light as with a garment: who stretchest out the heavens like a curtain....*"

Akhnaton: "*...Thou art very beautiful, brilliant and exalted above earth, Thy beams encompass all lands which thou has made....*"

Solomon: "*...Who layeth the beams of his chambers in the waters: who maketh the clouds his chariot: who walketh upon the wings of the wind...They go up by the mountains; they go down by the valleys unto the place which thou has founded for them....*"

Akhnaton: "*...The cattle all rest in their pastures...Where grow the trees and herbs....*"

Solomon: "*...He causeth the grass to grow for the cattle, and herb for the service of man: that he may bring forth food out of the earth....*"

Akhnaton: "*...Every lion cometh forth from his den, And all the serpents then bite; The night shines with its lights....*"

Solomon: "...*Thou makest darkness, and it is night: wherein all the beasts of the forest do creep forth... The young lions roar after their prey, and seek their meat from God....*"

Akhnaton: "...*Throughout the land they do their labours....*"

Solomon: "...*Man goeth forth unto his work and to his labour until the evening....*"

There is no reasonable doubt but that Solomon did live and study in Egypt for some years and took some of the things he learned there home with him to Israel. Solomon did create the Blue Lodge, which taught the first three degrees of AMORC studies or what at that time were called the Lesser Mysteries. Today, they are called the Freemasonic teachings.

There are all kinds of stories advanced by the Christian church and others about the perceived evils of Freemasonry. What and who are the Freemasons and what do they stand for? Are they a threat to the teachings of Master Jesus the Christ? Certainly not.

In fact the true teachings of Master Jesus the Christ and the true teachings of the Freemasons are one and the same thing. Are the Freemasons a threat to the political goals and aspirations of the Christian church? Most definitely yes, just as the teachings of Master Jesus the Christ are the downfall for all of the priesthoods of the world.

Exhibit 35: The Seal of the Oklahoma Freemasonic Grand Lodge. The "G" stands for God.

This is exactly the reason Master Jesus was hated by all the priesthoods in his time, and it is exactly the same reason that the Freemasons are also hated by all priesthoods of the world today. There is only one way for a Freemason to view a priest, and that is from above with understanding, compassion, love, and hope for his future enlightenment. A lodge of Freemasons is merely an assemblage of Freemasons, duly congregated, having the sacred writings, and the proper authority to do work. The physical room or place of a meeting of Freemasons is symbolically a part of King Solomon's Temple in Jerusalem.

What is meant by being duly congregated and having sacred writings and proper authority to do work could fill many books. The sacred writings do include the **Bible**,

180 TRUE ESOTERIC TRADITIONS

but also include the **Koran**, the **Bhagavad-Gita**, the **Zend-Avesta** and the holy books of all religions. It is this universality of view that results in severe criticism of the Freemasons from the Christian church.

In all Freemasonic lodges, in the east over the Master, enclosed in a triangle, is the symbol of the One True God. In the first lodges in Israel this letter was Yod; in the later French lodges it was the letter **D** for Dieu or God; and in English and American lodges, it is the letter **G** for God. All of these letters merely symbolize the One True God in the various languages.

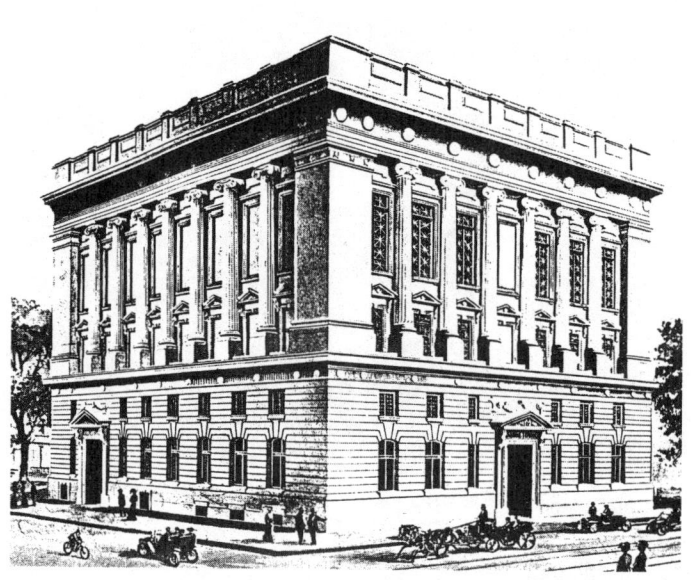

Exhibit 36: Indiana Freemasonic Grand Lodge, Indianapolis, Indiana USA

Are the Freemasons a secret society? Certainly their teachings have been available to the public for at least 5000 years and are not secret. If this were not so, the author could not know of them, since he is not now, has never been, and will never be a Freemason.

Certainly, the identity of Freemasons has been kept secret for the last 1700 years or so in countries dominated by the Christian church for a very practical reason. That reason was to keep Freemasons from being killed by the Christian church. This is the reason that all Freemasons consider it tantamount to treason to reveal anything about the lodge. Throughout history, a loose tongue by a Freemason could mean death to his fellow Freemasons. Under the rose or sub rosa was a rule to live by and violation often meant death.

The Blue Lodge of Freemasons begun by King Solomon of Israel had three degrees of work. These were the first three degrees of work of AMORC in Egypt and they included what was generally described as the Lesser Mysteries. These first three degrees required about four years of study to complete. In broad outline they covered all the teachings of AMORC which required one thousand weeks, or roughly twenty years, to complete.

Degree number one was the neophyte, or what today is called the **apprentice degree**. In this degree the student learned the basic ten rules of conduct for the Freemason.

They are:

1. God is Eternal and Omnipotent; has Immutable Wisdom, Supreme Intelligence, and Exhaustless Love. Thou shalt adore, revere, and love Him! Thou shalt honor Him by practicing the virtues!

2. Thy religion shall be to do good because it is a pleasure to thee, and not merely because it is a duty. That thou mayest become the friend of the wise man, thou shalt obey his precepts! Thy soul is immortal! Thou shalt do nothing to degrade it!

3. Thou shalt unceasingly war against vice! Thou shalt not do unto others that which thou wouldst not wish them to do unto thee! Thou shalt be submissive to thy fortunes, and keep burning the light of wisdom!

4. Thou shalt honor thy parents! Thou shalt pay respect and homage to the aged! Thou shalt instruct the young! Thou shalt protect and defend infancy and innocence!

5. Thou shalt cherish thy wife and thy children! Thou shalt love thy country and obey its laws!

6. Thy friend shall be to thee a second self! Misfortune shall not estrange thee from him! Thou shalt do for his memory whatever thou wouldst do for him, if he were living!

7. Thou shalt avoid and flee from insincere friendships! Thou shalt in everything refrain from excess. Thou shalt fear to be the cause of a stain on thy memory!

8. Thou shalt allow no passions to become thy master! Thou shalt make the passions of others profitable lessons to thyself! Thou shalt be indulgent to error!

9. Thou shalt hear much! Thou shalt speak little! Thou shalt act well! Thou shalt forget injuries! Thou shalt render good for evil! Thou shalt not misuse either thy strength or thy superiority!

10. Thou shalt study to know men; that thereby thou mayest learn to know thyself! Thou shalt ever seek after virtue! Thou shalt be just! Thou shalt avoid idleness!

The Law of the Rose, which is silence about AMORC matters, is the first lesson taught in the first degree and has been indispensable to the good of the Order up to this point in history. The second degree was known as the Brotherhood Degree, or what today is called the Fellowcraft Degree.

182 TRUE ESOTERIC TRADITIONS

The Freemasonic teachings of the Blue Lodge of King Solomon in Israel presented an imperfect image of the brilliant AMORC teachings of Egypt. The three most notable differences then, as now, were that the Blue Lodge did not accept females, slaves, or the progeny of slaves, as members.

The Freemasons taught the doctrine of brotherhood or fraternity. The later Christian church created by Roman Emperor Constantine also taught brotherhood but rejected the idea of political brotherhood by teaching obedience to Caesar and to others in authority which, of course, included the Christian-church priests. Freemasonry teaches equality. This was not just equality of Freemasons but equality in potential of all of the human species.

All humans are not equal in any way except one, and the one item all share in common is potential. It is exactly this Freemasonic idea of equality of potential that Thomas Jefferson wrote into the Declaration of Independence of the United States of America, even though the Rosicrucian Jefferson was not himself technically a member of a Freemasonic lodge.

In the Christian church there is fraternity but not equality. A layman is not equal to the priest; a priest is not equal to a bishop, and a bishop is not equal to the chief priest or pope. There cannot be true brotherhood unless there is equality and there cannot be

Exhibit 37: Scottish Rite Cathedral, Indianapolis, Indiana USA. This is one of the most beautiful buildings in the world.

true equality unless there is true freedom. There can be no true freedom unless there is the liberty of man to have control over his own inner self. These are the teachings of the Brotherhood Degree of the Freemasons and are the basis for the philosophy set forth in the Declaration of Independence.

After the American Constitutional Convention of 1789, Ben Franklin was asked what kind of a government the convention had given to America. Franklin, who was both a Rosicrucian and a Freemason, responded that they had given the people a republic if the people were wise enough to keep it. Franklin was paraphrasing the wise law-giver Solon who lived in Greece from about 630 to 561 BC. Solon was asked if he had given his countrymen the best laws. He answered that he had given them the best laws that they were capable of receiving.

The third degree of the Blue Lodge taught the folly of believing in death. Here is where one mastered the idea that there is something in man that never dies. Every time a student masters this idea and is raised to new enlightenment, transmutation takes place in him, because then he knows in his own inner being that he will live forever in some form on some plane. The physical body does pass away, but man is forever.

This is the symbolic story of Hiram Abiff, Christian Rosenkreuz, and Lazarus. A true Master Mason is one who has attained this level of enlightenment, and has mastered the fear of death. Mastership is not a political status in a lodge.

Solomon built the first temple and thereby made the Jewish religion into a political institution. Understand this logic. The **Bible** says a good Jew must attend temple services. The priesthood controls the temple, so one must pay money to the temple priesthood in order to obtain favor from the Jewish god. This made an excellent business arrangement.

The same idea was later used to sustain and maintain the Christian-church priesthood. Indeed, it is still in use today. The Roman Church and its descendants also teach that one must attend church and support the priesthoods of those churches.

To the present day, the Christian-church priesthood has tried to maintain the same political support system. All human beings feel an inward urge to communicate with God and to do God's work. The priest will say: "*You do want to do God's work, don't you?*" And of course all human beings do. Then the priest will say: "*Here is what God wants you to do -- give your money to me.*"

It is amazing that more people have not perceived the hypocrisy in such a position. For any church or institution or priest to suggest that it or he does God's work, or that he knows God's will is, of course, the height of hypocrisy. More money has been spent on such uses than for any other on Earth in the history of man. Even more money has been spent on religious institutions than on wars, and with about the same benefits for mankind.

The Christian church has been a much more deadly opponent of a true belief in the One True God than communism could ever be. Why is that so? Communism tells man that there is no God. Man knows better, from his own inner being. So man can easily perceive that error and reject the communist teachings. The Christian-church teaching is much more subtle and much more devious. The Christian church recognizes God, but then totally mis-reports God's laws.

This is why AMORC, the Blue Lodge, and Master Jesus have been so hated by the priesthood. They all teach that priesthoods are not needed or desirable. It is easy to hate someone who says that you should stop sponging a living from other people and go to work and feed yourself. Remember, the teachings of AMORC have never been for sale to anyone, at any price; never. Even King Solomon and Emperor Constantine could not buy them. All priesthoods who thus attempt, in effect, to sell knowledge of God are violating Cosmic Law before they even get started. Such efforts are doomed to failure, as indeed they have been since the dawn of history.

In setting up the Blue Lodge, Solomon prescribed that only free men could be masons, or what are now called Freemasons. This was completely different from AMORC in Egypt where anyone could be a member, if he or she could qualify.

Moses Moria-El was certainly an initiate of AMORC. But was he the son of slaves? The Hebrews in Egypt were anything but slaves, and Moses Moria-El was part Egyptian in any event. This requirement of being a free man has kept many blacks from membership in the Blue Lodge. Of course it has kept all females from membership, except in a very few non-regular Masonic lodges in France. These non-regular French lodges do have affiliates in some other countries.

Solomon's negative attitude toward women has had very widespread and powerful consequences for all women in Western culture. He believed that females were the prisoners of their own sex organs and could not develop both good sex organs and good brains at the same time. This attitude has carried down through history to our present culture and even up to the present time.

The pagan Christian church took the idea one step further and added that a female could not develop good sex organs and develop morally at the same time. These were absurd teachings to be sure, but still they are taught by the Christian church even to the present day. These teachings violate the Law of Balance taught in AMORC. Solomon reportedly had 700 wives and 300 mistresses, which shows his attitude toward women quite well. That negative attitude was later picked up and reported in the **Bible**. From there it passed to both the Christian and Muslim cultures.

Eastern cultures already had a negative view of women and so, for the most part, women have been mistreated in almost all religions and in all cultures of the world.

Consider the following:

1. "*I will greatly multiply your pain in child bearing, in pain you shall bring forth children, yet your desire shall be for your husband, and he shall rule over you.*" Source: The **Bible, Old Testament, Genesis 3:16**, Revised Standard Version.

2. "*...You are quite right...in maintaining the general inferiority of the female sex...gifts of nature are alike diffused...but in all of them a woman is inferior to man....*" Source: Plato (427-347 BC) **Republic, Book V, Five Great Dialogues**, Page 340, Walter J. Black, Inc., 1942.

3. "*In childhood a woman must be subjected to her father; in youth to her husband; when her husband is dead, to her sons. A woman must never be free of subjugation.*" Source: **Code of Manu** (c. 400 BC - AD 200).

4. "*...Through succession on intestacy (ab. intestato) the inheritance devolved to those members of the family...under his paternal power. ..In the absence of such heirs relatives tied with the deceased by descent from a common ancestor through males (agnates) received the most inheritance. ...*"[This is Praetorian law and was liberalized by Justinian to allow wills.] Source: Roman law, **Encyclopedia Americana**, Vol. 23, Page 646, Copyright 1971 by Americana Corporation.

5. "*...Allah lays commandment on you in the matter of your children. The male shall have the same portion as two females...Now those among your women who commit whoredom...Shut those women up in the houses till death take them....*" Source: **The Koran**, Sura 4, Page 194, **Surat an-Nisa: The Woman** (Translated from the Arabic by Arthur Jeffery) The Heritage Press, New York, 1958.

6. The Apostle Paul was blatantly anti-female. The Christian church founded on his teachings is anti-female. From **1 Corinthians 7** (Scofield Reference Edition): "*...For a man indeed ought not to cover his head for as much as he is the image and glory of God, but the woman is the glory of man. ...*" The **New Testament** is replete with Paul's anti-female attitude. It is there to be seen by any reasonable person who wishes to perceive it.

7. Compare the above with the comments of Pharaoh Akhnaton of Egypt. To woman, Akhnaton said: "*...Remember thou are man's reasonable companion, not the slave of his passion; the end of thy being is not merely to gratify his loose desire....*" And to man concerning women he said: "*...Consider the tenderness of her sex, the delicacy of her frame; and be not severe to her weakness but remember thine own imperfections....*"

186 TRUE ESOTERIC TRADITIONS

It is indeed grievous that Plato, an initiate of AMORC in Egypt, would hold the views set forth above. Actually, he had the true facts just backwards. In gifts of nature the female surpasses the male in all of them except physical strength. Plato was a great man, but he faltered here. However, it may be that the text was tampered with to conform to Christian teachings. Such tampering did happen with the **New Testament**.

Master Jesus, in line with the teachings of AMORC, taught the equality of women. Nearly half of Master Jesus' 73 disciples were women. And Master Jesus taught publicly, whereas AMORC teachings were private. It is sometimes said that Christianity existed long before Master Jesus. Although this sounds like a contradiction, it is in fact true. The teachings Master Jesus taught were, for the most part, also taught by Joseph-Yuya, Hermes, Akhnaton, and Moses Moria-El. Master Jesus gave them new meaning and new impetus, and did so in public.

Exhibit 38: Master Mason George Washington, Indiana State House lawn, Indianapolis, Indiana USA

In the United States the proposed Equal Rights Amendment provided: *"Equality of rights under the law shall not be denied or abridged by the United States or by any state on account of sex."* One would think that such a statement could cause no argument, but it has yet to become the law of the land. The reason it has not become law is mostly because of the rise in power of the Christian church in America during this period. And anyone who understands the history of the Christian church expects it to oppose anything which is truly Christian.

This anti-female bias has been given great support in this century from the field of psychology by Freud and Jung. Freud saw sex as the driving force in human relations and about the same as among the less-developed animal species. Jung modified Freud some, but he still felt that the female works through her emotions and a male works with his mind.

The female is intrinsically different from the male both biologically and psychologically. This fact is beyond dispute. These differences become negative in connotation only when they are perceived as being either inferior or superior to that of the male. Different, yes; but neither better or worse.

A very interesting thing is that even with the very negative female attitude of the Christian church, the one major distinctive characteristic that Western culture has over Eastern culture is its more positive attitude towards women.

As long as women look to organized religion to protect their rights, they will be the slaves of men. The **Bible** was not written by women. It was not written for women. Women have been the most misused and abused creatures of all time. Women are still not qualified to become priests in the Roman Church, even to the present day. Absolutely unbelievable! The real slaves throughout history have been the females, not just black people. The reason for this is that women are morally superior to men, but physically weaker than men. As Gandhi stated:

> *"To call women the weaker sex is a libel: it is man's injustice to woman. If by strength is meant brute strength, then indeed, is woman less brute than man. If by strength is meant moral power, then woman is immeasurably man's superior. Has she not greater intuition, is she not more self-sacrificing, has she not greater courage? If non-violence is the law of our being, the future is with women."*

To Gandhi's observation the author would add: If Love indeed be the most powerful force in the universe, is not the female more in tune with the Law of Love than the male? And if this be true, then would not the female in the final analysis be more powerful than the male?

All people are entitled to their own view of the wisdom of Solomon. Certainly, he did some good things. His Blue Lodge has been a source of knowledge and enlightenment for Western culture for nearly 3000 years. But his negative attitude towards women has been the source of much cruelty for the physically weaker but morally superior sex. On this, well-informed persons cannot reasonably disagree.

All the
major religions
on earth and all
the major cultures on
earth must have a common
source. This simply must be true.

CHAPTER TEN -- THE BIBLE

The story of the creation of man and the physical world had been told in most ancient cultures prior to the great Hebrew culture of 1000 BC.

There are two distinct stories of creation in **Genesis** of the **Bible**. In the first three chapters of **Genesis** the god named Elohim created day and night on the first day; on the second day, the firmament; on the third, Earth, the sea, grass, trees, and so on; on the fourth, the sun, moon, and stars; on the fifth, the whales, fishes, and winged fowl; and on the sixth, cattle, creeping things, and man; both male and female.

This particular scenario of the creation appears to have come from the ancient Persians-Iranians. In the **Zend-Avesta** it says that their god, named Ormuzd, created the universe and man in six successive periods of time. First, the Heavens; second, the waters; third, Earth; fourth, the trees and plants; fifth, the animals; and sixth, man. Likewise then, Ormuzd rested. This story pre-dates the account in **Genesis** by some 1500 years.

An even older but similar account is found in an ancient Etruscan legend. Their god created the world in 6000 years. In the first thousand, Heaven and Earth were created; in the second, the firmament; in the third, the waters; in the fourth, the sun, moon, and stars; in the fifth, the animals, birds of the air, water, and land; and in the sixth, man alone.

Beginning with the fourth verse in Chapter 2 of **Genesis** is a second creation story where the tribal god named Jehovah created the Heavens and Earth and man from the dust of the ground. After taking Eve from the rib of Adam, this god lied to them when it told them not to eat of the tree of life or they would die. After eating of that tree, however, they did not die, but instead their eyes were opened and they became as gods themselves, knowing good from evil.

This story of the tree of life may have been taken either from Egyptian or Hindu legends. The Hindu tribal god named Siva dropped a blossom of a fig tree from Heaven to tempt man. Man then, instigated by his wife, captured the blossom and was cursed by Siva with a life of misery and degradation. The Egyptian tribal god named Osiris ordered that the names of some souls be written on a tree of life, the fruit of which made those who ate of it become as gods. This is more likely the source of the second **Genesis** version.

The story of the creation of man set forth in the **Bible** in this second scenario sets forth that man was created as a physical being and then, after physical creation, man became a living soul. The **Bible** states in **Genesis** 2:7 *"And the Lord God formed man of the dust of the ground, and breathed into his nostrils the breath of life; and man **became** a living soul."*

This version is the one taught in AMORC in Egypt, by the Blue Lodge of ancient Israel, and by Master Jesus the Christ. This teaching is that man is both a physical and spiritual being, and our main concern is for man the spiritual being because man the physical being will surely pass away.

Most of the Christian churches, however, teach a different and pagan version which is that man is primarily a physical being and only becomes a living soul at the time of physical conception, and not with the first breath of life, as taught in the **Bible**.

This ancient pagan view held by the Christian church gives rise to much heated debate relative to abortion in countries dominated by that church. The incorrect pagan version taught by the Christian church cannot prevail in the end because man is, and has always been, primarily a spiritual being exactly as stated in **Genesis 2:7**.

The opposite views on abortion are extreme. On the one hand is the standard set forth in **Genesis** of the **Bible,** which is that anytime prior to the first breath of life abortion would be moral, or at least not murder.

On the other extreme is the view taught by much of the Christian church, which is that any time after conception, abortion is murder. The Christian-church view has always been based on a very real political-economic expediency. As more babies are born there are more people to work and pay money to support the Christian-church priesthood. Perhaps the Christian-church stand on abortion can yet be salvaged if it is being based on something more than those usual political goals. For example, studies now show that some people can actually remember events going back to their own physical conception and even before. This, too, shows that the human spirit is something outside of, and distinct from, the physical body it inhabits.

If one follows this logic back far enough, he comes to the proposition that it could be considered abortion to refrain from sex, and therefore not create physical bodies for humans to be born into. Perhaps, the Jewish religion recognizes this idea when it encourages every good Jew to marry and have children.

The United States Supreme Court has tried to strike a middle ground on the subject. During the first three months of pregnancy the mother's right to privacy prevails and abortion is legal. During the last three months, the fetus' right to life prevails and abortion is not legal, unless it is for health reasons of the mother.

Where does the right of privacy of the mother end and the right to life of the fetus take over? The Supreme Court says that this happens at the point of viability, or at that point where the fetus can live independently, outside the mother's body. At this time in the development of our technology, that happens at about the end of the sixth month. The Supreme Court position would seem to be a reasonable balancing of the rights of each.

The story of the fall of man is told in many different ancient cultures from around the world. The Chinese have their Garden of Eden story along with a doctrine of original sin. This story also incorrectly puts all the blame for the fall of man squarely on the woman.

The islands of the South Pacific have similar legends with the woman named Ivi. The Scandinavians have a similar story where all was well and good until woman came on the scene and caused man to fall.

It is upon this fall of man caused by woman, set forth in the first eleven chapters of **Genesis**, that much of the Christian-church theology of today is based. The doctrine of the fall of man and the redemption of man by the Christian-church priesthood is the very foundation of Christian-church theology. The church would have its adherents believe that man has been damned by the woman but saved by the priests. This is the basis of the discrimination against women taught by the Apostle Paul and the Christian church throughout its history and up to the present time. Certainly, Master Jesus the Christ never taught any such theology.

How is it that all cultures have these nearly identical stories and legends? All of the major religions on Earth and all of the major cultures on Earth must have a common source. This simply must be true.

The author suggests that at some time back in prehistory a clan, gathered around a camp fire, ran out of water. One fellow, who was smarter than the rest, told his buddy that he had been talking to his god and his god wanted man to make only the female carry water from the river. That sounded reasonable to man who was tired and lazy anyway. Since man was bigger and stronger than the female he could easily compel her obedience to the god's will. Slurring womankind with the guilt of causing man's fall is purely an attempt by male priests to justify mistreatment of the more evolved but weaker sex.

The second step was that the smart fellow told his clan that again he had been talking to his god, and the god wanted him to be the priest of the clan. Sure, why not, since god wanted it that way? Now comes the ringer. Then the priest said, "*I am lazy and don't like to work for my food and water, so when you send your female for food and water for yourself, have her also bring a little for me.*" And, since there were many men sending many females for food and water, the priest lived very well and without working. What about women who objected to the god's will? The priest had the perfect answer: "*Beat them for sure, and even kill them if you must, because it is god's will.*" So goes Christian-church theology.

The natives in the South Seas express Christian-church theology quite accurately. They say that the Christian-church missionaries came there to do good and did very well. Now the missionaries own everything.

The story of a great flood is also universal among all ancient cultures. The one in the **Bible** was probably taken from Chaldea. The Chaldean god named Cronos appeared to Xisuthrus and warned him that on the fifteenth day of the month Oesius, there would be a great flood that would destroy all of mankind. The god, Cronos, told him to write a history of the beginning and conclusion of creation and bury it at the city of Sippara. After that, he was instructed to build a boat and take on board his friends and two each of the animals and birds, along with sufficient food. After the flood had been upon Earth and some time had passed, Xisuthrus sent out some birds which at first came back; but on a third try, they did not return. The boat then came aground on a mountain side. The people all left the boat and offered sacrifices to Cronos.

The similarities with the Noah story are almost complete. Noah and Xisuthrus were each just men; each was told by his god to build a boat and to take his friends, animals and food on board; each sent out birds three times; each landed on a mountain; each was the tenth king or patriarch of his race; each had three sons and each, upon leaving the boat after the flood was over, gave sacrifices to his god.

The Noah story is substantially repeated in Hindu legend, in Chinese legend, in Persian-Iranian legend, in Greek legend, among the Celts of Britain, among the Scandinavians, among the Mexicans, and on and on among over a hundred different peoples from all around the world. There must, at some time on Earth, have been a great flood of some kind. The author suggests that this did in fact happen about 8000 BC when an asteroid hit Earth in the Gulf of Mexico, near Yucatan.

The priests of the world teach a doctrine of the fall of man and original sin because then every person needs the priest in order to be redeemed. With no fall and no original sin, there would be no need for a priest. However, these theologies overlook the flood story and how a god in each of these cultures found one just man who, along with his family, was saved from the flood.

All of mankind on Earth today have descended from these good and just families and not the fallen Adam and Eve. Thus the original fall of Adam and Eve would seem to have been long ago paid for and wiped out. Such thinking is not compatible with the priests' need for employment. Likewise, the teachings of Master Jesus the Christ that each person has a direct relationship to God and does not need an intermediary priest is also not compatible with the priests' needs. That is the very reason that Master Jesus was so hated by the priests of all religions, both in his own lifetime, and even yet today. This is particularly true of the priests of the Christian church which bears his name.

The story of the Ten Commandments in the **Bible** was taken from the story of Zoroaster in the **Zend-Avesta** of the Persians-Iranians. Zoroaster was on a mountain praying when the god Ormuzd appeared to him in thunder and lightning and delivered to him the Book of the Law. This book is called the **Zend-Avesta** which signifies the Living Word. The Persian-Iranian people were assembled together Zoroaster came down from the mountain unharmed and delivered the Ten Commandments to them. They are the same as the Ten Commandments in the later Hebrew **Bible** except that the name of the god has been changed from Ormuzd to Jehovah in the Hebrew version.

Buddha, the founder of Buddhism, also had ten laws for his people to live by. Not to kill, steal, lie, swear, bear false witness, avenge one's self, or be superstitious were the first seven. The other three were positive in command; to be chaste, to be disinterested, and to avoid impure works.

Almost all nations of antiquity had similar stories of a holy man ascending a mountain to ask counsel of his god and bringing back down from the mountain to the people a set of rules for them to live by.

Many of the stories in the Hebrew **Bible** have counterparts in the sacred teachings of other older cultures. This is true of the stories of Sampson,

Exhibit 39: The Bhagavad-Gita, The Egyptian Book of the Dead, The Tibetan Book of the Dead, Holy Bible, and The Holy Koran

Jonah and the great fish, the dreams of Pharaoh interpreted by Joseph, Moses Moria-El being put into the Nile River, Elijah ascending to Heaven, David killing Goliath, and Joshua's command to the sun to stand still, among many others.

It is not true that the majority of the ancient Hebrews worshiped only the One True God of the universe. The majority of mankind in all cultures including the Egyptian and Hebrew worshiped many gods. They were not monotheists. The ancient Hebrews, like other pagans, worshiped the sun, the moon, fire, stones, a queen of Heaven named Astarte, a bull named Apis, gods named Baal, Molock, and Chemosh, and even offered up human sacrifices to those gods. It was only during the 50 years of the Babylonian captivity, from 587 to 538 BC or so, that the ancient Hebrews finally gave up many of their pagan ways.

When, where, and why was the **Bible** written? The **Bible** was written down about 450 BC and the **New Testament** between AD 50 and 400. Ever since it was written, the **Bible** has been one of the most influential books in Western culture. People have studied it, admired it, worshiped it, disdained, and cursed it, certainly argued about it, and many have loved it. Many have died defending it, and some have murdered many people because of it. Some few have intentionally amended and changed it for their

194 TRUE ESOTERIC TRADITIONS

own political or financial purposes. A few others have perhaps unintentionally altered it when making translations into other languages.

The story of the **Bible** actually began in Egypt. Only the Hebrew family of the patriarch Joseph-Yuya, who was in Egypt, was involved in the Exodus of Hebrews from that land.

The mother of Moses Moria-El was Hebrew and of the family of Joseph-Yuya. His father was Egyptian, and also of the Egyptian royal family. This explains how Moses Moria-El had an Egyptian name and why he was considered Hebrew because the Hebrew blood line ran through the female side of the family. Even today, people of **mixed blood** are considered Jewish if the mother is Jewish. Moses Moria-El was able to be initiated into the highest level of AMORC.

Exhibit 40: The Ten Commandments

The author has been trying for twenty years to identify Moses Moria-El in Egyptian historical records. There almost seems to be a conspiracy of history to keep him from being so identified. The Egyptian royal families are now fairly well known from most of this period, with one exception -- the exact period when Moses Moria-El lived. Scholars will eventually come to understand this, and he will be identified by his Egyptian name in the not-too-distant future. It is probable that Moses and the great teacher Moria-El were one and the same man. The author assumes that they were one and the same in this book.

Historically, there were four different versions of much of the Old Testament. The oldest of these versions was the one in which the deity is named Elohim. We do not know the exact author or authors, but we do know that it was written shortly after 922 BC in the northern tribe of Israel. This, of course, was almost 500 years after the events happened. This version favored Moses Moria-El, the prophet, over Aaron, the priest, and it was later filtered down to the tribe of Judah in the south.

The **Bible** version written in Judah came shortly after 848 BC, and in this version the deity is named Jehovah. Some modifications were made from the Elohim text to favor the priest, Aaron, over Moses Moria-El. The exact identity of these authors is also not known.

The Assyrian empire destroyed the tribe of Israel in 722 BC. Then, only Judah and the Jews survived and they were very weak. These political changes meant economic and social changes and also the need to further revise and amend the **Bible**, which is exactly what happened. The third or priest version of the **Bible** was written in Jerusalem by King Hezekiah and his scribes about 700 BC.

The book of Deuteronomy and several following books in the **Bible** were part of the fourth version. They were written by the prophet Jeremiah who lived in exile in Egypt after the Babylonian destruction of Judah in 587 BC. In 538 BC, this fifty-year exile was ended by Cyrus the Great, and the Jews were allowed to return home and re-build their temple. Some 80 years later, in 458 BC, a politician-priest followed the other Jews home. He was Ezra, the politician, the priest, the scribe, and the real father of the **Bible**. He was appointed co-ruler over Judah by the Persian-Iranian king.

The situation when politician-scribe Ezra returned from Babylon to Jerusalem was such that there were these various versions of the ancient records, and obviously all could not be the words of God since in many cases they contradicted each other. To keep all of these various versions would challenge the authoritative quality of each of them.

Thus about 450 BC, Ezra, the ruler of Judah, decided to make Judah once again into a theocracy. The second temple was built; the priesthood was set up and protected by law. All of these diverse and sometimes contradictory versions of the **Bible** were merged into one. Some parts were stories imported from Sumer and some were from

Egypt. They included laws, genealogy lists, architectural instructions, poems, and prose. Ezra merged them all together with great literary skill. He created a document of history and literature sometimes at harmony within itself and sometimes not, but after that time, never to be separated again until the present time.

In addition, Ezra inserted some new material into the **Bible** of his own making. Among the things Ezra inserted into the **Bible** text was the idea that the Israelites, a name appropriated from AMORC, were God's chosen people. This gave the Jews an ideal to rally around and to follow, but it also lowered them from the worship of the One True God to a worship of the Jewish tribal god, Yahweh. The One True God would never favor Jew over Gentile or Gentile over Jew. This theology created a schism between the Jews and the rest of humanity that continues to the present day. Certainly the God of the universe would not favor one of his people over another of his people. To suggest such a thing was to return to tribal gods and tribal religion.

It also set the worst of very bad precedents and one that still haunts the Jews to this day. They altered the **Bible** for their own political purposes. The Roman Church would later use this example to do some altering of its own, only this time the altering worked against the Jews.

In the early Roman Church about AD 300, when the church got hungry for money, it looked around for those who had lots of money. Then, as now, it was the Jews. The Church wanted to seize their money, but it needed a reason. Some bright fellow suggested that the Church could alter some records to make it look as if Master Jesus died on the cross and that the Jews were responsible for his death. Then, with the idea of original sin, the Church branded the Jews as Christ killers and could and did seize their property. The Church's theory was that he who lives by the forgery of Holy Writ shall also die by the forgery of Holy Writ; and many Jews did die. Later, many non-Jews also died.

A thousand years later, Muhammad accurately accused the Jews of altering the old historical records. The changes made by Ezra were forged Holy Writ. Thus began a conflict between the Jews and Muslims that embroils the world to the present day.

The story of the Hebrews and Jews is the story of mankind. Man has the capacity for both good and evil. The Hebrews produced some of the finest and some of the wisest men who ever lived. That the Jews followed the bad men, rather than the good men, is a summary of Jewish history up to this time. But elements of the good, as always, remain and shall ultimately prevail.

CHAPTER ELEVEN -- MASTER JESUS THE CHRIST

The Roman Church as a political institution began with Constantine around AD 325. The major thrust of the Roman Church has always been to keep its followers ignorant in order to maintain its control over them. That effort has succeeded beyond the wildest dreams of Constantine and his successors. It is not true that over the centuries all Roman-church leaders have been mean and ignorant, but it certainly is true that many have been. Just a partial list of some of the things it was necessary for a good Roman Catholic to believe include:

1. That Master Jesus the Christ died on a cross in Israel;

2. That the Jews were responsible for the crucifixion and death of Master Jesus the Christ;

3. That knowledge was sinful and the burning of the great library at Alexandria, Egypt, was necessary in order to protect Christians from the sinful knowledge contained therein;

4. That sin could be forgiven by the Roman Church, and the right to sin could be bought in the marketplace;

5. That Earth was flat and was the center of the solar system and universe;

6. That Earth and man were created in 4004 BC;

7. That hundreds of thousands of people, mostly women, were witches and should be and were burned alive in some of the most cruel and sadistic mass murders the world has ever known. The reason that those witches had to be burned to death is that in AD 1163, at the Council of Tours, the Roman Church made it a part of the Canon Law that the Roman Church abhors bloodshed. But by burning, no blood was shed -- theoretically -- according to Roman-church logic. More than nine million people were tortured to death as witches over the centuries;

8. That abortion is murder even though the **Bible** itself in **Genesis** teaches that the soul enters the body only with the first breath of life;

9. That all knowledge was contained in the **Bible** and **New Testament** and only the Roman Church could properly read and interpret that **Bible** and **New Testament**; and,

10. That the pope could not be wrong on questions of morals.

Many scholars today would not agree with the Roman Church on any of those required beliefs. The odds are very high that not even one of those required tenets was ever in fact true. Yet millions of people were cruelly murdered by the Roman Church for not believing those untrue matters. The preface of volume two of the **Book of Canon Law** published in Rome in 1901 actually states: *"The death sentence is a necessary and efficacious means for the Church to attain its ends..."* That such an institution would claim association with Master Jesus the Christ is the height of hypocrisy.

Perhaps the gravest error of the Roman Church was its repudiation of the teachings of Master Jesus the Christ and its adoption of the philosophies of Aristotle and the Apostle Paul. There is no question that the teachings of Paul, as reported in the **New Testament** are much inferior to and contradictory to those of Master Jesus. But the Roman Church at that time knew that the Hebrew Ezra had rewritten the **Bible** for Jewish political purposes, so they felt justified in also rewriting the **New Testament** for its own political purposes.

The seven sacraments of the Roman Church are political expedients and have nothing to do with right living, right morals, or the teachings of Master Jesus the Christ. Master Jesus never taught that the level of learning and consciousness he had achieved was for himself alone, and he did not ask that we worship him. Rather, he wanted us to follow in his footsteps and to emulate and imitate and learn from his example and for us really to become like himself.

The Apostle Paul taught that man should turn to the Christian church for guidance, and that higher church officials know more about the desires and wishes of God than the ordinary person. For example, in **Hebrews, Chapters 13-17**, Paul says: *"Obey them [Church authorities] that have the rule over you, and submit yourselves: for they watch for your souls, as they that must give account..."* The Christian church used this authority and those teachings to lead the world away from learning and into the Dark Ages for more than a thousand years.

These teachings were exactly opposite to the teachings of Master Jesus the Christ, who taught inductive reasoning rather than deductive. The inductive method is the method of arriving at the comprehension of general laws by the observation and analysis of particulars. It progresses from results to cause, step by step, logically.

His inductive reasoning was to the effect that whatever Master Jesus did and achieved, any other person could also do and achieve, if that person could learn to be like Master Jesus. This was and certainly is a formidable task, but also was and certainly is a desirable goal. Master Jesus taught that man has a direct relationship with God, and thus no intermediary or go-between is necessary. This suggests that no Christian church was necessary. That did not and does not fare very well with the priesthood of the church. So the Church profaned the teachings in order to retain its political position.

An Essene, that is to say, a Rosicrucian couple gave birth to their first boy-child in May of 7 BC. They named him Joseph, after his father. Later they had several other children also. They were an Aryan family, not Hebrew, but they lived in a Hebrew

MASTER JESUS THE CHRIST 199

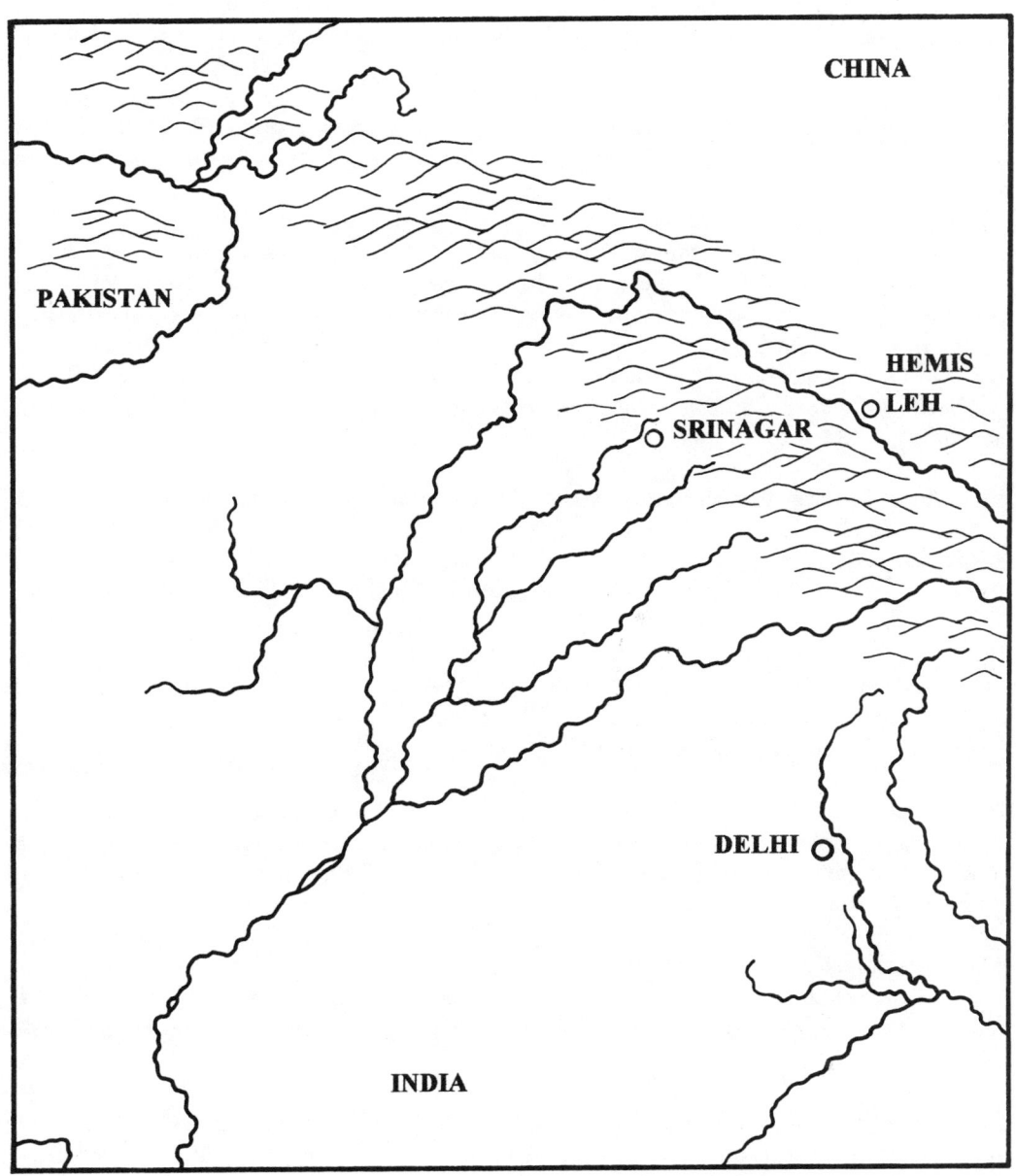

Exhibit 41: Kashmir, northern India. Note the town of Srinagar where Saint Issa is buried and Hemis Monastery where Saint Issa came from Israel to study.

state and were subject to Hebrew law. Many Aryans also lived in the Kashmir area of northern India. That could be one reason why Master Jesus later made his home there.

On May 29th in 7 BC there was the first-noted and a most impressive conjunction of Jupiter and Saturn. Then on October 3rd a second conjunction occurred. Still later, on December 4th, a third and last conjunction of these same two planets took place, all in the constellation of Pisces.

Any modern planetarium can show these conjunctions to the exact time, even to the hour. By February of 6 BC, the planet Jupiter had moved out of the constellation of Pisces and into the constellation of Aries. These conjunctions would have been clearly visible in the Middle East. A Jewish legend was that the Messiah would appear when there was a conjunction of Saturn and Jupiter in the constellation of Pisces, exactly as happened in 7 BC. A few years earlier, Halley's comet came by Earth in 12 BC, according to Chinese records.

The author believes that the real reason why the man Joseph of Galilee, known to us as Master Jesus the Christ, was never accepted by the Jews was that while Master Jesus was Jewish by law, he was not of the Hebrew race. Master Jesus was an Essene, which is to say he was an Israelite, Rosicrucian, Freemason, and Kabalist in his religious views.

The term Israelite has nothing to do with the Hebrews or Jews. Master Jesus understood the true meaning of Israelite; that it applied only to a person of enlightenment. In **John 1:47** Master Jesus reportedly said in reference to Nathanael: *"Here is a true Israelite, in whom there is nothing false."*

The gospel writer Matthew said that we had seen his star in the East. When properly translated, this should say that we had seen his star in the first rays of dawn, which rather clearly referred to the May 29 event, in the year 7 BC. If the **New Testament** is accurate, Master Jesus was born in May of 7 BC.

Where was Master Jesus born? Perhaps in an Essene house in Bethlehem as suggested in the **New Testament.** We do know that the Essenes, or Rosicrucians, did maintain houses all over the world of that day that were used by their members when they were traveling.

The story of the three wise men, or Rosicrucians, who came from the East is probably true. They probably came when Master Jesus was four or five years old, not right after he was born. The reason they came was to arrange for Master Jesus' education when he reached puberty, or about twelve to thirteen years of age.

The **New Testament**, which was not written until long after Master Jesus' time, seems to imply that the family of Master Jesus lived in Galilee in the town of Nazareth. The people of Galilee were mostly Aryans, not Hebrews, even though they were subject to

Jewish law. We do know that Master Jesus and his family did not live in Nazareth at the time of his birth, very simply because Nazareth did not even yet exist at that time in history.

We also do not know for sure when or where Master Jesus died. The exact place and the exact time of his death are totally irrelevant. The message Master Jesus was teaching was the important thing, and remains so to the present day. As Master Jesus himself reportedly said in **Luke 14:34** "*He who has ears to hear, let him hear.*"

At age five, Master Jesus was sent to the Mount Carmel Monastery of the Essenes, or Rosicrucians, to attend school. This school was located near the eastern Mediterranean shore in the present country of Lebanon, not very far from Master Jesus' home in Galilee. He attended school there for seven years, until age twelve, which was in about AD 5.

The story in the **New Testament** about Master Jesus, at age twelve, having heated discussion with the priests at the Temple in Jerusalem is also probably true. Master Jesus would have been taught, and would have known by age twelve, that priests are not even needed, or desirable, in order for man to be saved. Throughout history, the priests of all religions have taken serious, and often violent, exception to the proposition that they, and their profession, are totally unnecessary to the salvation of mankind.

When Pharaoh Akhnaton took away the power of the priests, the priests were angry. When Master Jesus suggested the same thing again, 1300 years later, the priests were even more angry. And the priests have not changed very much in the last 2000 years.

There are no records, in our Western culture, of what happened to Master Jesus from age twelve to 36 or so, because no one in Western culture knows. We presume that he helped his father in the carpenter trade during that time. Did Master Jesus work as a carpenter until age 36, then disclose to the world the greatest teachings this world has yet known? Certainly not.

In 1953, the author was in the hospital for about three days, having his tonsils removed. While reading only the red printed statements of Master Jesus in the **New Testament,** the author realized that Master Jesus was obviously a student of both Buddhist and Chinese philosophy. But how could this be, for a man who lived only in the Middle East during this period of history? With that realization, the author began a quest that has taken over 40 years, and he has traveled over much of the world several times.

Buddhism, Judaism, and the Roman Church all teach that in the beginning God created man. These teachings are to the effect that there does exist a linear time frame. This is to say that man had a beginning, which of course also logically implies, that he will have an end. Not so, said Master Jesus, and which Einstein much later proved to be true scientifically.

Time applies only to this physical universe. Since man is not of this physical universe, man had no beginning; will have no end; and, will live forever. This is true, and there is nothing man can do to keep from living forever. Of course man can, and most of us do live on in ignorance, but live on forever we must and shall. The teachings of AMORC and Master Jesus affect only the quality of that living and not at all whether or not it happens.

The author had just been reading some of the philosophy of the Chinese teacher named Laotse, who lived in China about 604 BC, and taught the Law of Love. He taught that by the accident of fortune a man may rule the world for a time, but by virtue of love he may rule the world forever. Laotse gave his teachings to the world and then went silent, which is to say that he disappeared from public view, and lived only a very private life thereafter. No one seems to know when or where Laotse died.

This was similar to the great teacher Moses Moria-El, who had also disappeared 700 years earlier. After the crucifixion of Master Jesus in Israel in AD 33, he also went silent and thereafter lived only a private life, and no one seems to know for sure just when or where he died. In Master Jesus's case, at some point he seems to have gone back to his boyhood home in Srinagar, Kashmir, where he spent the rest of his life.

In AD 1626, Francis Lord Bacon, also went silent in England and moved to Europe where he lived out the balance of his life. No one seems to know when or where Bacon died, but the author suspects he died in AD 1642.

One of Laotse's teachings was called **Nothing Weaker than Water.** It is as follows:

"There is nothing weaker than water, But none is superior to it in overcoming the hard, For which there is no substitute. That weakness overcomes strength, And gentleness overcomes rigidity, (What) No one does not know: No one can put into practice."

Therefore, the Sage says:

"(He) Who receives unto himself the calumny of the world, Is the preserver of the state. (He) Who bears himself the sins of the world, Is the king of the world. Straight words seem crooked."

In reading the first ten Beatitudes of the Sermon on the Mount by Master Jesus, The author felt that there might be some connection. Those Beatitudes are reported in the **New Testament**, in **Matthew 5:1 to 11**, as follows:

"1. And seeing the multitudes, he went up into a mountain; and when he was set, his disciples came unto him:

2. And he opened his mouth, and taught them, saying,

3. Blessed are the poor in spirit: for their's is the kingdom of heaven.

4. Blessed are they that mourn: for they shall be comforted.

5. Blessed are the meek: for they shall inherit the earth.

6. Blessed are they which do hunger and thirst after righteousness: for they shall be filled.

7. Blessed are the merciful: for they shall obtain mercy.

8. Blessed are the pure in heart: for they shall see God.

9. Blessed are the peacemakers: for they shall be called the children of God.

10. Blessed are they which are persecuted for righteousness' sake: for their's is the kingdom of heaven.

11. Blessed are ye, when men shall revile you, and persecute you, and shall say all manner of evil against you falsely, for my sake...."

Laotse says "...*That weakness overcomes strength. and gentleness overcomes rigidity....*" Master Jesus says that "...*Blessed are the meek: for they shall inherit the earth....*"

Laotse says that "...*(He) who bears himself the sins of the world Is the king of the world.*" Is this not exactly what Master Jesus did, or at least tried to do? These similarities did raise a serious question as to whether Master Jesus knew about Laotse. The author, much later, concluded that he did.

How does one summarize the thousands of volumes on the Buddhist teachings into something comprehensible for our purposes of tracing the source of Western cultural values? Buddhism is really a way of living, more than a formal religion. Very generally, while there are many sects, there are two main branches of Buddhist teachings.

One is called the Narrow Way and is austere, has a very narrow outlook, and leads to achievement of personal enlightenment by following the undeviating example of another. In other words, it is a cult religion. There are fundamentalists like this who refuse to think for themselves in every religion. Such people are intellectually lazy. They turn to some excuse, always outside of themselves, to try to justify their excessively negative behavior. They try and try but always without success.

The other branch is called the Great Way and calls upon a person to progress to enlightenment by his own efforts. According to this teaching, an Untouchable can achieve enlightenment just as easily, or even more so, than a king or high priest. The Great Way is the Eightfold Path, which means correct views, aspirations, speech, conduct, work, efforts, thoughts, and contemplations.

Is not the Eightfold Path exactly what Master Jesus was trying to bring to the world? **The Notovitch Manuscript**, about Saint Issa or Master Jesus at the Hemis Monastery, also indicates that this was the mission of Master Jesus. However, we also know that Master Jesus had an even higher mission, and that was to teach the Law of Love.

Have you ever met any person who could even come close to meeting any of the tests of the Law of Love as taught by Master Jesus? One example for parents: Can you love some young Iranian, as much as your own child? Could you still love him just as much as your own child, if he murdered your child? You must, if you follow the teachings of Master Jesus.

Master Jesus enunciated the most difficult rules for human conduct ever presented to mankind. Master Jesus is reported as saying in **Mark 3:33 - 34** "*Who are my mother and brothers?*" He then shows that blood relationship has no meaning when he answers his own question as follows: "*...Whoever does God's will is my brother and sister and mother.*"

Master Jesus is perhaps most loved and best remembered for his teaching of the Golden Rule. The Golden Rule was the basis of the philosophy of AMORC in Egypt. Beginning in 1202 BC, when missionaries were first sent out from Egypt, that teaching of the Golden Rule has been passed down to almost all cultures on Earth.

    1300s BC White Lodge: "*May I do others as I would that they should do unto me.*"

    500s BC Confucianism: "*What you don't want done to yourself, don't do to others.*"

    500s BC Buddhism: "*Hurt not others with that which pains thyself.*"

    500s BC Zoroastrianism: "*Do not do unto others all that which is not well for oneself.*"

    500s BC Jainism: "*...refrain from inflicting upon others such injury as would appear undesirable to us if inflicted upon ourselves.*"

    400s BC Plato in Greece: "*May I do to others as I would that they should do unto me.*"

300s BC Hinduism: *"Do naught to others which if done to thee would cause thee pain."*

100s BC Judaism: *"What is hateful to yourself, don't do to your fellow man."*

AD 30s Master Jesus the Christ: *"Whatsoever ye would that men should do to you, do ye even so to them."*

By the AD 400s and thereafter, the Roman Church had perverted the Golden Rule into the Rule of Gold. The Rule of Gold stated that you should do unto the Roman Church as the pope thinks that you should do unto it; and if you don't, he may burn you to death at the stake.

One of the most outstanding accomplishments of Master Jesus the Christ, that he was never given credit for, was the development of the theory of inductive logic. At that time in history the Western world was dominated by the thinking of Alexander the Great's Greek teacher, Aristotle. Aristotle was the pupil of Plato but did not follow his philosophy.

Aristotle taught deductive reasoning. Deductive reasoning consists of logical steps forward from the primary idea to its ultimate conclusion. The Roman Church, using this system of thinking, taught that the **Bible** and the **New Testament** contain all truth and that only the Roman Church could interpret them and be the source of truth.

Is it not one of the great tragedies of all time that the Roman Church chose to follow the philosophy of Aristotle and the Apostle Paul, rather than the teachings of Master Jesus the Christ?

Aristotle's logic did not require a person to think much for himself. He was given a general principle, then all he had to do was to search for, and discover for his own use, the specific rule for his own conduct from within that general rule. By definition, the use of deductive logic requires the exercise of less and less knowledge all the time. Deductive logic requires that man know less and less about less and less until he knows nothing about nothing. This later caused the Dark Ages to descend upon Western culture.

Master Jesus, however, taught a completely new revolutionary idea of thinking that was then known as the Christ teachings and is now partly known as inductive logic.

The inductive method is the method of arriving at the comprehension of general laws by the observation and analysis of particulars. It progresses from results to cause, step by step, logically.

Inductive logic allows one to arrive at knowledge by simply showing a very small particular thing to be true, and then from that particular truth generalizing to a larger universal truth. True genius is the ability to look at a particular but perceive a generality; to look at a tree, but see a forest.

Master Jesus was the foremost and greatest genius of all time. Read again the first ten, very beautiful, Beatitudes set out above. Note that in every one of them, Master Jesus first notes a particular truth, but then generalizes to a larger universal truth. In Beatitude three, from the **poor in spirit** to **Heaven**; in Beatitude four, from the **mourners** to the **comforted**; and in Beatitude five, from the **meek** to the **inheritors of the earth**. And so on.

Note, however, that in **Matthew 5:11** it completely reverses course and jumps from inductive logic back to the old deductive logic of Aristotle and says: *"for my (Jesus') sake."* This method of reasoning was later used by the Roman Church with such disaster to the world. This is one way you can tell that Master Jesus was not the author of **Matthew 5:11**. Another is that **Matthew 5:11** promotes a cult religion, which Master Jesus would never do. Yet another is that Jesus had the ability to reduce truth to something very simple that could be understood by everyone. This included the Untouchables as well as the priests and kings.

Perhaps the best example of the use of inductive logic by Master Jesus, and the very one which makes the teachings of Master Jesus the very unique thing that they are, is in **John 14:3** where Master Jesus reportedly said, *"And if I go and prepare a place for you, I will come again, and take you to be with me; that where I am, there you may be also."*

Note that Master Jesus cites a particular truth to-wit: *"Where I am"* and then generalizes from that particular truth to a much larger universal truth, which is that, where Master Jesus has gone, all of mankind may also go sometime. For those Roman-church priests who would like to think that Master Jesus may have believed in a hell, read **John 13:36** where Master Jesus says: *"Where I am going, you cannot follow now, but you will follow later."*

Note that Master Jesus says very specifically and without exception that you, which is all of mankind, will follow me. Again, Master Jesus teaches from a particular, himself, to a generality, which is all of mankind. He says nothing about anybody going to hell. If we can believe Master Jesus, he says that everybody will sooner or later follow him.

His inductive reasoning was to the effect that whatever Master Jesus did and achieved, any other person could also do and achieve, if that person could learn to be like Master Jesus. This certainly was and is a formidable task, but also certainly was and is a desirable goal.

In the AD 1600s, Francis Lord Bacon formalized some of these inductive teachings of Master Jesus into what is now known as inductive logic or simply as the Scientific Method.

Is Master Jesus' Sermon on the Mount, as reported in the **New Testament** in **Matthew 5**, etc., and in **Luke 6:20** etc., accurate? Obviously, both cannot be totally accurate since they are in some ways different.

In **Matthew 5:10** it says that "*...Blessed are they which are persecuted for righteousness' sake....*" In the very next verse in **Matthew 5:11** it says "*...Blessed are ye, when men ... persecute you ...for my sake....*"

Matthew 5:10 sounds like something Master Jesus could have said. **Matthew 5:11** sounds like something some priest, who was trying to start a cult, inserted into the Sermon on the Mount at a later time. Certainly **Matthew 5:11** sounds contrary to the teachings of Master Jesus. However, the Sermon on the Mount was Master Jesus' effort to make AMORC teachings public again. After that sermon, Master Jesus was a marked man and eventually had to leave the country.

There is no intent to go into **New Testament** analysis here. However, a few items are important for our consideration:

1. It is usually taught by the Roman Church that the Gospels of **Matthew, Mark, Luke**, and **John** were written in the AD 60 to 90 time period. Probably not. The earliest fragment, of any actual record of any Gospel, is about AD 125. But the Gospels were not finalized until much later.

The Gospels were only put into final form about AD 400, which is the same time that the great library at Alexandria, Egypt, was burned by the Roman Church. In that library were the records which would show the inaccuracy of the Gospels, and that is exactly one of the reasons why the 700,000 volumes of that great library were destroyed by the Roman Church.

2. **The Revelation** of Saint John the Divine was not by the great disciple John, who was the friend of Master Jesus. **The Revelation** was written about AD 66 to 70 in Jerusalem, not on the island of Patmos about AD 95.

3. It is reported in the **New Testament** that Master Jesus both prayed himself, and taught to his disciples, a Lord's Prayer. Not so. Certainly Master Jesus was the greatest exponent of prayer ever. But, he taught people to pray in private, and that such prayer was a very private matter between each man or woman and God. Many Christian churches have different versions of a Lord's Prayer. The Lord's Prayer was composed by one of the early Roman-church fathers, but long after the death of Master Jesus.

4. The real teachings of Master Jesus the Christ are the highest and most profound teachings ever exposed to mankind. Those teachings have survived in the world, in spite of the Christian churches and not because of them.

Also in the early 1950s, the author read the book entitled **The Aquarian Gospel of Jesus the Christ**. This book was written by Levi Dowling and tells of the eighteen or so years that Master Jesus spent traveling and studying in India, Persia-Iran, Greece, and Egypt. This fitted exactly into the author's theory, but where did Levi get his information?

Levi says that he got the information from reading the **Akashic Records**. What in the world are the **Akashic Records**? It is a Sanskrit word, and there is no single English word into which it will translate. The author's very limited knowledge of Sanskrit would translate it into English as being like a giant video camera, that has run continuously since the beginning of time, and records everything that happens, everywhere, to everybody.

This camera also records the thoughts and also the Quantum or statistical probabilities of what will happen in the future. Because God and man both enjoy free will, and can cause their own future to happen, no one, not even God, knows what will happen in the future.

All of these videos tapes are stored in a vast library or computer memory bank, and those who know and understand the storage system, can easily go into that vast library and read everything recorded there. Like a giant computer, once a person knows and understands the software that controls it, he or she can easily retrieve the information stored there.

The ancient mystics said that all this information was stored on the ether waves, and all humans have the capacity, in meditation, to consult those records and read therefrom. It is said that some high Rosicrucians, such as Master Jesus the Christ, knew how to read from the **Akashic Records**.

So, if everything is written in the **Akashic Records**, a person who could read those records, such as Master Jesus, would know everything about everybody.

Because of the source, the author rejected Levi's material completely. But many years later, the author would learn that the Rosicrucians have used many ways to expose truth to the world, sometimes without getting themselves murdered by the Roman-church priests in the process.

One method used was that some brave soul would find some old long-lost manuscript that exposed the priesthood. The author of the material had supposedly been dead for some time, so there was not much that could be done to him. Of course, the brave soul who happened to find the manuscript couldn't be blamed either, because he or she was only the finder. The finder would even admit that the negative Roman-church information in the manuscript obviously could not be true, because it was contrary to Roman-church teachings. The priest would tell you, both then and now, that everybody knows that Master Jesus never left Israel.

Another method used was that the Rosicrucian would report some teaching that attacked the Roman-church position but would, himself, defend the church position. But, the true teaching was presented for those readers who were enlightened enough to perceive it. And it was hard for the Roman Church to murder somebody who was gallantly defending its position.

Another method used was that the Rosicrucian would write under the name of a person who would never be taken seriously by anyone. This was the method that Francis Lord Bacon used in writing many of his works, the most notable of which were those by Shakespeare. The actor, William Shakespeare, from Stratford-upon-Avon in England was a drunken actor who could neither read nor write. He could only barely sign his name on his own Last Will and Testament, which was actually written by someone else. Even then, he did not spell his own name correctly.

In that Last Will and Testament, William Shakespeare took the trouble to mention his bed as a gift, but never, of course, mentioned any of the Shakespearean works. The reason for this was that, very simply, he knew he did not own them. Actually, some of the Shakespeare works were not even yet published at the time of Shakespeare's death in AD 1616.

Yet, another method used was to put the material into a fantasy situation that no one would take seriously. Yet truth was presented for those readers who were enlightened enough to perceive it. All other readers would chuckle and go on their way. But truth was impressed into their consciousness in the process. This was the method used by the Rosicrucian, Frank Baum, in writing the book entitled **The Wizard of Oz.** The Christian churches mounted vicious attacks against Baum's work, but because his book was so very well done, those attacks were not effective.

Another method used was that truth would be presented as a dream, or as having been read from the **Akashic Records.** But, the important point was that truth was presented for those readers who were enlightened enough to perceive it. Actually, the source of truth is totally unimportant. Even an atheist or a communist could speak truths. And even a priest, or a pope, can and often do speak non-truths. Man should never judge truth because of its source.

Levi Dowling spent a lifetime of study, and obviously came across some fairly good material someplace, somehow. He was born in Ohio in 1844, attended seminary in Indianapolis, Indiana USA, and became a minister of the Disciples of Christ. He served in the armed forces during the War Between the States, and later graduated from two medical colleges. He practiced medicine for some years and then retired to write his only book. Levi died in 1911. Levi's material was never taken seriously by very many people including the author. Where he actually obtained his material is not known, but at least some of it is accurate.

About the same time that Levi was writing his material in the 1800s, a very wealthy Russian by the name of Nicolas Notovitch was traveling in northern India near Srinagar in Kashmir. Notovitch kept hearing legends about a Saint Issa, or Master Jesus, who had lived and taught in the Srinagar area about 1800 years earlier, and whom the Hindu priests had tried to murder. Notovitch was naturally intrigued.

Notovitch broke his leg and so was confined at the monastery at Hemis for some time. He persuaded the chief priest to allow him, and his interpreter, to translate the document pertaining to Saint Issa, from Tibetan into Russian. This material, now known as **The Notovitch Manuscript**, was later translated into French, and still later into English.

Notovitch tells a very interesting story about the legends of Saint Issa, or Master Jesus, in the Srinagar, Kashmir area. The story is that the Buddha, or as we would say, the Christ, had incarnated into a Great Lama, or teacher known as Saint Issa, or Master Jesus, who was the true son of God. Saint Issa taught the only true religion throughout the entire world, without resorting to force. It is interesting to note that these legends are to the effect that Master Jesus actually taught throughout the entire world. Compare this to Roman-church theology that Master Jesus was born, lived, taught, and died only in Israel.

H. Spencer Lewis, the world head of the Rosicrucian Order in the early part of this century, wrote two books about Master Jesus which are entitled the **Mystical Life of Jesus** and **The Secret Doctrines of Jesus**. Much of Lewis' material was probably taken from the works of a Finnish scholar. Lewis also tells a similar story about Master Jesus. But again, the question is: Where did Lewis get his information? The Rosicrucians do have access to lots of ancient documents. Lewis leaves the inference that he certainly does have access to much private information. Whether that is true or not, we do not know for sure. It is true that some Rosicrucians do have knowledge of, or access to, some very ancient and very good private information.

The author spent a great deal of time tracking down this Notovitch document. In June of 1976, the author spent time in Srinagar, Kashmir, looking for **The Notovitch Manuscript**. It was not found at that time, but what was found, was a claimed grave site of Master Jesus, and also a legend about the actual grave site of Moses Moria-El.

The **Bible** says that Moses Moria-El went to the East to die, so if the **Bible** is correct, he obviously has a grave someplace east of Israel. Possibly this legend could lead to it.

The site is supposed to be about 60 miles north of Srinagar, and ten miles north of Bandipur, near the small village of Hasbal.

Travel in this area of the world can be difficult. The Hindus control the government, but the Muslims control the territory. The author was near the town of Zebak in northeastern-most Afghanistan, and looked down into the former Soviet Union. Srinagar is less than 300 miles to the southeast, but across the boundary in India. In order to get to Srinagar, it was necessary to travel south to Kabul, Afghanistan, then on south to Karachi, Pakistan, then east to New Delhi, India, and then north again to Srinagar in Kashmir. This is a distance of more than 1500 miles in order to cover less than 300 miles in actual distance.

The author has not visited Moses Moria-El's supposed grave site because of the Hindu-Muslim conflicts in that area. However, the German author Holger Kersten in his recent book entitled **Jesus Lived in India: His Unknown Life before and after the Crucifixion** says that such a grave of Moses Moria-El is indeed there.

Several years prior to visiting Srinagar in 1976, the author did learn that Master Jesus did not die on a cross in Israel in AD 33 at age 39. The **New Testament** went through some serious political editing in the AD 300s. This was done in order to justify a basis for the new pagan-style Roman Church that was being created by Roman Emperor Constantine and his successors.

It took up to a week for a healthy person to die from crucifixion. Master Jesus was very healthy and was only on the cross about five hours at most. The **New Testament**, even as politically edited, still does not say that Master Jesus died at that time. The reader may easily check this for him or herself. Actually, quite the contrary. The **New Testament** reports on many people who talked with Master Jesus after the crucifixion. The **New Testament** reports Master Jesus as saying:

1. **Matthew 26:32** *"But after I have risen, I will go ahead of you into Galilee."*

2. **Matthew 28:10** *"Do not be afraid. Go and tell my brothers to go to Galilee; there they will see me."*

There were many people who saw and talked with Master Jesus within a few days after the crucifixion event. The idea that Master Jesus actually died at that time is Roman-church theology, not history.

Both the Buddhist world and the Muslim world know very well that Master Jesus did not die in Israel in AD 33. The **Koran** states at Chapter 4:157:

"That they said (in boast), 'We killed Christ Jesus The son of Mary, The Apostle of God,' -- But they killed him not, Nor crucified him, But so it was made to appear to

*them, And those who differ Therein are full of doubts, With no (certain) knowledge, But only conjecture to follow, For of a surety **They killed him not.**"*

Did the Apostle Paul ever, in fact, meet Master Jesus? We really do not know for sure. Paul, who hated Master Jesus, does tell about meeting him on the road to Damascus, and of being converted and transformed by that meeting. But is this an accurate report?

We do know this. Master Jesus was living in the area, at Mount Carmel Monastery, about this time and could easily have met with Paul. We know that Paul did become a changed man. But we also know that if Paul did, in fact, meet Master Jesus, as stated in the **New Testament**, he did not learn much from that meeting.

Master Jesus taught that a priest is not necessary for salvation, but Paul taught just the opposite. Master Jesus taught that all people are equal in potential, but Paul taught that women are inferior to men. These are only two examples, but they are sufficient to make the point. The Apostle Paul was not a follower or student of Master Jesus the Christ.

The idea that the Jews were responsible for the death of Master Jesus is also Roman-church theology and is not historically true. Such an idea has been used to discredit the Jews for almost 2000 years now. It is high time this ceased forever.

The author believes that the idea that Master Jesus actually died at that time, and that the Jews were responsible for his death, was inserted into the **New Testament** about AD 300, so that the Roman Church could have a reason, even if only a very weak one, to justify seizing Jewish assets for the Roman Church. The pope could then say that Christ killers should have their assets seized by Christ's representative on Earth, who is the pope. Certainly, the Roman Church has used the Jews as scapegoats since the AD 300s. Throughout that time, the Roman Church has seized the property of Jews as well as the property of many non-Jews as well.

The Roman Empire was the most finely structured empire ever in the history of mankind. This was one reason that it lasted so very long. Roman justice put many people to death, particularly anyone who was perceived as being a threat to the Roman government. The Roman government did not turn Roman criminal-justice over to anyone else to administer and certainly not to the Jews in Israel.

There is much contradictory material about Master Jesus. The author has contemplated most of those contradictions for many years, and has arrived at some tentative conclusions about them.

Master Jesus did go to the Kashmir area of northern India to live, and spent most of the rest of his life there. He did study and achieve mastership there, which is to say, he mastered the highest studies that could be taught by the high Buddhist priests and lamas. He learned many languages and many philosophies, including that of the Buddhists, the Hindus, the Chinese, and others.

Exhibit 42: Tomb of Saint Issa in Srinagar, Kashmir. Saint Issa was born in Israel in 7 BC, taught over the whole world, and died in Kashmir in AD 74.

At about age 21, he fell into disgrace with the Hindu priests for teaching against the caste system. In the Hindu caste system there were four levels of people, with the Untouchables being the lowest. Master Jesus taught that these Untouchables were equal in potential to the priests. This made the priests very angry, and they tried to murder him. His friends helped him escape and go to Persia-Iran.

Master Jesus was more like a Buddhist than like a member of any formal religion at that time. However, he also perceived the errors in that teaching and set out to correct it.

214 TRUE ESOTERIC TRADITIONS

Even yet today, there are isolated communities high in the mountains in that area who are true Christians that were converted by Master Jesus himself as a young man. Of course, those Christians would have little in common with members of the Roman Church, as later created by Roman Emperor Constantine. Since AD 300, the Roman Church has tried to murder and exterminate all of those earlier Christians.

Exhibit 43: Footprints at the Tomb of Saint Issa in Srinagar, Kashmir.

At about age 22, Master Jesus arrived in Persia-Iran. Again, he studied and completed the things he could learn there in only about two years, and then began his teaching. Again, he fell into disfavor for teaching that man has a direct and personal relationship with God and does not need an intervening priest as a go-between. The priests wanted him killed for teaching such an obviously, to them, false doctrine. Master Jesus was outlawed by the king.

The term **outlaw** is a very old one and was used in many ancient countries in their criminal-justice systems. Instead of locking a criminal up, which required buildings, jailers, food, and expense, the king would merely outlaw the person. This put him outside the law, and it was not a criminal offense to kill the outlaw.

This was a cheap and effective system of criminal justice. Outlaws were usually killed by someone within a week or so. There was almost always someone around who would kill a person for his coat or shoes, or just for the fun of it. In tough cases, the king or the priests would add a little bounty money, which caused sure death to the outlaw by someone very quickly. This method has been used throughout history and was popular in the early years of the American West. An unusual thing happened to Master Jesus.

Even though he was an outlaw, he was loved by so many that they shielded him from all harm and he safely left the country.

Master Jesus arrived back in Israel at about age 24. You should not think of him as merely coming home. Any young person who moves away at age twelve, and comes back at age 24 or so, does not consider it coming home. His home was now where he spent his formative years. For Master Jesus, that was in northern India.

Even if Master Jesus lived to be only 33 years old, as taught by the Roman Church, he still spent only fifteen years, or less than half of his life, in Israel. And most of those fifteen years was as a child. But if he lived to be 81, then Israel was his place of birth, and a place that he came back to teach for two or three years, and really was not a significant part of his life. Such a statement may shock some Western readers, but that has always been common knowledge to the Buddhist lamas in the East.

Consider also, that by this time Master Jesus had world-wide fame among the Freemasons, Essenes, and Rosicrucians. He was achieving mastership in so much, at such a young age, that there had to be talk and speculation that he would fulfill AMORC predictions of a great teacher who would come in the Age of Pisces and take the Christ initiation. Remember, Master Jesus was the man and **Christness** was the level of consciousness he achieved. Could this finally, after all these centuries, be the man who would teach the world the 33rd law of AMORC -- the Law of Love?

The Sanhedrin, or Council of 73, which ruled the Essene, or Rosicrucian Order, world-wide was anxiously awaiting his appearance in all parts of the world. Obviously, all Freemasons and all Essenes, or Rosicrucians, wanted very much to meet him.

In **Luke 10:1** of the **New Testament**, it refers to this Sanhedrin as follows:

> *"After these things the Lord Appointed other seventy also, and sent them two and two before his face into every city and place, whither he himself would come."*

The Sanhedrin had a total of 73 members. There were 70 ordinary members who were spread out all over the world, plus two chief administrators, plus the 73rd person who was the leader. The world-wide leader at that time was Master Jesus the Christ.

At about age 24, Master Jesus spent a very brief time in Israel, perhaps seeing his family again and also laying the frame work for his world-wide work. Actually, there already existed a world-wide network of people, ready and waiting to follow him. That network of people has existed throughout history. It still exists today. But, Master Jesus did need to meet them so that they would really know who he was and that soon he would become the Christ.

Master Jesus did not get into any trouble with the authorities in Israel at that time. From Israel, he went back to Mount Carmel, where he had spent about seven years in school, and then on to Greece.

In Greece, again he studied and mastered all the teachings available there at that time. It is there that he probably took the sixth or Master's initiation and symbolically was born again as a new man. Remember, that those teachings had been brought to Greece by Solon several centuries before the time of Master Jesus. The teachings were then and still are that man must be born again. As Master Jesus has reportedly stated in **John 3:3** "*I tell you the truth, no one can see the kingdom of God unless he is born again.*"

It was probably at that time that Master Jesus actually took initiation and changed his name from Joseph to Master Jesus, to honor his symbolical rebirth as a new man. From that time on he would be Master Jesus, but not yet Master Jesus the Christ. The time would now be about AD 18, and Master Jesus was about 25 years of age. He had taken the sixth initiation at a much younger age than anyone in history.

What happened to Master Jesus over the next ten years? We do not know. We do know that in about AD 27 or 28, at age 35 or so, Master Jesus was in Egypt and took the Christ initiation in the Great Pyramid or Masonic Temple of Giza.

Apparently, Master Jesus already had achieved the sixth initiation in Greece before arriving in Egypt. He spent only about three years in Egypt, at most, and that was in testing for the Christ initiation. When it did happen, word spread immediately throughout the world that the initiate Master Jesus was now Master Jesus the Christ.

This happening was not a shock to anyone. AMORC members the world over, who knew Master Jesus, had known for some years that this was probably going to happen, and it did. The Messiah had at last come. Much joy prevailed among initiates the world over. At last the man had come who could and would reveal to the people of Earth a new and higher level of understanding of God's love. Master Jesus concentrated on the highest law for his teachings: the Law of Love. Only initiates understood the true nature and purpose of his teachings. The profane or uninitiated did not know his program and incorrectly perceived him to be a priest or politician. The priests incorrectly perceived it to be a situation where God had incarnated in the form of a man, when what had actually happened was that a man had raised his level of consciousness to the level of Christ consciousness in order to show mankind how it could be done.

Graduates of the Lesser Mysteries were able to recognize each other by the passing and receiving of certain signs. Initiates of the sixth degree could recognize each other immediately by other methods, without signs. This is how John the Baptist immediately recognized Master Jesus without any introduction or signs between them. Of course, initiates the world over had already heard the good news and were eagerly waiting to meet Master Jesus. Many already knew him well. Master Jesus spoke several languages fluently. He had already taught in India, Persia-Iran, probably Greece, maybe Italy and England, and very possibly other countries of which we now have no record.

Tradition is that Master Jesus went from Greece to Italy, then to Carthage in North Africa, and then to southern France. After the first crusade of AD 1095, the true followers of Jesus in southern France became known as the Cathars. They were later murdered in mass and completely exterminated by the Roman Church during the Albigensian Crusades, the only crusades against other Christians.

In all those places where Master Jesus went, he both studied and taught, and he became known as the greatest and wisest of men, which he indeed was. Did Master Jesus visit England? Certainly a great deal of legend and tradition in England says that he did. The author has spent much time in Ireland, Scotland, and particularly at Glastonbury, in England, looking for clues.

No actual hard facts have been found, but the author feels that Master Jesus was indeed in the British Isles. There are some logical reasons for this opinion:

1. Master Jesus would have known that the British Isles were in fact the legendary Atlantis, and the source of our Western culture. He probably could not become the Christ without mastering the ancient knowledge taught there. Obviously, becoming the Christ was his goal and he did achieve it. So, for that reason alone, he probably was there.

2. It is true that throughout history, any legend which has the energy to survive and persist and grow is in fact based on some truth. Note that the legend is not totally true, but is only based on some truth. This also would suggest that Master Jesus was there.

3. In the teachings of Master Jesus, it is inherent that he had a complete knowledge of all the religions of Asia and the Far East. The same thing is true of the mysteries of the Druids in the British Isles. It is evident that Master Jesus did have an intimate knowledge of those teachings. While he could have learned those teachings in other places, the logical place to learn them would have been in England.

4. Another reason was that Master Jesus both wanted and needed to meet any member of the Sanhedrin who lived in the British Isles. It would later require a vote of that Sanhedrin to acknowledge that he was Master Jesus the Christ.

5. After the crucifixion event, Master Jesus went silent in about AD 33, at age 40. Some members of his group went everywhere to tell the news, that Master Jesus was now Master Jesus the Christ. That was the real story of the twelve disciples being

sent everywhere to spread the news. Everywhere they went, members of the Sanhedrin were expecting them.

But everywhere they went, they ran into the same problems Master Jesus had experienced earlier. Many of them were not so lucky and were killed by the priests who had tried to kill Master Jesus earlier. Joseph of Arimathea went to England from Israel in about AD 35 or so, and apparently died and was buried at Glastonbury. This was the beginning of the Church of England whose roots are older than the Roman Church.

About AD 33 Master Jesus was crucified and run out of Israel; he just barely escaped with his life. He returned to Mount Carmel to recover and regain his strength. How long did he stay at Mount Carmel? Only a year or so, or many years? We do not know. Did he go back to England? Did he visit the North American continent, as the Mormon Church teaches? Certainly the Essenes knew about the North American continent, so it is quite possible that Master Jesus did visit there sometime after about AD 35. The important thing that was happening at that time was the dispersal of all of the disciples to spread the message that the Christ had come at last.

What did Master Jesus teach? He taught AMORC teachings. His emphasis was on the Law of Love. It was very difficult for Master Jesus to interpret those teachings into lay language that even the Untouchables could understand. But teach the Law of Love Master Jesus did. Almost 2000 years later, the world is finally just beginning to comprehend a very little of those teachings.

CHAPTER TWELVE -- THE ROMAN CHURCH

The story of the Roman Church is the most tragic story ever told in the history of Western culture. How did that all come about? The Jewish lawyer from Rome, known to us as the Apostle Paul, did not comprehend the teachings of Master Jesus. He Romanized and paganized them to the point that they lost their wisdom and value.

Roman Emperor Constantine, for his own purposes, transformed the Roman Church into a political system. Following that, Saint Augustine transformed that same church into a business enterprise designed to support the professional priesthood. Ignorance became the required quality of Roman-church membership, which it remains to the present day. The combining of politics and finance with religion in the government led to the decline and fall of the Roman Empire.

AMORC taught the Law of Compensation. This Law of Compensation is also sometimes called the Law of Karma, and is very close to the Law of Cause and Effect. Simply stated, it said that Cosmic Law is perfect, and all things done by anyone and everyone, either good or bad, must, without fail, create karma and must be compensated for, every last thing.

Master Jesus the Christ knew how to overcome this Law of Compensation. The first step was for a person to forgive the sins of self. This was one of Master Jesus' highest and greatest teachings. However, the forgiving of sins of self was not easy. It required an absolute knowledge, in the sinner's soul, of the fact that his previous conduct was wrong. And it required a genuine seeking of forgiveness for wrongs done.

History is replete with examples of the Law of Compensation at work. It will continue to be so unless and until mankind learns the teachings of Master Jesus. Here are some noteworthy and tragic examples:

1. The biblical Ezra forged Holy Writ about the Jews being God's chosen people, and made up a number of other things in the **Bible** as well. As a result of the example set by Ezra and the Jews, the Roman Church, about AD 300 and afterwards, also forged Holy Writ. This was done in order to make it appear in the **New Testament** that the Jews had killed Master Jesus. So, exactly the thing that the Jews used for centuries to lord it over their neighbors was then used by the Roman Church to lord it over the Jews. This was simply the Law of Compensation at work.

This forging of Holy Writ by Ezra and the Jews has been the source of much conflict between the Jews and the Muslims. The **Koran** states in Chapter 2:79:

"*Then woe to those who write The Book with their own hands, And then say: 'This is from God,' To traffic with it For a miserable price! -- Woe to them for what their hands Do write, and for the gain They make thereby.*"

The Jews did falsely represent their own writings to be those of the One True God.

2. From the time of Roman Emperor Nero, in AD 64, up to the time of Roman Emperor Constantine, in AD 312 or so, the Roman emperors murdered tens of thousands of Christians because of their belief system. Many Christians actually looked for earlier death in order to get to Heaven sooner. Then the tables turned, and the Roman Church came into control. How did it respond? It took on exactly the same characteristics as those of its previous oppressors, and for the next thousand years or so murdered, not thousands, but millions of people because of their belief systems.

One of the great ironies of all time was that many of those millions were murdered by the Roman Church in the name of Master Jesus, when in reality, many of those people wanted only to be followers of Master Jesus, but not of the Roman Church. The Albigensian Crusades is one example.

3. A modern example of the working of the Law of Compensation is the current situation in the United States of America. That great country was founded on the principles of a defensive nation. Those principles were set forth symbolically on the Great Seal of the United States, where thirteen arrows were shown in conjunction with the olive branch to be used only for its own defense.

Master Mason George Washington warned against aggressive war, which he termed foreign entanglements in his farewell speech as president. In other words, the United States of America, when it was created by the founding fathers who were mostly Freemasons, pledged that it would never be other than a defensive nation. It kept that pledge for nearly two hundred years.

This position was very similar to that of Egypt during the time when the Hebrews controlled that country, prior to the Exodus. As a result of those high principles, America enjoyed the position of moral leadership in the world. Then in the early AD 1960s all that changed, and America became a country waging aggressive war in Vietnam, in Central America, and in the Middle East into the 1990s.

Why were the American leaders not put on trial for war crimes like the German leaders after World War II? Very simply, only because there was no policeman in the world big and strong enough to do it. That fact of supreme military power did not make America less guilty. Morality cannot be decided by military power and popular elections.

America now must pay for all of that violence unleashed against those defenseless peoples, each and every one of them. What used to be great American cities are now drug-crazed war zones that are unfit for human habitation. Does the American public even faintly perceive why there is so much violence in America today? The end of the violence is not yet in sight, because the price has not been paid, and the lessons have not been learned. This is simply the Law of Compensation at work.

THE ROMAN CHURCH   221

4. In the AD 1930s, Germany murdered many of its citizens and neighbors, and particularly the Jews. The Jews were murdered, not because of their conduct or misconduct, but only because of their status as Jews. In 1948, the Jews seized the homeland of the Palestinians. Any claims the Jews made on homeland rights in Israel, based on forged insertions in the **Bible,** were totally fraudulent and without merit. The Jews copied their oppressors.

One of the forgeries Ezra inserted into the **Bible** was in **Genesis 15:18,** which states:

> "*On that day the Lord (note that this was only the Jewish tribal god) made a covenant with Abram (who was a Hebrew and no relation of any kind to the Jews ruling Israel today) and said, 'To your descendants I give this land, from the river (the Nile) to the great river, the Euphrates'....*"

This simple forgery has created untold bloodshed throughout history and even to the present day. Once again, the oppressed became the oppressors. The Jews must pay for every wrong committed against the Palestinians -- every single wrong. All their propaganda to the contrary and all their guns supplied by America notwithstanding, they still must pay in full. Sadly, America must also pay for its part in these matters.

Again, and again, and again, history repeats itself. All causes create multiple effects. All effects are the result of multiple causes. It will continue to be so until the causes cease and the effects of those causes play themselves out. It will continue to be so until the debts are all paid and the lessons are all learned.

There is one, and only one, alternative. That alternative is to allow the teachings of Master Jesus the Christ to enter the world and its institutions. This could conceivably include even the Roman Church and the Jewish community in Israel.

How all of this came about in the Roman Church is a very interesting story. It is the story of the source of Western cultural values. In AD 64, Nero set fire to the older part of Rome. The capital of the world was in flames. For six days and nights great fires raced out of control throughout the imperial city. Insane Roman Emperor Nero played his harp and enjoyed the sights from atop his palace roof. In order to divert suspicion from himself as the arsonist he began one of the most violent extermination efforts in the history of mankind. This persecution continued, off and on, until the time of Roman Emperor Constantine the Great, in AD 312 or so. Nero died in AD 68.

From the time of Nero on, the Christians in the Roman Empire lived on a roller-coaster. There were now and then a few years of relative peace, and then, without warning, another blood bath. In AD 95, Roman Emperor Domitian, the younger son of Roman Emperor Vespasian, and the brother of Roman Emperor Titus, who was the destroyer of Jerusalem, launched a short but very severe persecution of the Christians. Thousands more were slain in this reign of terror.

Again in AD 109, Roman Emperor Trajan launched a short but brutal extermination of the Christians. Bishop Ignatius of Antioch in Syria was thrown to the lions in the Roman Coliseum in AD 110. This was the man who demanded that elders obey the bishop, and the regular congregation obey both the elders and the bishop. This thinking followed the teachings of the Apostle Paul and steered the Roman Church toward becoming a political institution. Such thinking by the bishop had nothing to do with right living or the teachings of Master Jesus the Christ.

Also about this same time in AD 110, a church leader in Rome inserted the Last Supper narrative into the Roman-church mass. The year AD 110 saw the beginning of the complete Romanization and politicization of the Catholic Church. The Last Supper, while it probably did happen, was and is totally irrelevant to the teachings of Master Jesus. This was also just more political hyperbole.

In AD 161, Roman Emperor Aurelius ordered the most harsh persecution of the Christians since Nero. Thousands of Christians were executed. About this same time, in AD 167, Bishop Soter fixed Easter as a holiday on the Sunday following the 14th of the Jewish month Nisan, which is the day of the Jewish Passover. Again however, this formalization of teachings of the Roman Church were totally unrelated to the teachings of Master Jesus. More political hyperbole.

In AD 193, Roman Emperor Severus continued the persecution of the Christians, and thousands of Christians were burned at the stake, crucified, or beheaded. Again in AD 235, Roman Emperor Maximin continued the persecution of the Christians, and thousands more were killed in one way or another. Yet again, in AD 250, Roman Emperor Decius decided to completely exterminate all Christians in the Roman Empire. Again, thousands of Christians were put to death.

In AD 255, **Pope** Stephen I decided to make it appear that the Roman Church actually was the legitimate child of Master Jesus the Christ and one of his assistants known to us as Peter. He inserted into **Matthew 16:18 and 19** the following forgery:

"And I say also unto thee, That thou art Peter, and upon this rock I will build my church; and the gates of Hell shall not prevail against it. And I will give unto thee the keys of the Kingdom of Heaven: and whatsoever thou shall bind on earth shall be bound in heaven: and whatsoever thou shall loose on earth shall be loosed in heaven."

This was an obvious forgery for the one very simple reason that Master Jesus did not teach belief in a hell. **Matthew 16:19** purports to delegate from God to the Roman-church pope the power to decide who goes to Heaven and who goes to hell. That such assertions are forgeries should be apparent to all, and really require no proof. Surely such assertions could not be accepted by any serious-minded person. But they were, unfortunately, accepted by most Roman-church priests.

Pope Stephen I was a very egotistical and uncompromising priest. In 450 BC, Ezra had forged Holy Writ, and Pope Stephen I had learned his history well. He also learned forgery well. What the Jews had done to other people would in the very near future also be done to them. All swords do indeed seem to have two edges.

About AD 285, Roman Emperor Diocletian put into effect another attempt to exterminate all Christians within the Roman Empire. The blood flowed, and tens of thousands of Christians were put to death.

Roman Emperor Constantine the Great was born in AD 288 in central Europe. He would later literally create what is now called the Roman Catholic Church as a basically pagan institution.

About AD 297, Pope Marcellinus, along with three of his assistants who would be future popes, offered pagan sacrifices at the order of Roman Emperor Diocletian. The Roman Church has tried about everything to wipe this obvious blight from its family tree. The historical fact is that four early Roman-church popes were practicing pagans. But that fact should really surprise no one.

The Roman Church first tried to create forged records to show that Pope Marcellinus never existed, then later, that he was not really a pope. When this did not work, they tried to show that he was a church martyr. This same tactic was later used throughout church history. The most prominent example was a second Pope John XXIII in AD 1958. The first Pope John XXIII was such a complete scoundrel that the Roman Church tried hard to pretend that he never was a pope. He was so bad that no other pope adopted the name of **John** for many centuries.

Remember also, that previously in Egypt, Pharaoh Horemheb had also tried to wipe four of his preceding Hebrew-dominated pharaohs from the history books of Egypt. Such playing with history can and sometimes does work, but only when being sold to ignorant, uninformed, and dominated people.

About AD 310, Emperor Constantine was refused admission into AMORC. He later created the Roman Church to exterminate both AMORC and the Blue Lodge. The reason Constantine was refused admission was that he was found to be totally unfit. This was a morally correct decision, but very bad politically, as subsequent events clearly showed.

The Nicene Council met in AD 325 at Nicaea. This town is presently named Iznik and is located in northwest Turkey. The pope at that time was the almost non-person Silvester I. Silvester is best remembered for a forged document known as the **Donation of Constantine**. This document came into being in the AD 800s and stated that Constantine had granted or donated the number one position in the Roman Church to

Silvester and his successors. This document was exposed as a forgery 700 years later in the AD 1500s.

Roman Emperor Constantine did many things, and most of them were bad. The various things started by this one man have produced more murders and more misery for more people in Western culture than any other human being who has ever lived. Some of the things that he did were:

1. He made Christianity into an acceptable state religion of the Roman Empire. A few years earlier, in AD 320, he had prescribed a prayer in the manner of the ancient pagan observance, which tends to show that he was creating the Roman Church as a pagan institution. In AD 380, his successor, Theodosius I, made the Roman Church into the only state religion. This government approval and adoption sealed the church's fate against ever being an institution associated with the true teachings of Master Jesus the Christ.

2. At the infamous council of Nicaea, Constantine called all the Roman-church hierarchy together in order to settle the question of whether God was a trinity, as taught by the pagans and the Apostle Paul, or only a single entity as taught by Master Jesus the Christ and both AMORC and the Blue Lodge. Constantine felt that the issue was totally unimportant, but naturally took the side of the Apostle Paul, and the Roman Church and most Christian churches yet to this day teach a trinity of gods.

This is another example where pagan teachings of the Roman Church put it into conflict with both AMORC and the Muslim world. The **Koran** states in Chapter 9:31 as follows:

"They take their priests And their anchorites to be Their lords in derogation of God, And (they take as their Lord) Christ the son of Mary; Yet they were commanded To worship but One God: There is no god but He. Praise and glory to Him: (Far is He) from having The partners they associate (With Him)."

3. The idea of atonement also was picked up from the Apostle Paul. Paul taught that all men, and particularly women, were evil and doomed to go to hell. Paul liked pagan blood sacrifices. And so he picked up the Greek idea that all heros had to die and created the myth that Master Jesus died as a blood sacrifice, or atonement, for the evils of mankind. Any person who believes in blood sacrifices cannot be a follower of Master Jesus. Any person who is a follower of the Apostle Paul, cannot at the same time, be a follower of Master Jesus. The idea of Master Jesus making some kind of pagan blood sacrifice for mankind was the most vicious libel ever leveled against Master Jesus by the Roman Church.

4. In Rome, Constantine endowed the Basilica of Saint Peter's and basically provided for the papacy, which has now lasted over 1600 years and has spread so very much suffering to everyone, but particularly to women. During the AD 1600s, it is

estimated that one hundred thousand women were burned alive as witches by the Roman Church in Germany alone.

5. Constantine made himself the head of both church and state. In AD 1535, King Henry VIII used this example to make himself head of both church and state. The British monarch remains so today. It was these two events that caused the framers of the Constitution of the United States of America to insert a provision requiring the separation of church and state.

6. Constantine updated the art of war to a new level of success. He started the process of replacing foot soldiers with mounted cavalry, which was much faster and more efficient at killing people.

7. In AD 326, Constantine had his own wife, Fausta, and his eldest son, plus his deputy emperor, Crispus, all murdered. He also had tens of thousands of other people murdered for one perceived reason or another. Yes, this is the man who created the Roman Church in his own image.

8. In earlier times, prior to AD 110, church laymen and the church leaders were considered equal, but by this time only the church bishops could perform some church rites. The Roman Church was now only another oppressive and decadent social institution totally out of touch with its source.

9. The gnostics, or people of knowledge, were barred from the Roman Church. People of knowledge have remained barred from the Roman Church even down to the present day. From that period on, until even today, the most important quality for any Roman-church member to have was ignorance. Only church leaders had access to knowledge, and they might share a little of that knowledge with others, but only for a usurious fee, which they called a tithe.

A Roman-church priest will tell you that all men should help do God's work on Earth. That is true. Next, the priest will tell you to give ten percent of your income to the Roman Church, which, it is implied, does God's work. This, of course, is patently false. Can anyone imagine the debt incurred under the Law of Compensation by a priest who lies to some poor innocent soul and leads him to believe that he, the priest, knows God's will, and that he, the priest, is doing God's work. No man on Earth knows God's will, and no man on Earth knows for sure whether he is doing God's work or not. Man can think, hope, and believe, but man cannot know God's will. All priests who imply otherwise do not tell the truth. Any man who says that he knows God's will is really saying that he is equal to God. Such a position taken by anyone should require the most extraordinary proof.

Roman Emperor Constantine the Great died in AD 337. Water was poured on his forehead and he was declared baptized on his death bed and was therefore saved from all of his many sins, according to the pagan Roman Church.

The Roman Church yet today honors Constantine the Great, who was one of the most evil men in the history of Western culture. Not to be out-done by the Roman Church, the Jews still today honor King David of Israel, who was also a very evil person. It must be true that humans honor those whom they, themselves, would like to emulate.

Adolph Hitler was also an evil person. There are few people around today who honor him, but who knows what will happen in the future? Is it conceivable that history will forget the 50 million or so people that Hitler murdered, and only remember some of the great technical advances created during his reign of terror? Perhaps not, but do not forget King David, Emperor Constantine, and Saint Augustine. History does indeed repeat itself, over and over again. Man simply does not learn, except only with the most extreme pain and suffering.

Certainly, none of those changes happened overnight. Some had been in the process of development prior to Constantine, and some came only into full use after him. But Constantine was the one man, more than any other, who made the Roman Church into the very political and financial institution that it became over the next 1600 years or so. Constantine provided the politics and money and Augustine supplied the theology. Saint Augustine later inserted the theology into the church political institution created by Constantine. After that, the Roman Church became a completely pagan institution, a mighty power promoting murder, deceit, suffering, and ignorance for all mankind down to the present day. And the end is not yet in sight.

Even as we write, the Roman Church still teaches the inferiority of women and the power of the priests to control women's bodies. It still sometimes threatens a sentence to hell for persons who disagree with it. The Roman-church pope still actually believes that he can sentence people to hell, even though he must know that those insertions into the **New Testament** granting him such powers are forgeries. What karma this all creates! The Roman Church has not changed very much since the time of Constantine. If Master Jesus the Christ appeared on Earth again today, he would be persecuted by the Roman Church the same as he was by the priests the last time he was here.

Saint Augustine was born in AD 354. He fathered an illegitimate son at age eighteen. He became a professor of literature and rhetoric in both Carthage and Rome. Augustine converted to Christianity in AD 387, at age 33, and became the man who would most control Roman-church theology up to the present day. The great library at Alexandria was burned in AD 400 by the Roman Church, and Western culture devolved into the Dark Ages.

Although AMORC teachings of Master Jesus the Christ had been taken to Carthage by Hannibal in about 200 BC, Augustine never came into contact with those teachings and so he knew them not. That was an unfortunate turn of historical events. With his ability, had he known Master Jesus' teachings, Augustine could have become a powerful tool for good in the world. However, he knew them not and the things he came to believe and teach sealed the fate of the Roman Church as a more-or-less criminal organization throughout the next thousand years. This situation did not change until the Reformation in the AD 1500s, and then only very little. Some of Augustine's teachings, which still prevail in the Roman Church, were:

1. That sex was evil and women were the transmitters of original sin through their sex organs. Augustine, who was a whoremonger himself until his conversion, probably came to this opinion because of his own excessive sexual appetite. He gave up marriage, and very shortly thereafter, priests were also expected to forego marriage. Just like the Apostle Paul, Augustine held women in very low esteem, which only reflected on his own lack of enlightenment and not at all on the quality of women in general.

Later, priests were barred from marriage, and the Roman Church tried very hard to make it appear as though Master Jesus had never married. This was the source of the Roman-church dogma of original sin, which has no basis in anything except paganism. Master Jesus certainly taught and believed in marriage, so those teachings were just the opposite from the teachings of Master Jesus. The Roman Church opposed the teachings of Master Jesus.

2. Augustine endorsed the policy of the Roman Empire to use force to suppress what Augustine and the Roman Church considered to be heresy. Obviously, such views were totally the opposite of those of Master Jesus, and they eliminated completely any association the Roman Church still had with his teachings. This rationale later was used by the Roman Church to set up the infamous and dreaded Inquisition, which was authorized to use torture to exact confessions from its defenseless victims. This practice was the opposite of the teachings of Master Jesus, who spread knowledge of God without the use of force. Again, the Roman Church opposed the teachings of Master Jesus.

3. Augustine was a follower of the apostle Paul, who we have already seen was not a follower of Master Jesus. Master Jesus taught and believed in baptism as symbolic of a rebirth of man, who must be born again. Master Jesus was himself baptized as an adult. Adult baptism, such as Master Jesus experienced, was a proper rite. Infant baptism as taught by the Roman Church was done in order to rid the child of the original sin transmitted to it by its mother's sex organs at birth and to obtain money.

The doctrine of original sin was a political expediency created in order to maintain and support the Roman-church priesthood economically. It had nothing to do with right living or the teachings of Master Jesus. Again, the Roman Church opposed the teachings of Master Jesus.

4. Augustine also adopted the ancient idea of a trinity of gods as taught by the ancient Egyptians and Hindus, but he tried, through some hocus pocus, to merge these three gods metaphysically into one. The term hocus pocus comes from the words of the Latin mass: "*Hoc est enim corpus meus*" (...for this is my body). Certainly, a trinity of gods was never the teaching of Master Jesus. Again, the Roman Church opposed the teachings of Master Jesus.

5. Augustine developed and approved the idea of the just Holy War. This teaching was that it was okay and moral to kill people in order to convert them. Augustine never explained the obvious contradiction of how you convert dead people.

About 200 years after his time, the Muslims used Augustine's idea of a just Holy War to slaughter tens of thousands of Christians. The Holy War against the Christians by the Muslims was okay and very moral, according to Roman-church teachings. However, the Roman Church, in taking serious exception to the Muslims' Holy War, violated its own teachings. How could a Holy War be just by Christians, unless it was also just against Christians?

The Shiite Muslims and their holy wars are a scourge on modern civilization. Where did they learn such conduct? Correct: from the Roman Church. And again, the Roman Church opposed the teachings of Master Jesus.

6. Augustine also believed and taught that all men were doomed to hell. The only way man could avoid burning in hell throughout eternity was by God's grace, which could only be delivered to man by the Roman Church. Obviously, this was another political expediency that kept mankind economically committed to support the Roman-church priesthood, and had nothing to do with right living or the teachings of Master Jesus. Quite the contrary, Master Jesus taught that all of mankind will someday be saved. The idea that all of mankind will eventually be saved was also the prediction set forth in **The Revelation**, in the symbolism of 666. And yet again, the Roman Church opposed the teachings of Master Jesus.

Over a period of several hundred years the Apostles' Creed slowly developed. It did not evolve into final form until about AD 750. The text, as reported much later in **Martin Luther's Small Catechism**, with inserted observations by the author, is as follows:

"*I believe in God the Father Almighty, Maker of heaven and earth. I believe in Jesus Christ, His only Son,...*" Not true: all men and women, including Master Jesus the Christ, are equally children of God.

THE ROMAN CHURCH 229

"*...our Lord, who was conceived by the Holy Ghost,...*" Not true: Master Jesus was conceived by his parents, Joseph and Mary.

"*...born of the Virgin Mary,...*" Mary may have been a virgin, but virgin, at that time, only meant a young girl who had not yet started her menstrual cycle.

"*...suffered under Pontius Pilate, was crucified, dead,...*" No, Master Jesus did not die at that time.

"*...and buried;...*" He was placed in a room above ground, but was not buried in the usual sense.

"*...He descended into Hell;...*" Hell exists only as a state of mind, and since there is no hell Jesus certainly never went there.

"*...the third day He rose...*" It was more likely that he left the so-called tomb later that same day. In any event, Sunday was only the second day after Friday.

"*...again from the dead;...*" Dead, Master Jesus certainly was not, as many people talked to him in person within the next two or three days, all as is reported in the **New Testament.**

"*...He ascended into heaven, and sitteth on the right hand of God the Father Almighty; from thence He shall come to judge...*" Master Jesus never, ever, judged any person.

"*...the quick and the dead. I believe in the Holy Ghost;...*" Master Jesus taught only the One True God of the universe.

"*...the holy Roman Church,...*" Master Jesus did not teach that man needed a go-between with God.

"*...the communion of saints; the forgiveness of sins;...*" Yes, the sins of self.

"*...the resurrection of the body;...*" How gross; the physical body has little importance and must pass away, back to the dust of Earth whence it came.

"*...and the life everlasting....*" Yes, life everlasting; that is true. It is true regardless of man's merit or lack thereof. "*...Amen....*"

The Apostles' Creed was not exactly first class literature, but it was believed by many uninformed Roman-church members. Some still do, even today.

230 TRUE ESOTERIC TRADITIONS

Constantine and Augustine created the Roman Church as a political and financial institution based on ancient pagan theological belief systems. That church has been an instrument of terror to mankind, even to the present day.

How many of the teachings of the Roman Church still had anything to do with the teachings of Master Jesus the Christ by the time of Saint Augustine? Not very many. The Roman Church taught:

1. That the pagan holiday of December 25 was the birthday of Master Jesus. Not so.

2. That Easter was the day of Master Jesus' resurrection from the dead. Not so.

3. That a trinity of gods ruled the universe. Not so.

4. That man needed the Roman Church for salvation. Not so.

5. That man needed a priest for salvation. Not so.

6. That men were more moral than women. Not so.

7. That proper marriage could only take place in the Roman Church. Not so.

8. That infant baptism was needed to save babies from the original sin transmitted to them from their mothers. Not so.

9. That popes were more moral than ordinary people. Not so.

10. That bishops were more moral than ordinary people. Not so.

11. That priests were more moral than ordinary people. Not so.

12. That Master Jesus was a blood sacrifice for mankind. Not so.

13. That the Roman Church taught about Master Jesus. Not so.

14. That the Roman Church was a lineal descendent of Master Jesus. Not so.

15. That the Roman Church taught about God. Not so.

16. That the Freemasons were enemies of Master Jesus. Not so.

17. That the Freemasons were enemies of the Roman Church. Yes, very true.

18. That the Rosicrucians were enemies of the Roman Church. Also very true.

19. That the Roman Church did more good than evil. That was and is an open question!

Note that the Roman Church has been used as an instrument of terror. Any institution which has been used as an instrument of terror can also be used as an instrument for good. That had to be one of the hopes of mankind as the world enters the so-called Age of Aquarius. Seeds are planted by people such as Mother Theresa.

AMORC taught that in the Age of Aquarius a new world teacher will come whose name will be John and who will also take the Christ initiation. The Christ will come again, it is predicted. It is said that this prediction is set forth symbolically in the seal of the United States as shown on the back of a dollar bill. John's symbol is the eagle.

Is it possible that a third John XXIII could incarnate as pope of the Roman Church? Is it possible that this could be the John predicted by AMORC? We wonder.

At this time the Roman Church, for the most part, simply is not a very respectable institution. Is it possible for the Roman Church ever to gain respectability, either within itself or with its neighbors? It is possible, but is not likely to happen in the near future. Two things are essential for that ever to happen:

1. The Roman Church needs to get out of politics. This means getting out of the baby-breeding business, the government-policy business, and beginning to concentrate on helping individual people achieve enlightenment. Truly-enlightened people can and will produce only good governmental policy.

2. The Roman Church needs to stop sponging off its neighbors which, in truth, is pure theft. Without exception, to the author's knowledge, all Christian churches throughout the world demand and accept police and fire protection and other services from local communities without paying for them. This is theft pure and simple. It is very difficult for a thief to convince others not to steal.

When the Roman Church gets out of politics, and stops its very immoral thievery, mankind might look to that church for true leadership in the future.

This was the pagan Roman Church created by Roman Emperor Constantine and his successors, based on the teachings of the Apostle Paul. Can such an institution founded on deceit, oppression, murder, and about every evil known to mankind ever really change?

A woman's
right to control
her own body is fundamental.
Without that right, women have no rights.

As long as
women look to
organized religion
to protect their rights,
they will be the slaves of men.

There are
things worse than
death and one of them
is life without dignity or purpose.

CHAPTER THIRTEEN -- THE DARK AGES

It is not possible even to discuss Western civilization after the time of Constantine without taking into account the actions of the Roman Church. The story of the Roman Church during the next thousand years was one of complex political and military intrigue beyond any ever recorded in earlier history.

All Freemasons and Rosicrucians that could be identified were tracked down by the Roman Church and executed. Speaking only under the rose, or sub rosa, once again became a rule for survival for both Freemasons and Rosicrucians. That is, a rose hanging in the center of a meeting room indicated that all present were sworn to secrecy.

In most of those intrigues, the pope in Rome eventually won out, either by hook or by crook. The cause of those victories was usually a lack of competent leadership in the opposition, and the persuasive power of the forgeries in the **New Testament** stating that the Roman-church pope was the official representative of Master Jesus on Earth. The Roman-church popes have always claimed Master Jesus because of the power this gives them over other people, but they have never yet accepted or taught his teachings.

Actually, the pope claimed to be more important and more powerful even than Master Jesus himself. The pope claimed the power to decide who would go to Heaven and who would go to hell. That was a very potent weapon in AD 400 and throughout the next thousand years of the Dark Ages. Master Jesus certainly never had and did not claim any such power for himself. In fact, Master Jesus taught just the opposite, which was that each human must determine his or her own destiny.

The devolution of the Roman Church finally reached the point of the creation of the so-called Holy Roman Empire on Christmas Day of AD 800. The Holy Roman Empire was the effort to put all of Western culture under one leader in a theocracy, the same as Ezra did to the Jews in 450 BC.

The pope wanted to head the Empire and have all local kings serve only at the pope's pleasure. The plan was first to subjugate all of the Western governments and then eventually the whole world. To carry this off would require the destruction of all knowledge and the sources of all information in the entire world. This was the curse, not the donation, of Roman Emperor Constantine.

While the Roman Church consolidated its power more and more in the hands of fewer and fewer people, an event was unfolding which would become a force to split asunder the Roman Church a thousand years later.

In AD 409, after the Roman legions left Britain, a breakup of all society and a tremendous vacuum occurred there. England was not created until the time of King Alfred the Great in AD 871. Consequently, into that vacuum in Britain and southern Scotland, in AD 490, the legendary King Arthur the Great came to the throne.

Until recently, Arthur was thought to have been only a legendary king who never actually existed. Only recently has it been determined that Arthur was indeed a real king. In 1986, after years of research, Norma Lorre Goodrich wrote her book **King Arthur**, which clearly showed that Arthur certainly did exist and that he was king in the Scottish lowlands.

The legendary Christian King, Arthur the Great, was born in AD 475 on what is today the southern-most tip of Scotland, just south of present day Dumfries, on the coast of Solway Firth. Camelot Castle was located just west of the present city of Carlisle, near the western end of Hadrian's Wall on Solway Firth.

King Arthur's kingdom comprised mostly the Scottish lowlands, much of which was actually ruled over by his wife and queen, Guinevere. The southern border was a line running generally from Newcastle Upon Tyne on the east to Morecambe Bay on the west. The northern boundary ran generally from Dumbarton on the west to the River and Firth of Forth on the east.

The marvelous magician Merlin made his home at the site of the famous legendary round table and the so-called Grail Castle, on the Isle of Man which, in King Arthur's time, was called Avalon. The Grail Castle was on the west side of the island facing Ireland. Merlin was a very wise man and probably was a Druid priest. This means that he was privy to the teachings of AMORC and Master Jesus the Christ. Lancelot's castle was located near Sterling, northwest of Edinburgh, on the River Forth.

King Arthur was crowned king about AD 490 at the tender age of 15 years. He led the Celts in many bitter battles against the pagan Saxons and apparently won them all. He did put an end to war for a while, so that there was peace in his kingdom over a substantial period of time, perhaps for as long as 40 years.

King Arthur was married to the beautiful Guinevere, who was a queen in her own right and chief of state over her own territory. The queen was kidnapped, and King Arthur sent Sir Gawain and Sir Lancelot to recapture the queen and bring her back home again. The stories of the queen's sexual capers are probably not historically true. Those romantic stories were created by writers more than 500 years after the queen's death.

The mighty King Arthur was seriously injured in a battle near Hadrian's Wall in AD 542. He was removed from the field of battle and taken by boat to the Isle of Man. Apparently, King Arthur died from his wounds on the Isle of Man very soon thereafter. Stories about King Arthur being buried at Glastonbury in Western England, and about the Holy Grail Cup, supposedly taken there by Joseph of Arimathea, are not historically accurate. That was all just a big tourist promotion that took place about AD 1160 or so and was encouraged by King Henry II.

Exhibit 44: The northern area of England and southern Scotland showing the area where King Arthur the Great reigned

The legends about King Arthur, who was a great military and civilian leader, and his sage advisor Merlin, created an image of a Camelot where both church and state were joined into one center of enlightened leadership. This joining of church and state, but without the enlightenment, was what Emperor Constantine had also done earlier in the Roman Empire. Later, Henry VIII did the same thing.

Henry VIII's joining of church and state was not as ideal as King Arthur's because he did not have a Merlin as advisor, but it was much better than that of Constantine. Henry VIII was an effective, but totally ruthless, ruler who murdered anyone who got in his way, including two of his wives. Henry would have fitted into the mold of Roman-church pope perfectly.

In AD 570, a few years after Arthur's death, a man was born who would start a new religion that would be a much more massive threat to the Roman Church than Henry VIII. The man was Muhammad, the religion was Islam, and the followers of that religion were called Muslims. The Muslims use a calendar beginning with AD 622 as year one. That was the year Muhammad made his escape and flight from Mecca to Medina.

Islam followed the teachings of the six major prophets: Adam, Noah, Abraham, Moses, Master Jesus, and Muhammad. Unlike the Roman Church, which taught a trinity of gods, and Judaism which taught only a Jewish tribal god, Islam taught One True God for all of mankind, the same as Master Jesus.

In Islam, there were no sacraments, no idols, and no corporate rituals. No public worship was required. The Muslims taught fasting and the giving of 2.5% of income to the poor. Up to this point, Islam was almost identical to the teachings of AMORC and Master Jesus the Christ. That was one very good reason why AMORC teachings survived in the Muslim world after the burning of the great library at Alexandria, Egypt, by the Roman Church in AD 400.

The Muslims also knew all about Ezra and the Jews, and how the Jews forged Holy Writ by adding false material to the **Bible**. Islam was a much higher and much holier religion than Christianity, Hinduism, or Judaism in many ways. That was exactly the reason that within a hundred years Islam spread like wild-fire across north Africa, the Middle East, into India, and even into Europe. That rapid expansion into Europe came to a screeching halt at the Battle of Tours in France in AD 732.

The Muslim Army came out of Spain in vast numbers with all of their families and movable property as though they intended to stay in France forever. The Frankish Army, led by Charles Martel, after seven days of bloody fighting finally prevailed. This stopped the Muslim advance into Europe.

The estimates of the men killed in this battle vary greatly, but probably up to 350,000 or more men were actually killed in the battle. That would make it the bloodiest single battle in history. Some results of the Battle of Tours were the Christian Crusades to Jerusalem, beginning in AD 1095. Because of the extremely good fortune of the Christians under Charles Martel in winning this victory against overwhelming odds, the Roman-church popes got the mistaken idea that a few good Christians, with God's help of course, could whip any number of Muslims, regardless of the time, place, or circumstances.

In spite of their loss at the Battle of Tours, Islam remained a powerful force opposing Christian expansion, even up to the present day.

The rapid success of Islam can be attributed to at least four things:

1. Its devotion to a single universal deity without partners;

2. Its absolute simplicity without symbols and sacraments;

3. Its belief in a future life to come; and

4. Its fanaticism.

Islam also taught that Muhammad was a prophet of God, but he was only a man and should not be worshiped. Muhammad also disdained grandeur and miracle working and shunned them both in his own very simple life. He personally gave most of his own income to the poor. He also taught against betting and usury and the use of wine and pork, and also of meat killed in certain ways. This also included prohibiting the use of drugs and coffee. And like most other religions, he also taught against murder, theft, sexual excess, and slander.

The holy book of Islam is the **Koran**. It was written entirely by Muhammad and was in its present form within twenty years after his death. Compare this to the **Bible** and the **New Testament** which were both written over several hundreds of years by many different people and which have been edited, re-edited, translated, and re-translated, added to and subtracted from, to such an extent that it has been very difficult, if not impossible, to decipher the meaning of the original teachings.

However, the fact that the **Bible** was impossible to interpret made it possible for Western culture to advance. On the other hand, the **Koran** was crystal clear in its meaning and that has made it impossible, up to this point, for women to achieve equality in Muslim countries.

But not all of Muhammad's teachings compared favorably with those of AMORC and Master Jesus the Christ:

1. Prior to Muhammad's time, in what is now Saudi Arabia, many new-born girl babies were destroyed by being buried alive. Muhammad forbad such practices, and he also taught that females should inherit one-half of a male's share. However, women were still thought to be sinful creatures by nature and were required to be veiled. That meant that like the Apostle Paul, but unlike Master Jesus, Muhammad did not teach the moral equality of the sexes.

2. Muhammad adopted the idea of the just Holy War from Saint Augustine of the Roman Church and used it very effectively against that same church. He who sows violence does indeed inherit the wind. The Roman Church has inherited the wind.

3. Muhammad believed fervently in the One True God, as did Master Jesus. However, he also believed that the end can justify the means, and that force was acceptable in order to require a belief in the One True God. Master Jesus never accepted or taught the use of force.

4. Muhammad taught belief in a hell with very vivid and man-conceived punishments. Master Jesus did not. Muhammad's description of Heaven with jewels and beautiful women certainly lowers the image of the religion he taught. However, he was a very poetic man, and so perhaps he was only exercising poetic license.

5. Muhammad taught that every Muslim should, once in his or her life-time, make a pilgrimage to Mecca, if he or she were able to do so. This was an economic concession to the religious leaders in Mecca. A rose by any other name would smell as sweet, and a priest by any other name would still be a priest.

6. Muhammad also seemed to teach predestination, which denied free will to man, but he equivocated on those ideas somewhat. The teaching of a totally powerful and totally controlling God can easily lead to the error of predestination. Master Jesus taught that man, like God, does have free will and not even God knows what man will do until he does it.

7. Muhammad taught that a man was allowed four wives, apparently to make use of the many girl babies no longer killed at birth.

Whereas, Master Jesus was the most educated man of his time, Muhammad was brilliant, but he probably could neither read nor write. Both Master Jesus and Muhammad tried to teach the Jews and both failed. Like Master Jesus, Muhammad was a man of striking appearance and features, and he had an attractive, powerful personality. His teachings remain some of the most important concerns of mankind to the present day.

Shortly after the defeat of the Muslims in AD 732 at the Battle of Tours, the Roman Church assumed almost total control of Western culture. This was about AD 750, the same time that the Apostles' Creed became a fixed dogma.

In AD 754, the Frankish King Pippin legitimized the rule of the Roman popes over the papal states in central Italy. Pippin's son, Charlemagne, was a great king in many ways. First, he was seven feet tall, which, in that day, would be the equivalent of being eight feet tall today. He was truly a dominating figure, the average height of European males in the AD 800s being only about five feet.

Charlemagne's empire included most of what today is Western Europe. He made Latin the official language of his diverse realm, and ordered all bishops to set up schools. He totally reconstituted the social, political, and religious unity of Western Europe.

On Christmas Day in AD 800 at mass in Saint Peter's in Rome, Pope Leo conned Charlemagne into being crowned emperor of the Romans by the pope; and thus the Holy Roman Empire was born. The emperor had allowed himself to be subordinated to the pope. That act would haunt the kings in all the countries of the West until King Henry VIII in England in AD 1535. Indeed, it haunts the rulers of many countries of Central and South America even to the present day.

Even though South America enjoys natural resources greater than those in the United States, it has never been allowed to develop and prosper like the United States. The reason for this has been that the Roman-church popes still today control South America, and have kept it under-developed and under-educated in order both to control it and to siphon off its wealth to Rome. The real story of the revolution in Nicaragua, in the 1980s, had to do with the resistance by the people to the pope and to domination by Rome. That revolution had nothing whatever to do with communism.

Charlemagne heard rumors about AMORC and Blue-Lodge teachings of the Freemasons and Rosicrucians. He was intrigued and sent out agents to search for them. Actually Charlemagne, although uneducated himself, was a true seeker after knowledge.

It was perhaps unfortunate that Charlemagne never located AMORC or its teachings. However, Charlemagne was much too close to the Roman Church to be trusted, and he never was allowed access to any AMORC teachings. The reason for that was simple enough. If Charlemagne found out and then told the pope, all exposed Freemasons and Rosicrucians could expect to be executed. Sub rosa was the law of AMORC and it was enforced at that time.

The reader might well ask: Has the Roman-church papacy ever been accused of any evil act for which it was not guilty? The answer is yes, and the story concerns a mythical female pope named Joan. During the AD 1200s, the story was circulated that a beautiful and learned Anglo-Saxon girl began her career disguised as a monk.

According to the story, she ultimately went to Rome and was elected pope in AD 855. In AD 858, Pope Joan supposedly gave birth to a baby during a public procession in Rome and shortly thereafter died from grief and shame.

The story is not true, but it is interesting from several points of view. The Roman popes had murdered literally millions of people. Some of the popes were themselves murdered, but none ever died from grief or shame for his evil deeds.

The Roman Church accepted and could accommodate mass murder, but not the birth of a human child. How strange! This shows once again that the Roman Church believed and taught that females were basically evil because of original sin, and so they could not conceivably ever have qualified as popes. The Roman Church was a morally bankrupt institution at that time.

Nuns and many other women accepted such foolishness, and still do to the present day. In point of fact, some female popes would have been the best thing that could have happened to the Roman Church and Western culture during the Dark Ages.

The story of a Pope Joan probably evolved from a very powerful lady named Marozia who actually ruled Rome from AD 926 to 932. She was an extremely brilliant, sexy, and immoral lady. Really, except for her sex, she would have fit right in as a pope. She wedded several men, murdered some of them, and bedded down with several more. Her bastard son, her grandson, and her great-grandson inherited Marozia's qualities and all became popes. She was over-thrown by her own son, Alberic, who held her in a dungeon totally isolated for the rest of her life. Such was the disgrace of the already morally defunct Roman Church at that time.

Meanwhile, over in England, some things had happened that would make it possible for the Roman Church to some day rid England of almost all of those pre-Roman-church Christians whose descendants still survived there. These were the cultural descendants of King Arthur, Merlin, and the Druids.

The king known as Alfred the Great came to the throne in AD 871. He was described in the **Anglo-Saxon Chronicles** as the first king to reign over all of England. He was a great scholar. It was during his reign that the **Anglo-Saxon Chronicles** were assembled and distributed. Since Alfred had unified all of England under one authority, it would now be possible for the Roman Church, through William the Conqueror, to subjugate all of England in one big campaign. Alfred reigned until AD 899 and spent most of his life defending England from the Danish Vikings, most of whom were pagans.

It was Alfred who first grew weary of continual warfare in the English country-side. He made peace with the Danes. He constructed a fleet of ships and headed England toward becoming the sea-faring nation that it has remained for the last thousand years. Since AD 1066, England has fought its wars with external enemies on the oceans and in other countries; but not in England. The Roman Church, in the form of William the Conqueror, finally did capture England in AD 1066, when William defeated King Harold at the Battle of Hastings. Halley's comet also visited the Solar System in that same year and helped further the legend that the comet was an evil omen of bad things to come.

A very long, very detailed, and very beautiful tapestry called the Bayeux tapestry was made at that time. It concerns all of the details of the Battle of Hastings. That well-preserved tapestry may be seen yet today in Normandy. It was not historically accurate, but was very beautiful and very well done.

The Roman Church had been trying to stamp out the descendants of the original Christians in the British Isles who were there prior to the establishment of the church in Rome. That work had been partly carried out earlier by Augustine of Canterbury in Britain and Saint Patrick in Ireland. This was just one more effort to finalize that extermination process, but it never completely succeeded, as later events showed.

One result of the Norman conquest was that the English courts were now forced to use French, while the local population spoke Old English and Danish. This resulted in double-talk by the lawyers who wrote documents in both the French and English languages so that both the court and local people could understand them.

Exhibit 45: Bayeux Tapestry made in the late 1000s. Note the minute details of the Battle of Hastings in AD 1066

That double-talking still haunts legal documents throughout the English speaking world even to the present day. Such double-talking phrases as Last Will and Testament, null and void, wedding and marriage, devise and bequeath, heirs and legatees, and on and on, are still used in legal documents today.

William the Conqueror was also the man who created what has become known as the **Domesday Book.** That was a complete census of all of the property in England which William caused to be made in AD 1085 so that taxes could be properly assessed and collected. If one's property was listed in the **Domesday Book,** then one had to pay -- and pay -- and pay. And thus, the internal revenue services of the English-speaking world were born and still prosper even to the present day.

In AD 1160 or so in England, King Henry II tried to create a Camelot, but he was not able to take the church leadership away from Rome. He surrounded himself with educated men who obviously would not hold the Roman Church and its priesthood in very high regard. About this time one scornful poem about the Roman Church priesthood that was allowed to circulate stated in part:

"...*The lion is the* **Pope,** *that useth to devour,*
And laiethe his bookes to pledge and thirsteth aftir gold,
And dothe regard the marke, but sainct Marke dishonor,
And while he sailes alofte on coyne takes anker holde.

"*And to the* **Bisshoppe** *in the caulfe that we did see,*
For he dothe runne before in pasture, feild, and fenne,
And gnawes and chewes on that where he list best to be,
And thus he filles himselfe with goodes of other men.

"*Th' Archdeacon* *is likewise the egell that dothe flie,*
A robber rightlie cald, and sees a-farre his praie,
And aftir it with speed dothe follow by and by,
And so by theft and spoile he leades his life awaie.

"*The* **Deane** *is he that hathe the face and shape of man,*
Withe fraude, desceipt, and guile fraught full as he may be,
And yet dothe hide and cloke the same as he best can,
Undir pretense and shewe of plaine simplicitie.

"*And theis have winges to flye, eche one of these said foure,*
Because they flye abrode, and lie about affaires,
And they have eyes eche one, because that everye houre,
They looke about for gaine, and all that may be theires...."

After the time of King Henry II, England remained opposed to the Roman Church. Henry's son, Bad King John of Robin Hood fame, tried even harder to join church and state but also without success. It remained for King Henry VIII, in AD 1535, to finally get the job done.

By the early AD 1300s troubadours in England were denouncing the pope and priests as traitors to their sacred trust. Here is a poem by Raimon de Cornet in AD 1310:

"...I see the pope his sacred trust betray,
For while the rich his grace can gain alway,
His favors from the poor are aye withholden.
He strives to gather wealth as best he may,
Forcing Christ's people blindly to obey,
So that he may repose in garments golden.
The vilest traffickers in souls are all
His chapmen, and for gold a prebend's stall
He'll sell them, or an abbacy or miter.
And to us he sends clowns and tramps who crawl
Vending his pardon briefs from cot to hall --
Letters and pardons worthy of the writer,
Which leaves our pokes, if not our souls, the lighter.

"No better is each honored cardinal.
From early morning's dawn to evening's fall,
Their time is passed in eagerly contriving
To drive some bargain foul with each and all.
So if you feel a want, or great or small,
Or if for some preferment you are striving,
The more you please to give the more 'twill bring,
Be it a purple cap or bishop's ring.
And it need ne'er in any way alarm you
That you are ignorant of everything
To which a minister of Christ should cling,
You will have revenue enough to warm you --
And, bear in mind, the lesser gifts won't harm you.

"Our bishops, too, are plunged in similar sin,
For pitilessly they flay the very skin
From all their priests who chance to have fat livings.
For gold their seal official you can win
To any writ, no matter what's therein.
Sure God alone can make them stop their thievings.
'Twere hard, in full, their evil works to tell,
As when, for a few pence they greedily sell

*The tonsure to some mountebank or jester,
Whereby the temporal courts are wronged as well,
For then these tonsured rogues they cannot quell,
Howe'er their scampish doings may us pester,
While round the church still growing evils fester.*

"Then as for all the priests and minor clerks,
*There are, God knows, too many of them whose works
And daily life belie their daily teaching.
Scarce better are they than so many Turks,
Though they, no doubt, may be well taught -- it irks
Me not to own the fullness of their teaching --
For, learned or ignorant, they're ever bent
To make a traffic of each sacrament,
The mass's holy sacrifice included;
And when they shrive an honest penitent,
Who will not bribe, his penance they augment,
For honesty should never be obtruded --
But this, by sinners fair, is easily eluded.*

"'Tis true the monks and friars make ample show
*Of rules austere which they all undergo,
But this the vainest is of all pretenses.
In sooth, they live full twice as well, we know,
As e'er they did at home, despite their vow,
And all their mock parade of abstinences.
No jollier life than theirs can be, indeed;
And specially the begging friars exceed,
Whose frock grants license as abroad they wander.
These motives 'tis which to the Orders lead
So many worthless men, in sorest need
Of pelf, which on their vices they may squander,
And then,* **the frock protects them in their plunder....**"

Germany, like England, was also becoming anti-Roman Church. About this same time in Germany a poet named Walter von der Vogelweide made similar sport at the pope's expense:

"*...St. Peter's chair is filled to-day as well
As when 'twas fouled by Gerbert's sorcery;*

"**For he consigned himself alone to hell,**
*While this pope thither drags all Christentie.
Why are the chastisements of Heaven delayed?*

How long wilt thou in slumber lie, O Lord?

"Thy work is hindered and thy word gainsaid,
Thy treasurer steals the wealth that thou hast stored.
Thy ministers rob here and murder there,
And o'er thy sheep a wolf has shepherd's care...."

The **Gerbert** referred to above is Pope Sylvester II, who was pope from AD 999 to AD 1003, and who reportedly practiced sorcery. From this it can be seen that the Roman Church, even at this early time period, had become pretty much of a farce among educated people.

In AD 1215, Henry II's youngest son, Bad King John, was forced to sign the Magna Carta, which was one of the great documents of all time. This Great Charter provided, or really only implied, freedom of the church, strict administration of justice, including due process of law, the protection of life, liberty, and property, consent of the people to taxation, and trial by a jury of peers. It became much of the basis for the **United States Constitution** and many other laws in the United States of America.

The real story of Magna Carta began on October 14, AD 1066 when William the Conqueror landed at Hastings, on the southeast coast of England, and killed the English King Harold. William attended mass before joining the battle and carried the papal banner which showed the pope's blessing on his expedition. William was coronated king of England at Westminster on Christmas Day in 1066.

William immediately appropriated most of the real estate in England and gave it to his followers. About 500 years later, Henry VIII followed this example when he also seized much of this same real estate, by now owned by the Roman Church, and gave it to his followers. William also decreed a nation-wide tax, based on the **Domesday Book**, which provided the English government with a substantial treasury.

The major cause of the conflict in England, which gave rise to Magna Carta, was Richard the Lionhearted. He seized the throne from his father, Henry II, after defeating him in battle in AD 1189. England was a wealthy nation when Richard became king but he squandered the treasury on crusades and other domestic and foreign misadventures, much like the United States is doing in the late AD 1900s.

Richard was the worst king England ever had in its long history. He was bad to everyone, worse still to his friends, and worst of all to himself and his country. He left his younger brother, Bad King John, with a bankrupt country, and thus John had to beg, borrow, and even steal money from the English people. John was a much smarter and much better king than Richard, but both men suffered from ungovernable rage, an unquenchable thirst for both women and money, and both had consummate arrogance. And thus, Magna Carta became necessary.

Bad King John agreed to the original Magna Carta in AD 1215. John died and the Great Charter was re-done in AD 1216, followed by a very comprehensive revision in AD 1225. Over the years, the British Parliament amended and repealed several sections of Magna Carta; however, some parts still remain the law of the land in most all English-speaking countries, including the United States of America, even to the present day. The following quotations from Magna Carta are the author's literal translation thereof, translated into Modern English. In the following discussion, we do not distinguish among the various versions of the document.

Magna Carta provided:

> 1. *"FIRST, we have granted to God, ...that the English Church shall be free, and shall have all her rights entire and her liberties inviolate; ... We have also granted to all freemen of our kingdom, ...all the liberties set forth herein, to be had and held by them and their heirs, ...for ever...."*

Magna Carta began with a grant of freedom to the English church. Note that it states the **English Church** rather than the Roman Church. This particular section was substantially copied from the coronation charter of Henry I, more than a hundred years earlier, in AD 1100.

The grant of liberties to **freemen** applied only to perhaps ten per cent of the population at the time. During the reign of Elizabeth I, in the late AD 1500s, Edward Coke stated that the Magna Carta grant applied to **all** Englishmen and that interpretation became fully accepted. Since that time, all Englishmen, which includes Americans, have enjoyed the liberties granted by Magna Carta.

On the issue of religion, England and the US took exactly opposite courses. England supports state religion, whereas the US shuns official sanction of all religions.

> 2. *"A WIDOW, shall have her marriage portion and her inheritance immediately and without obstruction, nor shall she give anything for her dower or for her marriage portion, or for her inheritance, which inheritance her husband and she held on the day of the death of her husband: ... And her dower shall be assigned to her ...the third part of all the lands of her husband which were his during the marriage unless she had been endowed of less at the church door (by pre-nuptial agreement)...."*

In this time period, men did not often live to ripe old ages. The constant wars left many widows. Bad King John had a nasty habit of stealing the inheritances of widows and orphans, and this section was meant to curb John's stealing habits. Other sections also provided that widows could not be forced into re-marriage, which was another ruse often used to steal their property from them. Magna Carta set the widow's dower portion at one-third, which has been carried down to current times in jurisdictions that follow the common law.

3. *"NEITHER we nor our bailiffs shall seize any land or rent for any debt, so long as the present personal property of the debtor are sufficient for the payment of the debt ..."*

By this provision, real estate could not be seized and sold to pay creditors until the personal property had first been sold. This is still the law today in many jurisdictions which follow the common law.

Debts were usually owed to the king for taxes or assessments and, then as now, debts owed to the king or Internal Revenue Service were very serious matters. Bad King John would seize a vast estate worth perhaps thousands for a debt of only a very few dollars and then keep it all. This provision was meant to limit such practices. The Internal Revenue Service in the US employs tactics almost identical to those of Bad King John, and the US Congress is continually faced with requests to curb the abuses. Some things have not changed very much since Bad King John.

4. *"COMMON PLEAS shall not follow our court, but shall be held in some place certain...."*

The Common Pleas were the courts of the day that handled disputes among the population. In earlier times, litigants had to wait until the king or his representative traveled to town. This section provided for courts to be set up in certain places which would be open to all without bribes being required. In the United States, minor matters could be handled by a justice of the peace, but murders and other serious matters were handled by judges who rode a circuit. Many states in the US still have circuit courts, to the present day.

5. *"A FREEMAN shall not be fined for a small offence, except in proportion to the measure of the offence; and for a great offence he shall be fined in proportion to the magnitude of the offence, ...and none of the above fines shall be imposed except by the oaths of honest and lawful men of the neighborhood...."*

The right to trial by jury had already been clearly established by King Henry II, father of Richard and John, in the Statutes of Clarendon in AD 1166. This provision sets up a fundamental constitutional right to all Englishmen and, much later, to Americans. It imposes restraints on the use of arbitrary governmental authority. The amount of fines had to be determined by a jury and they had to be commensurate with the offense committed. There could be **no cruel and no unusual** punishments. What does that mean? Is the death penalty cruel or unusual? In the US such decisions are left to the Supreme Court of the United States.

The ban on cruel or unusual punishments is a crucial concept of law that was not present in French law, giving rise to the sad and unfortunate story of Jean Val-Jean who stole a loaf of bread to eat and spent most of his life in prison as a result. Val-Jean's life story is told in the book and stage play entitled **Les Misérables**. The lack of this concept of law was a major cause of the bloody French Revolution in AD 1789.

The Founding Fathers of the US embodied this concept into the US constitution in the Eight Amendment, which states:

> Amendment VIII: *"Excessive bail shall not be required, nor excessive fines imposed, nor cruel and unusual punishments inflicted."*

The Eight Amendment has been very important in keeping Congress and the legislatures from, at times, over-legislating.

> 6. *"IF any person holding an interest in real estate from us shall die, and ...owe us ... it shall be lawful for our sheriff or bailiff to attach and enroll the personal property of the deceased ... to the value of that debt, in the view of lawful men, provided nevertheless that nothing be removed thence **until the clear debt to us (i.e. the king) shall be paid**; and the remainder shall be left to the executors for the fulfillment of the will of the deceased; ...except to his wife and children for their reasonable shares...."*

This provision is mostly still the law today. If a decedent owes the king or Internal Revenue Service money, the king or Internal Revenue Service comes first. Next, the widow gets a share; but today, adult children can usually be disinherited. After the government and the widow are paid, plus of course the funeral director and the lawyers, the balance of the decedent's estate, if any is still left, is distributed as set forth in the decedent's will.

> 7. *"NO constable or bailiff of ours shall take anyone's grain or other personal property ... **without immediately paying for them in money**, unless he is able to obtain a postponement by permission of the seller. If, however, he lives in the same town, he need only receive his payment within forty days...."*

Another of Bad King John's nasty habits was that when he traveled to a town, both he and his staff lived in the best inns, ate the best food, drank the best wine, and often appropriated the prettiest women of the town for their own private use for several days, but never ever paid for anything. Some towns were so fearful of a visit from the king that they would send out messengers to the king's party, warning them that the town was under quarantine for smallpox.

In the United States, eminent domain laws have always required that any property seized by the government for public use shall be paid for at market value. Every person whose property is taken has the right to have the value determined by a jury. These laws come into play when new roads or airports are built by the government.

8. "**NO** freeman shall be taken or imprisoned or dispossessed of any ...or outlawed, or banished, or in any other way destroyed, ... except by the legal judgment of his peers or by the **law of the land. To no one will we sell, to no one will we deny, or delay right or justice....**"

The current legal concept of **due process of law** can be traced back to this provision in Magna Carta. This is just one example of where English law and, later, American law imposes a **higher law** that is not clearly defined but is left to the court system to decide as circumstances indicate.

This idea is embedded in the Fifth Amendment to the US Constitution, which states:

"No person shall be held ... unless on ...indictment of a Grand Jury ...Nor shall any person be subject for the same offence to be twice put in jeopardy of life or limb; nor shall be compelled in any Criminal Case to be witness against himself, nor be deprived of life, liberty, or property, **without due process of law;** nor shall private property be taken for public use, without just compensation."

What is due process of law? The concept is probably impossible to define but most people have a sense of when due process of law is being violated.

9. "*IT* shall not be lawful from henceforth to any to give his lands to any religious house, ...nor shall it be lawful to any house of religion so to take the lands of any..."

These prohibitions against leaving property to the Roman Church were generally known as Mortmain Statutes. In that time period about the only people who could read and write were the clerics of the Roman Church. It was sometimes easy for such clerics to convince some ignorant soul that he would burn in hell for eternity if he did not leave his property to the church.

By law, property had always passed to the decedent's heirs, so the church advanced the idea that everyone should make a will and, of course, leave property to the church. The church had gone so far as to say that dying without a will was actually a sin, and by reason of that sin, the church could seize a decedent's property to pay for the sin.

This provision was meant to limit gifts to the church and curb such abuses, but by AD 1534, when Henry VIII confiscated most church property, the church had become the largest owner of real estate in England. And yet again, by the late AD 1900s, the Roman Church is the largest land owner and the single richest institution in the entire world. Deception is still used by clerics to acquire real estate from people for all churches, even to the present day. This deception is repeated every time a new Methodist Church is built. This anti-church provision of Magna Carta, most unfortunately, has not remained law in the United States.

By the AD 1900s in England, the courts had decided that all of Magna Carta had either been repealed or superseded. By the time of the signing of the Magna Carta, King John had humbled himself before the pope, so he asked his new friend for help. As should be expected, the pope responded by nullifying Magna Carta. Notwithstanding the pope's nullification, Magna Carta remains, to this day through its off-spring, the law of the land in most English-speaking nations of the world, including the United States of America.

Why did the pope create a crusade against the Muslims? Was it for religious reasons? Was it for economic reasons? Or, was it only to delay reform?

By AD 1095, the Roman-church popes were so evil that they were repulsive, even to their own priests who also shared in the spoils. Throughout history, all dictators who wielded absolute power would, when they felt themselves slipping, create an external enemy. That would turn people's attention away from the internal failures and concentrate their attention and energies externally, on a common enemy. That is probably what happened here. The popes wielded absolute power. By AD 1095, the Roman Church had sunk to such moral lows that the priesthood could not even stomach itself.

Pope John XII was the son of Alberic, who had imprisoned his own mother for life. This pope was an outright sex fiend. He even raped women who had come to pray inside Saint Peter's. He was finally thrown out of office and lost his job as the representative of Master Jesus on Earth. This Pope John was pope the same year as the mythical Pope Joan, AD 955.

Pope Benedict IX was pope on three different occasions. He actually sold the papacy for 1500 pounds of gold to Pope Gregory VI in AD 1045. Within two years, three different popes were all in office at the same time. There have often been two popes in office at the same time, but three was a rarity.

Pope Benedict V, in AD 964, ruled for one month and was thrown out of office. Pope Boniface VII and Pope Leo VIII were both popes on two different occasions. Pope John XIV, Pope John XVII, and Pope Gregory VI each served only six months as the official representative of Master Jesus during this time period. There was a Pope John XIX and also XXI, but no Pope John XX. There have been two different persons with the title of Pope John XXIII.

By AD 1088, Pope Urban II was the 33rd pope to sit on the throne in Saint Peter's since only AD 955, the supposed date of the female Pope Joan. This was a period of only 133 years, or an average of a little over four years per pope. In the 1850 years from Pope Pius I, in AD 144, to the present Pope John Paul II, a total of 289 popes have served on average a little more than six years per pope. Job security is not a major asset of the job.

About 94 popes or almost one-third served two years or less. The longest serving pope was Pope Pius IX who served from 1846 to 1878 or about 32 years. There have been several popes who served only a few days and one of the shortest in history was that of John Paul I who served only 33 days in 1978.

In the Middle Ages prominent persons, including cardinals, who visited the Vatican in Rome often carried their own food with them to keep from being poisoned by the Vatican Bureaucracy. Many times this did not work. The food guards were bribed and the visitors were poisoned anyway. Also, often when a pope was selected that was not acceptable to the Vatican Bureaucracy they simply poisoned him, much like the ancient Egyptian Pharaohs were poisoned, and then a new compliant successor was selected. Rumors persist among the Roman-church clergy that John Paul I was poisoned in order to keep him from making radical changes within the church.

While it is true that there have been a very few Roman Church popes who were good men, the sad truth is that almost all popes have been bad people and several have been the most vicious criminals to ever live on Earth. It is estimated that the German Nazi murdered twelve million Slavs, Gypsies, and Jews. It is also estimated that the Roman-church popes have murdered nine million people, mostly women. However, the Nazi killed their helpless victims in only a few minutes in gas chambers whereas the Roman-church popes burned their victims very slowly to death over an open fire in the most sadistic murders the world has yet known.

These were some of the men that the Roman Church presented to the world as the representatives of Master Jesus the Christ on Earth. How corrupt can human beings become? As bad as some of these men were, they were saints compared to some who followed.

Pope Urban II, by AD 1095, had some hard choices to make:

1. Reform the church: This was one possibility but was immediately rejected because there was no one within the church hierarchy who knew anything at all about the true teachings of Master Jesus the Christ. There was no standard by which to gauge reform. Reform within the church was rejected for another 400 years.

2. Renounce power over people: The leaders of the Roman Church, from the pope down to the most common priests, were all drunk with the power that they wielded over peoples' lives. Such power was not easy to surrender. Indeed the popes in the late AD 1900s are still drunk with that same power, and they still give out the same answer; retain the power over people. Any pope who would suggest surrendering that power would not be at all popular among his own priesthood. So, it probably will not happen soon, but it must happen.

3. Give up praying for pay: Roman-church priests were men who lived, taught, and preached very self-serving doctrines to poor, ignorant, unsuspecting souls who looked to them for leadership. What did those people get from the priests? They got lies and more lies, and for those lies they paid money and more money. A law of AMORC was that no one should charge for sharing knowledge about God. Master Jesus never, ever charged. Any time a person accepts money for sharing knowledge of God, he accumulates karma under the Law of Compensation. Any priest who is truly sincere can show his sincerity by earning his own keep from his own efforts in the market place, like the rest of mankind. Any priest who accepts things of value for sharing knowledge of God should never expect to be, and should not be, honored for his work.

4. Create a diversion: Pope Urban could feel the hot breath of reform beginning to pressure him. What does any despot do? He turns the attention of his country or in this case his church, to an external enemy; the Muslims. That was what Pope Urban II did and the blood of tens of thousands of people flowed in the streets and gutters as a result.

In AD 1095, Pope Urban II issued a summons for the First Crusade, which lasted until AD 1099. He called on all Christians to go to Jerusalem, exterminate the inhabitants, and rid it of Muslim domination. With that edict, the Roman Church became a power waging aggressive war. If such an international crime were committed in the current century, the pope could be executed as a war criminal.

The pope's personal army and personal bankers were a group known as the Knights of the Temple of Jerusalem or more commonly called the Knights Templar. The Knights Templar were wealthy beyond comprehension. They owned the banking system in Europe and built and paid for many of the great cathedrals. They also led and financed the First Crusade for the pope.

When the Roman-church army, led by the Knights Templar, entered Jerusalem they killed everybody; men, women, and children alike. Can anyone imagine the horror of 10,000 women and children beheaded in the streets in a single day? Blood literally ran in the streets of Jerusalem ankle deep. The pope was ecstatic. Good job, well done, Knights of the Temple. The plan of the Roman Church to control the world took one big step; one very bloody big step forward. Much karma was created in the First Crusade by the Templars and the Roman Church.

But then a very strange thing happened to the knights in Solomon's Temple. They apparently discovered some very ancient documents and teachings in King Solomon's Temple. Over time, they became truly transformed. They were partially converted to the teachings of AMORC and Master Jesus the Christ. This was very bad news for the pope.

In a little over 200 years, by AD 1314, the situation had deteriorated to the point that the Grand Master of the Templars, Jacques de Molay, was burned to death at the stake in Paris. Seventy of his assistants were burned to death at the same time. The torture ordered by the pope was inhuman beyond anything known on Earth either before or since. The teeth, fingernails, and eye balls of the victims were all gouged out. Hot pokers were inserted into the sockets.

An incision was made in the abdomen and the intestines were slowly pulled from the person's body and roasted on a fire while still connected to the victim. The legs, feet, and ankles were put into a vise and savagely broken. Red hot pokers were applied to the genitals of men and women alike. Their broken feet were oiled and then slowly burned off over a slowly burning fire. They were chained by a neck iron too high on the wall for them to sit without choking and some were chained in the cesspool and forced to drink the urine of other prisoners. A Nazi gas chamber would have been a welcome relief to victims of the pope.

Tens of thousands of humans were inhumanely murdered in this manner by the popes and their accomplices. Hardly any of those popes or their accomplices were ever brought to justice in a court of law. The worst crimes ever committed on the face of Earth were committed by the popes in the name of Master Jesus.

It was in response to such sickening horror that some secular rulers in Europe began to put a limitation on Roman-church torture called the third degree. Today if anyone put another person through the third degree, they themselves would probably spend many years in prison, as did the Nazi criminals after World War II.

However, in that day, the three degrees of torture the Roman Church was allowed to use were a blessing to the popes' helpless victims. The three degrees of torture allowed to the Roman Church were as follows:

First Degree: The victim had his thumb placed into a thumb screw and the screw was tightened down until the thumb joint was crushed.

Second Degree: The victim had his hands tied behind him and then a rope was tied to the hands and put over a high rafter. The victim was then raised off the floor several times until the arms were pulled from the shoulder sockets. Often the priests would swing on the victims' ankles in order to increase the pain.

Third Degree: The person was stripped and the hands were tied high up on a wall. Then the torturer would hold a candle to the victims chest, sides, or back until the helpless victim was scourged with third degree burns over much of the body.

Still today, some people suffer third degree burns, but hardly ever intentionally inflicted. The very term **third degree** today means unreasonable persuasion.

However, if the victim survived the third degree, he or she was judged to be innocent and was released to live out his or her life as a maimed person. Such maimed persons often could not make a living and starved to death.

The self-appointed representatives of Master Jesus the Christ on Earth were not very nice people. He who sows violence shall inherit the wind. The Templars did sow violence, and they did inherit the wind. The Roman Church has sowed untold violence, and it too must inherit the wind. However, in those days the third degree, as mean and savage as it was to the victim, was perceived as showing the Christian mercy of the Roman Church.

This is the history of the Roman Church, the most evil institution ever known to mankind. But as for the Templars and their countless murders for the Roman Church in Jerusalem, those same murders were visited back upon them by that same church, and the Law of Compensation was again upheld.

The pope and the king thought that they had extinguished the secret Sanhedrin along with de Molay, but they were both wrong. The ancient Sanhedrin, or Council of 70, had ruled AMORC world-wide. Within one year, as de Molay predicted from the stake just before his death, both the French king and the pope joined him in death. Was de Molay psychic? Probably not. He probably, very simply, left a message for the pope and king to be killed, and they were. This statement cannot be proven, but it is highly probable. He did call for it, or he did predict it, and it did happen. If it did happen that way, then the Templars violated the teachings of AMORC and Master Jesus the Christ, which was an immoral thing to do on their part.

What happened to all of the Templar wealth? Perhaps no one knows. At least no one who knows will talk about it. We do know that shortly before de Molay was burned, eighteen ships laden with gold and other Templar valuables sailed away from France and have not been seen or heard of since. Was it taken to Scotland? Perhaps so, perhaps not. Another possibility is that the treasure was taken to Oak Island, just off of the east coast of Nova Scotia, in Canada.

There must be persons alive today who know the answers. The secret has perhaps been passed down through a line of Freemasons for almost 700 years. Only four Freemasons at one time ever know. When one of those four dies, a new younger person is carefully selected, to whom the knowledge is passed.

The Knights Templar still exist, but most of the books and stories about them are not accurate. A true Rosicrucian never brags that he is, in fact, a Rosicrucian. Under the rule of sub rosa, a Rosicrucian may properly deny being a Rosicrucian. This has been a valid rule of self-preservation for Rosicrucians throughout history.

The author suspects that the same may be true of the Templars. Any group that publicly claims that it is Templar probably is not. Any group that claims to be a continuation of the Order of the Temple can make money. France abounds with many such money-seeking organizations. Perhaps the world will know the answer to these questions in the near future.

What was the net result of the many bloody crusades sponsored by the Roman Church? There were two major results:

1. Reform within the Roman Church was delayed for an additional 400 years, to the AD 1500s.

2. AMORC teachings of Master Jesus the Christ were brought to the West.

Eventually, AMORC teachings will compel a complete renewal within the Roman Church. This is in the process of happening today.

An American jurist has observed that "*Power corrupts, and absolute power corrupts absolutely.*" That seems to be true, and the Roman-church papacy reached the zenith of its power and corruption in the person of Pope Innocent III, who died in AD 1216, about the same time as Bad King John in England.

During his reign, Pope Innocent put both John of England and Phillipe of France under papal interdict, and brought those kings to their knees. In addition, he instituted the dreaded Inquisition, which murdered thousands upon thousands of helpless, innocent victims, most of whom were women. In some cities in southern France whole populations of non-Roman-catholic Christians were murdered without compunction or remorse by the evil pope. Non-Christians, including Jews, were required to wear distinctive clothing, and were not even allowed to leave their homes during the week of Easter. If Master Jesus had lived at this time, he would have been imprisoned by the church bearing his own name.

In matters of theology, Pope Innocent also was very busy. The absurd doctrine of transubstantiation was implemented as a sacrament. This sacrament celebrated, as truth, the absurdity that during the Eucharist the bread and wine actually and literally become the body and blood of Master Jesus. Since the bread and wine were now the actual body and blood of Master Jesus, the ceremony was performed by the priests and only witnessed by ordinary lay people. They were not allowed to participate, except once each year.

Even to the present day, the priest often places the wafer of bread on the tongue of the Christian adherent so that it theoretically remains untainted by his or her touch. Priests were required to remain celibate, to wear distinctive clothes, and speak Latin, which very few people at that time could even begin to understand.

The Eucharist was the central sacrament of the seven sacraments of the Roman Church. Is it not interesting that none of those seven sacraments had any connection whatsoever with the teachings of Master Jesus the Christ? Very strange, but very true. Any person who could really believe that bread and wine actually and literally turned into the flesh and blood of Master Jesus certainly would not be able to comprehend the teachings of Master Jesus the Christ.

The Roman-church priesthood would perhaps retort that the Eucharist goes much deeper and can only be truly understood on a subjective level. Some Roman-church members might say that the Eucharist is symbolic only, but it is still deeply meaningful. Of course that could be true. Subjectively, any person could attend any kind of rite that one can imagine, and it could have a very deep and satisfying meaning for that person. But that begs the question. Such a person could also go into his own closet and pray, as Master Jesus recommended, and obtain a similar satisfying result. That would merely be saying that a person gets out of it what he or she puts into it which, of course, is obviously true.

But the issue is that the Roman Church teaches that the bread and wine literally changes into the body and blood of Master Jesus. That teaching is an obvious absurdity that needs no further discussion. To those who know that it really is the actual body and blood of Master Jesus, and that belief sustains their lives, so mote it be.

Infant baptism, as we have already noted, was corrupted to the purpose of symbolically washing away original sin that tainted a person by his or her mother's sex organs at birth. Baptism, as taught by Master Jesus, was for adults and was a diploma or public recognition of accomplishments already achieved. Once a person achieved a certain level of enlightenment, he or she was baptized and publicly acknowledged to have attained that level. It was never ever possible for a person thereafter to become unenlightened below that level. Once man or woman knows, he or she cannot, ever thereafter, not know.

Could one person have several baptisms? Surely yes. The same public recognition could be awarded in many different communities. For example, Master Jesus was already baptized as The Christ in Egypt before he met John the Baptist at the Jordan River. But Master Jesus at that time again accepted baptism from John. Infant baptism, as practiced by the Roman Church, was only an economic expediency used to command both commitment and money to the church in order to support its priests.

The Sacrament of Confirmation was another economic expediency designed by the church to sustain its priests monetarily. The church destroyed the major collection of knowledge in the world when it destroyed the great library at Alexandria, Egypt. The church then agreed to share small bits of that knowledge with lay people in return for a moral commitment to keep paying the church and supporting its priests forever. That sacrament also violated the teachings of Master Jesus, which were to the effect that every human being has the obligation, without charging for it, to share knowledge about God when asked. Master Jesus never, ever, demanded pay for sharing his teachings; never once.

The Sacrament of Marriage was another economic expediency designed by the church to sustain its priests monetarily. Two people could morally marry themselves and no priest or church would be necessary. However, according to Roman-church rules, if even a million people lived in a community and there was no Roman-church priest present, no proper marriage could be consummated. This was obviously absurd.

Master Jesus taught and favored marriage. But the Roman Church forbad marriage to its priests and nuns. Unmarried priests and nuns were a necessity in order for the church to maintain its control system over women and, consequently, over all of society. A married woman with a husband and family is less likely to give a male priest complete control over her life, as do unmarried nuns.

A married man would know that the female is more attuned than the male to the Law of Love taught by Master Jesus. Married men ultimately would not be able to retain a belief in the inferior moral status of women.

Another reason that marriage was included by the church as a sacrament was so that at the time of marriage the priest could exact a promise from the couple to indulge in required sex and have lots of babies. Those babies would then grow up to work and pay money to maintain the church and its priests. Surely a most cynical and self-serving propaganda scheme! The **Bible** only says in **Genesis 1:28** "...*Be fruitful, and multiply, and replenish the earth,...*" It does not say to create a population increasing by geometric progression without limitation.

The Sacrament of Penance was another economic expediency designed by the church to sustain its priests monetarily. Any action that any person takes may result in multiple unforseen consequences. A consequence becomes wrong only when and if that consequence was intended and does harm to another person. The Roman Church taught that when that happened, the person must come to the priest and confess -- and pay -- and the priest would then forgive them. Wrong!

Master Jesus taught that a person must begin by first forgiving the sins of self. If talking to a priest, or a psychologist, or even a lawyer helped that process, this would be good. However, no priest or other go-between was really needed. Master Jesus taught that a person should go into his or her own closet and pray to God -- directly one-on-one -- with no go-betweens and no payment of fees required. Such a teaching was pure horror to the Roman Church.

Another holy sacrament of the Roman Church was the very unholy one called Holy Orders. This was a structure set up by the church to dispense so-called Christian teachings and traditions, but of course for a fee. In order for the priest to be allowed to ply his trade, he first had to jump through seven hoops. These hoops included: first, being a door-keeper or door mat; second, a lecturer on traditions; third, an exorcist; fourth, an acolyte priest; fifth, a sub-deacon; sixth, a deacon; and seventh, a full-fledged priest. Only a priest could administer the Sacrament of Extreme Unction.

There were heavy penalties to be paid if a person missed the unholy sacrament of Extreme Unction. It could mean burning in hell for eternity at worst, or being well scorched in half-hell or purgatory for a while, at best. To get out of purgatory was very expensive. Had Master Jesus died at that time, he might still be languishing in purgatory unless he could have raised the money to pay his way out. Absurd? Yes. Believed by many Christians? Sadly, also yes. And still believed by some less-educated Christians even to the present day.

The seven sacraments of the Roman Church were really seven ways to cheat your brother. Is it any wonder that Muhammad started a new religion based at least on some moral principles? Is it any wonder that enlightenment continued to survive in the Muslim world at a time when it was only barely still breathing in the Christian world? Is it any wonder that a revolt eventually had to come in the Roman Church? And is it not understandable why the Roman Church, its cousins and its step-children, continue to oppose most of the teachings of AMORC and Master Jesus the Christ, even to the present day?

But, into all that darkness some light had to come. It is sometimes true that out of the weakest, comes the strongest; out of the least enlightened, comes the most enlightened; and out of the worst, comes the best. The Roman Church did exactly that. It produced Francis of Assisi. Saint Francis, as he was called, prayed:

> "Lord, make me an instrument of Thy Peace. Where there is hatred, let me sow love. Where there is injury, pardon. Where there is doubt, faith. Where there is despair, hope. Where there is darkness, light. Where there is sadness, joy.
>
> O Divine Master, grant that I may not so much seek to be consoled as to console; to be understood, as to understand; to be loved, as to love; for it is in giving that we receive, it is in pardoning that we are pardoned, and it is in dying that we are born to Eternal Life."

This was new philosophy for the Roman Church at that time. Far better to light one small candle than to live forever in the dark. Saint Francis was one very small fluttering candle in the Roman Church.

But there were also some other small candles being lit. Working outside the church were the Rosicrucians Dante in Italy and Roger Bacon in England. These two men also turned on a couple of very small lights in Western culture. Darkness cannot be absolute in the presence of even a small light, ignorance cannot remain complete in the face of even a little knowledge, and corruption cannot continue totally unabated in the presence of even a little virtue.

Power and the center of gravity of Western culture began shifting from the Continent to England after the Magna Carta in AD 1215. Several things happened in England, causing it to avoid a bloody social revolution and, instead, to evolve into a much broader-based and more open society.

One reason for this shift of the center of gravity to England was the great Rosicrucian Roger Bacon, who lived from AD 1220 to 1292. Bacon held a Master's Degree from the University of Oxford and the University of Paris, and was well versed in philosophy, religion, and natural science.

Bacon suggested eyeglasses, horseless carriages, and flying machines. He computed the inaccuracy of the Julian calendar, showed that light travels faster than sound, experimented with chemical analysis, and performed countless other investigations. Bacon's credo was to experiment, experiment, experiment. Like many Rosicrucians, Bacon spent most of the last twelve years or so of his life in prison for heresy. His books were suppressed by the Roman Church and were not finally published until 450 years later, in AD 1733.

In the AD 1200s, the thinking of men like Saint Francis of Assisi, Dante Alighieri, and Roger Bacon began to have impact. Magna Carta was signed and later, in the AD 1500s, the Rule in Shelley's Case became law, which allowed everyone to own land in England.

In AD 1348, the Black Death spread across Western culture, including England, and perhaps as many as one-third of the entire population died. This cut significantly the number of people available to support the royal family and other non-producing members of society. Very suddenly workers and artisans were much more important in the society and thus also much more powerful.

In AD 1381, the Freemasons in England led a miniature civil war which lasted only a week or so, and killed but very few people, but it was enough to get the attention of the royal family and other leaders in England, and to convince them that some change was required. And some changes were made for the better.

To some extent, the Dark Ages are still with us even today. The Roman Church still loots Central and South America and demeans women. Some of the Protestant sects are even worse than the Roman Church in demeaning women and selling religion commercially in the marketplace.

260 TRUE ESOTERIC TRADITIONS

But all of those evils must eventually pass away. It finally started in Western culture when Columbus sailed the ocean blue in AD 1492. The time was ripe for the Rosicrucians once again to expose the teachings of AMORC and Master Jesus the Christ to the world. Next, came the Rosicrucian enlightenment which would eventually lead Western culture out of the Dark Ages and into the so-called Age of Aquarius.

```
            Darkness cannot be
          absolute in the presence
        of even a small light, ignorance
        cannot remain complete in the face of
      even a little knowledge, and corruption cannot
     continue totally unabated in the presence of even
                  a little virtue.
```

CHAPTER FOURTEEN -- THE ROSICRUCIAN ENLIGHTENMENT

What is the Rosicrucian Enlightenment? What time period does it cover? Who were the people that caused it to happen? What have been the effects of that enlightenment in terms of science, technology, economics, health, and religion? Why have the countries of Europe, from France and Switzerland northward, plus England, enjoyed more from that enlightenment, while southern European countries such as Spain, Portugal, and Italy enjoyed less?

After AD 1535, England became the center of learning in Western culture and dispensed that knowledge to the rest of the world. Part of that knowledge, going from England to Europe, included Rosicrucian publications written by a group headed by Francis Lord Bacon, which were anti-Roman Church. The Roman Church frustrated itself trying to track down these publications and trying to ban and burn them and those responsible therefor.

Some of these publications were the **Laudable Fraternity of the Rosy Cross**, **Confessions of the Fraternity**, and the **Chemical Marriage of Christian Rosenkreutz**. These publications made reference to a very mysterious **Book M**, which was purported to be in Damascus. Who was Christian Rosenkreutz? Did such a person even exist? What was the mysterious **Book M**?

If it were in Damascus, **Book M** must be in Muslim hands which would not be serious for the Roman Church because both the Buddhists and Muslims have always known that Master Jesus did not die by crucifixion in Israel in AD 33. But that information in Europe, in Christian hands, could be disaster. One has to wonder why the Roman Church would be so paranoid and in utter panic about such an innocuous reference to **Book M**, but it is a fact that the Roman Church was in complete panic. The author pondered this question for many years and finally came up with a possible answer.

Rosicrucian sources have always **publicly** stated that Christian Rosenkreutz was only a mythical person. They do this to avoid persecution. That is not really true any more than Mark Twain was only mythical. Mark Twain was a pseudonym for Samuel Clemens, and Christian Rosenkreutz was a pseudonym for a very brilliant German by the name of Christian Von Germelshausen, whose family had been murdered by order of the Roman Church when he was only a youth. Christian had been reared by monks who obviously were very well informed.

As a young adult, Christian traveled to Italy, Greece, Israel, a center of learning near Damascus, Cairo, and Spain. When he returned to Germany he brought back the ancient knowledge of the Rosicrucians and established the Order in Germany. Although there are dates given that Christian died in the late AD 1400s, those may not be reliable because the Rosicrucians often applied earlier dates to people in order to frustrate the Roman Church in searching for them.

The reader will remember that the Buddhists have always revered Master Jesus as a saint, and the Muslims have always honored him as a prophet, but both groups have always known that most certainly Master Jesus was a man, howbeit the very greatest of men. It would seem that such a view would need little affirmation, and only those who maintain otherwise would be required to present overwhelming evidence of their claims. As already reported herein, the holy book of the Muslims, **The Koran**, states in Chapter 4:157:

> "That they said (in boast), 'We killed Christ Jesus The son of Mary, The Apostle of God,' -- But they killed him not, Nor crucified him, But so it was made to appear to them, And those who differ Therein are full of doubts, With no (certain) knowledge, But only conjecture to follow, For of a surety **They killed him not**:"

Throughout its history, the Roman Church had always destroyed all information and exterminated all people who had information that could expose the misinformation the church had foisted on Western culture. The burning of the great library at Alexandria in Egypt in AD 400 is the best single example.

So what information was in **Book M**? The author suggests that it was nothing less than the record of a meeting between Master Jesus and the Apostle Paul near Damascus, late in both their lives, when Paul came face to face with the reality that his life's work had been all wrong. When did it take place? The time would be after Paul wrote all of his letters in the **New Testament**, and only shortly prior to his death.

What took place at the meeting? First of all, Paul recognized Master Jesus from their meeting on the road to Damascus, shortly after the crucifixion event. So he had no choice, none whatever, but to admit that Master Jesus was alive and had not died as he, Paul, had been preaching to the world.

What else happened? What did Master Jesus tell Paul at that meeting? The author's hypothesis is as follows:

1. The worst of Paul's teachings was that Master Jesus had died on the cross, rose from the dead, and was a blood sacrifice for mankind. This item alone gave rise to many of the pagan teachings of the Roman Church which still prevail in much of the world to the present day. That never was true and now Paul knew it.

2. Another big error in Paul's teachings was that women were inferior to men. Master Jesus taught that all people are equal in the sight of God, and Paul finally accepted this teaching; however, the damage he had already done could not be reversed.

Paul, even though a Jew, did not marry until late in life; after he left Rome, gave up public preaching and moved to Damascus. This may account for his negative attitude toward women in his younger life. Almost without question, Master Jesus did marry and probably more than once. Paul was forced to face his own negative fixations of mind concerning sex.

3. Paul came to know the true teachings of Master Jesus and the incredible meaning they have for mankind. Paul had earlier taught that God had **devolved** down into a man in the form of Master Jesus. Now he knew that Master Jesus was indeed a man and the most marvelous man who has ever lived because he showed how man can evolve up to, and re-unite, with God.

4. Paul finally learned that Master Jesus was important because of what he taught, not because of who he was or how or when he was born.

Can anyone imagine the agony Paul must have suffered on learning these things? He suffered pure agony because of the people he had led astray, but he rejoiced in his new knowledge. Now Paul really did know the truth; now he really had a much more profound message for mankind.

But it was not to be. Paul was too old, and it was too late. It should be stated here that very few would have believed Paul even if he had preached his new message. Master Jesus had already recognized this fact before he went silent. People who could believe the teachings of the Roman Church and its off-spring would not yet be able to comprehend the teachings of Master Jesus the Christ. It was true then, and it remains true to the present day.

Now, the panic of the Roman Church can be easily understood. They knew the contents of **Book M**, and they knew that if that knowledge became well known in Western culture, it could mean the complete downfall of the Roman Church. To the priests, it might mean going to work and nothing could be worse than that. Their paranoia can be understood.

Is there now danger in sharing this information with others? The answer is, **perhaps yes**; and that is one reason the author has waited these many years before doing so. All who feel that the resurrection story is true and important in their lives should go ahead and believe it as they always have in the past. When their time is right, they too will come to know the truth of these matters, and that truth will truly set them free.

As Master Jesus knew, gaining enlightenment is no easy matter. In the Western Hemisphere, why have the countries of the United States and Canada enjoyed more enlightenment than Mexico and Central and South America? What specific event, if any, can now be viewed as the snapshot in time where those differences first began?

These are all interesting questions and are not easy to answer. Indeed there is no single answer. The author suggests some reasons other than those most analysts would select, and some events, that others might not even consider. Again, however, this is a brief and not a treatise. Much of the detailed history of Western culture since the time of Columbus is well known to most readers and need not be repeated here.

In the Western Hemisphere, there are basically three languages in use. The United States and Canada speak mostly English and are more secular societies. That is, those two countries are not totally dominated by the Roman Church.

Mexico, Central and South America, except for Brazil, all speak Spanish and are totally dominated by the Roman Church. Brazil speaks mostly Portuguese, but is also totally dominated by the Roman Church.

In early AD 1492, Ferdinand and Isabella defeated the Muslims and created modern Spain and made it into a theocracy. The Jews were forcibly converted or expelled from the country. The Jewish bankers in Spain did nominally convert to Christianity, for appearance's sake only.

Christopher Columbus, with Jewish financial backing, re-discovered the Western hemisphere. All Jews had been ordered to leave Spain or convert to Christianity by July 31, 1492, and Columbus set sail for the West on August 3, 1492. Very little is known about Christopher Columbus. We don't know really where he came from or where he is buried.

We do know that Columbus was smart enough to negotiate a very liberal employment agreement for himself. In these negotiations, Columbus had a big advantage over Ferdinand and Isabella because he really knew that the Western hemisphere existed and how to get there, as was shown by his sailing south rather than west. His employment agreement entitled *"PRIVILEGES AND PREROGATIVES GRANTED BY THEIR CATHOLIC MAJESTIES TO CHRISTOPHER COLUMBUS--1492"* is dated April 30, 1492, and states:

> "...*Our will is, That you, Christopher Columbus, after discovering and conquering the said Islands and Continent in the said ocean, or any of them, shall be our Admiral of the said Islands and Continent you shall so discover and conquer; and that you be our Admiral, Vice-Roy, and Governour in them and that for the future, you may call and stile yourself, D. Christopher Columbus,* **and that your sons and successors in the said employment**, *may call themselves Dons, Admirals, Vice-Roys, and Governours of them; and that you may exercise the office of Admiral, with the charge of Vice-Roy and Governour of the said Islands and Continent, which you and your Lieutenants shall conquer, and* **freely decide all causes, civil and criminal**... *as you shall think fit in justice, and ...you have power to punish offenders...*"

You will note that Columbus is to have the authority to decide all matters of government which one might think could eventually result in Jewish people being welcome in the new lands unlike they were in Spain. The document is redundant in granting total and complete governing rights to Columbus and his family in perpetuity. Obviously, Ferdinand and Isabella did not know that Columbus was being backed by, and represented, Jewish interests.

But, many people were in the Western hemisphere and even in Kentucky, southern Indiana and Illinois, long before Columbus arrived. All types of ancient artifacts have been discovered in the area. These include a Hebrew coin dating to AD 100 or so, a mummy, and other skeletons. These mysteries may be solved by the turn of the next century and it will be shown that a few people, worldwide, have long been in contact with the Western hemisphere.

Some students of Kabala say that the ancient teachings clearly say that Earth spins as a sphere; that when part of it is up the other is down, and when one side is lit up the other is dark, and that the day and the night change positions.

The Kabala, even in its present form, dates to the AD 1100s, or more than 300 years before Columbus. However, the Kabala actually goes back to 1300 BC and earlier.

Columbus did know, from Rosicrucian sources, that the currents in the Atlantic Ocean move west at the Equator and then rotate clockwise around and up through the Gulf Stream in the North Atlantic to Western Europe. This is probably caused by Earth's rotation to the east. The same thing is true in the Pacific where the current moves west toward Asia at the Equator and then rotates clockwise around and up through the Japanese current to northwestern North America.

In the Southern hemisphere, the currents rotate counter-clockwise. For example, the current moves from Africa west to Central South America along the Equator, and then counter-clockwise, back toward south Africa in the south Atlantic. This is also the general route that cyclones seem to travel. However, in the Northern hemisphere the winds rotate counter-clockwise whereas in the Southern hemisphere, they rotate clockwise.

It was this knowledge of Earth's currents, plus knowledge of the use of the magnetic compass and the position of the North Star, that allowed first Columbus, and then all Western countries, to break the economic grip of the Arabs and put control of world affairs into the hands of Europeans, where it remains to this day.

Only in this century have the Japanese, through their technology, been able to loosen the grip of Europe and America on world affairs. This was really the reason for World War II in the Pacific. The Japanese were trying to restore Asia to the Asians.

As always, all swords have two edges. The United States is the true land of milk and honey, as predicted in the **Bible**, and was discovered where not only Jews but all people can worship, or not worship at all, as they see fit. But the Spanish and Portuguese with Christian-church blessing slaughtered tens of thousands of natives found living in the Western hemisphere. Many of these were sadistically slaughtered, even after converting to Christianity.

Actually, Rosicrucians around the world had perhaps known about the Western hemisphere even before the time of Aristotle. Master Jesus certainly knew about the Western hemisphere and may well have visited here, as the Mormon Church teaches.

Spain, as the dominant influence in Western culture, lasted less than a 100 years. That short period of dominance came to a screeching halt in AD 1588 when the Spanish Armada was soundly defeated by the English, under Queen Elizabeth I. After AD 1588, the English culture and the English language spread over the entire world, until today English is approaching the status of a universal language.

France is a special case. The French have always been nominal members of the Roman Church, except for a brief period after the French Revolution. Unlike many other countries, the French have never been totally dominated by that church. Quite the contrary, France has often, instead, dominated the Roman Church.

Even today while the Roman Church harangues against abortion in many countries of the world, France, which is 90 per cent nominally Roman Catholic, develops and markets the abortion pill. This is quite a contradiction, but that is France. Likewise, the French have persisted, without much success, in trying to maintain French as a universal language.

Over-population is the world's worst problem; still, the abortion pill is controversial because of the adverse economic impact it has on churches. Even more controversy may come about when a suicide pill is developed and marketed. It has to happen. Medical technology has surpassed our legal system. We now have the knowledge and technology to keep people alive long after they should have experienced a peaceful and dignified transition or death. Any rational person can perceive this by visiting some of the thousands of nursing homes, or human vegetable warehouses, in America.

It is the legal system's duty to construct a procedure where each individual can decide these very serious matters for him or herself. There are things worse than death and one of them is life without dignity or purpose. The Christian churches need to re-think their position as to what is in the best interests of the individual rather than the best financial interests of the church. That will eventually happen, but not soon.

The French lost their dignity, and much of the world's respect, during World War II when they collaborated with the Germans against their own Jewish citizens, without even a struggle. On the other hand the English, under Churchill, were determined to resist German domination to the bitter end. It is interesting to note that London was heavily damaged and Berlin was almost totally destroyed in that war, but Paris suffered not a single bomb during the entire war.

Is it not also interesting that Hitler caused the death of some 50 million people and untold physical destruction, trying to dominate Europe. And now only 50 years later, Germany dominates all of Europe without having fired a single shot. That domination of Europe by Germany will become more complete by the turn of the century.

On the other side of the world Japan tried almost everything, in bloodshed and destruction, it could muster to capture Pearl Harbor. And now only 50 years later, it has taken possession of much of Hawaii, except for Pearl Harbor, also without firing a single shot.

Why has the English culture spread world-wide? In the AD 1500s, a rather insignificant event took place which has had world-wide impact and has been the single most important factor in separating Western culture from Eastern culture. That event is what is known by lawyers as the **Rule in Shelley's Case**.

Be aware that throughout history, until the Industrial Revolution, most of the wealth in the world was in the form of the ownership of land. And most land was owned by families, not individuals. That is, the children, often male children only, inherited the land from their parents, who had inherited it from their parents, and so on back through the centuries.

The point is that owners could not sell land because it was owned by their yet unborn descendants. Thus, no matter how hard one ever worked and tried, he or she could never acquire land, and therefore could never acquire wealth. The wealthy families who were very few in number always remained wealthy, regardless of their merit or lack thereof. And the very poor families, which were 95 per cent of the population, always remained poor, regardless of their merit or lack thereof. Both merit and effort were not important values in those societies. These were not good rules by which to govern a society.

In the rule of law laid down in Shelley's Case, the judge ruled that if a person owned real estate, he or she could mortgage it or even sell it to someone else, if he or she so chose. And the buyer, or mortgagee who loaned money on the land, did not have to worry about the owner's descendants, because unborn descendants no longer had any legal interest in their parents' land.

The owner's interest became known as a **fee simple absolute** and is familiar to almost every person in the English-speaking world who has ever owned a farm, a house, or a condominium. From the fee simple absolute concept, developed the further idea that a person's home was his or her castle, and peaceful possession thereof was sacrosanct under the law.

The Rule in Shelley's Case and the fee simple absolute are the reasons that there has never been a social revolution in an English-speaking nation. Never once. Many countries, including the United States of America, have broken away from England but those were all for political purposes, not social. As a result of that rule of law, ownership of land and thus wealth became distributed among more and more people. If one worked hard enough, he or she could own land. And if one inherited land, he or she could lose it. Society in English-speaking countries became broader based.

Many of the states in the United States of America are repealing the Rule in Shelley's Case. This is unfortunate and unwise. This is happening because the law professors and lawyers want to set up long-running trusts in order to avoid taxes and keep both law professors and lawyers employed.

In Russia, until 1917, less than five percent of the population owned all of the land and wealth, while the other 95% of the population were mere peasants. Exactly the same thing was true in India until 1947, and in China until 1949. Those countries never had the Rule in Shelley's Case and the idea of the fee simple absolute in their law. Likewise in France, until the bloody French Revolution in AD 1789, the French king claimed ownership of all land. It was really the model of the French Revolution that inspired the revolutions in Russia, India, and China.

In India, Gandhi, who was an English-trained lawyer, knew how to use the English rule of law against the English themselves and was able to separate India from England without significant bloodshed. However, the Hindus and Muslims then promptly shed much blood in trying to divide India between them. The priests in all religions simply cannot resist the temptation to try forcibly to control the minds of other persons.

The differences between a political revolution and a social revolution are profound. In a political revolution, the only disagreement concerns who will be the boss. The Americans did not like King George and the badly spoiled royalty, but almost all Americans at that time had families in England. Many of the English, especially the Freemasons, supported the Americans in their revolution against King George. The Americans adopted the English law and language, but chose the republic, as espoused by Thomas Jefferson, as the best form of government.

In France, Russia, India, and China it required over-turning the entire social order. Some of those countries have been criticized for executing the royal families and some of the very wealthy in their societies, but really they had no reasonable alternatives.

History shows that the very wealthy have seldom consented to change in the social order by giving up their wealth and control, and only continue the status quo as long as possible. Executing thousands who refused to alter their conduct was not desirable, but it was better than having millions forever oppressed by those few thousands.

In most cases, the elite that were executed had the option to alter their conduct and chose not to do so. So, for the most part, those elitists sealed their own fate by their own misconduct.

An excellent example of elitists who refused voluntarily to change their conduct were the southern states of the United States on the slavery issue, which eventually led to the very bloody War Between the States.

The American-French idea of the republic as the best form of government has spread over the entire world in the last 200 years. Only in the last few years, most of the countries in Eastern Europe, and even the former Soviet Union, have adopted republican forms of government. By far the best exports that the United States has are its ideas, not its military might. Very sadly, America has forgotten that simple fact of its own history.

Another event that has had a profound effect was the re-establishment of the English Church in AD 1535 by King Henry VIII. The English Church actually pre-dates the Roman Church by some years, but the Roman Church had successfully suppressed that historical fact for some 1500 years. Most unfortunately, the English Church continued to use the Roman-church theology created by the Apostle Paul, Constantine, and Saint Augustine instead of reverting to the true teachings of Master Jesus the Christ.

King Henry also seized most of the Roman-church wealth in England and divided it up among his friends and supporters. This was one reason why King Henry was so popular, even though he was a murderer and a complete scoundrel.

However, the most lasting result of that act was that England became a land of learning where the Rosicrucian teachings could surface and be openly taught and discussed in the public forum. With that intellectual freedom, knowledge grew rapidly in England, while Spain, Portugal, and Italy began lagging behind and have continued to do so to the present day.

France also lagged behind for another 250 years until its own revolution. This advance in knowledge gained from intellectual freedom gave rise to advances in science and technology, which gave birth to the Industrial Revolution. The cutting of the umbilical cord with the Roman Church by King Henry was the single most important event leading to the Rosicrucian Enlightenment.

The export of that Industrial Revolution from England to the rest of Western culture has for some 300 years pushed Western culture ahead of the rest of the world. For example, the export of that Rosicrucian Enlightenment has resulted in the following advances throughout Western culture:

1. There has been a growth trend in Western culture for 300 years, while the rest of the world has remained mostly stagnant.

2. Personal incomes of the middle class have increased many times and that middle class has been open to all who chose to join it.

3. Infant mortality has declined significantly.

4. The average life span has almost doubled.

5. John Deere developed the first truly effective plow, and food production increased to the point that great famine is now a thing of the past in the West. Food production which at one time required about 90 per cent of the population, now occupies less than five per cent.

6. Knowledge of health and sanitation has increased to the point that great plagues, such as the one that ravished England in AD 1348, and again in 1666, have now been completely overcome, but new plagues, like aids, are appearing.

7. Urbanization and ever-increasing wealth has led to changes in living and working standards to the point that the ever-growing middle class have better living conditions than the elite in most other cultures.

The second most important economy in the world is Japan, which has almost no natural resources. The countries of South America, Indonesia, and the former Soviet Union have vast natural resources, but stagnant economies. The difference between cultures lies not in the amount of natural resources.

The author suggests that the reasons that Western culture, which includes Japan since World War II, has been so very successful are:

1. The large amount of money allocated by both business and government to science and discovering the secrets of nature. When science solves problems intellectually, technology implements those solutions to the betterment of mankind.

2. The large amount of money allocated to education and the high value placed on youth.

Many things have changed, but not all are for the better. The blacks in America should demand quality schools. Busing of black youths to achieve racial balance is a slur against the black race and should not be tolerated. It is the worst kind of discrimination not to demand equal performance from black youths. Teachers need to be honored and rewarded as they are in Japan. America will continue its rapid decline as long as athletes make millions and good teachers can barely make ends meet. It is a misplacement of values and a very sad situation.

3. The relative freedom of the individual to pursue knowledge in spite of opposition from the Roman Church.

Here too, many things have changed, and not all for the better. The churches should not be allowed to insist that poor people have children that they do not want and cannot provide for. The churches should be told to attend to their own business, which should be to enlighten people, and not to forcibly impose their views on others.

4. The ability of nations to pursue their own ideals without, at the same time, trying to impose their values on others.

This too has changed, but not for the better. America needs to return to its earlier status as a defensive nation.

During the last generation, America has spent itself to near bankruptcy, trying to impose its will on others militarily, with nothing but failure to show for those vast expenditures. In only a very few years the former Soviet Union and Eastern Europe have turned to the idea of the republic voluntarily, and completely on their own. America's great military might was scarcely a factor in those decisions; in fact, it was probably a negative factor.

For 200 years the United States of America followed Rosicrucian and Freemasonic ideals and became the number-one country in the whole world. During the last generation, it has lost those ideals and deserted those values, and as a consequence, it is rapidly declining into a second-rate nation. It has created extensive violence among its own people and seems not to know the cause of this violence or how to stop it.

Who are those who have brought Rosicrucian enlightenment to Western culture? There have been millions, of course, but some few have contributed more than others.

Dante Alighieri was born in Florence in AD 1265. He devoted much of his life to self-education, and became a Rosicrucian. In AD 1302, he was condemned to death, but instead went into exile. He held typical Rosicrucian views of the Roman Church and held up a mirror to expose the Roman Church to the world. In his book, **The Divine Comedy,** he takes a trip to hell and purgatory, neither of which he believed in, and then finally to Paradise. On that trip he met many familiar people in the lower circles of hell.

Dante held women in high esteem, as do all Rosicrucians, and as the Roman Church does not. He, more than any one other person, started the trend towards the Renaissance and the Reformation. Dante appears to be the man who started the move toward adding new degrees to the earlier Rosicrucian seven degrees. Dante symbolically suggested that the Rosicrucian Order now needed nine degrees, instead of only seven, to save mankind from the low status to which it had devolved under the Roman Church.

Dante may have been inspired by Saint Francis of Assisi who was born in the same area of the world in AD 1182. Saint Francis was a youth at the time King Richard the Lion-Hearted of England led the murderous Third Crusade from England to Israel. Dante died in AD 1321.

When the Jews were persecuted in Spain in AD 1492, they financially supported Christopher Columbus in his quest to re-discover the Western hemisphere. This resulted in opening up Western culture to a vastly-expanded world and is still expanding even to the present day.

Shortly thereafter in AD 1517, the Roman-church priest, Martin Luther, began the Reformation in earnest when he nailed his **95 Theses** on the door of the Roman Church in Wittenberg. In some ways, Luther was as intolerant as the popes he was condemning, but he did create a distinct and separate power base opposed to the Roman Church. That breaking of Roman-church power later proved to be the salvation of Western culture.

In his **95 Theses**, Luther set forth the idea that one could achieve Heaven or relationship with God through faith alone. This made the indulgences, or licenses to sin, sold by the Roman Church at that time unnecessary. This was a big step forward toward the obsolescence of the priesthood. If one could establish a relationship with God through his own faith alone then a priest as go-between was no longer necessary.

Such teachings were pure heresy to the Roman Church. Luther also dealt a heavy blow to the economic foundation of the Roman Church. It was the sale of these indulgences that actually raised the money to complete the building of Saint Peters in the Vatican. Luther would have been burned at the stake, like many before him, except that he had too many powerful friends. And thus was lit one more small candle that became the Reformation, and the Dark Ages gave way to the light of day.

In AD 1543, the Polish astronomer, Nicolaus Copernicus, published his theory that the sun, not Earth, is the center of the Solar System. This event had serious repercussions throughout Western culture and, indeed, the whole world.

King Henry VIII, scoundrel that he was, broke the death-grip of the Roman Church on England and did provide a relatively safe haven where knowledge, but not politics, could be pursued without fear of execution by the Roman Church. This was a pivotal event in the history of Western culture.

At the beginning of the AD 1600s, the Italian Galileo said that the sun, with all its planets moving around it, can ripen the smallest bunch of grapes as if it had nothing else to do. Why then should I doubt God's power? Galileo discovered the four largest moons of Jupiter, using a telescope, and confirmed Copernicus' theory that the sun, not Earth, is the center of the Solar System.

In order to avoid death at the stake by burning, Galileo was willing to admit that the Law of Continuity did not operate in the higher truths of the Roman Church. The Law of Continuity simply stated that if something is true, then it is always true. This created a false division between science and religion that remains to the present day.

In the early AD 1600s, Francis Lord Bacon of England re-discovered inductive logic from the teachings of Master Jesus the Christ and also created the Scientific Method. This has been one of the greatest contributions to mankind, ever. He also publicly exposed many of the long-suppressed Rosicrucian teachings to the world, using many pen names, including that of Shakespeare and others.

About AD 1605, King James set up a group of scholars to translate the **Bible** and the **New Testament**. The more than 50 translators worked until AD 1609 and then turned their work over to the king, who referred it to Francis Lord Bacon for final review. Bacon loved the use of codes. In much of the Shakespearean literature Bacon secretly implanted his own name in code. Bacon did the same thing to the King James version of the **Bible**. For example, in **Psalm 46**, if you read 46 words down from the beginning you will arrive at the word **shake**; and if you read 46 words up from the end, you will come to the word **spear**. Thus, we find **shakespear** down 46 and up 46, in the **46th Psalm**. Bacon could not resist implanting his signature, in code, on his work.

In the King James Version of the **Bible** and the **New Testament**, the word **shake** appears 90 times and the word **spear** appears 65 times. Probably, there is some kind of message encoded in these if someone has the time and inclination to decipher it.

Bacon was probably the greatest mind to live on Earth since Master Jesus the Christ, but he was not perfect by any means. Very wrongly, he failed to support those wanting to replace the monarchy with a republic after the death of his mother, Queen Elizabeth I. Instead, he helped to bring the morally corrupt James to the throne of England. The monarchy still impedes development in that country to the present day. This was a very bad decision by Bacon. He also failed to support Sir Walter Raleigh when he should have, even though his help probably would not have saved the innocent Raleigh from execution.

Bacon was also accused of taking bribes and deserting his own brother, Lord Essex, but he was not guilty of either of these. Queen Elizabeth I had her own wayward son, Lord Essex, beheaded for treason. Elizabeth was truly a chip off the old Henry VIII block.

274 TRUE ESOTERIC TRADITIONS

Bacon was the head of both the Freemasons and Rosicrucians in England and gave much to both groups. Here are some of his thoughts about **truth**:

Exhibit 46: Francis Lord Bacon

"...Truth, which only doth judge itself, teacheth, that the inquiry of Truth, which is the love-making, or wooing of it; the knowledge of Truth, which is the presence of it; and the belief of Truth, which is the enjoying of it; is the sovereign good of human nature.

"The first creature of God, in the works of the days, was the light of the sense; the last, was the light of reason; and His Sabbath work, ever since, is the illumination of His spirit. First He breathed light, upon the face, of the matter or chaos; then He breathed light, into the face of man; and still He breatheth and inspireth light, into the face of His chosen.

"The poet, that beautified the sect, that was otherwise inferior to the rest, saith yet excellently well: It is a pleasure to stand upon the shore, and to see ships tost upon the sea: a pleasure to stand in the window of a castle, and to see a battle, and the adventures thereof, below: but no pleasure is comparable, to the standing, upon the vantage ground of Truth: (a hill not to be commanded, and where the air is always clear, and serene;) and to see the errors, and wanderings, and mists, and tempests, in the vale below: so always, that this prospect, be with pity, and not with swelling, or pride.

"Certainly, it is Heaven upon earth, to have a man's mind move in charity, rest in providence, and turn upon the poles of Truth...."

Following Bacon, the great Rosicrucian, Sir Isaac Newton, made gigantic contributions to knowledge. Some were:

1. AD 1665: Discovered differential calculus.

2. AD 1666: Discovered integral calculus, separated the colors of the rainbow with a prism, and calculated the orbit of the moon.

3. AD 1668: Built the first reflecting telescope.

4. AD 1687: Published his **Principia,** the most important book in science until the current century. He set forth his three laws of motion, the motion of bodies in the universe, and his theory of gravity which stood unchallenged until Einstein.

5. AD 1690: Proposed a particle theory of light, which was later proven to be true. There is also a wave theory of light that is also true.

6. AD 1698: Calculated the speed of sound. A German scientist had earlier in, AD 1675, calculated the speed of light as being a finite number.

7. AD 1704: Published his **Opticks**, summarizing his work on the nature of light.

As a Rosicrucian, Newton never took holy orders. He was appointed head of the mint as a channel through which to reward him for his many contributions. He died in AD 1727.

The year AD 1717 is the year that some Freemasons of the Blue Lodge seem to think that their lodge actually came into existence. The Roman Church would also like to think that the Blue Lodge was a post-Middle Ages organization. After all, if you have enjoyed total power for 1000 years, and mighty kings like Charlemagne could not locate AMORC or the Blue Lodge, then surely they must not have even existed at that time. Not true.

If some organization, such as the Roman Church:

1. Burned first your parents and then all of their acquaintances.

2. Burned your parents' marriage license and all other official birth records.

3. Accused you of being a bastard and demanded that you prove otherwise.

4. Refused to allow you to use Muslim and Buddhist records, just how would you go about proving your innocence?

Answer: Only with great difficulty. But that is exactly the situation for both AMORC and the Blue Lodge in Western culture.

The author suggests that the Roman Church and some of its progeny do not have the standing even to make any such demands against AMORC and the Blue Lodge. Let him who is without sin cast the first stone. The Roman Church stands accused of being a bastard child itself. Let it prove, not to its own choir, but to an impartial jury of outsiders such as perhaps, the Buddhists, the Muslims, or the Blue Lodge itself, that it has some honest connection to Master Jesus the Christ. It will not do that because it cannot.

Master Jesus the Christ is most highly honored as a saint by the Buddhists; as a prophet by the Muslims; and certainly, both AMORC and the Blue Lodge honor him as the best and highest person ever among themselves.

The Roman Church and its descendants have done little except to dishonor Master Jesus the Christ. The time is quickly approaching when they will want to do otherwise, we hope. Those who suggest that America is a **Christian** nation know not of which they speak; or, they seek deliberately to mislead the unknowing. The United States of America was set up as a secular nation under the One True God but not under the Christian church gods. It was designed and set up by Freemasons to function pursuant to the teachings of Master Jesus the Christ -- not the Christian church. Jews, Muslims, Buddhists, and others have equal religious rights and freedom with Christians and others.

Thomas Jefferson became a legend in his own time. Einstein may be the smartest American ever, but Jefferson must be the smartest native-born American yet to this time in history. Jefferson was like the biblical Joseph in that he had a coat of many colors, which is to say that he was a genius in many different areas of human endeavor.

Jefferson wrote the Declaration of Independence, as well as other documents, on the rights of man. In these, he created the idea of the brotherhood of man directly from the second degree teachings of the Freemasonic Lodge. Jefferson stated in *"THE UNANIMOUS DECLARATION of the thirteen united STATES OF AMERICA"* that:

> "...We hold these truths to be self evident, that all men are created equal, that they are endowed by their Creator with certain unalienable Rights, that among these are Life, Liberty and the pursuit of Happiness...."

The Declaration was passed and went into effect on July 4, 1776. This gave birth to the United States of America, which is the greatest country the world has ever known. Jefferson's thinking on equality of potential of the human species has so permeated the American psyche that Americans do not realize that such thinking does not yet exist in other parts of the world, including even Great Britain.

The idea of the republic has now spread almost world-wide, and is the very idea that has crumbled the communist dictatorships that, in their turn, had earlier crumbled the aristocracies of Eastern Europe and Russia. The republic must be the greatest political idea of all time.

Jefferson truly understood the need for education and created the University of Virginia. He was America's foremost educator. He was also the leading architect of early America and a physical scientist in several areas. Jefferson is the man who expanded the United States from the original thirteen colonies to the vast nation it later became. If Nobel Prizes had been awarded in those days, he might well have collected several: all in different fields.

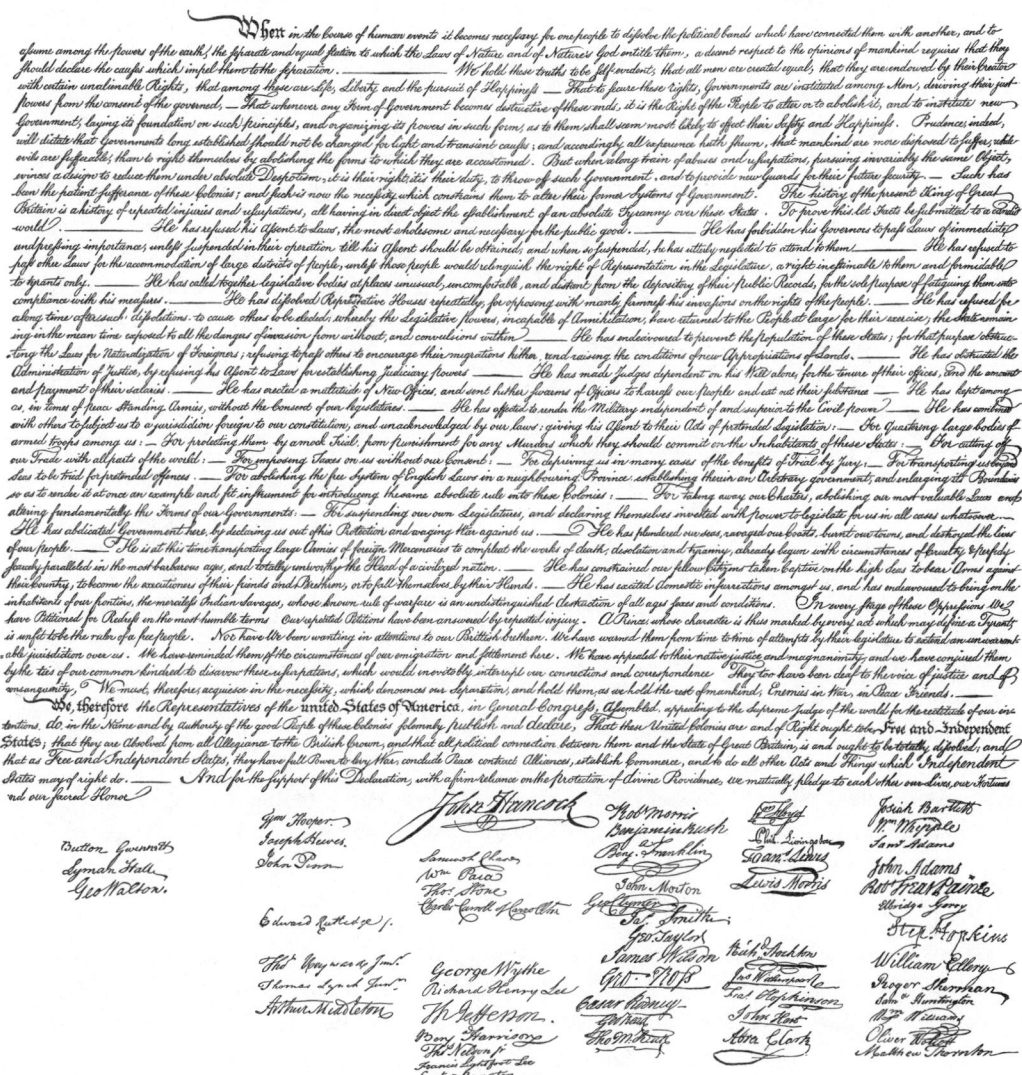

Exhibit 47: The Declaration of Independence of the United States of America which was written by Thomas Jefferson in 1776. Note that John Hancock signed first with his signature large enough that the British King could read it without his glasses.

Jefferson also knew and understood very clearly that times change and that while basic government foundations should be built on sound principles, they must also have flexibility to change with the times. In that regard he stated:

> *"Some men look at constitutions with sanctimonious reverence, and deem them like the ark of the covenant, too sacred to be touched. They ascribe to the men of the preceding age a wisdom more than human, and suppose what they did to be beyond amendment. I knew that age well; I belonged to it and labored with it. It deserved well of its country. ...But I know also, that laws and institutions must go hand in hand with the progress of the human mind. As that becomes more developed, more enlightened, as new discoveries are made, new truths disclosed, and **manners and opinions change with the change of circumstances, institutions must advance also, and keep pace with the times.**..."*

Does Jefferson's view of the Constitution perhaps give Congress the power to impose gun control?

Most of the New England states were religiously dominated, not by the Roman Church but instead by the Puritans. They were as intolerant and ignorant as the Roman Church, but without a pope. In the early AD 1690s, in Salem, Massachusetts several people, mostly women, were put to death for being witches. Holy Toledo! That was the infamous Inquisition right here in America.

In AD 1705, Virginia passed a law which disqualified a person from holding office if he denied the existence of God, **the trinity**, or asserted that there are more gods than one; denied the Christian religion to be true; or, if he denied that the **Bible** is divine authority. Note that a person was required to believe, both, that there is only one God, and also that there are three gods which, of course, is a contradiction on its face by its own terms.

This was a detestable statute and Jefferson made no secret of the fact that he wanted it repealed. Jefferson fervently believed that our civil rights have no dependence on our religious opinions, any more than our opinions on physics and geometry. Jefferson shocked some of his friends when he stated:

> *"The legitimate powers of government extend to such acts only as are injurious to others. But it does me no injury for my neighbor to say there are twenty gods, or no god. It neither picks my pocket nor breaks my leg."*

In AD 1777, Jefferson drafted the Virginia Statute for Religious Freedom, which today is America's most unique contribution to the good of mankind. In drafting this statute, Jefferson stated, in some of the more profound observations yet made, that we are:

"well aware that Almighty God had created the mind free; that all attempts to influence it by temporal punishments or burthens (burdens), or by civil incapacitations, tend only to beget habits of hypocrisy and meanness, and are a departure from the plan of the Holy Author of our religion, who, being Lord both of body and mind, yet chose not to propagate it by coercions on either, as was in his Almighty power to do."

"The impious presumption of legislators and rulers, civil as well as ecclesiastical, who, being themselves but fallible and uninspired men have assumed dominion over the faith of others, setting up their own opinions and modes of thinking as the only true and infallible, and as such endeavoring to impose them on others, **hath established and maintained false religions over the greatest part of the world, and through all time.***"*

"To compel a man to furnish contributions of money for the propagation of opinions which he disbelieves is sinful and tyrannical." or, *"Even forcing him to support this or that teacher of his own religious persuasion..."*

Jefferson felt that such would deprive man of his liberty and is a violation of his natural rights. The statute then stated:

"Be it therefore enacted by the General Assembly, That no man shall be compelled to frequent or support any religious worship, place or ministry whatsoever, nor shall be enforced, restrained, molested, or burthened (burdened) in his body or goods, nor shall otherwise suffer on account of his religious opinions or belief; but that all men shall be free to profess, and by argument to maintain, their opinions in matters of religion, and that the same shall in no wise diminish, enlarge, or affect their civil capacities...."

"And though we well know that this Assembly, elected by the people for the ordinary purposes of legislation only, have no power to restrain the acts of succeeding Assemblies, constituted with powers equal to our own, and that therefore to declare this act irrevocable would be of no effect in law, yet we are free to declare, and do declare, that **if any act shall be hereafter passed to repeal the present, or to narrow rights hereby asserted such act will be an infringement of natural right...***"*

The brilliant Jefferson knew that future legislatures could undo his work, but he made it very difficult for them ever to do so. This has to be one of the great achievements of the human mind and yet it exactly follows the teachings of Master Jesus. Copies of this statute were printed and circulated in Paris and from there it spread throughout the entire world. In his life, Jefferson did many great things, but this was the single greatest achievement of his life, surpassing even the Declaration of Independence. It made Jefferson a legend in his own time.

In AD 1784, the Commonwealth of Virginia had agreed to transfer the Northwest Territory, now composed of the states of Ohio, Indiana, Illinois, Michigan, and Wisconsin, to the US. Jefferson made a report on the matter to the Virginia Assembly but his report failed to be adopted by one vote. Later, the Northwest Ordinance of 1787, taken from Jefferson's earlier report, was passed by the Continental Congress on July 13, 1787, which was prior to adoption of the US Constitution. It is one of the great pieces of legislation of all time.

There were six articles in the ordinance which covered the rights of citizens in the territory so that the US would not make the same mistakes with the territory that England had made with the thirteen colonies.

The fourth article covered general government rule-making for the territory, and article five set out the geographic size of the new states and required that the governments in the territory be republican in form.

Articles 1, 2, 3, and 6 provided:

> Article 1: "*No person demeaning himself in a peaceable and orderly manner shall ever be molested on account of his mode of worship or religious sentiments in the said territory...*"
>
> Article 2: "*The Inhabitants of the said territory shall always be entitled to the benefits of the writ of **habeas corpus**, and of the **trial by Jury**; of a proportionate representation of the people in the legislature, and of judicial proceedings according to the course of the common law; all Persons shall be **bailable** unless for capital offences, where the proof shall be evident, or the presumption great; all fines shall be moderate, and **no cruel or unusual punishments** shall be inflicted; no man shall be deprived of his liberty or property but by the judgment of his Peers, or **the law of the land**; and should the public exigencies make it necessary for the common preservation to take any person's property, or to demand his particular services, **full compensation shall be made** for the same; and in the just preservation of rights and property it is understood and declared, that no law ought ever to be made, or have force in the said territory, that shall in any manner whatever interfere with, or affect private contracts or engagements, bona fide and without fraud previously formed.*"
>
> Article 3: "*Religion, Morality and knowledge being necessary to good government and the happiness of mankind, Schools and the means of education shall forever be encouraged....*"
>
> Article 6: "*There shall be neither Slavery nor involuntary Servitude in the said territory otherwise than in the punishment of crimes, whereof the Party shall have been duly convicted:...*"

What a document! It would be well to remember that all people in the Northwest Territory had rights in 1777 that were not granted to all people in the US by the US

Exhibit 48: Jefferson Memorial, Washington DC, USA

Constitution until after the War Between the States in the AD 1860s, more than 80 years later. Note that Article 6 prohibits indentured servants as well as slaves in the territory and the new states.

Virginia had already passed legislation against importation of slaves into Virginia. And now, strange as it may seem, slavery was actually illegal in the Northwest Territory which, until 1787, had been a part of Virginia.

In these matters, Jefferson left much of the work of obtaining passage to his proteges, James Madison and James Monroe. Both men were totally dedicated to Jefferson and to putting into effect his ideas and programs.

Thomas Jefferson was the foremost thinker among all the Founding Fathers of the US even though he was among the youngest of the group. He was a Rosicrucian but, unlike almost all the others, was not a Freemason. Even though he owned slaves he was strongly opposed to slavery and frequently borrowed pocket change from his own personal slave who often traveled with him. Had slavery been prohibited in the Declaration of Independence, as he wanted it to be, the US might have avoided the horribly bloody War Between the States some eighty plus years later.

Jefferson did obtain a prohibition on slavery in the Northwest Ordinance of 1787 which prohibited slavery in a large part of what was then Virginia, but is now the states of Ohio, Indiana, Illinois, Michigan, and Wisconsin. Other parts of Virginia such as Kentucky and West Virginia also later became anti-slavery although Kentucky had some mixed feelings on the subject.

The importance of Jefferson's position on slavery cannot be over-stated. With the US Midwest legally bound to anti-slavery, this anti slavery concept carried then on to the West as people from the North moved west and settled the rest of the United States. Slavery became isolated to less than a dozen states in the southeastern US. Even the English courts adopted Jefferson's views on slavery in 1832.

Jefferson also believed in the full equality of women. He said:

> *"The women are submitted to unjust drudgery. This I believe is the case with every barbarous people. With such, force is law. The stronger sex therefore imposes on the weaker. It is civilization alone which replaces women in the enjoyment of their natural equality."*

Two very powerful men, Ben Franklin from Pennsylvania and John Adams from Massachusetts, backed Jefferson emphatically and totally. Why? Because both men recognized the younger Jefferson as the premier philosopher and mind in the whole group. In short, in terms of history and as Freemasons, they knew he was right.

Either John Adams or Ben Franklin would have been the logical choice to draft the Declaration of Independence but both begged off. Franklin felt that he had long ago quit trying to counsel public bodies because such bodies seldom listen very well, which is quite true.

John Adams in his usual blunt fashion told Jefferson that he, Adams, was obnoxious and unpopular, which was not totally true, whereas Jefferson was very popular and well-liked, and also because Jefferson could write ten times better, which was true. Adams also wanted a Virginian to head the group just as later Adams wanted George Washington, rather than his friend and neighbor John Hancock from Massachusetts, to be commander-in-chief of the armed forces.

Why did John Adams always push Virginians into the forefront of leadership in the American Revolutionary cause? There are two reasons. One was economic and the other was intellectual. Even in 1776 the Commonwealth of Virginia was a very old, well established government over a large territory, to-wit: Virginia, West Virginia, Kentucky, Ohio, Indiana, Illinois, Michigan, and Wisconsin. Incidentally, Virginia was a commonwealth on its own for almost as long as it has been a part of the US.

In gross national product Virginia was equal to or greater than all the other states combined. But, the biggest difference was in brain-power. Virginia had a lot of very well educated men. Just a few were George Wythe, Patrick Henry, George Mason, the entire Randolph family, Richard Henry Lee, John Marshall, George Washington and, of course, Jefferson and his proteges, James Madison and James Monroe, to name only a few. John Adams knew that for the American cause to succeed they had to have Virginia's leadership and money.

If Jefferson was the heart and soul of the American Revolution then John Adams was the rock upon which it was built. On July 3, 1776 Adams wrote to his wife, Abigail, about the Declaration of Independence in glowing and prophetic terms:

> "...*The second day of July, 1776 will be the most memorable epoch in the history of America. I am apt to believe that it will be celebrated by succeeding generations as the great anniversary festival. It ought to be commemorated as the day of deliverance, by solemn acts of devotion to God Almighty. It ought to be solemnized with pomp and parade, with shows, games, sport, guns, bells, bon-fires, and illuminations, from one end of this continent to the other, from this time forward for evermore....*"

Adams was so right except that when the public announcement was made on July 4th that is the day that is celebrated yet to the present day, and celebrated exactly as Adams predicted it should be.

It would be well to remember that Congress deleted about one fourth of Jefferson's Declaration of Independence before it was voted on and approved. Jefferson was very upset about the deletion of his passage on abolishing slavery which he denounced for the rest of his life. Again, Jefferson was right and Congress was wrong. Indeed, Congress did desecrate his masterpiece. Even so the Declaration of Independence stands as the outstanding political document of all time.

There is some controversy, but no doubt, about what Jefferson really meant about all people being created equal. He meant that all people are created equal, morally and potentially, in the eyes of God. All human beings share equally the ability to judge between right and wrong and this is true without regard to economics, education, or conditions of birth. Modern courts would do well to remember this when isolating juries which, in itself, should be unconstitutional. When judges are the triers of fact they are not locked up. Why then juries? Are jurors less bright or less honest than judges?

In 1785, Jefferson went to Paris as the US Ambassador to France where he remained until 1789 shortly after the French Revolution broke out in which he was deeply involved. While in Paris, the genius Jefferson traveled around Europe meeting other Rosicrucians and surveying everything Europe had to offer, including the women. Jefferson was a prolific letter writer and much of his tremendous influence derived from the clarity and logic of his written communications. While in Paris, he fell and broke his wrist which hampered his writing for several months.

Jefferson was much interested in agriculture and collected seeds and plants. He made sketches of all the unique buildings and methods of construction he encountered. He also developed very close friendships with several European ladies, and had a love affair with at least one married woman. However, allegations by his opponents that he fathered children by one of his slave girls were not true.

He also held meetings with revolutionary leaders from Brazil and was in constant meetings with the leaders of the revolution in France. He was present and deeply involved with the French National Assembly in the spring and summer of AD 1789.

Although Jefferson found fault with about everything in the French government he did put his confidence in the National Assembly, which he felt was **cool, temperate, and sagacious**. He attended the assembly every day as though a shepherd caring for his flock. On June 2, 1789, Jefferson actually drafted a charter granting to the National Assembly sole power and authority over both taxes and appropriations. When bread riots erupted in Paris, the report circulated through the city that Jefferson had offered to ship grain from America but the French government had refused.

The arrogant and malicious French queen, Marie Antoinette, upon hearing of the bread riots made her infamous statement that if the people could not find bread then let them eat cake instead. She was the daughter of the Austrian king who was also the employer and sponsor of musical genius and leading Freemason, Mozart. The queen's cake comment may be the last straw that actually cost her and the French king, Louis XVI, their heads.

The author offers the hypothesis that after the French queen was beheaded, and Mozart published his famous **Magic Flute**, which praised the virtues of Freemasonry, the Austrian king came to believe that Mozart was either directly involved, or at least in sympathy, with the French Revolution and with Marie's execution. In retaliation, the king had Mozart poisoned.

Jefferson's friend, Lafayette, who had helped lead the American armies to victory over the British was trying to draft a Declaration of Rights for the French similar to the Virginia Declaration of Rights and the US Declaration of Independence. Jefferson helped him with this effort. In violation of the rules of conduct for foreign diplomats, he actually had the leaders of the National Assembly to his home for dinner when many of their revolutionary plans were discussed and agreed upon. He was also actually out in the streets of Paris on the night of July 14 when the French civil war began in earnest. Was Jefferson in danger from the mobs that were hanging people from lamp-posts in the streets? Not at all; Jefferson was their hero and he knew it. The French National Assembly did adopt a Declaration of Rights patterned after the two documents from the US.

Jefferson was then presented with a shock from one of his daughters; she wanted to become a Catholic nun. To the Rosicrucian Jefferson, this would happen only over his dead body. Before enrolling his daughter in the school, he had exacted a promise from the Catholic sisters that they would not try to convert his daughter to catholicism but something went wrong.

In October, 1789, Jefferson took his daughter out of school, and, with his family, returned to the US where a constitution had been put into effect, but the US Constitution also needed a Bill of Rights which it would very soon have.

In AD 1800, Jefferson defeated John Adams for the presidency and he and his protegès controlled that office for the next 24 years. Jefferson's election was the closest and most controversial in all US history. It resulted in the death of Alexander Hamilton when Aaron Burr killed him in a duel.

Jefferson was Republican, anti-royalty, and anti-church to the very core of his being. He emphasized his anti-royalty image by walking from his boarding house to the capital for his inauguration as president of the US. President William **Jefferson** Clinton recently copied Thomas Jefferson by walking to the capital. Jefferson was opposed to tobacco even though for economic reasons he was forced to grow it. It has been said that the only **vice** Jefferson ever had was when he was **vice**-president and he lost that one by becoming president. Strange as it may seem, Jefferson never considered being president of the US as one of the major accomplishments of his life.

Perhaps most fitting to both John Adams and Thomas Jefferson is that not only did they both live to ripe old ages, but both died on the same day: July 4, 1826, the 50th birthday of the Declaration of Independence. Is that not strange? The two men were near and dear friends throughout their lives except for a brief period of mis-understanding around 1800 when Jefferson defeated Adams for the presidency. Even in that contest, Jefferson and Aaron Burr tied for first and President Adams came in third on the first ballot. President Adams then threw his support to Jefferson who won.

Jefferson, being the complete man that he was, wrote his own epitaph. In that epitaph he failed to mention that he had been president of the United States because he did not view that as one of the major achievements of his life. Jefferson was a Rosicrucian. He was also falsely accused by priests and preachers of his time as being an atheist. Would they so accuse today? Probably, most would not. That does not mean, of course, that Jefferson's views ever changed; only that the priests became sufficiently enlightened to understand him.

It is difficult to pinpoint exactly when and where it was decided that America would have a vastly different value system from that in Europe, from whence the people came. **The Mayflower Compact**, signed on November 11, 1620, states:

> "...IN The Name of God. Amen. We, whose names are underwritten... Do by these Presents, solemnly and mutually in the Presence of God and one another, covenant and combine ourselves together into a civil Body Politick, for our better Ordering and Preservation, and Furtherance of the Ends aforesaid. And by Virtue hereof do enact, constitute, and frame, such just and **equal** Laws, Ordinances, Acts, Constitutions, and Offices, from time to time to time, as shall be thought most meet and convenient for the general Good of the Colony..."

The Compact was signed by William Bradford, Miles Standish, John Alden, and 38 other men of the group. One can see the idea of **equality** in this very early American document.

All the founding fathers of America were Freemasons and men of God, but were not necessarily supporters of the Christian churches. George Washington, a Master Mason, once observed:

> "...Flattering as it may be to the human mind, and truly honourable as it is to receive from our fellow citizens testimonies of approbation for exertions to promote the public welfare, it is not less pleasing to know that the milder virtues of the heart are highly respected by a Society (Freemasonic Order) whose liberal principles must be founded in the immutable laws of truth and justice. To enlarge the sphere of social happiness is worthy of the benevolent design of a Masonic institution; and it is most fervently to be wished that the conduct of every member of the Fraternity, as well as those publications that discover the principles which actuate them, may tend to convince

mankind that **the great object of Masonry is to promote the happiness of the human race....**"

Ben Franklin was not particularly religious in the **churchy** sense, but he had a profound belief in God. Franklin stated his belief to be:

"*Here is my Creed. I believe in one God, Creator of the Universe. That he governs it by his Providence. That he ought to be worshipped. That the most acceptable service we render him is doing good to his other children. That the soul of man is immortal and will be treated with justice in another life respecting its conduct in this....*"

He also recognized that in Western culture people could not learn about God from the churches, so the Freemasonic Lodge was essential. Franklin stated:

"*...Freemasonry has tenets peculiar to itself. They serve as testimonials of character and qualifications which are only conferred after due course of instruction and examination. These are of no small value; they speak a universal language, and act as a passport to the attention and support of the initiated in all parts of the world. They cannot be lost as long as memory retains its power. Let the possessor of them be expatriated, shipwrecked or imprisoned, let him be stripped of everything he has got in the world, still those credentials remain, and are available for use as circumstances require.* **The good effects they have produced are established by the most incontestable facts of history.** *They have stayed the uplifted hand of the destroyer; they have softened the asperities of the tyrant; they have mitigated the horrors of captivity; they have subdued the rancour of malevolence; and broken down the barriers of political animosity and sectarian alienation. On the field of battle, in the solitudes of the uncultivated forest, or in the busy haunts of the crowded city, they have made men of the most hostile feelings, the most distant regions, and diversified conditions, rush to the aid of each other, and feel a special joy and satisfaction that they have been able to afford relief to a Brother Mason....*"

It is obvious from the above that Franklin knew that the Freemasonic Lodge is an ancient and universal institution. Franklin, like Jefferson, also recognized that the US Constitution was less than perfect because people are less than perfect. Franklin thought that the US government would serve the people well for a time, but then would degrade into corruption and issued a sober warning:

"*...I agree to this Constitution, with all its faults, if they are such; because I think a general government necessary for us, and there is no form of government but what may be a blessing to the people if well administered; and I believe farther that this is likely to be well administered for a course of years,* **and can only end in despotism as other forms have done before it, when the people shall become so corrupted as to need despotic government, being incapable of any other.**"

Washington was acutely aware of the dangers lying ahead for his beloved country. His farewell address was read to the House of Representatives on September 19, 1796. One paragraph of that address pointedly warned against excessive militarism and foreign entanglements. Washington warned:

*"...While then every part of our Country thus feels an immediate and particular interest in Union, all the parts combined in the united mass of means and efforts cannot fail to find greater strength, greater resource, proportionably greater security from external danger, a less frequent interruption of their Peace by foreign Nations; and, what is of inestimable value! they must derive from Union **an exemption from those broils and wars between themselves, which so frequently afflict neighboring countries**, not tied together by the same governments; which their own rival ships alone would be sufficient to produce; but which opposite foreign alliances, attachments, and intrigues would stimulate and embitter. --Hence likewise they will avoid the necessity of those **overgrown Military establishments, which, under any form of government, are inauspicious to liberty, and which are to be regarded as particularly hostile to Republican Liberty**. In this sense it is, that your Union ought to be considered as a main prop to your liberty, and that the love of the one ought to endear to you the reservation of the other...."*

"...The great rule of conduct for us, in regard to foreign Nations, is, in extending our commercial relations, to have with them as little Political connection as possible. -- So far as we have already formed engagements, let them be fulfilled with perfect good faith. -- Here let us stop. -- ..."

Are there serious people who would dispute that excessive militarism and foreign entanglements have brought the United States to the edge of financial and moral bankruptcy? Surely few.

Truly, many great men set up the United States of America. Which men exerted the most influence in that effort? The author's list of the seven most influential would be in order: Thomas Jefferson, John Adams, Ben Franklin, George Washington, John Hancock, James Madison, and Patrick Henry. In later years, one could add John Marshall, Andrew Jackson, and Abraham Lincoln.

As early as 1815, the United States government legally bound itself to stop the slave trade. Article ten of the treaty with Great Britain, which ended the war of 1812, stated:

"Whereas the traffic in slaves is irreconcilable with the principles of humanity and justice, and whereas both His Majesty and the United States are desirous of continuing their efforts to pronounce its entire abolition, it is hereby agreed that both the contracting parties shall use their best endeavours to accomplish so desirable an object...."

This treaty became effective in February, 1815, and addressed the issue of trading in slaves, but not slavery in the United States itself.

These principles were all available to Lincoln when he decided to emancipate the slaves. Lincoln knew he was right and that his view ultimately would prevail. Without the approval of Congress or anyone else, on January 1, 1863, Lincoln forever freed the slaves. His very simple but most profound proclamation said it all:

> "...Whereas, on the twenty-second day of September, in the year of our Lord one thousand eight hundred and sixty-two, a proclamation was issued by the President (Lincoln) of the United States, containing, among other things, the following, to wit:
>
> *'That on the first day of January, in the year of our Lord one thousand eight hundred and sixty-three, all persons held as slaves...shall be then, thence forward, and forever free;...*"

The North already enjoyed a political and economic advantage over the South. Now it had a decided moral advantage as well.

The Rosetta Stone was discovered at Rosetta, Egypt, by the French in AD 1799. This made it possible to translate Egyptian hieroglyphics for the first time since the Roman Church burned the great library at Alexandria, Egypt. The vast knowledge of that ancient culture became available to the general public in Western culture. This too was a pivotal event in Western culture. For the first time in almost 2000 years, Western culture could get a true glimpse of its own source.

Albert Einstein was a German and a Jew. He was probably one of the most enlightened men who has ever lived, but he had to leave his home in Germany in 1933 because he was a Jew. This one man:

1. In 1905 developed the Special Theory of Relativity which gave rise to atomic energy and the understanding of many other secrets of nature.

2. In 1916 developed the General Theory of Relativity which corrected Newton's theory of gravity and is usually considered the single greatest intellectual achievement of all time.

3. In the 1920s helped develop Quantum Theory which forever destroyed determinism, and which, Einstein could never intellectually accept even though he was responsible for some of its development. Quantum Theory is the most successful and useful theory in the history of physical science.

The very name **Einstein**, yet today, is synonymous with high intelligence.

290 TRUE ESOTERIC TRADITIONS

In 1947, some old documents were located in a cave in Jordan. Those documents have become known as the Dead Sea Scrolls. A small group of scholars have been studying those scrolls since 1947. Although there have been many partial analyses; as yet, no over-all summary of them has been published.

Exhibit 49: Cave in Jordan where the Dead Sea Scrolls were found by a shepherd boy in 1947. They have been the source of raging controversy ever since their discovery.

Throughout history the Rosicrucians, or in this case the Essenes, moved their records from place to place in order to keep them out of the hands of the wrong people. This happened in 1335 BC at the time of the Exodus event, when the Israelites went underground and left Egypt.

It did not happen at the time of Alexander the Great because Alexander approved of learning and was himself a student of Aristotle. Although Aristotle was wrong in some of his ideas, he did favor learning.

The hiding of documents also happened at the time of the fall of Jerusalem in the AD 66 to 70 period at the same time the Jewish army general Josephus, later a historian, was captured by the Romans. Some of the scrolls were written on copper, obviously to be preserved over a long period of time.

Most of the world, at this time, seems to think that the Dead Sea Scrolls were merely the teachings of a small sect of Jews known as the Essenes. Some few Jews were Essenes, but not all Essenes were Jews, by any means.

The author offers the hypothesis that the Dead Sea Scrolls, when fully and finally analyzed will prove to be a diverse body of knowledge; and not just the documents of a small Jewish sect. The Dead Sea Scrolls may not fit the current orthodoxy of either the Jews or the Christian churches. Very understandably, the editors need to be very sure of their work because they will be crucified and vilified. That is probably the real reason that no major summary has yet been published. A wise editor might publish his analysis only the day before he dies. Hell hath no fury like a priest scorned.

AD 70 was also the same time that the Essenes disappeared from history. The reason for that disappearance was that the Essenes were one and the same thing as the Gnostic-enlightened Christians, and were thereafter known under that name. They continued under the Gnostic name until again they had to go underground because of Roman-church persecution in about AD 400 and thereafter. At that time, copies of the records were removed to Tibet. Apparently, some were also hidden in the cave in Jordan.

For more than 1000 years, the Rosicrucians stayed completely underground and have only very slowly resurfaced during the last 400 years or so.

In AD 1314, the pope and king wanted two things from the Knights Templar. First, they wanted their vast treasury; and second, they wanted their secret manuscripts brought to France from Israel during the First Crusade. They burned Jacques de Molay and 70 of his fellow Templars (they thought to be the Sanhedrin) to death, but they obtained neither the vast treasury nor the secret documents.

In AD 1939, a removal of many documents from France took place only days before the German army took control of that country. History indeed proves that sharing knowledge with the world is a very dangerous business. Master Jesus proved that. Hopefully, those tendencies are abating as we head toward the next century.

The AD 1930s, in Europe, saw the rise of the most evil human being ever to live upon Earth. Hitler was perhaps no more evil than some Roman-church popes, but he did have a mechanized military force so that he could torture and murder more people more quickly and more economically.

For centuries, the popes tortured and murdered millions of innocent victims and stole all the property they could get their hands on. Recent studies show that the Roman Church, over several hundred years, tortured to death as many as 9,000,000 people. Dear God, what a horribly evil institution! Hitler simply murdered the people and destroyed the property.

Among the many contributions of Albert Einstein was that of atomic energy, including atomic bombs in the AD 1940s. While the atom bomb is viewed as a scourge on mankind by some, it made man finally begin to realize that wars usually solve very little and are often counter-productive to the evolution of mankind.

Is it not an irony of history that, since AD 1945, both Germany and Japan have become more Americanized, while the United States of America has become as Germany and Japan used to be. Japan now enjoys the benefits of the original dream of America, with a free enterprise economy and the historic American ideal of a non-aggressive nation. Germany also enjoys those same benefits of a free enterprise economy and the historic American ideal of a non-aggressive nation.

In AD 1961, America began its illegal and immoral intrusion into Asia, and also began irresponsibly to spend itself towards financial bankruptcy. Even worse, America committed mass murder and raised the level of violence in the world to new highs. Under the Law of Compensation this created violence in America in return. This was also simply the Law of Cause and Effect at work. The cause was America's violence unleashed against the Far East, the Middle East, and Central America. The effect was naturally enough that the same amount of violence was unleashed within America itself, in return.

America wrings its hands in dismay at the violence in its own streets and seems not even to perceive the cause. Where are the Freemasons when America needs them so desperately? America has appointed itself the policeman of the world. But who will protect the world from the policeman? Moral leadership of the world is passing from America to the former Soviet Union, Germany, and Japan.

America, for only a short time, has been the self-appointed and brutalizing policeman of the world, but in the process it lost its much higher position as conscience for the world. And now America has also become the fireman of the world. A good fireman tries to pour water on a small fire and put it out. But America has a new way to handle a small fire. It pours gasoline on it until it eventually becomes a roaring inferno. America spends money it does not have to create violence where it has no business and, as a result, visits both violence and bankruptcy upon its own people.

Many Americans have died trying to bring violence to America. Literally, billions have been spent in order to bring violence to America. We have worked for it and we have paid for it, and we are entitled to have it right here in our own land. By Cosmic Law it is our due, and we demand justice. We want our violence because we honor and love it so. It will be so. And the end is not yet.

However, man must always retain a positive outlook on life and prospects for the future. Things can be better than they now are. As the late and very prominent Freemason, Dr. Norman Vincent Peale, has stated:

> "...train your mind never to accept the thought of defeat about anything. That verse from the **Bible** makes an unbeatable inspiration in any situation: 'If God be for us, who can be against us?' Hold it habitually in mind and it will train you to believe in yourself by constantly reminding you that you have extra power available."

And in the end it will be so.

It would seem
that love and religion
should have something in
common. In fact, they seldom do.

Abraham Lincoln
Gettysburg, Pennsylvania USA
November 19, 1863

-- "that this nation,
under God, shall have
a new birth of freedom -
and that government of the
people, by the people, for the
people shall not perish from the earth".

CLOSING STATEMENT

Dear readers, you have now heard my case. I say that you can be free. Free to set aside many of the unenlightened teachings forced upon mankind by the Christian churches. And free also to seek out the true teachings of Master Jesus the Christ. He or she who earnestly seeks shall be rewarded. If it were not so, Master Jesus surely would have told us.

I began this book with the purpose of tracing the source of our Western cultural values. Hopefully, some information has been presented which will help the reader in understanding that source. I do understand that some of the thoughts presented here may be discomforting to some Christian readers. So mote it be.

We know that God does exist, but the truth of only One True God is very difficult for many people to comprehend. The Hindus and Christians still teach a trinity of gods, and the Jews still teach a private tribal god. We, in Western culture, stand amazed at the power of Islam and seem not to realize that Islam, almost alone, teaches only One True God for all mankind. This is true even though Islam is degrading to women as are also the Christian churches. All the major religions degrade women. Is it not a disgrace that a pope and other religious leaders living in the AD 1990s could still be trying to justify such a blatant anti-female bias?

The idea of One True God perhaps goes back even to the Garden of Eden, but I have traced it only to the biblical Hebrew Joseph in Egypt and the teachings of the Sons of Light, or what I have called the White Lodge. The idea of one God left Egypt in an Exodus event, about 1335 BC, and has been passed down to us from the Hebrew Kabalists into the teachings of Master Jesus the Christ.

It was Thomas Jefferson who performed two great services for mankind. First, he revealed to the public, in the Declaration of Independence, the brotherhood teachings of the Freemasonic Lodge: that all the human species, if not equal now, are at least equal in potential, and therefore equal in the eyes of God.

Jefferson also understood, and I believe that he was the first person to so perceive, that religion and government should **not** be co-mingled. This is one of the best things that has ever happened to free man's mind from imposed belief systems and allow him to come to seek the One True God. Jefferson was also instrumental in abolishing slavery and involuntary servitude in the US Midwest about 50 years before the English courts did so in England. However, it required a bloody civil war to achieve freedom for all Americans, 80 years later, in the AD 1860s.

The idea of the jury trial first began with Solon about 600 BC in Greece, but was lost during the long Dark Ages imposed on Western culture by the Roman Church. The idea resurfaced in England about AD 1166, then was adopted into Magna Carta in AD 1215, and was passed on down into the US Constitution. Trial by a jury of peers is a concept and right that is crucial to limited government. We should never, ever let the law professors take it away. The misuse and abuse of the jury trial system in places like California has ground justice almost to a halt. Lawyers are literally raping the public treasury, and they destroy anyone who tries to limit their thievery.

There is no reason why most trials could not and should not be handled in two weeks time. The US Constitution guarantees to all Americans the right to a speedy trial and that right is being trampled on and abused by lawyers for their own selfish gain. These are the people who should be protecting that right, but they default. The media supports such abuses for their own selfish reasons. The legal system and the media make money through long, drawn-out, and non-speedy, **unconstitutional** trials. Never, ever allow lawyers to have the final say on matters of justice.

The right of all citizens to use all institutions and facilities owned by the government is a very basic right that has only become a part of our law since the Brown school desegregation case in 1954. When I began college, blacks did not have the right to attend quality schools. Even today, black children are being bused all over the countryside like cattle, in some of the most blatant race discrimination the US has yet seen. Even our court system has defaulted here, and allows, and even mandates, such race discrimination. Blacks will never, ever achieve full equality until their children are allowed to be educated in good quality schools without unreasonable bussing.

A sizeable percentage of the world's population is now and has always been non-heterosexual or what today is called **gay**. This is not a matter of choice; people are simply born that way. Why is it so very difficult for these people to achieve equal treatment under the law? Many religions openly teach hatred towards such people. If Thomas Jefferson was correct in the Declaration of Independence -- that all people are created equal -- equal, that is, in potential, and therefore equal in the eyes of God, then such hate-mongers in the churches and elsewhere are wrong. It is the absolute and unequivocal duty of the Supreme Court of the US to uphold the Declaration of Independence in this respect.

All Americans have the right to control their own minds and their own bodies. We must fight every day and in every way to keep those rights. There are always some people around who will take them away. A woman's right to control her own body is fundamental. Without that right, women have no rights. The biggest danger to these rights is the professional religionists; that is, the people who make their living from teaching the abuse of those rights. Always beware of priests!

Freedom of religion, freedom of speech, freedom of the press, freedom to peaceably assemble, and freedom to petition the government for redress of grievances was first clearly set forth and mandated in the US Constitution. These are all precious rights and must be zealously defended and protected. This is true even though the print media became overly abusive in exercising its rights. We should be thankful for television, which is beginning to balance the scales.

Certainly blacks have been abused, but even black men had the right to vote long before women did. Women in the US won the right to vote only in 1921, and now, have the power to protect their other rights if they will only use it.

There is another Constitutional right that is **not** being protected at all. That is the right of taxpayers to not be required to pay taxes to provide roads to, and fire and police protection for, non-public properties that do not also pay their fair share of taxes. This includes the Christian churches and others. Members of these groups are stealing from their neighbors and the author pleads guilty. How can a church that steals teach the young not to do so? Very simply, it cannot.

However, even if I had the power to do so, I would not destroy the Christian churches. All churches are merely vehicles that lack any moral quality on their own. They are whatever they are led to be by the driving forces behind them. The Christian churches, as a whole, possess the largest capacity for good or evil of any institutions in the world. In the past much of that tremendous capacity has been used for evil purposes because the pope and other church leaders were not enlightened people.

But there is no law that says that such evil objectives must always and forever be the case. Someday, when the third Pope John XXIII, or Joan XXIII, takes over the papacy, everything could change. Just think of the power for good that the Roman Church, led by an enlightened third Pope John XXIII, could be in the world. It can and will happen someday, but perhaps not soon.

When will that Age of Intelligence begin? Not even the world's greatest optimist can seriously suggest that it has yet begun. Some students of Kabala compute that the world entered the Current Age in about 6 BC, or about the time Master Jesus the Christ was born. An interesting coincidence perhaps. If true, then the world will enter the Age of Aquarius or Intelligence about AD 2150. Certainly, the sooner the better.

It is worth recalling here that some teachings of AMORC indicate that in the coming so-called Aquarian Age, or what is called the Age of Intelligence, the Christ will come again to Earth. Also, they teach that in the next coming, the Christ will be known as John or Joan the Christ. Very interesting.

The author is reasonably convinced that when the Christ does indeed appear again in bodily form on this Earth, he or she, as the case may be, will not be so recognized by most people. This is particularly true of the so-called religious people.

As he was last time, the Christ will still be a threat to all religious leaders. As he did last time, the Christ will again try to show the world that man can become better than he now is. As he did last time, he will try to teach man how this can be done.

Also as happened last time, he will be recognized by a few and damned by many. And as happened last time, the religious leaders will not be among those who do recognize him. But more people will recognize him than did last time, and fewer will damn him. And then we will know that the world has come a long way during this Current Age, even though it still has a long way to go.

The coming of this new age will also mean that scientists must reformulate science to take into account the possibility of a lot of new knowledge. Much of this so-called new knowledge is really only ancient teachings rediscovered.

I would point out that Lord Bacon, who formulated the Scientific Method, also rediscovered and postulated inductive logic which gives us access to so much knowledge beyond the Scientific Method. Incidentally, Lord Bacon was also head of the worldwide Rosicrucian Order at that time, and that is why I have named the chapter of my book covering that period, **The Rosicrucian Enlightenment**.

The corner stone of the Scientific Method is that new experiments must be such that they can be duplicated, which allows us to predict with certainty the results. However, with inductive logic, we discover only one small truth and then generalize from that one small truth to a more general truth.

Very simply, some things at this time cannot be duplicated. The big bang is one example. The cosmic consciousness achieved by Master Jesus the Christ is another. And just maybe, communication between dimensions of reality between loved ones is yet another. But, because these things cannot be duplicated, and thus do not meet the standards of the Scientific Method, are we to discredit the knowledge learned therefrom? I think not, and the scientific community needs to broaden its views just as the religions of the world need to do likewise.

The most successful physical theory of all time is Quantum Mechanics. And yet, it is Quantum Mechanics that brings subjectivity into science and replaces determinism. It is Quantum Mechanics that replaces objectivity with subjectivity. It is Quantum Mechanics, and the Uncertainty Principle, that teaches us that some things are not always capable of being duplicated. It is likewise Quantum Mechanics, and the Uncertainty Principle, which teaches us that the Scientific Method, which has lifted Western Culture out of the superstitious malaise fostered by the Christian churches, still is not a sufficient methodology for the work that lies ahead.

Several years ago I read some of Stephen Hawking's material wherein he discussed, what he thought to be, a **new** concept about Superstring Theory, which theory suggests that there may exist multiple universes above or beyond this physical universe. I pointed out to Hawking that the idea of multiple universes is hardly a **new** idea since it was taught more than 3000 years ago in the ancient White Lodge of Egypt. Hawking did respond to my letter but seemed unaware that the idea of multiple universes has such an ancient history.

Hawking's application of Quantum Theory to the black holes suggested by calculations from Einstein's Theory of General Relativity is a most brilliant piece of work. Supposedly, Einstein's black holes have such dense gravity that nothing can escape from them, not even light. Incidentally, such a result would violate the Law of Cycles taught by the ancient White Lodge.

Hawking pointed out, correctly I think, that Quantum Theory would over-ride General Relativity and some radiation or energy would necessarily escape even from black holes. Perhaps black holes should instead be called gray holes. Again, the Law of Cycles does prevail. Again, it is an indeterminate universe in which we live. And also again, that sheet of paper we discussed earlier has no black and no white but, in reality, is all in shades of gray.

If one of the basic teachings of the White Lodge, which tells us that initiates could communicate with persons in other dimensions of reality, has any possibility of being true, why can't science at least investigate such a possibility? Such investigation cannot be done by priests and lawyers so it must be done by scientists. And if those ancient teachings are correct, and such communication is possible, then it must be possible to create scientific tools with which to do it. Knowledge on such profound matters must somehow be moved from the exclusive domain of the right-brained people of this world and made available to us left-brained creatures as well.

I do not possess the knowledge or ability to communicate with persons in other dimensions of reality. However, I do know several people who do have that ability and have done so, or at least, so they say. Most of them are very rational, very honest, and very well-educated individuals. I am persuaded that not all of those people can be deluded or totally wrong.

I do know that I am a living soul and separate from the body I inhabit. I know that other dimensions of reality do exist. Master Jesus also assures us these things are true. And since other dimensions do exist, there must be those amongst us who have some knowledge of such matters. To suggest otherwise is to leave ourselves with those who are color blind and feel sure that rainbows do not exist.

If even one of those people is correct, then such communication must be possible. If such communication is possible, then it must be possible to do it under laboratory conditions; and, even if not done to the standard of the Scientific Method, at least to some new standard to which we could generally agree upon, and which has validity.

This is the new hurdle for the scientific community, and it is one that must be met and conquered. And if it isn't conquered then science will continue to lose creditability until, like the Christian churches, it ceases to have relevance to much of human experience.

However, the biggest impediment to the moral advancement of mankind is the religious leaders of the world. The biggest impediment to the advancement of the teachings of Master Jesus the Christ is the leaders of the very churches that bear his name.

In the language of deductive logic, Master Jesus set forth his major premise that God does exist. He then followed with a minor premise, set forth in inductive logic, that all people can come to know God, using the same methods that he, Master Jesus, used. And his conclusion followed from the major and minor premises; that those who followed this teaching would some day realize reunion with God.

Materialists begin with a false major premise which is that God does not exist. When the major premise is not correct, then the minor premise and any conclusion drawn therefrom, by definition, is invalid. This is why communists are not, and have never been, a threat to anyone.

A much more subtle and dangerous threat to **truth** is all the major religions of the world. Christians begin with a very true major premise that God does exist. They then follow with a false minor premise that all people must become Christians, and then follow with the obviously false conclusion, that all true Christians, as a result, will realize reunion with God.

All Christians, Jews, and Hindus share in this false theology. Master Jesus perceived the error in these theologies and attempted to correct them. That is the very reason that Master Jesus is now so shunned by the priests of all major religions, just as he was when he lived on Earth. Truly, hell hath no fury like a priest scorned. This was true at the time of Moses Moria-El and Master Jesus, and is almost as true yet today. May it not always continue to be so.

I am not a Freemason; however, I make the statement herein that Master Jesus the Christ was both a Freemason and a Rosicrucian. Now, how can one know that to be true? Actually, quite simply. A true Freemason was a person who had mastered the Lesser Mysteries. One could not enter the Greater Mysteries until one had mastered the Lesser Mysteries. And one could not study for the Christ Degree until one had mastered the Greater Mysteries. Master Jesus did become the Christ, so he had to have mastered both the Lesser and the Greater Mysteries.

If you point out a complete stranger to me and tell me that the person is a medical doctor, then I can pretty safely guess that he is also a high school and college graduate. The same is true concerning Master Jesus. He became the Christ, so he had to have mastered both the Freemasonic Blue Lodge and AMORC teachings before reaching that highest of goals.

This book did not start out to be, and is not intended to be, propaganda for either the Freemasons or the Rosicrucians. I receive no pay from either of those groups. However, we must give them their due and one cannot get very deep into the values of Western culture without running headlong into both the Freemasons and Rosicrucians. They battle with the Christian churches and all religions for the hearts and souls of mankind.

I hope the reader has become convinced:

1. That God does exist outside this physical universe, but has heretofore interceded in this universe, and man is the best evidence of that intercession. I think, therefore God exists. Consciousness did not evolve from this physical universe. On the contrary, this physical universe evolved from consciousness. This is a subjective universe.

2. That Master Jesus the Christ taught the truth that man shares some equivalence with God and, while he is presently and temporarily living in this physical universe as a physical being, he is, in reality, a spiritual being and not really of this physical universe.

3. That man originated in the Middle East, which is to say in the Garden of Eden, and many of our cultural values come to us through the Exodus of the Hebrews out of Egypt.

4. That the second degree teachings of both the Blue Lodge and AMORC were promulgated to the public by Rosicrucian Thomas Jefferson in the Declaration of Independence.

5. That everyone on Earth, while not equal now, is equal in potential and must some day, at some time, come to know the teachings of AMORC and Master Jesus the Christ.

6. That the teachings of Master Jesus the Christ continue to survive in the world in spite of, rather than because of, the Christian churches.

7. That all the major religions of the world share a common source, and a common goal, which is to attain to the knowledge and practice of the teachings of Master Jesus the Christ.

8. That we live in an indeterminate universe and man must, and shall, for better or worse, create his own future. That future is not known, either by man or God, at this time. This also tells us that God is all good, but is not all knowing or all powerful.

9. That living the good life is possible here and now in this physical universe, and need not be delayed until later times. Master Jesus the Christ tried to show us how this could be done.

10. That all men and women must and shall be born again, and all men and women do indeed live forever. This is a fact, and man cannot change that regardless of what he does. Man will live forever, and the only decision man can make is what the quality of that living will be. Man will live in truth or in ignorance, as only he decides for himself.

In the end, things will work out, but until then it will be violent and very painful. You will remember that the Law of Compensation of AMORC states that for each sorrow or joy we bring to others, we shall have experience in like degree and manner, at the most appropriate time, so that the lessons to be gained will teach us our error so as to increase our understanding.

America has dispensed much violence in the world and must now pay the price; this is only true justice and the Law of Compensation at work. Why such true justice would be a mystery to America is unclear to the author. Earlier leaders who were well versed in Freemasonic teachings certainly understood this. This is exactly the reason why Master Mason George Washington, in his farewell address to the nation, warned us against foreign entanglements.

Has America dealt with the human beings of Southeast Asia, Central America, and the Middle East according to the most basic of human values? Have we dealt with those people with love, with truth, with non-violence, with right action, and in peace? No, clearly not.

Why is it so difficult to look at Japan and see that what it tried to achieve with violence failed? Japan tried to control Asia and the Pacific Rim with force and violence but could not. Now, in peace, it has come to almost control both. The same is true of Germany. It tried to control all of Europe with force and violence and failed miserably. Now it largely dominates Europe, also in peace.

We condemned and executed the leaders of Germany and Japan for waging aggressive war. Then we immediately took on the characteristics of our former enemies and began waging aggressive war throughout the entire world. We called their aggressive leaders criminals; and now we call our own aggressive leaders great men, even heros.

America is now the nation waging aggressive war, just as Germany and Japan did earlier in this century. Germany and Japan are now the hard-working economic leaders of the world who try hard to mind their own business, much as America did earlier in this century. They became us, and we have become them.

We run our own economy like drug addicts, while our former enemies pay not only their own debts but many of ours also. Our armed forces are now mere mercenaries who are for hire to the wealthy dictators of Arabia. The lives of a hundred or so American men and women should be worth perhaps 50 billion dollars or so, which is a mere pittance to Arabia's wealthy dictators.

A few years ago, the former Soviet Union was depicted as the Evil Empire. Without question, the government of the former Soviet Union was the cause of many mass murders and the source of repression in an important part of the world. Could that ever change? Only a few years ago, many people would have said no. The former Soviet Union was an evil empire for only 65 years and is now deceased. The Roman Church has been an evil empire for 1600 years and is now very slowly beginning to reform.

One of our presidents spoke of moral leadership, then accepted millions of dollars from the Japanese for allowing transgressions of the Japanese against his own people. Another of our presidents, with pompous pride, blocked the importation of drugs from France that could have saved thousands of American women from cancer. That same president went searching for a kinder and gentler nation and, on the road to that kindness and gentleness, murdered thousands of largely innocent souls in Iraq.

We pay millions of dollars to our athletes who can barely read, write, and speak the English language, while good school teachers are paid barely enough to make ends meet. In our major cities, we pay millions of dollars to politicians, preachers, lawyers, drug addicts, and other leaches on society. However, we pay barely a living wage to garbage collectors, firemen, policemen, and teachers, who struggle valiantly, but fight a losing battle, as our cities turn into cesspools.

Our president said that the Iraqi president is another Hitler and our only enemy in Iraq. Our president also said that we do not believe in targeting an individual, so he ordered thousands of innocent Iraqis killed instead. We note that the Iraqi president is an evil dictator and then sent American men and women to die in order to replace him with an equally evil royal family. Evil man that he may be, the Iraqi president will one day die, but, the royal family of Kuwait may go on for centuries. We go half way around the world to expel thousands of Iraqis from Kuwait, but are unwilling to expel millions of illegal immigrants from around our own homes.

Our morally corrupt, egotistical leaders accused Iraq's morally corrupt, egotistical leaders of being morally corrupt and egotistical. Our leaders accused their leaders of criminal conduct without much thought of their own even more criminal conduct. We accused their leaders of using terror and violence and then unleashed twice as much terror and violence to teach them how wrong they were.

We accused them of having many weapons for death and destruction while we are the ones who gave them many of those very same weapons. We accused them of having the capacity to build even more weapons of death and destruction while we, ourselves, produced and now possess most of the world's great weapons of death and destruction. We accused them of using violence against their neighbors with whom they had disagreements; then, we went half-way around the world to use twice as much violence against people who are not our neighbors, and with whom we had no disagreements.

We use our tremendous food supply to gain political power throughout the world while thousands are destitute in our own land. We verge on the edge of bankruptcy ourselves and yet ship borrowed money and guns to the Middle East to beget even more violence.

We recognized that our soldiers on the battlefield in Arabia and elsewhere were safer than ordinary citizens on the streets in our major cities. We decry the violence in our own land and seem not to comprehend that such violence is merely the result of our own violence unleashed around the world. We may intimidate the entire world, but not the Law of Compensation.

We wage aggressive war in a search for peace. We know not our own history and seem to care not for our own future. Violence begets only more violence. He who sows violence shall inherit the wind. America has sowed unbelievable violence and now must inherit the winds of its own actions because, very simply, it is the law. Great violence in defense can be justified; even mild violence in aggression cannot.

We Americans spread more violence in the world than any other nation on Earth. Such crass disregard for lives and property has to be evil. Worst of all, is that we take pride in our evil ways. The great public support for our own aggression is reminiscent of the great public support for the Third Reich in Germany in the mid-1930s. Also, as in Germany, the Christian churches gave passive support to this violence and aggression. Was that not because the dead were Muslims rather than Christians?

We Americans begin our argument with a truth; that the rule of law needs to be made binding throughout the entire world. We then follow with the dubious conclusion that this entitles us to go anywhere and do anything to make others remain subjected to oppressive leaders that we would not tolerate here at home. We then somehow imagine that by killing thousands indiscriminately, there will be peace. Of course, there may indeed be peace in those areas where we impose it, but all we really accomplished was to transfer their violence back home to our own people. Why is this so difficult for Americans to accept and understand?

We tend to honor presidents who lead us to war and have not yet come to the realization that going to war demonstrates a failure of leadership. We honor a legal system that actually promotes law suits and division in the land and seem not to comprehend that the best legal system would be one that diminishes such controversies. Lawyers seem to forget that the true function of lawyers is to settle controversies

CLOSING STATEMENT 305

Exhibit 50:: Machupicchu, the lost city in the Andes Mountains in Peru. It was rediscovered only in 1909.

created by others. Instead, lawyers now originate and create controversies in order to get paid to settle them.

We pray to our American god to sanction our acts. Is there a person alive, anywhere, who could seriously suggest that Master Jesus the Christ would approve of America's aggressive actions in the world? Surely not. Is there any American who could seriously suggest that Thomas Jefferson would so approve? Again, surely not.

America now must suffer war and rumors of wars, but these wars will be right here in our own streets, among our own people. The violence we shipped abroad now must be visited back upon us. When this happens we shall cry and wonder why. And when our irresponsibility leads us to moral and financial ruin, we shall look back and perhaps then will shed a tear.

I have traveled this world over several times trying to make sense out of things that seem to make no sense. I sat in northern India at the grave of Saint Issa, and wondered if this really is the final resting place of the body of our beloved Master Jesus the Christ.

I have been in China and seen the teeming masses of people who, more and more, seem to resemble so many ants, and understood, as they now seem to understand, that over-population is the world's worst single problem. And this is true, notwithstanding the teachings of the Roman Church. The religious fanatics who encourage over-population are worse criminals to the planet than the misguided souls who steal cars at the local shopping centers.

I have climbed to ancient Machupicchu in the Andes Mountains of Peru and marveled at the high culture of those native people who were sadistically slaughtered by a Christian church of which I am a member. I then faced the realization that the fighting in Nicaragua and Central America had nothing to do with communism, but only with those poor souls trying to shed the control of the Roman Church so they can use their resources for their own people.

I have visited modern Israel and listened to the guides explain how that country is being re-claimed by the people to whom their Jewish god gave the land in the time of Abraham. All our guides were of European descent. They were either blue-eyed or fair-haired, or both. They had no more relationship with the ancient Hebrew, Abraham, than the Palestinians they are displacing. In fact, they have less. The ruling Jews in Israel today are Aryan; not Hebrew. The abused have become the abusers.

Israel is much like America, the guides told us, in that they teach no religion in the public schools. When I challenged the guide, he admitted that they did teach the **Bible**, but claimed such teaching was only historical; not religious. Don't believe it.

I have sat on the Acropolis at Athens and wondered at the teachings of Socrates, Plato, Aristotle, and the other great sages of ancient Greece. Plato theorized the ideal republic, and now, 2500 years later, Jefferson's republic, rather than Plato's, is becoming the government of choice throughout much of the world.

I have sat on Red Square in Moscow and grieved at the pain and suffering required there to overthrow the corrupt czars. It took an evil communism to remove an even more evil royal family; now, both evils are hopefully gone forever. Will the Christian church also re-impose itself on the backs of the people? Hopefully not, but don't bet on it. Look at Poland which seems to have learned nothing in the last fifty years. They merely exchanged a new dictator, the Roman Church, for the old communism.

Exhibit 51: The Acropolis in Athens, Greece where Socrates, Plato, Aristotle, and the Greek sages brought together the mighty Greek culture.

308 TRUE ESOTERIC TRADITIONS

I have sat in the King's Chamber in the Great Pyramid at Giza and marveled at the thought that this is the exact place where Master Jesus, and many of the world's great minds, have come to study, to learn, and to take initiation. This chamber is awesome.

I have sat in the out-back of Australia, looked at a sky so vast and beautiful, and wondered how the ego of man could allow him to contemplate that he is alone in this universe. Thinking we are all alone in this vast universe is only man's egotism. I have also sat at Stonehenge in England and marveled at the work done by those people so long ago to construct an observatory in order to discover the secrets of God's universe.

The rains came -- and I wonder why so many of these lessons of history are not known to our present leaders. Our best people will no longer go to the forum. We also realize

Exhibit 52: Stonehenge on a gloomy December day in England. It was constructed, beginning about 2700 BC, as an astronomical observatory. Note the winter sun approaching the solstice.

that we, who do not learn our history, are damned to re-live it. We may be taught, but we will never learn, unless we can hear the ring of intuitive truth in our souls. And -- the rains came.

We need now to apologize to those who follow us in this land, for leaving to them such a legacy of moral delinquency. Ben Franklin expressed the idea well; those who will not be counseled cannot be helped. And America listens not. Much pain, suffering, and violence now must be experienced in America before there can be a rebirth. It will get much darker before we will again see the dawn. We must pass through a dark night of the soul. Oh my country, I do grieve for thee!

But there is a way out of our dilemma. There is one, and only one, way out. This will be the supreme challenge for America since its beginnings, throughout its entire existence. That way out is for America to turn to the teachings of Master Jesus the Christ. There are many things that need to happen; they can and will, happen swiftly when the time is right, which is not quite yet.

First, and closest to home, is that we Americans need to sober up from our drunken spree; return to the principles of our own form of government, and the basic values that served this country so well for so long.

The Christian churches need to undergo evolution internally and convert to the true teachings of Master Jesus the Christ. The world cannot reform until the largest Christian church -- the Roman Church -- reforms. The ball is now in the court of the Roman Church.

The Jews need to turn from the worship of their own private tribal god, and recognize that there is only One True God in the universe. This means admitting their claim as a chosen people is a hoax and their claim to real estate in the Middle East is a fraud. Most of the Jews the author has met are some of the smartest, hardest working, most honest, most congenial, and most generous people on Earth. They have no need to make false claims about being a chosen people or to real estate owned by others. In fact, such claims are counter productive to their own image. The Jewish religion contains some of the finest teachings and finest people on Earth. Unfortunately, it also contains some fanatical religionists.

The Muslims must recognize that all people have the right to religious freedom and the right to live as they see fit. This also means learning that the Holy War, they copied from the Roman Church, is not at all holy; and the republic, not the Islamic Republic, is the best form of government.

All the major religions need to come to the realization that females are equal to men as human beings, and are entitled to an equal voice in world affairs. Obviously, they are entitled to control their own bodies. That's elementary.

All women need to demand fair and equal treatment throughout the world. Women have much economic power if they will only use it. The quickest way for women to gain equality is for them to patronize and support female doctors, lawyers, accountants, politicians, and priests. Collectively, these professions run the world. The males in those professions, including even the pope, will get the message quickly.

This also means that all the established religions in the world must experience the pain of a complete rebirth into the new realities or go out of existence. A new comprehension of religion must spread throughout the entire world. This will not come easily, but it will eventually come. And in the end, man finally will be saved from destruction, exactly as is predicted in **The Revelation**. I rest my case.

M. Dale Palmer

APPENDIX: THE ROMAN CHURCH POPES

It is not possible to give an exact listing of the popes of the Roman Church. The first pope that can clearly be identified as such was Stephen I who held the job from AD 254 to AD 257. Some argument can be made that Pius I, who was a leader in the Roman Church from AD 144 to AD 155, was the first pope. Any popes prior to Pius I in AD 144 are pure fiction. This was, of course, long after Master Jesus, Apostle Peter, and Apostle Paul had all died. Also keep in mind that by this time there were Christian groups over much of the world. The Church of England was already over one hundred years old. Almost all of these other Christian groups were later exterminated by the Roman Church.

In about AD 175, Irenaeus wrote the Gospel of John and also created the fiction that the Apostle Peter was the first pope. The reason he had to create such a fiction was that under the rules laid down by the eleven remaining apostles in Jerusalem the only people who could qualify as apostles were persons who had actually met Master Jesus. This disqualified Paul and thus Irenaeus felt that the Roman Church, as a political matter, had to be **fictionally** built on Peter rather than Paul, even though it would follow Paul's theology. This also may be the reason for the story about the Apostle Paul meeting Master Jesus on the road to Damascus. Paul wanted very much to be accepted by the eleven remaining apostles as a true apostle of Master Jesus, and he could not be so accepted unless he had actually met Master Jesus in person. Paul hoped that his purported meeting with Master Jesus on the road to Damascus would be acceptable, but most of the eleven apostles never bought the story and never accepted Paul as one of them. It is also possible that Irenaeus knew that Paul eventually left Rome and went to Asia Minor, probably Damascus, married, had a family and gave up the traveling preacher work.

The Apostle Peter, as the senior apostle, did travel around visiting and checking on the other newer churches outside of Jerusalem. He visited the second largest city in the Roman Empire, Antioch, where the local Christian group wanted to make him their local bishop, but, of course, he declined and continued his inspection tour. Peter visited Rome but was never bishop there. Even if such a position as bishop even existed at the time and even if it had been offered to Peter he would never have accepted. Peter was, after all, the senior apostle at the home of the Christian church in Jerusalem. At this time period, Rome was considered the Babylon of the West and Nero was depicted as the anti-Christ. It would be like today the president of the US resigning to accept the presidency of North Korea. No way.

The fictional popes created by Irenaeus were Peter from an unknown date to AD 64; a Pope Linus from AD 66 to 78; a Pope Anacletus from AD 79 to 91; a Pope Clement I from AD 91 to 101; a Pope Evaristus from AD 100 to 109; a Pope Alexander I from AD 109 to 116; a Pope Sixtus I from AD 116 to 125; a Pope Telesphorus from AD 125 to 136 and a Pope Hyginus from AD 138 to 142. In some years there were no popes and in some years two and even three popes. Later popes of course could not easily explain more than one pope at the same time so they simply decreed that some of the earlier popes were not even popes. It would require thousands of pages, and would be far beyond the scope of this book, to try and evaluate all of those competing claims. They are all largely irrelevant in any event. Regardless of who won those arguments Western Culture always lost.

This listing of the Roman Church popes is substantially in accordance with **The Oxford Dictionary of Popes**, which has been adopted largely from the work entitled **Annuario Pontificio** and the five-volume treatise entitled **Geschiche der Päpste**, except in the very early years of the papacy, where the author states that Pius I was the earliest possible Roman-church pope. The author's listing of the Roman-church popes and the probable years they served is set out left to right chronologically. All dates are AD.

Pius I: 144 - 155	Anicetus: 155 - 166	Soter: 166 - 174
Eleutherius: 174 - 189	Victor I: 189 - 198	Zephyrinus: 198 - 217
Callistus I: 217 - 222	Hippolytus: 217 - 235	Urban I: 222 - 230
Pontian: 230 - 235	Anterus: 235 - 236	Fabian: 236 - 250
Cornelius: 253 - 253	Novatian: 251 - 258	Lucius: 253 - 254

Stephen I: 254 - 257
Felix I: 269 - 274
Marcellinus: 296 - 304
Miltiades: 311 - 314
Julius I: 337 - 352
Ursinus: 367 - 385
Innocent I: 401 - 417
Boniface I: 418 - 422
Leo I: 440 - 461
Felix III: 483 - 492
Symmachus: 498 - 514
John I: 523 - 526
Boniface II: 530 - 532
Silverius: 536 - 537
John III: 561 - 574
Gregory I: 590 - 604
Boniface IV: 608 - 615
Honorius I: 625 - 638
Theodore I: 642 - 649
Vitalian: 657 - 672
Agatho: 678 - 681
John V: 685 - 686
Paschal: 687 - 692
John VII: 705 - 707
Gregory II: 715 - 731
Stephen II: 752 - 752
Constantine: 767 - 768
Hadrian I: 772 - 795
Paschal I: 817 - 824
Gregory IV: 827 - 844
Leo IV: 847 - 855
Nicholas I: 858 - 867
Marinus I: 882 - 884
Formosus: 891 - 896
Romanus: 897 - 897
Benedict IV: 900 - 903
Sergius III: 904 - 911
John X: 914 - 928
John XI: 931 - 935
Marinus II: 942 - 946
Leo VIII: 963 - 965
Benedict VI: 973 - 974
John XIV: 983 - 984
John XVI: 997 - 998
John XVIII: 1003 - 1009
Gregory VI: 1012 - 1012
Silvester III: 1045 - 1063
Demasus II: 1048 - 1048
Stephen IX: 1057 - 1058
Alexander II: 1061 - 1073
Clement III: 1080 - 1084
Paschal II: 1099 - 1118
Silvester IV: 1105 - 1111
Callistus II: 1119 - 1124
Innocent II: 1130 - 1143
Celestine II: 1143 - 1144
Anastasius IV: 1153 - 1154
Victor IV: 1159 - 1164

Sixtus II: 257 - 258
Eutychian: 275 - 283
Marcellus I: 306 - 308
Silvester I: 314 - 335
Liberius: 352 - 366
Siricius: 384 - 399
Zosimus: 417 - 418
Celestine I: 422 - 432
Hilarus: 461 - 468
Gelasius I: 492 - 496
Lawrence: 498 - 499
Felix IV: 526 - 530
John II: 533 - 535
Vigilius: 537 - 555
Benedict I: 575 - 579
Sabinian: 604 - 606
Deusdedit: 615 - 618
Severinus: 640 - 640
Martin I: 649 - 653
Adeodatus II: 672 - 676
Leo II: 682 - 683
Conon: 686 - 687
Sergius I: 687 - 689
Sisinnius: 708 - 708
Gregory III: 731 - 741
Stephen III: 752 - 757
Philip: 768 - 768
Leo III: 795 - 816
Eugene II: 824 - 827
John: 844 - 844
Benedict III: 855 - 858
Hadrian II: 867 - 872
Hadrian III: 884 - 885
Boniface VI: 896 - 896
Theodore II: 897 - 897
Leo V: 903 - 904
Anastasius III: 911 - 913
Leo VI: 928 - 928
Leo VII: 936 - 939
Agapitus II: 946 - 955
Benedict V: 964 - 964
Boniface VII: 974 - 984
John XV: 985 - 996
Silvester II: 999 - 1003
Sergius IV: 1009 - 1012
John XIX: 1024 - 1032
Gregory VI: 1045 - 1046
Leo IX: 1049 - 1054
Benedict X: 1058 - 1059
Honorius II: 1061 - 1064
Victor III: 1086 - 1087
Theoderic: 1100 - 1101
Gelasius II: 1118 - 1119
Honorius II: 1124 - 1130
Anacletus II: 1130 - 1138
Lucius II: 1144 - 1145
Hadrian IV: 1154 - 1159
Paschal III: 1164 - 1168

Dionysius: 260 - 268
Gaius: 283 - 296
Eusebius: 310 - 310
Mark: 336 - 336
Damasus I: 366 - 384
Anastasius I: 399 - 401
Eulalius: 418 - 419
Sixtus III: 432 - 440
Simplicius: 468 - 483
Anastasius II: 496 - 498
Hormisdas: 514 - 523
Dioscorus: 530 - 530
Agapitus I: 535 - 536
Pelagius I: 536 - 561
Pelagius II: 579 - 590
Boniface III: 607 - 607
Boniface V: 619 - 625
John IV: 640 - 642
Eugene I: 654 - 657
Donus: 676 - 678
Benedict II: 684 - 685
Theodore: 687 - 687
John VI: 701 - 705
Constantine: 708 - 715
Zacharias: 741 - 752
Paul I: 757 - 767
Stephen III: 768 - 772
Stephen IV: 816 - 817
Valentine: 827 - 827
Sergius II: 844 - 847
Anastasius: 855 - 855
John VIII: 872 - 882
Stephen V: 885 - 891
Stephen VI: 896 - 897
John IX: 898 - 900
Christopher: 903 - 904
Lando: 913 - 914
Stephen VII: 928 - 931
Stephen VIII: 939 - 942
John XII: 955 - 964
John XIII: 965 - 972
Benedict VII: 974 - 983
Gregory V: 996 - 999
John XVII: 1003 - 1003
Benedict VIII: 1012 - 1024
Benedict IX: 1032 - 1044
Clement II: 1046 - 1047
Victor II: 1055 - 1057
Nicholas II: 1058 - 1061
Gregory VII: 1073 - 1085
Urban II: 1088 - 1099
Albert: 1101 - 1101
Gregory VIII: 1118 - 1121
Celestine II: 1124 - 1125
Victor IV: 1138 - 1138
Eugene III: 1145 - 1153
Alexander III: 1159 - 1181
Callistus III: 1168 - 1178

Innocent III: 1179 - 1180	Lucius III: 1181 - 1185	Urban III: 1185 - 1187
Gregory VIII: 1187 - 1187	Clement III: 1187 - 1191	Celestine III: 1191 - 1198
Innocent III: 1198 - 1216	Honorius III: 1216 - 1227	Gregory IX: 1227 - 1241
Celestine IV: 1241 - 1241	Innocent IV: 1243 - 1254	Alexander IV: 1254 - 1261
Urban IV: 1261 - 1264	Clement IV: 1265 - 1268	Gregory X: 1271 - 1276
Innocent V: 1276 - 1276	Hadrian V: 1276 - 1276	John XXI: 1276 - 1277
Nicholas III: 1277 - 1280	Martin IV: 1281 - 1285	Honorius IV: 1285 - 1287
Nicholas IV: 1288 - 1292	Celestine V: 1294 - 1294	Boniface VIII: 1294 - 1303
Benedict XI: 1303 - 1304	Clement V: 1305 - 1314	John XXII: 1316 - 1334
Nicholas V: 1328 - 1330	Benedict XII: 1334 - 1342	Clement VI: 1342 - 1352
Innocent VI: 1352 - 1362	Urban V: 1362 - 1370	Gregory XI: 1370 - 1378
Urban VI: 1378 - 1389	Clement VII: 1378 - 1394	Boniface IX: 1389 - 1404
Benedict XIII: 1394 - 1417	Innocent VII: 1404 - 1406	Gregory XII: 1406 - 1415
Alexander V: 1409 - 1410	John XXIII: 1410 - 1415	Martin V: 1417 - 1431
Celment VIII: 1423 - 1429	Benedict XIV: 1425 - 1425	Eugene IV: 1431 - 1447
Felix V: 1439 - 1449	Nicholas V: 1447 - 1455	Callistus III: 1455 - 1458
Pius II: 1458 - 1464	Paul II: 1464 - 1471	Sixtus IV: 1471 - 1484
Innocent VIII: 1484 - 1492	Alexander VI: 1492 - 1503	Pius III: 1503 - 1503
Julius II: 1503 - 1513	Leo X: 1513 - 1521	Hadrian VI: 1522 - 1523
Clement VII: 1523 - 1534	Paul III: 1534 - 1549	Julius III: 1550 - 1555
Marcellus II: 1555 - 1555	Paul IV: 1555 - 1559	Pius IV: 1559 - 1565
Pius V: 1566 - 1572	Gregory XIII: 1572 - 1585	Sixtus V: 1585 - 1590
Urban VII: 1590 - 1590	Gregory XIV: 1590 - 1591	Innocent IV: 1591 - 1591
Clement VIII: 1592 - 1605	Leo XI: 1605 - 1605	Paul V: 1605 - 1621
Gregory XV: 1621 - 1623	Urban VIII: 1623 - 1644	Innocent X: 1644 - 1655
Alexander VII: 1655 - 1667	Clement IX: 1667 - 1669	Clement X: 1670 - 1676
Clement XI: 1700 - 1721	Innocent XIII: 1721 - 1724	Benedict XIII: 1724 - 1730
Clement XII: 1730 - 1740	Benedect XIV: 1740 - 1758	Clement XIII: 1758 - 1769
Clement XIV: 1769 - 1774	Pius VI: 1775 - 1799	Pius VII: 1800 - 1823
Leo XII: 1823 - 1829	Pius VIII: 1829 - 1830	Gregory XVI: 1831 - 1846
Pius IX: 1846 - 1878	Leo XIII: 1878 - 1903	Pius X: 1903 - 1914
Benedict XV: 1914 - 1922	Pius XI: 1922 - 1939	Pius XII: 1939 - 1958
John XXIII: 1958 - 1963	Paul VI: 1963 - 1978	John Paul I: 1978 - 1978
John Paul II: 1978 - ?		

How many of these men who claimed to be popes at the time were later disowned by the Roman Church? A close answer would be about 33. This would include: Albert, Anacletus II, Anastasius, the first Benedict XIII, Benedict XIV, Boniface VII, the first Callistus III, the first Celestine II, the first Clement III, the first Clement VIII, Constantine, Dioscorus, Eulalius, Felix II, Felix VI, the first Gregory VI, the first Gregory VIII, Hippolytus, the first Honorius II, the first Innocent III, John, John XVI, the first John XXIII, Lawrence, the first Nicholas V, Novation, Paschal, Paschal III, Philip, Silvester IV, Theordore, Theoderic, and both the first and second Victor IV.

Were any of the Roman-church popes not Christians? The answer is **yes**, at least four: Marcellinus, Marcellus I, Eusebius, and Miltiades who were practicing pagans and also were popes who served from about AD 296 to 314. For some time the Roman Church tried to disown these non-Christian popes but because their collective reigns totaled about eighteen successive years that was not feasible. The current fiction concedes that these pagan popes were popes but now maintains that they were not really pagans.

Have there been times when all Roman Catholics who died went to hell? According to Roman-church law there have been many such periods. In AD 1302 Pope Boniface VIII, in Papal Bull Unam Sanctum, decreed that ..."We, moreover, proclaim, declare, and pronounce that it is altogether necessary to salvation for every human being to be subject to the Roman pontiff." The decree is simple enough: no Roman Pontiff no salvation.

For example, after the death of one of Pope Boniface VIII's successors, Clement V, in AD 1314, there was more than a two year vacancy when there was no Roman pope. Thus, by Pope Boniface VIII's Papal Bull, Unam Sanctum, all Roman Catholics who died during that two-year period went to hell. Worst of all is that there have been hundreds of vacancies in the papacy throughout the history of the Roman Church. Is Papal Bull Unam Sanctum still the law in the Roman Church today? It is a real dilemma because if it isn't repealed an ever-growing number of educated Roman Catholics may say that Papal Bull Unam Sanctum is pure nonsense. However, if it is repealed this means that a pope has been grievously wrong on a matter of morals and the whole Roman Church faith structure could begin crashing down. Truly, a dilemma.

These are the 287 or so men who claimed to be the official representatives of Master Jesus the Christ on Earth. There may have been considerably fewer than this number but not more. If you throw out the some 33 popes now disowned by the Roman Church there would be only 254 or so popes. If you further eliminate the fifteen doubtful popes prior to Stephen I in AD 254 there would be only 239 popes in total.

Preface, Volume Two,
Book of Canon Law, Rome AD 1901

..."The death sentence is a necessary and efficacious means for the Church to attain its ends ..."

SELECTED ANNOTATED BIBLIOGRAPHY

Although the author has read thousands of volumes over the last 40 years or so, he refers the reader only to about one hundred of those volumes in this selected bibliography. Anyone who completes reading these volumes will be guided to others on the same subjects.

Ali, A. Yusuf, 1983, **The Holy Koran**, Amana Company, Brentwood, Maryland.

This is the best of the several translations of the **Koran**. It is well annotated and cross-referenced with the **Bible** and the **New Testament**. This book was a personal gift to the author from the English singer, Cat Stevens, who now uses his Muslim name, Yusuf Islam. Cat Stevens destroyed his own integrity when he endorsed the idea that the author Salman Rushdie should be assassinated. Right-thinking people would not be threatened by ideas. In this book, citations to the **Koran** are referred to as chapters. This is merely a convenient translation of the correct Arabic word **sura**.

The **Koran** states:

1. At note 119 that it is blasphemy to teach that God begat sons, like a man or an animal. In a spiritual sense, we are all children of God. The teaching that Master Jesus or any man is God is, of course, paganism.

2. At note 382 that all Christian sects, except the Unitarians, teach that Master Jesus was God and the son of God.

3. At note 516 that a male generally inherits double that of the female.

4. At note 663 that the theological doctrine of blood sacrifice and vicarious atonement of the Roman Church are repudiated by Islam, and also that Master Jesus was not crucified or killed by the Jews. Note here that the Muslims have a very low image of the Jews, but still know and realize that they did not kill Master Jesus.

5. At note 753 that even some of the ancient books that the Jews had, they twisted in meaning to suit their own purposes, and what they had were only small fragments of the original law of Moses.

6. At note 789 that true Christians are Muslims at heart, regardless of the label they apply to themselves.

7. At note 809 that attributing anger to God is ignorant and degrading to men and dishonoring to God.

8. In Appendix 2 that Moses was not the author of the first five books of the **Bible**. Further, that the laws were lost and most of the **Bible** was, in fact, written by Ezra about 458 BC, but some of it much later.

9. In Appendix 3 that world thought has learned much from Islam's protest against priest domination, class domination, and sectarianism.

10. In note 1072 that the pharaoh of the Exodus event was probably Tuthmosis I, about 1540 BC. The author discloses in this book, for the first time, that the pharaoh was Aye in 1335 BC.

Alighieri, Dante, AD 1265 to 1321, **The Divine Comedy**, the Harvard classics, P.F. Collier & Son Corporation, New York.

This book covers an allegorical trip through the various circles of hell, then purgatory and on to Paradise. It is the first big step forward out of the Dark Ages and the first serious public attack on the morality, or lack thereof, of the Roman Church.

Dante mentions several popes in various circles of hell, including Pope Clement V who transferred the papacy to Avignon in France and plotted against Jacques de Molay and the Knights Templar in AD 1314. Pope Clement himself also died in AD 1314. Dante alludes to the so-called Donation of Constantine, in which the pretended gift of the Lateran was donated to Silvester I and his successors. Dante exposed the Donation of Constantine as a forgery more than two hundred years before the Roman Church admitted as much.

Barnstone, Willis, 1984, **The Other Bible, Esoteric Texts from the Pseudepigrapha, the Dead Sea Scrolls, the early Kabbahah, the Nag Hammadi Library and other sources.** Harper & Row, New York.

This large volume contains many of the writings that were considered for inclusion into the **Bible** but which were rejected, for one reason or another, usually for political reasons.

On page 567 et seq., it also confirms that the thrice-great Hermes Trismegistus did live in Egypt shortly after Moses, and taught that the purpose of life is to free the soul from its low estate in the physical body, through enlightenment. It also states that there are seven universes above this physical universe, at the highest of which one meets God. Barnstone rejects these ideas and incorrectly says that Hermes was only a myth.

Bede, 1955, **A History of the English Church and People,** Dorset Press, New York.

Bede was probably born in AD 673 and spent his whole life from age seven on at various monasteries. He studied and wrote. This book is one of the sources for information in many other books, including the **Anglo-Saxon Chronicles.** Bede died in AD 735 at about the same time as the defeat of the Muslims by the Christians at the Battle of Tours in France.

Bellwood, Peter, **The Austronesian Dispersal and the Origin of Languages, Scientific American,** July 1991, page 88, New York.

Bellwood notes that the Austronesian languages of the Pacific spread very rapidly across some 6000 miles of coastline, in less then 1500 years.

This again shows that communication is faster across the water areas of the world than across the land areas. He also offers the attractive hypothesis that language dispersal follows agricultural populations as they replace the forager and hunter populations. In the United States, farmers and ranchers replaced the Indians, and their English language replaced the many Indian languages.

Bhagavad-Gita, the Hindu Holy Book.

The Bhagavad-Gita is a metaphysical treatise on the nature of God and the human species. Ralph Waldo Emerson and Henry David Thoreau were greatly influenced by the Gita. The Indian Lawyer, Mohandas Gandhi, was a student of Thoreau and Martin Luther King, Jr. was a student of Gandhi. There is nothing so potent as a truth whose time has come.

The Gita speaks of three qualities which bind the soul to the physical body. They are Sattva, Rajas, and Tamas. These Sanskrit terms translate only very roughly into English as truth, desire, and indifference, respectively. Although all three qualities are unlike each other, they are present in all human beings.

SELECTED ANNOTATED BIBLIOGRAPHY 317

There are literally thousands of volumes, by thousands of sages, commenting on and explaining this book. Many scholars feel that this is the oldest religion in the world; older even than those of ancient Egypt and the British Isles. While the author disagrees, there is no question but what Hinduism is a very old religion. Here are the comments of one especially troublesome Hindu cult group:

ॐ नमो भगवते वासुदेवाय
जन्माद्यस्य यतोऽन्वयादितरतश्चार्थेष्वभिज्ञः स्वराट्
तेने ब्रह्म हृदा य आदिकवये मुह्यन्ति यत्सूरयः ।
तेजोवारिमृदां यथा विनिमयो यत्र त्रिसर्गोऽमृषा
धाम्ना स्वेन सदा निरस्तकुहकं सत्यं परं धीमहि ॥ १ ॥

Remember, achieving **Krsna Consciousness** is something akin to being **in grace** or **sanctified** in the fundamentalist Christian sects. Several years ago, the author toyed with the idea of learning Sanskrit but, after buying the translation dictionaries, decided to leave the Sanskrit-to-English translating to the professional team working in Adyar, India.

A very literal translation of the above Sanskrit would be that I pray to my Lord Krsna, or Christ, son of God, because you are Absolute Truth and Creator of the manifested universe. You are the Ultimate Cause of all causes and the source of knowledge imparted to the original Adam. I pray to you Lord Christ because you are Absolute Truth.

The similarities to Christian-church teachings are self-evident. Both Christianity and Hinduism, unlike Islam, teach a more-or-less cult religion.

A free copy of **Bhagavad-Gita**, the Hindu Holy Book, may be obtained from Seth S. B. Jalan Charity Trust, 8, Dalhousie Square East, Calcutta - 700001 (India).

Blavatsky, H. P., **The Secret Doctrine**, The Theosophical Publishing House, Wheaton, Illinois.

This is a small abridgement of two large volumes. Blavatsky was a Russian mystic born in AD 1831. She was a linguist and musician and spent several years in Nepal, India, and Tibet. She claims to have met a master named Moria who taught her many secrets from materials in Tibet, probably taken there from Egypt when the great library at Alexandria was burned in AD 400 by the Roman Church. Her ideas are distributed throughout the world by the Theosophical Society.

The Theosophical Society sponsors a translation team in Adyar, India, which is translating many ancient materials into English from Sanskrit for the first time.

Buddha, The Teachings of, 1985, Buddhist Promoting Foundation, Tokyo, Japan.

There are many editions of this work, and millions of copies have been sold. It summarizes 2500 years and 5000 volumes of material into one volume. One printing is in both Japanese and English and another is in English alone.

Case, Paul Foster, 1985, **One True and Invisible Rosicrucian Order**, Samuel Weiser, Inc., York Beach, Maine 03910.

There are thousands of books on Kabala, and this is reputed to be one of the best. Many of the discussions are excellent; however, beware of the Tree of Life set forth on page 157 of the book. It is not accurate. It shows the Soul devolving down the Tree of Life. The Soul never goes in any direction but up. For 1500 years the Roman Church and its offspring have taught such pagan teachings, but they are not accurate. God never devolved down into man. If God could devolve down into a man, then man could devolve down into an amoeba. Such is not possible.

There are several small but good collections of materials on Kabala in Europe and the United States. The Rosicrucian Order in San Jose, California, has a collection of about 60 volumes, but those volumes are not available to the general public. The largest collection of Kabala materials in the world is at Hebrew Union College in Cincinnati, Ohio. As of 1985, they had approximately 1060 volumes, and these may be borrowed through an interlibrary loan.

Chadwick, Henry, 1986, **The Early Church,** Dorset Press, New York.

This is a good volume on the history of the Roman Church, from about AD 100 to 500. Chadwick makes the interesting observation that Roman officials were not baptized until near death because of their duties of torturing and executing people who disagreed with the authorities. Roman Emperor Constantine was a good example. But how could anyone have a duty to commit murder? A better word than **duties** would have been **responsibilities.**

Chamberlin, E.R., 1986, **The Bad Popes,** Dorset Press, New York.

This is a very well detailed book on only seven of the bad popes between AD 955 and 1534. They were John (not Joan) XII, Benedict IX, Boniface VIII, Urban VI, Alexander VI, Leo X, and Clement VII. These seven included rapists, thieves, and murderers, but they murdered fewer people than some other popes not reported on in this book.

Champion, Selwyn Gurney, 1959, **Readings from the World Religions,** Fawcett Publication, Inc., Greenwich, Conn.

The essence of man's spiritual wisdom, gathered from mankind's holy books, is presented in this book. The book covers Hinduism, Shintoism, Judaism, Zoroastrianism, Taoism, Confucianism, Janism, Buddhism, Christianity, Islam, and Sikhism. Each of these great faiths is summarized in a simple outline of its origins, evolution, and main doctrines. This would be a good book to have in any library.

Decter, Jacqueline, 1989, **Nicholas Roerich, The Life and Art of a Russian Master,** Park Street Press, Rochester, Vermont.

Nicholas Roerich was one of the more amazing men of our time. He was a genius in many areas but not in law or business. He was a Rosicrucian and close friend of AMORC Imperator Spencer Lewis, Albert Einstein, H. G. Wells, and George Bernard Shaw. Roerich was a Russian and was educated in Saint Petersburg. He spent his life traveling, painting, and working for peace. He was nominated for the Nobel Peace Prize in 1929.

Roerich, like his fellow Russians Nicholas Notovitch and Madame Helena Blavatsky, spent much time in the Far East, and with Notovitch and Blavatsky, comprise the three people most responsible for bringing the wisdom of the Far East into Western culture.

It was Roerich who suggested that the Great Pyramid on the seal of the US be placed on the US one dollar bill. This was approved and implemented by US President Franklin D. Roosevelt.

Roerich also re-discovered the so-called Notovitch Manuscript, which relates the life story of Saint Issa or Jesus. It was Roerich who discovered a couple errors in the earlier translation of the manuscript by the Russian Orthodox priests employed by Notovitch, about 50 years earlier.

Roerich collected many manuscripts in Asia and returned them to his museum in New York, as well as to other museums in Europe and Russia. Among these items were the monumental 333 volume **Kanjur-Tanjur** which are the holy scriptures of Tibet. Perhaps it should be noted, that the Notovitch Manuscript disappeared from northern India about the time of Roerich's visit there. No one seems to know at this time exactly what happened to that most interesting document.

Older American readers may remember that Roerich's name became prominent in the late 1940s because of his association with American politician Henry Wallace. His thousands of paintings may be found in museums and private collections throughout the world.

Devi, Savitri, 1981, **Son of the Sun**, Supreme Grand Lodge of AMORC, Inc., San Jose, California.

This is an excellent book on the history of Egypt during its greatest period, when the biblical Joseph was the prime minister. Joseph's daughter, Tiye, was first wife and queen of Amenhotep III, and actually ran the Egyptian government after the death of her father, Joseph.

The Hebrews must have had a very specific plan to take over and control the government of Egypt, and did exactly that. Fifteen years later, army general Horemheb overthrew the Hebrew royal family of Egypt and caused the Exodus event.

Devi incorrectly reports that Queen Tiye was not a monotheist. She definitely was. Devi also says that ancient Rosicrucian records show that Akhnaton died on July 24, 1350 BC. Akhnaton taught belief in the One True God of the universe who loved all his creatures equally. The Jews, to this day, worship only a tribal god and the Christian churches, yet to this day, teach a trinity of gods that prefer their own people over others of mankind.

Dodd, Alfred, 1986, **Francis Bacon's Personal Life Story**, Brookmount House, London WC2N 4NW.

This is a well-researched documentary and the best account of the many intrigues in the court of Elizabeth I, the so-called Virgin Queen. She was much like her father, Henry VIII, and was a complete scoundrel, but she did fight off the Roman Church, and allow considerable literary and academic freedom, although no political freedom. Elizabeth gave birth to three sons; Francis Lord Bacon being the second-born. She had her youngest son, Lord Essex, executed for purported treason.

Bacon was the head of the Freemasons and the Rosicrucians. He was also the leader of the group that wrote and published many literary works, including those published under the name of William Shakespeare. Brilliant man that he was, Bacon betrayed the Rosicrucian Order by favoring monarchy over a republic. He felt that a monarch, like a pope, could do no wrong, which was obviously nonsense. Bacon also failed to support Sir Walter Raleigh when his support might have saved the innocent Raleigh from execution.

The author of this book, Alfred Dodd, also has some very strange values. He states:

1. "...this great genius (Bacon) was forced to...beg for pecuniary assistance, to which he was justly entitled..."

Dodd apparently assumes that because Bacon was Queen Elizabeth's son, he was entitled to a free lunch. Not so.

2. "...Francis Bacon's ideal government was that of a monarchy similar to the one we enjoy today...."

Mr. Dodd, now deceased, was surely jesting. All Rosicrucians must believe only in merit as a basis for leadership, which excludes the idea of kingship. Bacon betrayed the Rosicrucian Order of which he was head, and as a result, Rosicrucian leadership moved to Continental Europe where it has remained most of the time ever since.

3. "...King James was not a Stuart at all ... Mary of Scotland's blood never flowed in his veins. ... a pretender sat on the English throne -- a usurper...."

Dodd criticized King James for being what he called a usurper, because of his blood-line, with no thought to the higher truth that all royalty are usurpers. To Dodd, being a bastard was worse than being a murderer. Very strange values.

However, once you get beyond the political propaganda, this is an excellent book that sets forth a crucial period in history in very realistic terms.

Dowling, Levi, 1907, **The Aquarian Gospel of Jesus, the Christ of the Piscean age**, DeVorss & Co., Santa Monica, California.

Levi tells about the life of Master Jesus. Levi says that Master Jesus lived and studied in many countries and was the greatest man who has yet lived, but certainly different from the Roman-church Jesus.

What is an Age? Earth wobbles on its axis and one such wobble takes about 25,920 years or what is called a Zodiac. Ancient astrology said there were twelve signs of the Zodiac and thus it takes 2160 years to move through each sign. According to those ancient teachings, the world will enter the so-called Aquarian Age about AD 2150 or so, and it is predicted that Christ, this time called John, will come again in the Aquarian Age to again attempt to teach mankind. The previous sign was the so-called Piscean Age which began about 6 BC. Master Jesus the Christ was the great teacher of the Piscean Age which will soon come to a close. The time will soon come for the Law of Love as taught by Master Jesus the Christ of the Piscean Age to really begin to take effect in the world.

The Roman Church has really had about 239 popes, most of whom were scoundrels, at best, and many who were outright criminals. It has had two popes named John XXIII, one who was a scoundrel, and the last in this century who was a great teacher. There has been no Pope John XX. AMORC teachings predict that in the AD 2000s the Christ will come again, and this time he will be called John. So, is it possible that in the coming years, during the AD 2000s, finally a Pope John XX the Christ will come? It is an interesting thought.

Will John the Christ be within the Roman Church or outside it? Who knows? At this time there is probably no church that could even recognize the Christ if he did appear. The author feels that the Christ, when he or she does appear, will do so inside the church and the Roman Church will, at last, become what it has long claimed to be.

Durant, Will and Ariel, 1953, **The Story of Civilization**, Simon and Schuster, New York.

This is in twelve volumes and contains almost 10,000 pages. It is much easier to read than Toynbee, but less objective.

Eddy, Mary Baker, 1902, **Science and Health with Key to the Scriptures**, Boston.

Mary Baker Eddy wrote more than fifteen books, but this one is by far the best known and most popular. Her first works were published about AD 1875. Her main theology is that if man lives by divine principles, the treatment of disease as well as sin will be taken care of by God. The sin part of her theology has not been a problem. However, when her followers failed to give even minimal health care to minor children, often letting them die, they very understandably came into conflict with criminal laws in the United States.

Each person has the right to believe as he or she wants. However, each person does not have the right to act as he or she wishes to act. The secular law should and does address actions, but not beliefs. This is one of many examples that shows the emptiness of the Christian-church theology which has caused some people to reach out for something new and, hopefully, better.

Eliade, Mircea, 1987, **The Encyclopedia of Religion**, Macmillan Publishing Company, New York.

This is the most complete study of the religions of the world ever produced. It is in sixteen large volumes and covers almost every religion ever known to mankind.

Eusebius, 1965, **The History of the Church**, Dorset Press, New York.

Eusebius was the historian of the Christian church and lived from AD 263 to 339. He was a very good friend of Roman-Emperor Constantine. He covered the early persecutions of the Christians as well as what the Roman Church considered to be the teachings of dozens of heretics. This book gives a good background of the events leading up to the Nicene Council in AD 325. One must remember that Eusebius was a bishop of the Roman Church and that the teachings of Master Jesus the Christ were some of those heresies the Roman Church suppressed.

Fell, Barry, 1989, **America B.C.**, Simon & Schuster, Inc., New York.

We usually think of the first Europeans coming to America with Leif Eriksson about AD 1000. However, Professor Fell shows that Europeans were in New England and the Midwest of America as far back as 800 BC.

Feng, Gia-Fu and English, Jane, 1972, **Tao Te Ching**, Random house, New York.

This is a book of 81 chapters and 5000 words, supposedly written by the Chinese sage, Laotse, shortly before he went away to die in private. He says that the total truth cannot be conveyed objectively but can be perceived only on a subjective level. He taught that rain falls equally on the just and the unjust and we should treat all people as equals, regardless of how they behave. Te or virtue lies always in Tao or natural law.

The author suggests that Master Jesus obtained some of his philosophy from Laotse and it is set forth in the first part of the Sermon on the Mount.

Gamkrelidze, Thomas V. and Ivanov, V. V., **The Early History of Indo-European Languages**, **Scientific American**, March 1990, page 110, New York.

Gamkrelidze is professor of linguistics at Tiblisi State University and Ivanov is professor of linguistics at the Institute of Slavic and Balkan Studies in Moscow. Their two-volume work was published in 1984 in Russian, and is now being translated into English. This is an excellent summary of a vast and complicated area of study. The study of linguistics is not unlike the study of the Exodus in the Sinai Peninsula. Each scholar has his own theory.

One of the big advances in the study of linguistics came in 1822 when Jacob Grimm formulated Grimm's Law, which stated that consonants displace one another over time in a very predictable and regular fashion. Grimm is better known and remembered for the fairy tales he wrote with his brother, Wilhelm, and which collectively are known as **Grimms' Fairy Tales.**

Gardner, John and Maier, John, **Gilgamesh,** 1984, Alfred A. Knopf, New York

This is one of the oldest pieces of literature available in Western culture and was discovered in Iraq in 1872 by George Smith of the British Museum.

Gilgamesh probably was an early ruler of a city in Sumer, about 2700 BC, which today is Iraq. Gilgamesh searches for eternal life and finally seeks out Noah who survived the flood for answers. The answer he gets is not good; eventually all people must die. So, Gilgamesh makes himself happy with love and being king and decides to take life as it comes and make the best of things.

Gelb, I. J., 1963, **A Study of Writing,** University of Chicago Press, Chicago.

This is one of many books on the source of written languages to appear since 1960. Gelb traces written languages back to three sources in about 3000 BC. They are Sumerian cuneiform, Egyptian pictographic, and proto-elamite.

Gibbon, Edward, 1979, **The History of the Decline and Fall of the Roman Empire,** Rand McNally & Company, Chicago.

This is the first comprehensive history written in modern times. The original is in six volumes and was published between AD 1776 and 1788. Gibbon pinpointed several causes for the decline and fall of the Roman Empire but failed to perceive the Roman Church as one of those causes, perhaps because he was a member of that church.

Glick, Carl, 1959, **A Treasury of Masonic Thought,** Robert Hale, London.

This is a collection of quotations from a very few of the great Freemasons of the world. These include Ethan Allen, James Boswell, Robert Burns, William Jennings Bryan, Lord Chesterfield, Samuel L. Clemens, Benjamin Franklin, Johann Wolfgang von Goethe, Edgar A. Guest, Alexander Hamilton, Nathan Hale, Patrick Henry, Rudyard Kipling, John Marshall, Wolfgang Amadeus Mozart, Norman Vincent Peale, Albert Pike, Alexander Pope, Will Rogers, Theodore Roosevelt, Sir Walter Scott, Count Leo Tolstoy, Voltaire, Lew Wallace, George Washington, and others.

Goodrich, Norma Lorre   1986, **King Arthur,** Franklin Watts, New York, Toronto.

Many people, over the years, have contributed to the deciphering of the legends surrounding King Arthur the Great. One such person was Indiana University Professor John S. Grimes, who first asserted to the author, about 1958, that King Arthur was not just a legend, but indeed was a very real man and king.

The most credit must go to Professor Norma Lorre Goodrich who has put most of the story together in this book.

Gribbin, John, 1984, **In Search of Schrodinger's Cat**, Bantam Books, New York.

This is one of the best little books anyone can have and read concerning Quantum Mechanics. Heisenberg's Uncertainty Principle is one of the greatest advances in human knowledge.

Some experimenters thought that Heisenberg was simply saying that their experiments were not accurate enough; not so. Very simply, it is in the nature of things.

The position and momentum of an electron cannot be determined at the same time, simply because there is no such thing as an electron that possesses both a precise momentum and a precise position at the same time. Down goes determinism. We live in an indeterminate universe.

Hall, Manly Palmer, The Philosophical Research Society, Inc., Los Angeles, California.

Manly Palmer Hall, a distant cousin of the author, was born in 1901 and passed through transition in August, 1990. He was a Protestant minister, a 33rd degree Mason, and the leading Masonic historian in the world for the last 60 years. Hall wrote many books, perhaps 175 or so, but only two are listed here:

1. **Freemasonry of the Ancient Egyptians,** 1965:

"Nothing is more pathetic in the history of religion than the ever ready assumption of Christian scholastics that the vices of the heathen are inherent, while their virtues are plagiarized from Holy Writ. The early church proclaimed itself the enemy of learning for it willfully destroyed a great library which had housed the accumulated wisdom of ten thousand years. The sacred books of the Hindus are far older than those of the Egyptians and the symbolism we know antedates the most ancient of languages."

"An early Roman-church father, Origen, was at heart a pagan philosopher, From them, Plato affirms, Solon was taught the Atlantean language ... seventy-two conspirators represent the three destructive forces as the murderers of the Master Builder. They are ignorance, superstition and fear,... The seventh grade (in the Greater Mysteries) was bestowed only at the pleasure of the Pharaoh and the high priest with the assent of all of the members of the Society ...The symbol of the Degree is the T surmounted by a circle.... only a few hundred people have ever passed successfully the Greater Mysteries."

Hall, much like historian Albert Pike, a 33rd degree Freemason in the 1800s, also traces Freemasonry back to Egypt.

2. **The Story of Christmas,** 1986. Mr. Hall traces the history of the December 25th holiday from pagan times down to the present. He also describes why and when it came to be considered the birthday of Master Jesus who was actually born in May.

Hallam, Elizabeth, 1986, **The Plantagenet Chronicles,** Weidenfeld & Nicolson, New York.

This is the story of King Henry II and his wife, Eleanor of Aquitaine, and their sons Richard the "so-called" Lion-Hearted and Bad King John. Much of the material in this book has been put into Modern English for the first time.

Henry II was one of the strongest kings that England had until Henry VIII in the early AD 1500s. The kings during that period were:

    AD 1066 to 1087: William the Conqueror
    AD 1087 to 1100: William II
    AD 1100 to 1135: Henry I
    AD 1135 to 1154: Stephen
    AD 1154 to 1189: Henry II
    AD 1189 to 1199: Richard the Lion-Hearted
    AD 1199 to 1216: Bad King John

Henry II solidified a large kingdom composed of England and much of what is today France. His intent was to create a Camelot, with a united church and state, similar to King Arthur the Great. Henry II appointed his life-long friend, Thomas Beckett, to be Archbishop of Canterbury, and Beckett immediately double-crossed his friend and king in favor of the pope. Henry II started the use of a twelve-man jury to determine the facts in court cases.

Richard the Lion-Hearted was a bad son who turned against his own father, a bad husband, a selfish ruler, and a vicious dishonorable man. He was really a worse king than his younger brother, Bad King John. The only reason he was better liked in England was because he was very seldom there, and he did make use of good public relations. Richard spent the country into bankruptcy. John was very greedy, and since the treasury was empty, he stole money from wherever he could, which usually was from widows and orphans. Because of Magna Carta, King John will always symbolize the worst in bad kings.

Higgins, Godfrey, 1836, **Anacalypsis, An Attempt to Draw Aside the Veil of the Saitic Isis; or, an Inquiry into the Origin of Languages, Nations, and Religions**, vols. 1 & 2, Longman, London.

Godfrey Higgins was a circuit judge in England and became an amateur, but very good, historian. This work of about 1400 pages was his best and is one of the best books on history. Higgins became convinced that India is the source of our cultural values. The author disagrees and feels that the Garden of Eden in the Middle East is more probably the source of those values which passed to Egypt, and then out of Egypt with the Hebrews in the Exodus.

Only 200 copies of these two volumes were printed in 1836, so they may be difficult to locate.

Hinde, Thomas, 1985, **The Domesday Book, England's Heritage, Then and Now,** Crown Publishers, Inc., New York.

In AD 1085, William the Conqueror ordered the compiling of this village by village, and household by household, census of all assets in England, down to the very last pig. The book, which was written in abbreviated Latin, was used for the purpose of assessing taxes and was the final word on amounts owed to the king. It was the most complete and detailed census of property in historical times. It sometimes listed the head of the household but not all the people living there.

One of the entries in **Domesday Book** for the county of Shropshire, which bordered Wales, was "Polemere Pole: Alward Son of Elmund from Earl Roger."

The name Polemere possibly later evolved into Palmer about the time of the First Crusade in AD 1095. The Master of Reading at Oxford in AD 1556 was a man named Julius Palmer. He was burned to death at the Smithfield fires by Bloody Mary for holding Protestant opinions.

SELECTED ANNOTATED BIBLIOGRAPHY

In AD 1621, a William Palmer sailed to America on a ship named **Fortune** and settled at Plymouth, Massachusetts. In the late 1600s, there were three Palmer brothers in England. One of them was hanged as a highwayman. The other two left England and came to New York. There were many Palmers who fought in the America Revolution including a total of fourteen who were officers.

The leading Masonic scholar in the world, the late Manly Palmer Hall, and the popular golfer, Arnold Palmer, are both descendants of that family line.

Johnson, Rossiter, LL.D., supervising editor, **The Great Events by Famous Historians**, No publisher or date of publication is provided.

These are reprints of originals in the Old Royal Collection at the British Museum. Volume III includes a general report on many of the events occurring between AD 13 and AD 409. This gives a report on the life of the man we know as the Apostle Paul. It reports that neither Peter nor Paul died in Rome, and that Paul later went to Asia Minor and had a family. Volume IV includes a general report on many of the events occurring between AD 410 and AD 842.

In these volumes are reprinted some of the works of many ancient and respected historians including; Tacitus, Farrar, Renan, Wise, Newman, Sienkiewicz, Pliny, Lytton, Merivale, Cox, Polycarp, Guizot, Rawlinson, von Mosheim, Stanley, Alzog, Marcellinus, Bury, Rudd, Gibbon, Knight, Ruskin, Josephus, Green, Creasy, Hodkin, Bede, Irving, Ockley, Hazlitt, Al-Markari, Creasy, Mann, and Hume.

Josephus, Flavius, **The Life and Works of Josephus**, composed of two books entitled **Antiquities of the Jews** and **Wars of the Jews**, Holt, Rinehart and Winston, New York.

One paragraph in the **Antiquities** book states:

> "Now there was about this time Jesus, a wise man, if it be lawful to call him a man; for he was a doer of wonderful works, a teacher of such men as receive the truth with pleasure. He drew over to him both many of the Jews and many of the Gentiles. He was [the] Christ. And when Pilate, at the suggestion of the principal men amongst us (Would a Jewish author make up a falsehood like this to indict his own people?), had condemned him to the cross, those that loved him at the first did not forsake him; for he appeared to them alive again the third day (Sunday is only the second day after Friday as most any rational person knows.); as the divine prophets had foretold these and ten thousand other wonderful things concerning him. And the tribe of Christians, so named from him, are not extinct at this day."

This paragraph was a later insertion into Josephus' book and is an obvious forgery.

Kelly, J. N. D., 1986, **The Oxford Dictionary of Popes.** Oxford University Press, New York.

This is an excellent book for any library. It gives a sketch of each of the popes of the Roman Church, from non-Pope Peter in AD 64 or so to John Paul II in AD 1978.

Kersten, Holger, 1986, **Jesus Lived in India -- His Unknown Life Before and After the Crucifixion,** Element Books, Ltd., Dorset, England.

Kersten lives in Freilburg, Germany and was trained in a Protestant college. Kersten spent several years in India and that area studying ancient material in order to write this book. He presents evidence that Master Jesus did return to northern India after the crucifixion

326 TRUE ESOTERIC TRADITIONS

event in AD 33. He says that Master Jesus did not return there until AD 49 or so, and had probably spent some of that time in England and France. Kersten presents evidence concerning the graves of Moses Moria-El, Master Jesus, and Mary, all of which he says are located near Srinagar, Kashmir. Kersten presents about the same story concerning Master Jesus that the author learned years before, but Kersten does present some interesting new data in support of that story.

Lauf, Detlef Ingo, 1977, **Secret Doctrines of the Tibetan Books of the Dead,** translated by Graham Parkes, Shambhala, Boulder & London.

This is an English translation of a poorly written German book. These books deal with the event of death and the experiences to be expected after death, all of which take place between either total liberation or reincarnation. This journey can be almost instantaneous for a very high lama, such as Master Jesus, or up to 49 days for an ordinary person. It is this journey that is referred to as purgatory in the Roman Church.

Many highly evolved persons such as Moses, Laotse, Master Jesus, and others, chose to experience death or transition in private where they could, and apparently did, pass through transition or death without ever losing consciousness. Most of us do lose consciousness temporarily and thus do fear transition or death. Transition or death is every bit as normal as birth and life and, at the appropriate time, is to be accepted and enjoyed.

Lewis, Dr. H. Spencer, 1929, **Mystical Life of Jesus,** Supreme Grand Lodge of AMORC, Inc., San Jose California.

Lewis, who was head of the external Rosicrucian Order in the United States, reports that ancient records of that Order tell almost exactly the same life story of Master Jesus as did Levi Dowling in his one and only book, **The Aquarian Age Gospel of Jesus, the Christ of the Piscean Age.**

Notovitch, Levi, Lewis, and several others from various parts of the world tell almost exactly the same life story of Master Jesus. The true story of the facts about Master Jesus have been suppressed by the Roman Church for more than 1600 years so that it could create a pagan-style Master Jesus who was some kind of magician or side-show freak who wasted his time going about dazzling the ignorant with magical tricks. There is no question but that Master Jesus could look at a person and tell immediately the kind of person he really was. However, this is fully explainable by physical law.

Lewis says that Master Jesus was an Aryan gentile, not a Hebrew, who studied and taught in many different countries and went silent, but did not die, in AD 33. Lewis failed to completely comprehend the role of women in those matters. The reason for this was that, then as now, women either were forced to or chose to express themselves more quietly through men, who were in the public view. Actually, Lewis copied much of this material from two Finnish books by Pekka Ervast entitled **The Esoteric School of Jesus** and **The Sermon on the Mount or The Key to Christianity.**

Mapp, Alf J. Jr., 1987, **Thomas Jefferson,** Madison Books, New York.

This is perhaps the best of many books on Thomas Jefferson.

Marsh, Henry, 1987, **Dark Age Britain,** Sources of history, Dorset Press, New York.

This is a collection of the most ancient historical works concerning Britain collected into one small volume of 200 pages. This would make an excellent college text on the history of England. It reports on the following:

1. **The Destruction of Britain,** by Gildas the Wise. This was written about AD 547 by the monk Gildas who was sort of a John-the-Baptist-type character. He passed severe judgment on all the people and events of his time. He covers the time period from the conquest of Britain by Julius Caesar to the mid-AD 500s. Gildas states that Britain converted to Christianity during the reign of Tiberius Caesar, which would have been about AD 35. This was some years prior to any claimed church in Rome which did not happen until about AD 144 or later. Whether true or not, Gildas and the people of his time period thought that it was true. Gildas supports the idea of Joseph of Arimathea coming to Britain in about AD 35. Gildas was born in Scotland and was thus a contemporary of King Arthur the Great. He knew King Arthur quite well. Gildas died in AD 570.

2. **The Welsh Annals** and the **Chronicle of the Prince of Wales.** These annals were written and kept in the mountains of Wales where the Britons were exiled after the Saxons shoved them to the west, out of England. They cover the time period AD 444 to 954. They also describe much conflict up to AD 517 and then a long period of peace similar to that in King Arthur's kingdom, to the north of Wales. It also describes the Great Plague which reached the area in AD 547. There is also a very specific entry about King Arthur and the Battle of Baden in AD 516.

It reports that, in AD 595, Augustine of Canterbury converted the English to the Roman Church and that there was great conflict between Augustine and the native church of the Britons. The local Christian bishops refused to accept the new Roman Church until forced to do so.

3. Nennius, **The History of the Britons.** Nennius, who lived about AD 858, like Bede, lived in a monastery and tried to write a history of the Britons. He also mentioned King Arthur and some of his wars against the Danes.

This volume also reports on **The Anglo-Saxon Chronicles, Bede's Ecclesiastical History of the English People, Bishop Asser's Life of King Alfred, William of Malmesbury, and Godfrey of Monmouth.**

Michel, John, 1983, **The New View over Atlantis,** Harper & Row, New York.

This is the best book in existence on the subject of the ancient ley-lines, or pre-historically marked boundaries, that seem to criss-cross Britain and several other countries. It also contains the ancient magic squares of the planets, including the sign of the sun, which is 666.

Norbu, Thubten Jigme and Turnbull, Colin, 1969, **Tibet,** Chatto & Windus Ltd., 40 William IV Street, London W.C.2.

This is one of the best little books on understanding Tibet that the author has located. It was purchased in Srinagar, Kashmir, in 1976. The authors are Thubten Jigme Norbu, the older brother of the Dali Lama and Colin Turnbull the noted anthropologist. Norbu taught at Indiana University, an alma mater of the author, for many years.

They relate the legends of a great teacher, Master Jesus, who came from the West and taught in the area at about the time period Master Jesus was living in that area of the world.

They also relate that the Russian Notwitch (Notovitch) took away the Saint Issa Manuscript from the Hemis Monastery in northern India. Although Notovitch later returned a translation of the document, this, too, was later taken away by a foreign traveler.

The Buddhists have two views of Buddha, just as the Christians have two views of Master Jesus. One group believes that God incarnated down into Buddha while the others believe that Buddha was a man who lived and suffered like any other man. This is exactly like the teachings of the Roman Church which teach that God incarnated down into Master Jesus. Such teachings are pagan. If God could incarnate down into either Buddha or Master Jesus, then man can reincarnate down into an amoeba. Such is not possible.

Notovitch, Nicolas, 1974, **The Unknown Life of Jesus Christ**, Gordon Press, New York.

This is the story of the great sage called Saint Issa in Sanskrit, or Jesus in Greek. Saint Issa was a child prodigy born in Israel who, at age 13, came to study in northern India. Saint Issa taught against the caste system, multiple gods, and gods that could be seen. He also taught against sacrifices and converted many pagans. The priests plotted his death.

Saint Issa studied and taught in the India area for about six or seven years and then moved on to Persia where his fame had already spread. The priests in Persia also plotted his death and the king outlawed him. Later, Saint Issa taught all over the world and then in Israel where he was crucified and put on a cross for a few hours by the Romans. However, he survived and later died at his home in northern India.

Saint Issa was hated by the priests of all religions and for very good reasons. He taught that man has a personal relationship with God and priests are not necessary as go-betweens. It's pretty easy to hate someone who says your occupation is not necessary and even counter-productive. But, it was true then and remains true today.

Osman, Ahmed, 1987, **Stranger in the Valley of the Kings, The Identification of Yuya as the Patriarch Joseph**, Souvenir Press, London.

The author, Ahmed Osman, is a Muslim scholar who was born in Cairo, Egypt, and presently lives and works in London, England. In this book, he takes a new look at the story of the biblical Joseph being prime minister of Egypt and concludes that the story is, in fact, true.

But could a Muslim from Egypt conceivably know anything about pharaonic or biblical history? Certainly not, argues an obviously jealous Professor Donald B. Redford of Toronto University in Canada. However, the professor himself seems totally ignorant of AMORC which played such a crucial role in the events of this time period.

About 30 years ago, the author concluded that it is not possible to even begin to understand the Akhnaton period of Egyptian history without at least:

1. Becoming familiar with AMORC or Masonic teachings which played a crucial part in the events of that time period; and,

2. De-**Bible**-izing his thinking somewhat, because while the **Bible**, which was written hundreds of years later, accurately reflects general themes of that time period, it simply is not accurate on details, because both the later Egyptians and also the later Hebrews tried very hard to pretend that the Hebrew family of Joseph-Yuya had no connection to the royal family of Egypt.

Osman's statement in his book that the **Bible** is the inspired word of God is, of course, a religious view and is not history.

Payne, Robert, 1989, **The Fathers of the Eastern Church**, Dorset Press, New York.

This is a good book covering the early Roman-church fathers from the East. It includes Clement of Alexandria, Origen, Athanasius, Basil, Chrysostom, and others.

Payne, Robert, 1989, **The Fathers of the Western Church**, Dorset Press, New York.

This is a good book covering the early Roman-church fathers in the West from the Apostle Paul to Thomas Aquinas. It includes Tertullian, Ambrose, Augustine, Benedict, Gregory, and others.

Pelley, William Dudley, 1950, **Soulcraft, a Post-graduate Education in the Eternal Verities**, Fellowcraft Press, Inc., Noblesville, Indiana (twelve volumes).

Pelley has written 156 scripts which are published in twelve volumes of thirteen scripts each. This is a monumental work. It is a study of the great cosmic principles on which the universe is run; on the mystical history of man on this planet; on the significance of Master Jesus the Christ in human destiny; on the continuity and survival of human consciousness, and the programs by which souls may aspire to gain perfection.

A somewhat strange situation exists concerning the acquisition of this set of books by the author. The author acquired volumes one, two, and three in the early 1960s and looked for the other nine volumes over a period of twenty-five years. In 1987, while visiting a well-known book store in Los Angeles, the author inquired about this set of books. The book dealer said that he did have a partial set composed of the last nine volumes. "I have had the last nine volumes of this set for many years but I have never been able to locate the first three," the dealer stated. He was dumbfounded when the author related that he had the first three volumes but had searched until that day to find the other nine.

Perry, Whitall N., 1986, **A Treasury of Traditional Wisdom**, Harper & Row, San Francisco.

This book is 1144 pages in length, including the index and acknowledgements; these take up 100 of the pages. While it is much too long for the average reader, it is an excellent collection of wisdom from the world's leading minds. While it is true that no amount of knowledge can add up to wisdom, this book is packed full of knowledge. It is almost a library in itself.

Pike, Albert, 1871, **Morals and Dogma of the Ancient and Accepted Scottish Rite of Freemasonry,** Supreme Council of the Thirty-third Degree for the Southern Jurisdiction of the United States.

Hundreds of books have been written about Freemasonry. For understanding the esoteric teachings of Freemasonry, this book probably is the best of them all. Pike says that about half of his material was taken directly from ancient manuscripts and the other half is his own analysis and commentary.

This may disturb some Christians but Pike also confirmed that Master Jesus was a Freemason. On page 97 he states: "The Holy Kabalah was ... revealed by the Savior to Saint John...." All Freemasons should know that their fraternity pre-dates Master Jesus by many centuries and certainly did not begin in Europe. The idea that the Freemasons were started only after AD 1200 or so was mere propaganda against them by the Roman Church.

Pike's book is 860 pages of very heavy reading concerning descriptions of the 32 degrees of the Scottish Rite. In 1925, a leading Freemason named Hugo prepared an index of Pike's book. The index is 218 pages long. Surely many Freemasons, and maybe even some of the 32nd degree, have not read this ancient material of their own fraternity.

Pope Boniface VIII, AD 1302, **Papal Bull Unam Sanctum,** Roman Church

"That there is one holy Catholic and apostolic Church we are impelled by our faith to believe and to hold -- this we do firmly believe and openly confess -- and **outside of this there is neither salvation nor remission of sins,** as the bridegroom proclaims in Canticles, 'My dove, my undefiled is but one; she is the only one of her mother, she is the choice one of her that bare her.' The Church represents one mystic body, and of this body Christ is the head; of Christ, indeed, God is the head. In it is one Lord, and one faith, and one baptism. In the time of the flood there was one ark of Noah, prefiguring the one Church, finished in one cubit, having one Noah as steersman and commander. Outside of this all things upon the face of the earth were, as we read, destroyed. This Church we venerate and this alone. ... It is that seamless coat of the Lord, which was not rent but fell by lot. Therefore, in this one and only Church there is one body and one head, -- not two heads as if it were a monster, -- namely, **Christ and Christ's vicar, Peter and Peter's successor** for the Lord said to Peter himself, 'Feed my sheep.' 'My sheep,' he said, using a general term and not designating these or those sheep, so that we must believe that all the sheep were committed to him. If, then, the Greeks, or others, shall say that they were not intrusted to Peter and his successors, they must perforce admit that they are not of Christ's sheep, as the Lord says in John, 'there is one fold, and one shepherd.'

"In this Church and in its power are two swords, to wit, a spiritual and a temporal, and this we are taught by the words of the Gospel; for when the apostles said, 'Behold, here are two swords' (in the Church, namely, since the apostles were speaking), the Lord did not reply that it was too many, but enough. And surely he who claims that the temporal sword is not in the power of Peter has but ill understood the word of our Lord when he said, 'Put up again thy sword into his place.' **Both the spiritual and the material swords, therefore, are in the power of the Church,** the later indeed to be used for the Church, the former by the Church, the one by the priest, the other by the hand of kings and soldiers, but by the will and sufferance of the priest.

"It is fitting, moreover, that one sword should be under the other, and the temporal authority subject to the spiritual power. For when the apostle said, 'there is no power but of God: the powers that be are ordained of God,' they would not be ordained unless one sword were under the other, and one, as inferior, was brought back by the other to the highest place. For, according to St. Dionysius, the law of divinity is to lead the lowest through the intermediate to the highest. Therefore, according to the law of the universe, **things are not reduced to order directly and upon the same footing,** but the lowest through the intermediate, and the inferior though the superior. It behooves us, therefore, the more freely to confess that the spiritual power excels in dignity and nobility and from whatsoever of earthly power, as spiritual interests exceed the temporal in importance. All this we see fairly from the giving of tithes, from the benediction and sanctification, from the recognition of this power and the control of these same things.

"Hence, the truth bearing witness, it is for the spiritual power to establish the earthly power and judge it, if it be not good. Thus, in the case of the Church and the power of the Church, the prophecy of Jeremiah is fulfilled: 'See, I have this day set thee over the nations and over the kingdoms,' etc. **Therefore, if the earthly power shall err, it shall be judged by the spiritual power; if the lesser spiritual power err, it shall be judged by the higher. But if the supreme power err, it can be judged by God alone and not by man,** the apostles bearing witness, saying, The spiritual man judges all things, but he himself is judged by no one. Hence this power, although given to man and exercised by man, is not human, but rather a divine power, given by the divine lips to Peter, and founded on a rock for him and his successors in him (Christ) whom he confessed, the Lord saying to Peter himself, 'Whatsoever thou shalt bind,' etc.

"Whoever, therefore, shall resist this power, ordained by God, resists the ordination of God, unless there should be two beginnings [i.e. principles], as the Manichæan imagines. But this we judge to be false and heretical, since, by the testimony of Moses, not in the beginnings but in the beginning, God created the heaven and the earth. **We, moreover, proclaim, declare, and pronounce that it is altogether necessary to salvation for every human being to be subject to the Roman pontiff.**

"Given at the Latern the twelfth day before the Kalends of December, in our eighth year, as a perpetual memorial of this matter."

Obviously, Boniface is talking about **every human being** and not just **Christians** as later claimed by his apologists. He also fails to tell his flock that the reference in the **New Testament** to the Apostle Peter being the first bishop of that church is a rather obvious forgery.

Pope Leo XIII, AD 1884, **Papal Bull Humanum Genus,** Roman Church

This papal bull is a very long venomous diatribe against the Freemasons and states only in part:

2"...The Roman Pontiffs, our predecessors, watching constantly over the safety of the Christian people, early recognized this capital enemy [Freemasons] rushing forth out of the darkness of hidden conspiracy, and, anticipating the future in their mind, gave the alarm to princes and people, that they should not be caught by deceptions and frauds.

"Clement XII., by the Apostolic constitution -- quo graviora -- recapitulating the acts and decrees of the above Pontiffs about the matter, validated and confirmed them forever. In the same way spoke Pius VIII., Gregory XVI., and very often Pius IX.

"The purpose and aim of the Masonic sect having been discovered from plain evidence, from the cognition of causes, its laws, Rites and commentaries having come to light and been made known by the additional depositions of the associated members, this Apostolic See denounced and openly declared that **the sect of Masons is established against law and honesty, and is equally a danger to Christianity as well as to society; and, threatening those heavy punishments which the Church uses against the guilty ones, she forbade the society, and ordered that none should give his name to it....**"

This papal bull is so grossly inaccurate, and much like the temper tantum of an overly spoiled child that, notwithstanding the Roman Church's well-known animosity to Freemasons, it is somewhat surprising that the Vatican advisors would even allow the pope to issue it because of the negative image created for the Roman Church.

Pyles, Thomas, 1971, **The Origins and Development of the English Language,** Harcourt Brace Jovanovich, Inc., New York.

332 TRUE ESOTERIC TRADITIONS

Since about 1960, there have been many new theories on the sources of languages. This is the most readable book on the subject of the English language. Pyles states that language is man's greatest intellectual tool, and it goes back as far as one million years, when man first used tools; whereas, the oldest known Sumerian writing goes back only about 5000 years. He puts the Old English period from AD 449 to 1100; the Middle English period from AD 1100 to 1500; and, the Modern English period since AD 1500. He also traces the modern alphabet forward from Semitic to Greek to Roman and to English.

Redford, Donald B., **Akhenaten, the Heretic King**, 1984, Princeton University Press, Princeton, New Jersey.

The author, Donald Redford, is professor of Near Eastern studies at the University of Toronto in Canada. Let us examine some of Professor Redford's conclusions on events around this time period.

   1. On page 223, Professor Redford says: "Before he came to the throne Horemhab (Horemheb) was a docile general...." Just the opposite was true. This was the revolutionary general who overthrew and ousted the royal family of Egypt and established the 19th dynasty. The general was an extremely aggressive man and was essentially in control of the government of Egypt even before taking the throne, possibly as early as the reign of King Tut. Professor Redford completely misinterprets the situation.

   2. On page 232, Professor Redford says of Akhnaton: "... Humanist he was not.... Nor is he the mentor of Moses." A reasonable interpretation of the history of this period would be just the opposite of Professor Redford's statement set forth above. Akhnaton was a fanatical monotheist even to his downfall, and very probably was the philosophical mentor of Moses Moria-El.

   3. On page 233, Professor Redford says: "We have no idea who or what influenced him (Akhnaton) in his formative years; but he was not brought into contact with his father's court...." The person who controlled Akhnaton's education was one of the most powerful women of all time, his non-Egyptian mother, Queen Tiye. What Akhnaton was taught were the teachings of the ancient White Lodge. Professor Redford seems totally uninformed on such teachings and the crucial role they played in those events.

   4. On page 233, Professor Redford again says of Akhnaton: "Though he was apprehensive about his own lack of resolve, be nonetheless espoused a lenient policy toward his northern provinces which deterred him from acting unhesitatingly in the Asian sphere." This statement is complete nonsense. The historical fact is that both Pharaoh Akhnaton and his mother, Queen Tiye, were fervently opposed to aggressive war and watched the mighty Egyptian empire crumble rather than violate that belief. However, only in our own time, at the Nazi war-crimes trials, was aggressive war determined to be a crime against humanity and legally punishable. Contrary to the Professor's implication, Akhnaton was not necessarily weak and he certainly was not wrong. In fact he was about 3300 years ahead of his time.

   5. On page 234, Professor Redford yet once again says: "... what Akhenaten (Akhnaton) championed was in the truest sense of the word, atheism." This statement clearly demonstrates a complete lack of understanding of the subject matter. Akhnaton an atheist; simply not true.

Any person who can study the history of this period and conclude that Akhnaton was an atheist or that General Horemheb was docile really forfeits any right to be taken seriously on the subject. Professor Redford seems to have learned more and more about less and less until he has come to know almost everything about almost nothing. His very impressive title to the contrary notwithstanding, Professor Redford is not academically qualified to objectively evaluate the Osman material about the biblical Joseph being prime minister of Egypt.

Reinach, Salomon, 1930, **Orpheus, a History of Religions**, Horace Liveright, Inc., USA.

This is an excellent book on the history of the world's religions. It appeared in 38 editions in French and this 39th edition has been translated into English. Reinach feels that religion was disguised under symbols that were taken literally by the uninitiated and erroneously accepted as an adequate expression of human knowledge. He also confirms that the famous paragraph in Josephus is a forgery and that the Jews were not responsible for the death of Master Jesus, because he was not killed.

The idea that Master Jesus died at that time in Israel and that the Jews were responsible, is Roman-church theology, not history.

Robinson, James Harvey, 1904, **Readings in European History**, Ginn & Company, Boston

The author was professor of History at Columbia University. This is a treatise. Professor Robinson reviews and reports on literally thousands of manuscripts in several languages for the 1200 year period from Constantine in AD 325 to the Protestant revolt in AD 1517.

Robinson, John J., 1989, **Born in Blood; The Lost Secrets of Freemasonry**, M. Evans & Company, New York.

This is an excellent book on some of the activities of the Freemasons in England from the time of de Molay in AD 1314 to the going public of the Freemasons in England in AD 1717. The Freemasons organized a mini civil war in England in AD 1381 which is well reported in this volume.

Robinson reports on the horrible and inhumane torture used by the Roman-church popes. The popes used torture worse even than the Nazi gas chambers in World War II.

Robinson presents the thesis that the Freemasons were an offspring of the Knights Templar. This is not correct. The Knights Templars were sort of an offspring or step-child of the Freemasons, although the Knights never completely changed to the Freemasonic teachings. The Freemasons pre-date the Knights Templar by at least 2000 years.

Robinson presents a complete English translation of the Papal Bull called **Humanum Genus**, a lengthy, false, and malicious diatribe against the Freemasons by Pope Leo XIII in AD 1884.

Rowse, Alfred Leslie, 1984, **The Annotated Shakespeare**, Arlington House, Inc., New York.

This is a complete set of the Shakespearean literature and contains almost 2500 pages, with commentary by Dr. Rowse who is sometimes considered one of the leading authorities on the Elizabethan era. It is therefore disappointing to see that Dr. Rowse seems not to know that the actor, William Shakespeare from Stratford-upon-Avon, was not actually the author of the literature published under that name.

Among the few knowledgeable people who still seriously maintain that the actor is the author of that literature is the Stratford Chamber of Commerce which, of course, includes the faculty of Oxford University which is just down the road and where Dr. Rowse was a teacher.

Professor Rowse reminds one of Professor Redford of Toronto University who tries to understand the Eighteenth Dynasty in Egypt without ever learning about the ancient White Lodge and its teachings.

The author is somewhat acquainted with some of the people involved in the reconstruction of the Old Globe Theatre in London. Certainly, many of those people do know the truth of the authorship, as well as some of the actors at Stratford-upon-Avon, the Chamber of Commerce and Oxford University notwithstanding.

Having a professor from Oxford write on Shakespeare is like having Oxford and Cambridge try to explain why the monarchy in Britain is not the best form of government, or why it is bad public policy to allow Oxford and Cambridge to own tens of thousands of acres of English farm land. It would be like having the pope sit as judge in a trial of the Roman Church for high crimes and misdemeanors.

Savage, Anne, 1983, **The Anglo-Saxon Chronicles,** Dorset Press, New York.

These chronicles purport to be the authentic voices of England from the time of Julius Caesar in about 45 BC to the coronation of King Henry II in AD 1154. The monks who compiled the **Chronicles** began their work in the late AD 800s probably during the reign of King Alfred the Great who was a great proponent of education. Their other sources are unknown, but Bede's **History of the English Church and People** was one important source. This is mostly the history of southern England and does not report the existence of a King Arthur. That is one reason that King Arthur was thought to be only a legend until very recently. Now it is known that King Arthur was king in the Scottish lowlands. Most scholars consider these **Chronicles** to be quite authentic in their reporting of events from about AD 800 forward.

Shaw, M. R. B., 1985, **Chronicles of the Crusades,** Joinville and Villehardouin, Dorset Press, New York.

This is actually two books in one. Villehardouin lived in about AD 1185 and wrote **The Conquest of Constantinople.** Joinville lived a little later in about AD 1250 and wrote **The Life of Saint Louis.**

In AD 1076, Jerusalem fell into the hands of the Muslim Turks who treated the local Christians badly. Pope Urban II needed some excuse to create an external enemy and this was it. The Jews and Muslims in Jerusalem were slaughtered in AD 1099 by the Crusaders, led and financed by the Knights Templar.

Again in AD 1189, a new crusade was led mainly by England's King Richard the Lion-Hearted, who was a son of Henry II and the older brother of Bad King John. After the capture of Acre, King Richard executed all the Turkish prisoners of war who had surrendered. Richard had the prisoners placed down on their knees and then had his solders pull their heads back while he cut their throats. Not really a nice fellow despite his name. Then followed the Fourth Crusade which is covered in detail in this book. It was another disaster.

Sitchin, Zecharia, 1976, **The 12th Planet,** Stein and Day, New York.

This Russian-born Jewish scholar, who now lives in New York City, has spent a lifetime studying the ancient pre-Egyptian culture known as Sumer. From that research, he develops the idea that advanced men came here from another as yet unidentified planet in the Solar System, to mine gold. This planet circles the sun once every 3600 years. While these advanced men were here, they cross-bred with the less advanced females on Earth and created today's mankind. Many of Sitchin's ideas are also perhaps alluded to in the **Bible.** This is a very interesting book that, if true, would explain much of our history that otherwise remains unexplained.

Smith, Joseph, translator, 1974. **The Book of Mormon,** The Church of Jesus Christ of Latter-day Saints, Salt Lake City, Utah.

The **Book of Mormon** contains fifteen chapters and covers the period from 600 BC to AD 421. At that time the book was secreted in New York state, where it remained until AD 1827, at which time the plates were delivered to Joseph Smith who interpreted them into the **Book of Mormon.** Joseph Smith was killed by an armed mob while he was in jail in Carthage, Illinois, on June 27, 1844. Brigham Young then led most of the Mormons to Utah.

The Mormon idea that a man could legally have more than one wife at the same time brought them into conflict with criminal laws in the United States. Utah was required to outlaw bigamy before it could become a state. This book was a gift to the author from Elders Robinson and Williams. This is one of many examples that shows the emptiness of the earlier Christian-church theology which caused some people to reach out for something new and hopefully better.

Straus, Barrie Ruth, 1987, **The Catholic Church,** David & Charles, Newton Abbot, London.

This is an apology for the Roman Church. Straus soft-pedals considerably the criminal history of the Roman Church and comes to the rather dubious conclusion that all is now well in Rome. She states that the present pope speaks powerfully on behalf of human dignity, social justice, and peace. However, she makes no effort to reconcile that statement with the Roman Church's political and financial objectives concerning its own nuns and priests, and the female population of the world.

Swindler, William F., 1965, **Magna Carta: Legend and Legacy,** The Bobbs-Merrill Company, Inc.

This is the best book on the events lending up to the drafting and re-drafting of this Great Charter during the period AD 1215 to 1225. Richard the Lion-Hearted was king of England for ten years but he spent only six months of that time in England. He literally bankrupted a very wealthy country left to him by Henry II. Both Richard and John had consummate arrogance, ungovernable rage, and unequaled hunger for money and women. The stories of Richard being a homosexual are not true. Quite the contrary, he was a womanizer to the extreme.

Taylor, Robert M. Jr., 1987, **The Northwest Ordinance 1787, a Bicentennial Handbook,** Indiana Historical Society, Indianapolis, Indiana.

This is an excellent little book on the facts and dates leading up to the adoption of "An Ordinance for the Government of the Territory North-west of the River Ohio." It was adopted by the Continental Congress on July 13, 1787. The new US Constitution went into effect on June 21, 1788 and the Bill of Rights was approved by Virginia on December 15, 1791, which made those first ten amendments part of the US Constitution.

Tedlock, Dennis, 1985, **Popol Vuh,** Simon & Schuster, Inc., New York.

This is the holy book of the Mayan Indians of Mexico. The accounts go back to the dawn of life. **Popol Vuh** means **Council Book.** It was also sometimes referred to as the light that came from across the sea. On page 210, it lists the great and ancient leaders in order of rank, with the head lord being "Keeper of the Mat." Remember, that in Egypt, **maat** meant **truth**, and **cromaat** meant that **the truth shall be**, or that, **it is done in truth**.

Tompkins, Peter, 1971, **Secrets of the Great Pyramid,** Harper & Row, New York.

This is the best single book on the Great Pyramid of Giza. Tompkins reviews all the theories on why and when the great pyramid was constructed. Theories that the Great Pyramid was built as a burial chamber simply do not stand up. There are many reasons, but one that is very apparent is the two air shafts that lead to the King's Chamber deep in the heart of this very unique building which, the author has concluded, was built as a Masonic Lodge and was used for initiations into the Ancient Mysteries. The Great Pyramid was built by Master Masons.

The only item in the King's Chamber is a granite casket-like box that is exactly sized for a man or woman to lay in in ancient days. The casket is only six feet three inches in length so it would not be long enough today, but it was more than adequate in ancient times. There is no lid and no ornaments so it could not have been a burial chamber. Its real purpose was for rituals involving the dying as a material person and being symbolically re-born as a new person, which has always been taught by the ancient White Lodge and its step-child, the Blue Lodge of Israel, and later still by Master Jesus the Christ.

The author can affirm that being in the King's Chamber does give one a most unique feeling that is long remembered. The pyramid itself was constructed to show many mathematical relationships. It appears that pi(π) or 3.1416 etc. is shown on two faces of the pyramid and phi(ϕ), or what is called the Golden Section, which is 1.6180 etc., is shown on the other two faces.

Phi(ϕ) can be obtained by dividing a line AB at a point C, in such a way that the whole line AB is longer than the first part AC, in the same proportion as the first part AC is longer than the remainder CB, or algebraically as:

$$\frac{AB}{AC} = \frac{AC}{CB} = 1.618$$

It can also be obtained from Pythagoras' theorem which will show that the value of ϕ will be ½ + $\sqrt{5}$/2, or 1.618. The dimensions of two faces of the Great Pyramid are in the phi(ϕ) relationship. The two computations for π and ϕ are very close to each other and are as follows:

	Pi(π)	Phi(ϕ)
Height of pyramid	481.1 ft.	480.8 ft.
Apothem (distance from top down a side)	611.8 ft.	611.6 ft.

Thus, it appears that the sides of the Great Pyramid were slightly skewed in order to project both these mathematical relationships. The builders of the Great Pyramid knew the dimensions of Earth. They could measure the year and the precession of the equinoxes, or the Great Year, of 25,920 years. They could calculate latitude and longitude at different locations on earth and they, of course, knew that the earth was a sphere and revolved on its axis. The ancient Egyptians perhaps obtained their knowledge from the Sumerians, but they had knowledge then that was not re-discovered until the Rosicrucian Enlightenment in the AD 1500s, and thereafter.

They calculated the year as 365¼ days and added an extra day every four years for leap year. They also computed cycles of 1460 years, caused by the precession of the equinoxes, going from 4240 BC to 2789 BC to 1320 BC to AD 140. According to some students these cycles went back in time to 25 times 1460 or 36,500 years, and then five times 36,500 or 182,500 years. It might be worth noting that 182,500 years ago is very close to the time that some modern scientists say that the biblical Eve lived in the Garden of Eden. We wonder.

The Descending Passage in the pyramid appears to have been constructed to point directly at Polaris the North Star. That passage is so accurately cut through the rock that the average error is less than 1/50th of an inch in its entire 350 foot length.

Toynbee, Arnold, 1979, **A Study of History**, Weathervane Books, New York.

This is the best study of history in the world. The complete set has twelve volumes and contains more than 7000 pages. It is very heavy reading.

Walsh, Michael, 1984, **An Illustrated History of the Popes: Saint Peter to John Paul II**, Bonanza Books, New York.

This book was written by a former Jesuit and was reviewed and cleared for publication by the censor of the Roman Church as being free from doctrinal or moral error. This obviously makes the book suspect.

It is beautifully done with many pictures and paintings. Walsh acknowledges that there were some misdeeds by popes in the Dark Ages, but rationalizes the misdeeds of the popes in current times. He acknowledges the reign of 263 different popes, but this number is not accurate.

In AD 1978, Pope John Paul I reigned for only 33 days, then promptly died. His death has never been satisfactorily explained. Walsh totally fails to focus on that event. Some priests in the church really believe that John Paul I intended to transform the church to the teachings of Master Jesus and that he was murdered by other officials in the Vatican to prevent that from happening.

Of the 239 popes, many have been criminals and most have been pretty unscrupulous people. A very few have been fine upstanding men; since the time of Roman Emperor Constantine, one can count the really good popes on one hand. It is almost impossible for a truly good man to become pope, just as in recent times, it is almost impossible for a really qualified man to become president of the United States. Sad, but true.

White, Ellen G. 1958, **Conflict of the Ages Series**, Pacific Press Publishing Association, Boise, Idaho. These five volumes are:

1. **Patriarchs and Prophets;**
2. **Prophets and Kings;**
3. **The Desire of Ages;**
4. **The Acts of the Apostles;** and
5. **The Great Controversy,**

which constitute the re-interpretation of the **Bible** by Ellen G. White, the founder of the Seventh-day Adventist Church.

Mrs. White adds very little to any new understanding of the **Bible**. She insists that the world was created in six 24 hour days, from Sunday through Friday, and so declares, that the Sabbath, Saturday, is a holy day. Like the Jews, she suffers from a very limited view of God, as though the One True God would care which day of the week is reserved for rest and meditation. This was yet one more of many examples that showed the emptiness of the Christian-church theology which caused some people to reach out for something new and, hopefully, better. This set of books was a gift to the author from Debbie Moen, a member of that church and a niece of the author.

Wilson, Epiphanius, 1982, **The Wisdom of Confucius**, Avenel Books, New York.

Confucius taught the Golden Rule as well as five other primary virtues. They were love, justice, reverence, wisdom, and sincerity. His teachings still dominate the thinking of almost one billion Chinese people yet today, which is about twenty per cent of the world's population.

Wright, Robert, 1991, **Quest for the Mother Tongue**, The Atlantic Monthly, Boston, MA.

This is an excellent, but short and concise, review of the search for the Eve language. Most linguists think that such an Eve language did not even exist, but a few are already piecing together reasonable proof that Eve did have a language.

> One of the great
> injustices man has
> committed against woman
> has been the taking away of
> her identity during life.

> Although there
> may be much pain
> leading up to transition,
> the transition process itself,
> is totally free of pain.

> Perhaps the most
> ignorant belief on Earth
> is that found among Christians
> who believe that they, and their religion,
> are closer than the other people of Earth to Master
> Jesus the Christ and his teachings.

> And -- the rains came.

INDEX

666 109-111, 228, 327

Abiff 183
Abraham 45-47, 57, 73, 114, 141, 143, 144, 236, 288, 294, 306
Absalom 177
Adams 63, 282, 283, 285, 286, 288
Age of Aquarius 22, 231, 260, 297
Age of Brahma 90
Age of Pisces 55, 215
Akashic Records 18, 208, 209
Alexander the Great 53-55, 168, 172, 205, 291
Alexandria 23, 26, 61, 72, 112, 113, 162, 197, 207, 226, 236, 256, 262, 289, 317, 329
Amenhotep 47, 48, 113, 119, 144, 146, 147, 161, 319
AMORC 10, 16, 17, 22, 23, 27, 29, 31, 33, 36, 39-42, 49-55, 57, 59, 61, 63, 66, 70, 78, 85, 113, 114, 119, 120, 122, 127, 130-132, 147, 162, 166, 177-182, 184, 186, 190, 194, 196, 202, 204, 207, 215, 216, 218, 219, 223, 224, 227, 231, 234, 236, 237, 239, 252, 254, 255, 258, 260, 275, 297, 300-302, 318, 320, 325, 328
Anastasia 74
Anglo-Saxon Chronicles 64, 240, 316, 326, 327, 334
Antoinette 73, 284
Apostle Paul 22, 29, 44, 57, 59, 185, 191, 198, 205, 212, 219, 222, 224, 227, 231, 238, 262, 269, 311, 325, 329
Apostle Peter 68, 311, 331
Apostles' Creed 228, 229, 239
Aristocles 54, 55, 119, 139
Aristotle 54, 55, 79, 198, 205, 206, 266, 291, 307
Assyria 51
Atlantis 21, 41, 77-80, 84, 85, 113, 148, 165, 217
Attila the hun 62, 117
Augustine of Canterbury 241, 327
Australia 72, 308

Babylon 44, 54, 100, 156, 195, 311
Bacon 24, 55, 70, 71, 73, 90, 120, 202, 207, 209, 258, 259, 261, 273, 274, 298, 319, 320
Baldwin 171
Bathsheba 51, 115, 118, 177, 178
Battle of Hastings 64, 241
Battle of Tours 23, 63, 236-238, 316
Bayeux Tapestry 241
Beckett 324
Bede 63, 316, 325, 327, 334
Bhagavad-Gita 180, 193, 316, 317
Bible 12, 21-23, 26, 27, 29, 40, 45, 46, 51, 52, 54, 55, 61, 70, 79, 81, 84, 93-97, 99, 100, 102, 111, 112, 114, 115, 117, 119, 127, 130, 141, 143, 144, 156, 165, 167, 169, 172,

174, 175, 178, 179, 183-185, 187, 189, 190, 192-198, 205, 210, 219, 221, 236, 237, 257, 265, 273, 278, 293, 306, 315, 316, 328, 329, 334, 337
Blavatsky   61, 317, 318
Blue Lodge   23, 46, 51, 59, 70, 72, 104, 113, 114, 118, 119, 150, 163, 177, 179, 180, 182, 183, 184, 187, 190, 223, 224, 275, 300, 301, 336
Bode's law   102
Book M   261-263
Boone   73
British Isles   21, 43, 79, 80, 113, 148, 176, 217, 241, 317
Buddha   52, 81, 193, 210, 317, 328
Buddhism   193, 201, 203, 204

Caesar   55-57, 60, 64, 182, 327, 334
Camelot   234, 236, 242, 324
Castaneda   95
Cathars   217
Champollion   84
China   24, 52, 65, 68, 112, 202, 268, 306
Christian Rosenkreuz   183
Circumcision   46, 161
Clark   72
Clausius   74
Code of Manu   185
Coke   246
Columbus   23, 55, 69, 260, 264, 265, 272
Confession to Maat   157
Confucius   52, 338
Copernicus   69, 272, 273
Cornwallis   73
Council of Laodices   61
Cranmer   69
Cromaat   158, 173, 336
Cronos   192
Crusades   217, 220, 237, 245, 255, 334

Dali Lama   112, 327
Dante   70, 258, 259, 271, 272, 315, 316
Dark Ages   23, 61, 63, 198, 205, 226, 233, 240, 259, 260, 272, 295, 316, 337
Darwin   93
De Molay   68, 253, 254, 291, 316, 333
Dead Sea Scrolls   290, 291, 316
Declaration of Independence   24, 25, 182, 183, 276, 277, 279, 282-286, 295, 296, 301
Deductive logic   55, 205, 206, 300
Deere   270
Democritus   54
Dionysius   60, 312
Domesday Book   242, 245, 324

Donation of Constantine 223, 316
Donnelly 80
Doss 11, 12, 14, 20, 31, 164
Durant 25, 320

Eddy 321
Egyptian Book of the Dead *157, 193*
Einstein 24, 37-41, 53, 54, 74, 118, 121, 122, 133, 134, 163, 201, 274, 276, 289, 292, 299, 318
Eisen 90
Elohim 51, 52, 117, 189, 195
Empedocles 124
Emperor Constantine 22, 23, 28, 59, 60, 178, 182, 184, 211, 214, 219-221, 223, 224, 226, 231, 233, 236, 318, 321, 336
Emperor Galerius 60
Emperor Hadrian 58
Emperor Valentinian 62
England 12, 16, 23, 24, 29, 44, 50, 58, 62-64, 68-72, 74, 90, 102, 111, 202, 209, 217, 218, 233, 234, 235, 239-246, 249, 250, 255, 258, 259, 261, 268-270, 272-274, 278, 280, 295, 308, 311, 321, 323-327, 333-335
Essenes 29, 30, 46, 56, 144, 200, 201, 215, 218, 291
Euclid 53, 55, 163
Eve 76, 81, 97, 98, 189, 192, 337, 338
Exiguus 60
Exodus 21, 23, 28, 46-48, 50, 65, 115, 144, 156, 158, 160, 165-167, 170, 173-177, 194, 220, 291, 295, 301, 315, 319, 322, 324
Ezra 22, 23, 53, 54, 100, 115, 143, 161, 165, 167, 174, 175, 195, 196, 198, 219, 221, 223, 233, 236, 315

Fibionacci series 132
First Crusade 64, 66, 217, 252, 291, 324
France 13, 23, 24, 55, 63, 65, 66, 69, 73, 74, 184, 217, 236, 254, 255, 261, 266, 268, 269, 284, 291, 303, 316, 324, 326
Franklin 72, 73, 183, 282, 283, 287, 288, 309, 319, 322
Freemason 11, 22, 27, 29, 71, 73, 163, 179-181, 183, 200, 282, 284, 293, 300, 323, 329, 330
Freud 87, 156, 186

Galileo 69, 70, 129, 273
Gamkrelidze 81, 321, 322
Gandhi 187, 268, 316
Garden of Eden 26, 42, 43, 77, 81, 84, 87, 93, 95, 156, 176, 191, 295, 301, 324, 336
Gardner 90, 322

342 TRUE ESOTERIC TRADITIONS

Germany   13, 55, 69, 74, 221, 225, 244, 261, 267, 289, 292, 302, 304, 325
Gibbon   25, 26, 322, 325
Godfrey of Bouillion   64
Golden Mean   88, 89, 132
Golden Rule   28, 204, 205, 338
Goodrich   234, 322, 323
Great Flood   43, 102, 176, 192
Great Pyramid   13, 16, 88, 89, 103-106, 137-139, 158, 162, 216, 308, 318, 336
Grimes   28, 322
Grimm   74, 322

Hall   152, 243, 323
Halley   63, 71, 200, 241
Hamilton   72, 285
Hannibal   55, 227
Hawking   39, 122, 298, 299
Heisenberg   24, 74, 133, 134, 323
Hemis Monastery   52, 57, 141, 199, 204, 328
Hermes   41, 46-50, 112, 114, 115, 143, 144, 147, 148, 155, 160, 173, 186, 316
Higgins   26, 113, 124, 324
Hitler   117, 132, 140, 226, 267, 292, 303
Holy Grail   66, 234
Holy Roman Empire   63, 233, 239
Holy War   228, 238, 309
Holy Writ   175, 196, 219, 223, 236, 323
Hyksos   26, 46, 146, 166, 167

Ignatius   80, 222
India   24, 26, 43, 51, 52, 57, 58, 61, 73, 112-114, 141, 142, 199, 200, 208, 210-212, 215, 217, 236, 268, 306, 317-319, 324, 325, 328
Inductive logic   24, 55, 130, 152, 205-207, 273, 298, 300
Inquisition   7, 227, 255, 278
Iraqi   13, 303
Isaac   24, 46, 47, 71, 111, 114, 143, 144, 274
Israel   22, 23, 28, 43, 47, 51, 53, 54, 56-58, 64, 65, 81, 84, 113-119, 132, 139, 143, 144, 162, 163, 175, 177-180, 182, 190, 195, 197, 199, 202, 209-213, 215, 216, 218, 221, 226, 261, 272, 291, 306, 328, 333, 336
Israelite   144, 150, 200
Ivanov   81, 321, 322

Jacob   47, 74, 119, 144, 322
Japan   267, 270, 292, 302, 317
Jefferson   24, 25, 63, 72, 73, 182, 268, 276-288, 295, 296, 301, 306, 307, 326
Jehovah   27, 51, 52, 117, 189, 193, 195

Jeremiah 46, 52, 195, 330
Jesus 12, 22-31, 42, 52-60, 62, 66, 80, 94, 95, 107, 111, 112, 117, 119, 120, 126-132, 134, 135, 139-143, 149, 150, 152-155, 157, 159, 163, 176, 177, 179, 184, 186, 190-192, 196-198, 200-222, 224, 226-230, 233, 234, 236-238, 250-258, 260-263, 266, 269, 273, 275, 276, 279, 292, 295, 297-302, 306, 308, 309, 311, 314, 315, 319, 320, 321, 323, 325-329, 333, 335-338
Jews 23, 26, 28, 51-53, 56-58, 62, 65, 66, 80, 114, 115, 118, 132, 150, 153, 165, 170, 175, 195, 196, 197, 200, 212, 219, 221, 223, 226, 233, 236, 238, 251, 255, 264, 265, 272, 276, 291, 295, 300, 309, 315, 319, 325, 333, 334, 337
John the Baptist 65, 66, 139, 154, 216, 256
John the Beloved 110, 111
Jones 73
Joseph 21, 26, 28, 29, 47-51, 56, 87, 99, 107, 111, 112, 115, 117, 119, 139, 141, 142, 144, 145-147, 155, 156, 160, 161, 165-167, 175, 177, 186, 193, 194, 198, 200, 216, 218, 229, 234, 276, 295, 319, 327, 328, 333, 335
Joseph of Arimathea 218, 234, 327
Joseph-Yuya 47-51, 99, 107, 112, 115, 117, 141, 144-147, 155, 156, 160, 161, 165-167, 175, 186, 194, 328
Josephus 26, 46, 146, 291, 325, 333
Jung 87, 186

Kabala 85-87, 89, 90, 111, 265, 297, 318
Kabalists 30, 51, 163, 176, 295
Kashmir 58, 141-143, 199, 200, 202, 210-214, 326, 327
Kersten 141, 211, 325, 326
King Arthur 62, 165, 233-236, 240, 322-324, 327, 334
King Darius 53, 54
King David 51, 115-118, 132, 163, 177, 178, 226
King Hammurabi 45, 156
King Henry II 234, 242, 243, 247, 323, 334
King Henry VIII 23, 225, 239, 243, 269, 272
King Herod 56, 57
King Hezekiah 195
King James 70, 71, 273, 320
King John 66, 243, 245-248, 250, 255, 324, 334
King Philip 65
King Richard 272, 334
King's chamber 16, 104, 138, 139, 158, 335
Knights Templar 66, 68, 252, 254, 291, 316, 333, 334
Koran 12, 63, 143, 180, 185, 193, 211, 219, 224, 237, 262, 315

Lake Moeris 13, 155
Lancelot 234

Laotse   *31, 52, 137, 202, 203, 321, 326*
Lavosier   *122*
Levi   *208-210, 320, 326*
Levitt   *81*
Lewis   *16, 17, 210, 318, 326*
Lincoln   *28, 29, 73, 288, 289, 294*
Long Count Calendar   *44*
Lord's Prayer   *207*
Lucas   *94*
Luther   *69, 228, 272, 316*

Machupicchu   *306*
Madame Blavatsky   *61*
Madison   *282, 283, 288, 326*
Magna Carta   *66, 90, 245, 246, 249, 250, 259, 295, 324, 335*
Marathon run   *54*
Marco Polo   *65*
Mark Anthony   *56*
Marsiglio of Padua   *68*
Martel   *23, 63, 236, 237*
Mathematical constants   *87*
Matthew   *12, 56-59, 200, 202, 206, 207, 211, 222*
Maya Indians   *44*
Mayflower Compact   *286*
McGuffey   *28*
Mckenna   *95*
Melchizedek   *139*
Merenptah Israel Stele   *51*
Merlin   *234, 236, 240*
Modern English   *24, 41, 43, 76, 81, 82, 84-86, 88-91, 113, 246, 323, 332*
Montsegur   *66*
Mormon Church   *218, 266*
Moscow   *307, 322*
Moses   *28, 48, 50-53, 99, 107, 115, 137, 141, 143, 144, 155, 156, 161, 165-167, 169, 173, 175, 177, 184, 186, 193-195, 202, 210, 211, 236, 315, 316, 326, 331, 332*
Moses Moria-el   *48, 50-53, 99, 107, 115, 137, 141, 143, 144, 161, 165-167, 173, 175, 177, 184, 186, 193-195, 202, 210, 211, 300, 326, 332*
Mount Carmel   *142, 143, 201, 212, 216, 218*
Mount Sinai   *172, 174*
Mozart   *72, 95, 284, 285, 322*
Muhammad   *196, 236-238, 258*

Nefertiti   *49, 147*
Nefertum   *107*

Nero 58, 111, 220-222, 311
New Testament 28, 56-58, 61, 69, 109, 111, 139, 143, 185, 186, 193, 197, 198, 200-202, 205, 207, 211, 212, 215, 219, 226, 229, 233, 237, 262, 273, 315
Newton 24, 38, 71, 111, 274, 275, 289, 335
Nicene Council 60, 223, 321
Noah 81, 101, 192, 236, 322, 330
Northwest Ordinance 73, 280, 282
Notovitch 204, 210, 318, 319, 328

Oak Island 254
Osiris 11, 40, 157, 160, 189
Osman 145, 155, 328, 329, 333
Outlaw 214, 215, 335

Papal Bull 66, 68, 313, 314, 330, 331, 333
Parah dish 43, 81
Peale 27, 29, 293, 322
Pharaoh Ahmosis I 146
Pharaoh Akhnaton 52, 61, 112, 146, 156, 185, 201, 332
Pharaoh Amenhotep III 48, 161
Pharaoh Amenhotep IV 119
Pharaoh Aye 50, 156, 160, 163, 173
Pharaoh Horemheb 50, 161, 162, 165, 168, 174, 223
Pharaoh Rameses II 175
Pharaoh Tuthmosis II 46, 47, 146
Pharaoh Tuthmosis III 104, 114
Phi 88, 89, 336
Pi 88-90, 103, 336
Pike 152, 322, 323, 329, 330
Plantagenet Chronicles 323
Plato 43, 53-55, 78, 79, 119, 139, 141, 148, 155, 163, 185, 186, 204, 205, 307, 323
Pluto 44, 97, 102
Poland 307
Pope Boniface VIII 66, 68, 99, 314, 330
Pope Eugenius III 65
Pope Joan 240, 250
Pope John XXIII 161, 223, 250, 297
Pope Leo 62, 63, 68, 239, 250, 331, 333
Pope Nicholas V 69
Pope Siricius 61
Pope Soter 59, 222
Pope Stephen I 59, 222, 223
Pope Urban II 64, 65, 250-252

Prince Gautama 52
Ptah 107, 112, 160
Purgatory 135, 258, 271, 315, 326
Pythagoras 12, 53, 141, 163, 336

Queen Elizabeth I 70, 266, 273
Queen Elizabeth II 99
Quetzalcoatl 44, 81

Ra 46, 109, 124
Raleigh 11, 19, 20, 70, 71, 273, 319
Romanov 74
Rosetta stone 74, 75, 84, 289
Rosicrucian 10-12, 16-18, 22, 27, 30, 31, 48, 56, 61, 70-73, 82, 85, 90, 106, 111, 131, 138, 152-154, 162, 164, 182, 183, 198, 200, 209, 210, 215, 254, 259-261, 265, 269, 271, 272-275, 282, 285, 286, 298, 300, 301, 318-320, 326, 336
Rosicrucian alphabet 27, 31, 82, 85, 90
Russia 24, 71, 74, 268, 276, 319

Sacraments of the Roman Church 198, 256, 258
Sagan 103
Saint Augustine 22, 62, 63, 219, 226, 230, 238, 269
Saint Francis 29, 258, 259, 272
Saint Issa 57, 58, 199, 204, 210, 213, 214, 306, 319, 328
Saint Jerome 61
Saint Mark 11
Saint Patrick 62, 241
Sanhedrin 56, 132, 162, 215, 217, 218, 254, 291
Sarah 46, 114, 141, 143, 144
Sarich 97
Satan 42, 107, 108, 111, 120, 131, 150
Scottish Rite 70, 119, 152, 182, 329, 330
Sekmet 107
Semenkhkare 47, 49, 50, 156, 159, 161
Sermon on the Mount 28, 52, 202, 207, 321, 326
Shakespeare 25, 70, 71, 209, 273, 319, 333, 334
Shelley's case 68, 70, 259, 267, 268
Sitchin 55, 77, 93, 96, 97, 102, 104, 334
Siva 189
Smith 70, 322, 335
Socrates 54, 307
Solomon 22, 48, 51, 53, 56, 64, 111, 113-115, 118, 142, 150, 163, 177-180, 182-184, 187, 252
Solon 52, 53, 78, 141, 183, 216, 295, 322

Spain 61, 69, 112, 236, 261, 264-266, 269, 272
Stonehenge 44, 308
Sub rosa 153, 180, 233, 239, 254
Sumer 43, 44, 93, 96, 97, 99, 100, 104, 195, 322, 334
Sun sign 109, 110

Tacitus 58
Tao Te Ching 52, 321
Templars 252-255, 291, 333
The Revelation 109-111, 207, 228, 310
Theosophical Society 317
Therapeuti 29, 46, 52
Tibetan Book of the Dead 135, 193
Tiye 47-49, 146, 147, 319, 332
Tomkins 89
Toynbee 24, 25, 321, 337
Tree of Life 70, 119, 130, 131, 149-152, 189, 318
Tut 47, 49, 50, 156, 159-161
Tyndale 69

Unam Sanctum 68, 313, 314
Uncertainty Principle 37, 38, 40, 74, 133, 298, 323
Usher 93

Virginia 70, 72, 73, 276, 278, 279, 282, 283, 285, 335
Vital Life Force 41, 128, 149

Washington 19, 73, 74, 163, 186, 220, 281, 283, 286, 288, 302, 322
Wasson 95
White Lodge 22, 23, 29, 30, 44, 46-49, 77, 80, 91, 104, 107, 109, 113, 114, 118, 135, 138, 140-144, 147, 148, 150, 152, 155, 156, 158, 159, 162, 204, 295, 298, 299, 332, 334, 336
William the Conqueror 64, 240-242, 245, 324
Wilson 97, 338
Wizard 209

Xisuthrus 192

Yahweh 117, 196

Zend-Avesta 180, 189, 192
Zodiac 320
Zoroaster 52, 192